Forget Me NOT

7 Steps for Healing Our Body, Mind, Spirit, and Mother Earth

Dr. Ani Kalayjian

Forget Me NOT
7 Steps for Healing Our Body, Mind, Spirit, and Mother Earth

Book design by Dr. Ani Kalayjian
This is a Non-Fiction Self-Help Book
Written by Dr. Ani Kalayjian
Visit my website at: http://drkalayjian.com and
http://meaningfulworld.com/

Printed in the United States of America
First Printing: October 2017
Published by: Sojourn Publishing, LLC

Paperback ISBN: 978-1-62747-132-9
Ebook ISBN: 978-1-62747-134-3

Dedication

I dedicate this book to my family: my Father Kevork, and my elder brother Arch-Priest Fr. Vertanes Kalayjian (God rest their souls), my mother Diramayr Zabelle, my sister Zarmine, brothers Kevork and Vasken for all their support, love, and compassion.

I also express deep gratitude to my friends, as well as my clients who were the source of my inspiration to heal and to serve. Finally, deep gratitude to all the survivors around the world.

Content

Introduction vii

Part I
Childhood and Generational Trauma 1
Childhood in the Village 1
School Age: Moving to Aleppo, Syria 2
Managing Parental Arguments 5
Gender Discrimination 6
Generational Transmission of Trauma 8
Self-Reflection 9

Part II
Embracing Adulthood: Being the Change We Want to See 11
Immigrating to America 11
Withholding Feelings 13
Culture Shock in American High School 16
Arranged Engagement 20
Generational Transmission of Trauma 20
Self-Reflection 23

Part III
Outreach to Families, Communities and the World 25
Workshop at the United Nations:
World Congress of Women, Beijing, China 25
Organize to Transform Global Traumas 26
Dialogue for Peace 28
Negative Impact of Anger 29
7 Steps for Empathic Listening 31
Self-Reflection 35

Part IV
Making Meaning out of the Nonsense 37
Training in Logotherapy: 37

Establishing a MeaningfulWorld 40
Naturopathic Healing 41
Self-Reflection 43

Part V
Healing Myself and Sharing This Knowledge with Others........... 45
Discovering the 7-Step Integrative Healing Model....................... 45
Step I: Identify and Assess Your Feelings 47
Assess your feelings and then measure 47
Step II: Express and Release Your Feelings................................... 53
Step III: Empathy and Validation.. 59
Step IV: Encourage Discovery and Expression
of Positive Meaning... 67
Step V: Provide and Gather Information.. 83
Here are some of the myths on forgiveness: 84
Step VI: Connecting with Mother Earth 95
Step VII: Healing Through Breath and Movement........................ 99

Part VI
Reflections.. 121

Part VII
Attachments.. 123
References... 153

Introduction

The goddess within me embraces and celebrates the god/goddess within you.
Let's hold hands and create the dance of our lifetime.
Dance is a metaphor for life—it helps us connect with love,
flow with grace, and step with caution and determination
while we gaze at one another with admiration,
validation and empathy—and with love and acceptance
we lead one another towards joyful enlightenment.
~ Dr. Kalayjian

This book shares concepts about self-care. Of course, you are thinking that you already have been caring for yourself for a long time. Yes, I am glad that you are caring for yourself. But this book will guide you to another level of caring, or a different way of caring—or it will support and enrich the practice that you already have. You may also tell me that there are so many books out there on self-care that another book will not be necessary. I would agree with you that there are lots of self-help books out there; however, this book shares concept like Horizontal Violence and Generational Transmission of Trauma, and ancestral healing, which are integral parts of self-care that you may NOT have heard about.

The first part of this book, Part I, is about my childhood—the roots of my issues, the traumas I experienced that have guided me to the healing modality that I share with you in the last part of this book. In Part II, I share my adolescence and the gender discrimination I endured. In Part III, I share my experiences of immigrating to the United States of America, the hopes and the dreams of being free and able to receive a good education, find a good occupation, and exercise my human rights. In Part IV, I share how I transformed some of my traumas, and began reaching out to help others and humanity around the globe through the Association for Trauma Outreach and Prevention, the Armenian American Society for Studies on Stress and Genocide, and Meaningfulworld, organizing more than 100 humanitarian relief missions to address human suffering from the mind-body-eco-spirit perspectives. In Part V, I share about healing another layer of myself. In Part VI, I share my healing tool that was transformative for me, and for thousands of people around the world, the 7-Step Integrative Healing Model. We have used this model in more than forty-five countries, with more than a million people who survived many human-made calamities, such as incest, domestic violence, and physical and emotional abuse on the individual level, as well as political wars, genocides, terrorism, and other state-sponsored violence on the national level. We also used this healing model after natural calamities, such as earthquakes, hurricanes, tornadoes, cyclones, tsunamis, and floods. We have used this model in more than forty-five countries around the globe with six religious belief systems—Buddhism, Christianity, Hinduism, Islam, Judaism, and Jainism—with great success. We have also used this model in the United States in more than twenty-six states.

The last part, Part VII, is full of important handouts that you can print, post, frame, and use for your daily emotional and health improvement needs.

When you read each part, take your time and reflect about your own childhood and your own relationships with your parents and siblings, considering your sibling order—what it means to you, and what it meant to your parents and other members of your extended family.

I also invite you to draw your own genogram, a map of your familial relationships. You will see a sample of Eugene O'Neill's family relationships in the last part of this book. This emotional family tree (genogram) will help you so much that I ask you to invite all your friends to do this exercise.

Are you ready to take this journey with me? Great! Let's start.

Part I

Childhood and Generational Trauma

Childhood in the Village

If you realize that all things change,
There is nothing you will try to hold on to
~ Lao Tzu

I remember being four years old and having to learn how to manage my two brothers—one three years older and one three years younger than Me. I also had a sister and another older brother, who were much older than we were, and they were away at boarding school and so were not living with us. We lived in a small village in Azez, in northern Syria, about fifty kilometers from the Turkish border. I remember only happy moments in that village. I remember being seated on the shoulders of my father and walking in the mountainous parts of Azez after dinner, and being able to see above his balding head. It may have been just a one-time event, but that memory holds me in a special place. It was the late 1950s, just over a decade after World War II, and of course it was many decades after the Ottoman-Turkish Genocide of the Armenians, of which the dark and sad memory lingered all around us, as my father was a survivor, and my mother was a child of survivors.

I remember being told that I was given a second chance to live when, as a baby of forty days, I had high fever that would not break, and my father had to travel to Aleppo, Syria, in the middle of the night because our village did not have antibiotics. My sister had to run to the doctor and beg for a prescription, and then my father had to travel all the way to Aleppo to buy it. My mother tells me the story of how she was kneeling down the entire night praying to God to keep me safe and alive until my father arrived in the morning from Aleppo. I was told that as the sun rose over the mountain, my dad arrived home with the antibiotics. God heard my mom's prayers, and Dad arrived home with the antibiotics in time for me to stay alive. Mom was very

1

concerned, as she had already lost two other children due to sickness and high fever. This became a pattern. Every time I was running even a low-grade fever, I remember Mom being afraid and running to the doctor to get antibiotics for me. I even remember her carrying me to the doctor in her arms when I was bigger, at about age six. This must be how my intestinal flora got weakened over time. At that time, no one knew how dangerous antibiotics could be; in addition, there were no probiotics to replenish what antibiotics destroyed.

I was told that at age four, I was the center of entertainment for my family. For example, when we had guests, they asked me to read the big Bible with small Armenian letters; apparently, I read it with confidence and fluency. I remember having my cheeks pinched a lot, by people who were strangers to me, while I visited relatives with my mom. Even among Armenians, an Indo-European nation, there was a clear preference for whiter skin, as they kept on pinching my cheeks and telling me how white and how beautiful I was. At the same time, they called my cousin, who was a little darker with olive-like skin, "esmer shirin," which meant darker skin but sweet (cute).

School Age: Moving to Aleppo, Syria

Between stimulus and response there is a space.
In that space is our power to choose our response.
In our response lie our growth and our freedom.
~ Viktor Frankl

My parents decided to move to Aleppo because Azez did not have higher education, which was necessary for us. Aleppo was a new experience for me. It was a big city, the second-largest city in Syria after Damascus, which is the capital. At seven years of age, I enrolled in Lazar Najarian Armenian Private School. I walked to school with my elder brother and sister. At this time, my sister Zarmine moved to live with us; prior to this, she had been going to school in Jerusalem with my elder brother Zaven. When I was born, Zaven, who was the firstborn son in our family, left our home to study in the Anthelias Seminary in Lebanon to become an Armenian priest. At fifteen years of age, Zaven became my godfather, and then he left to go to Beirut, Lebanon.

I was distressed growing up in Aleppo. My parents were very traditional, and the climate was full of fear and sadness as the emotional impact of wars lingered. Especially prominent in our memory was the Ottoman-Turkish Genocide (1885-1928) that had killed close to 2 million Armenians, with the rest forced to walk through the desert of Arabia until some—only one-third of the Armenian population—reached Syria. There was an unspoken tension among Arabs and Armenians as the latter were a Christian minority in an Islamic State. Although Syria opened its doors to the Armenians after the Genocide, there were many restrictions placed on the Armenians. One of the restrictions was in the realm of education: In Armenian private schools, we were not allowed to study Armenian history. We were only allowed one Armenian language class per day and one Armenian religion class per week. Armenian schools were mandated to have an Arab Muslim principal next to the Armenian principal—even though Armenians fully sponsored the education and did not receive funding from the Syrian government. Additionally, government/Arab inspectors popped into our classes (without notice) to make sure we were following their laws and not teaching Armenian history. Why were they so afraid of Armenian history? To this day, I am not certain.

This kind of fear had also permeated the society at large, and it was felt in the air. It affected my gut. I was not sure if I was allergic to milk, or intolerant of powdered milk; I had no problems with my mother's breast milk and enjoyed it until I was about two years old. Breakfast was a struggle in my house, as I could not drink the milk. My brothers made fun of me for this and teased me mercilessly.

I had a traumatic experience on my first day of school in Aleppo. I wasn't sure who was to pick me up after school—my sister Zarmine (nine years older than I) or my brother George (at the time, now Kevork, three years older than I). All I recall is walking around and around looking for familiar faces and then starting to cry out of fear and out of feelings of unfamiliarity. I was so fortunate that my Uncle Hovanness was a well-known businessman and a self-made entrepreneur in Aleppo, and many people knew of him. He was the pride of the family, the only son of my maternal grandparents, who had him after five girls. Males were and still are preferred in Armenian culture. Uncle Hovanness had a generous heart and was well known among the local government officials and the Armenians alike. I began calling his name, "Hovanness Keri," meaning Uncle Hovanness, and ladies who were hanging out the windows felt sorry for me and directed me to go to a local mechanic store, where they would call my uncle. In less than ten minutes, my uncle showed up and rescued me.

While at school, I felt another trauma: all the kids had gone through kindergarten together, but I joined them during the first grade. They all looked at me as kind of weird, not approving of my clothing that had been sewn by my mom. After all, we came from the village of Azez, so I was looked down upon as a village girl. When I told mom about it, she dismissed it and said not to pay attention to others, that school was not a place for a fashion show. My mother had, in a way, homeschooled us. I knew how to read, write, and do arithmetic and multiplication. Mom taught us while she was working at home. For example, she would be doing the laundry (using a small burner for boiling water to soak the white sheets and towels in, since we had no washing machine nor hot water or gas) and would then go up to the roof to hang the laundry to dry. (We had a one-story house with a small cement yard in the middle.) And while all this was going on, she was asking me and my younger brother Vasken (three years younger than I) to repeat the readings we had studied, to repeat the times table from one to ten, and to repeat the alphabet in Armenian and Arabic. When I received my first report card, I had straight A's, actually 100s. This made the girl who was the previous first of the class very angry, and she went home and told her mother that "This farm girl took my place, she had all 100s, and I hate her." Apparently, my neighbor knew the family, and they came and told my mother about this transaction, and I overheard them.

When I came home from school, I was not allowed to play outside with other children, although my brothers could. But I was a girl, so I could not. This double standard infuriated me. Mom was fearful of the abduction of girls, perhaps left over from the genocidal practices in which the Ottoman Turks targeted the most beautiful and the whitest children to abduct and enslave, or to use for sex trafficking. Mothers had to smudge their daughters with mud to make them look unattractive in order to avoid abductions. It was accepted that both of my brothers (George and Vasken) could play outdoors in the street, ride bicycles, and be like other children, but that was not allowed for me. All summer long I was to stay home and learn needlepoint, and crochet and do house cleaning but could not be outdoors.

Managing Parental Arguments

The black moment is the moment when the real message
of transformation is going to come. At the darkest moment comes the light.
~ Joseph Campbell

Later, during my teens, my time was spent at home managing the fights and arguments between my parents. At first, Dad continued working in Azez and joined us on weekends; those were the most peaceful times of my childhood. Later, when Dad opened up his own shoe repair shop in Aleppo and was living with us full time, the arguments occurred daily. The arguments centered on why my dad hospitalized my mom in a mental institution in Beirut for her postpartum depression (PPD). Mom was apparently suffering from PPD after Vasken's birth, and it became very severe. I was about three years old. She was not eating or drinking, she lost over fifty pounds, and she became paranoid, especially concerning her children's welfare. There was a severe stigma attached to emotional challenges and no understanding of PPD or any other mental issues in Syria. No one knew what to do, or how to help Mom. There was only one mental institution which was in Beirut, and it was called the "Khentanots" (the crazy house). There were no psychologists or psychiatrists in Syria. One had to travel all the way to Beirut, Lebanon (a six-hour drive at that time), to see a psychiatrist. Therefore, my maternal aunts and father had come up with an intervention: They fooled Mom and convinced her that she would visit her sister in Beirut, but they committed her to the mental institution instead. She was severely traumatized; most of all, she felt betrayed by my dad, her sisters, and other family members.

Arguments focused on themes such as, "Why did you fool me? Why did you take me to a mental institution?" Dad did not have a response, and over the years, whatever he said was not enough to remedy the sense of betrayal and sadness my mom was feeling. The stigma of mental illness was much more severe in the Middle East, and it still is on many levels. There are only a handful of psychologists in Aleppo, and throughout Syria, even now. (This country, Syria, is where the war started in 2010 and continues until today 2017. Some say it's a civil war, but most of it is a war between the USA, Russia, Turkey, Qatar, and Saudi Arabia, which happens to be taking place in Syria.) I was tired of hearing this argument over and over, and it was just a sad situation for both my father and my mother. Even now, in 2017, Mom has never truly understood PPD, nor has she forgiven my dad and her sister, even though he has been dead since 1983, and my aunt died this year. Although my mother is otherwise very spiritual and reads the Bible daily and prays daily, this is a very sensitive and sore spot for her and even today, at age 94, she feels challenged by this. She is still unable to forgive my father and her sister. I was delighted to hear yesterday, though, she said "God has forgiven them."

Gender Discrimination

You must learn one thing: The world was made to be free in…
Give up all the other worlds except the one to which you belong…
Anything or anyone that does not bring you alive is too small for you.
~ David Whyte

Gender issues, discrimination, and violence against women were prevalent all around us. Discrimination was more severe in the Arab Islamic communities. Both of my brothers were the victims of this, as they began to dump their observations of discrimination on me, the only sister at home. In our home there were double standards, as my two brothers George and Vasken could do anything they wished—play outdoors, ride a bicycle and even a motorcycle—while I had to stay home. Unfortunately, George had a severe motorcycle accident—his head was gashed in the middle—and if it weren't for my Uncle Hovanness's speedy intervention, George could have died. George was in a coma for about a month and had to be fed and taken care of. I was so sad, and I remember visiting him in the hospital, and while I was feeding him he used to say, "Feed me fast, feed me a lot." He was always hungry. After that accident, he was sent to a boarding school in Cyprus, the Melkonian Armenian Higher Education Center. I remember the first year when he returned for summer vacation, he was a different George. He was Kevork (Armenian for George), much calmer, much more into reading books and writing poetry, basically, he was transformed. In one summer month, I remember that he finished reading the entire series of Raffi's several volumes (Armenian books, more than 900 pages each). I was so impressed with him and appreciated him more, as he was no longer abusive toward me.

Prior to his leaving, George used to call me Chinese because I loved rice pilaf. Vasken used to wage big fights about how to divide our shared study desk evenly. Even my shadow was not tolerated and caused huge fights. One day they were both playing outside with each other with homemade slings. I was watching them from the door. They were extremely creative, and they burned an object and pulled the sling and threw it in the air. It lodged in my throat and made me stutter for a few days or weeks, I don't recall. I still have a scar on my throat from that traumatic incident—though I, even as a child, knew that it was an accident. From childhood, my mom had instilled in me the concept of being understanding and empathic toward my brothers. She used to say repeatedly, especially when I complained about my brothers' behaviors, "Ani, you are a girl, you should understand your brothers, they don't understand, they are boys." One day I rebelled and said in protest, "No, Mom, I don't understand anymore, and I am tired of this. It's not fair—you have to do something about this." I am grateful to have developed close relations with my brothers over the years, and I now enjoy their loving unconditional support and respect.

Looking back, I think the seeds of promoting human rights, especially for girls and women, began growing in me as a young girl, as well as the wish to transform all these conflicting messages and double-bind messages concerning male and female roles. I brought all

7

of my passion and frustrations with me to America, the land of opportunity, and began protesting against wars, against denial, and for the acknowledgment of the Ottoman-Turkish Genocide.

Generational Transmission of Trauma

This phenomenon, which includes feelings of guilt, shame, hatred and fear, occurs in many traumatized societies, such as Native Americans, Holocaust survivors, and Ottoman Turkish Genocide Armenian survivors. We found two variables unique to the Armenian survivor community—the meaning construed by the individual of the profoundly invalidating experience of the denial of the genocide by the Turkish & US governments, and the degree of the family's involvement in the Armenian community (Kalayjian et al. 1996). According to our research, the nightmares of second-generation genocide survivors who had experienced the devastating 1988 earthquake in Armenia were not of the earthquake, but of the Turkish gendarmes beating them on the forced death march—as they had heard the accounts of these horrors, which had happened some seventy-three years before, from their grandparents (Kalayjian 1995).

Part I

Self-Reflection Childhood and Generational Trauma

Review your childhood, review your family tree and respond to these questions in writing:

1. What is your earliest memory? What are you doing in this memory? What are you feeling? Kindly review the anger chart if your feelings are negative in nature. Who is involved in this memory? Write down as much detail as you recall. Ask your parents (if they are still alive) about this memory. How does this memory make you feel right now, when you are recalling it? If it is unresolved, I invite you to continue working on this.

2. What are your childhood memories (earlier than six years of age, if possible) of your parents?

3. What are your childhood memories of your siblings, if you have any?

4. Who were your caregivers, if not your biological parents? And what were your childhood memories of those caregivers, or adoptive parents?

5. If you had babysitters or nannies, what are your childhood memories of those caregivers?

6. If you were in daycare, what are your memories of caregivers in that setting?

7. Do you recall any bullying or traumatic experiences from your childhood? Who was involved? How did it end? How do you feel about it right now recalling those traumatic incidents?

8. Give a description of your father's and mother's (or caregivers') personality and his/her attitude toward you (past and present).

9. In what ways were you disciplined or punished by your caregivers?

10. Give an impression of your home atmosphere. Was there compatibility between parents and between children (if applicable)?
11. Did you feel loved and respected by your parents/caregivers?
12. Has anyone (parents, relatives, and friends) ever interfered in your occupation, career, dating, or marriage?

Part II
Embracing Adulthood: Being the Change We Want to See

Immigrating to America

We either make ourselves miserable or we make ourselves strong.
The amount of work is the same.
~ Carlos Castaneda

As soon as I was born, Zaven, my elder brother and godfather, left to go to Beirut, Lebanon, to study in the Armenian seminary. We saw him during some summers, when he would come home and spend a month in our house. Later on, from 1963 to 1964, he took a teaching position at the Giligian Armenian School in Aleppo, and he lived with us for a year. I had held on to him like a hero from afar all these years while he was in the seminary. He was looked up to by both of my parents; God was up above, and Father Vertanes (his name as a priest) was His representative on Earth. I enjoyed looking up to him as a big brother, someone who engaged in intellectual discussions and who attracted many people around him—young and old, men and women alike. I could not understand how the women were all hanging around and flirting with him, as at the time he was a celibate priest. He was full of life, full of passion, with a contagious laughter and a unique style of leadership. Shortly after, though, Father Vertanes was invited to take a priesthood position in Illinois, USA, and he left our home and Syria. He then married and became a married priest in the Armenian Church, which was in fact a first—because in the Armenian Church you have to decide ahead of time if you wish to be a celibate or a married priest, and you cannot change your status along the way. After his move to America, we were communicating only through letters. In the early 1970s, Father Vertanes was able to apply for our USA residency, and in June of 1971, we left Aleppo and moved to Fort Lee, New Jersey to live in his second house. The plan was to protect our brothers Kevork and Vasken from Syrian military drafting as the Syrian-Israeli war was inevitable.

My sister was married in 1966. Because of this, she could not immigrate with us to the USA. Before our move, my parents were planning to see me married quickly so that I could stay with my sister in Aleppo. In addition, they had misconceptions about the freedom of girls and women in America; they wanted to marry me off so I would not be a 'free' woman in America (which at that time they equaled to being a prostitute). I had to write a secret letter to my brother Father Vertanes to convince my parents to bring me with them to America, so I could get an education. I felt, and a few people had reinforced it, that if I did not leave Aleppo when I did, I would have been either killed or imprisoned. I was too outspoken, and unable to accept all the discrimination against women and the restricted and constantly monitored lifestyle there. Although I was certain that I did not want to stay in Aleppo, I was also very sad to depart from my only sister. This decision was especially hard for me since she had just experienced the traumatic loss of her beautiful one-year-old daughter Arpi, my first niece, who had a congenital heart defect and lived only one brief year. I felt a special connection with my sister, not only because I looked up to her as an elder but because she was and still is very caring and compassionate, and has always guided me with love.

First, my brother Kevork got married and moved out of the parental apartment in Fort Lee, and then Vasken got admitted to Pratt Institute, in Brooklyn, New York, and moved out, so I was left alone with my parents. I had to commute to Long Island University in Brooklyn from New Jersey, which became more and more challenging. My move out of my parental home became a huge struggle. My mother stayed by the door and physically prevented me from moving, telling me, "Over my dead body." My father did not want to talk with me, because in Armenian culture at that time (and in many families still today) independence was not tolerated. Moving out of the parental home was to be done only at the time of marriage. My move was very emotionally charged; thus I had to wait until Mom had gone to work the next day, and then move in her absence. The sad part is that my parents were too concerned about "What would others say about my move? You are moving out and living by yourself? Who is going to protect you?" Does that mean you are going to have sex before marriage?

Soon Mom began coming to visit me, bringing home-cooked food. She would take a bus and two subways to visit me and Vasken in Brooklyn. Vasken and I lived in the same building around the corner from Pratt Institute, in Clinton Hills. It was also close to Long Island University where I was enrolled with a full scholarship to become a Registered Professional Nurse, specializing in psychiatry and mental health. It was this that led me to merge into psychology, human rights, and mind-body-eco-spirit health.

If you think you're enlightened,
Go spend a week with your family.
~ Ram Dass

Withholding Feelings

One must have chaos within oneself
In order to give birth to a dancing star.
~ Friedrich Nietzsche

Expression of feelings was not at the top of our agenda in the Middle East. In the 1960's, people engaged in announcing what you have done wrong by criticizing one another, rather than celebrating the positive behaviors or giving constructive criticism. I was the first in my class from the first grade to the eighth grade. I noticed that other classmates received gifts from their parents for being the second or the third in our class, but I never received a gift or an acknowledgment from my parents for being the first. I knew we were poor, so gifts were out of question, but I did not even receive positive compliments. In the eighth grade, I remember rebelling and telling my mother, "Well, I am not going to be first any longer—I cannot tolerate that other classmates receive gifts for being second and third, and I don't get anything." I was told that I was expected to be the first, since I was capable of it and already proven myself for 8 years —why not continue?

Other expressions of love were also withheld, as my parents were of the antiquated (some say traditional or cultural) opinion that "children get spoiled if you show them compassion and outward expressions of love." It hurt me to hear from my father later on in life, before he died, that he used to kiss us at night while we were asleep and tell us that he loved us, because he did not want us to be "spoiled," and he did not want others in the community to hear of his love for us, especially to a girl child. I realized then that my parents were victims just as we were, and that they too suffered from the societal misconceptions. Here the trauma continued passing along from generation to generation, as my father shared that this is what his father had done as well—hence, the generational transmission.

Later on, I founded and volunteered with Meaningfulworld Humanitarian Outreach Programs in more than forty-five countries around the world, and in more than twenty-six states in the USA. I came to realize that withholding emotions is a continuing ill practice around the world, especially in developing countries, but also in the United States. A similar expression was given to us at our eleventh Meaningfulworld Humanitarian Mission to Haiti in June of 2016. A psychologist in his thirties stated that he prefers to show his feelings in his behavior rather than express his emotions verbally. Many other men agreed with him. We began educating these men and women about the importance of expression of feelings: letting family and friends know how one feels is important, it's positive, it's uplifting, and it's a learned behavior for the next generations. I am also perplexed as to why they weren't concerned about expressing their negative and judgmental feelings that poisoned us all energetically as well as emotionally. Even the Bible, among other religious philosophies, reinforces the importance of expression, as the Bible states that in the beginning there was the word, the word was God. Since God is love, the word is love. If the emotions are negative, and one is concerned about expressing those in order to not cause pain or suffering to the other person, then we could teach the assertiveness and empathic communication skills. See attachment 2, COPE Model of empathic and assertive communication.

From caring comes courage.
~ Lao Tzu

My mother was fifteen years old when she, against her will, was arranged to be married. She was pulled out of the eighth grade to marry my father, who was twenty-four years old; he too did not want to get married to my mom because she was too young. They were both forced into the arranged marriage due to their parents' relations; both Mom's and Dad's parents were forced out of their homes in Kilis, Anatolia, which is now occupied by Turkey. Both parents were subjected to the negative impact of the Genocide of the Armenians that killed close to 2 million Armenians, close to 1.5 million Greeks, and more than 230,000 Assyrians.

Fear and uncertainty permeated the Armenian communities in Syria. Therefore, my maternal grandparents felt that before another war took place, they should have all their five girls married. My parents had no say, no choice at all. In addition, the marrying couples had to be from the same town in ancient Armenia; for example, both sets of my grandparents, maternal and paternal, were from the town of Kilis in Anatolia (ancient Armenia). So, by that rationale, if you are from Fort Lee, New Jersey, you cannot marry someone from Englewood, although it is still in New Jersey, even if the person were of the same nationality (Armenian). It was apparent that Mom and Dad were not suited for each other, as Mom was from the town of Aleppo while Dad was from the village of Azez. Mom had to move from Aleppo to the village and basically move in with all the in-laws: two brothers-in-law, two sisters-in-law, a mother-in-law, and a father-in-law. She was like a servant servicing everyone in the family.

My mother's emotional breakdown is not surprising and it impacted all of us, but mostly my sister, who, as the elder in the house had to care for us, especially for Vasken, who was a baby. She had to wash all his diapers by hand, and she did not have a normal adolescence. Her hands would chap and bleed from the detergents and the pressure. Mom was oblivious to what was happening with her PPD, and she has never forgiven her sister and my father for their intervention in committing her to a mental institution. Fortunately, the psychiatrist noticed that Mom did not belong in that hospital, and she was discharged to a regular medical hospital in Aleppo, where she got much better.

I became my mom's spokesperson, or maybe the Syrian and Armenian women's spokesperson. I always argued with my mom and dad, protesting, "But it's not fair." I became the persistent voice of the silenced. I also grew angrier each day as I witnessed more discrimination and inequality between the genders.

Only years later I remembered how different we feel based on the place we hold in our sibling order, and the place we occupy in the society. I remembered this wonderful story: On one glorious morning, a teacher took his students outside to sit on the grass in a circle to meditate and pray. While the sun began rising, its rays reflected on the morning dew on the grass. The teacher went around the circle and asked each student what color the morning dew is. "Red," said the first with confidence, "orange," said the second with certainty, "yellow" asserted the third, and so on. Each one was confident that the color he or she saw was the truth and the only truth and the others were wrong. The teacher smiled and asked the students to change their seats in the circle. The students were shocked, as the first who was sure he saw red was now seeing purple, the second who was confident he saw orange was now seeing yellow, etc., and so the teacher concluded: Be mindful of your observations and convictions, as they depend on your position in life; where you are sitting, how you are observing, and the attitude that you are holding.

Culture Shock in American High School

The tongue has no bones; but it is strong enough
To cut a heart just like a knife.
So, let's be mindful when we think and
Manage the words uttered. Always asking mindfully, is it uplifting?
Is it positive? Will it make them happy?
~ Kalayjian

Here in America, I was starting to slowly experience and get in touch with my inner freedom, and freedom of choice. Of course, at home, we were still living as if we were in Aleppo; after all, my parents always reminded us "We are Armenian; we are not Americans," so the answer was always "no" when it came to permission to go to parties, field trips, or other gatherings. I was only allowed if one of my brothers could go with me as a chaperone, until they both moved out.

My first days in Fort Lee high school became very traumatic for me. During my first week, I was called a "dirty immigrant." When asked what I was, I responded "Armenian," and they asked in a demeaning way, "What's that?" I said that Armenia is partially a republic in the Soviet Union (it became independent in 1992). The other, larger part is occupied by Turkey.

They pushed me away, claiming I was a "communist." But I told them I was not even born in Armenia—I was born in Syria, as my father and his family were forced out of their home in Anatolia, after Ottoman Turks had forced the Armenians out of their homes and killed a million-and-a-half of them. "Where is Syria? You must be a terrorist," they responded! And they went on: "Do you have refrigerators? How about TV? Do you ride camels and donkeys?" They continued with their sly remarks, putting down who I was and where I was from....

Then the principal of the high school called me into his office. That was so embarrassing for me, for in Aleppo, if you were called into the principal's office, it meant you had done something wrong. I was crying, blushing from embarrassment, and couldn't make an eye contact. Meanwhile the principal, who was a friend of my elder brother Father Vertanes, was just welcoming me to the new school. Since I did not speak much English, this was hard for me to understand. The principal then called my brother and explained the situation, and my brother was then able to let me know the purpose of his visit, which made me much more relaxed.

Another shock at the high school was the attire. Since Fort Lee High School is a public school, uniforms were not mandatory; instead, students were wearing ripped clothes, mini short jeans, or long jeans with big holes in them. They were smoking cigarettes and drinking sodas. None of these behaviors would have been tolerated in my school in Aleppo. Many students there received harsh punishments for not having ironed shirts or proper uniforms. We stood up in respect when a teacher walked into our classroom, and we stood up when the teacher left. I guess this was the practice in America back in the 1950s, but not in the 1970s.

On the second day, when I needed to use the bathroom, I was not let in by the girls in the senior class, who told me I had to smoke cigarettes and only then would I be allowed to use the toilet. That was my culture shock. I was also amazed that students called their teachers by their first name, "Hey John," and not "Hello Mr. Smith."

I was accepted only after my younger brother had to use aggression and hit a bully in the locker room. After that he was respected, and then I was accepted and respected as his sister. I could not understand why aggression won respect and acceptance.

Going through the educational system was challenging, yet I persevered. I received a Bachelor's degree with honors, and then I received a full scholarship to continue my Master's and Doctoral degrees from Teachers College, Columbia University, while I worked nights to support myself financially as a Registered Professional Psychiatric Nurse at the Metropolitan Hospital in East Harlem, New York.

Having gone through all these experiences of trauma, shock, bullying, and harassment, I was intrigued to study suffering for my doctoral dissertation. My doctoral adviser at the time discouraged me and said, "If you choose a topic as large as suffering, you would be suffering by yourself, as I would not be your adviser, and you'd have to work by yourself." We then negotiated the topic to focus on the suffering of cancer patients' families and spouses.

At the same time, in the early 1980s, my father was suffering from cancer and the doctors had given him six months to live. Dad did not believe in medical doctors and medicine, and he had never been sick, never stayed home sick, and worked every day of his life, except on Sundays. He worked almost to the last day of his life, despite cancer. I was with him when he took his last breath. I actually had said goodbye to him, when I left for California to be a maid of honor at the double wedding of my twin cousins, Krikor and George. I saw Dad before I left for California, and he told me to go ahead and enjoy life. I asked if

I should stay behind to be with him, and he laughed and said, "Why, do you think if you stay here I would not die? When my time comes I will go, so let's say goodbye now." We laughed, and we said our goodbyes. I cried leaving the hospital, as I knew very well I would not see him in his funny state again.

Right after the wedding ceremony, in California, I received a phone call from my sister indicating that Dad was in a partial coma and was calling my name, and that he was at death's door, perhaps hours away. I took the next flight home, went straight to the hospital, drove my mom home so she could get some rest, and then returned to the hospital. I was with Dad when he pulled his own IV and feeding tube out. Although he was unable to communicate, I explained to him that without the IV and feeding tube he would die. I told him if that is what he wanted, and if he was ready, then he should squeeze my finger, in which case I would not call the nurse to replace the fluids, which was what my mom had been doing for the last couple of days. He squeezed my finger tight, we gazed at each other's eyes intensely, and then there it was—THE DEEP BREATH—and the exhalation. After that there was no more breath. It was about 5 a.m., and out of the silence grew the chirping of the birds. The sun began rising, and there was this halo of light surrounding my father—his spirit had lifted and was watching over us. What a peaceful ending, after he'd struggled with prostate and lung cancer that had spread to his bones. Before his death, he asked that I keep a close watch over my mom and take good care of her; I realized then how much he cared and had grown to love Mom through the years.

After Dad's transition, Mom and I grew closer, as I chose to be geographically near her in New Jersey. I helped her with many things—her social security paperwork, supplements, communications, writing—as well as taking care of her bills, doctor's appointments, shopping, etc. Nonetheless she was still the same mom as always: tough, demanding, critical, feisty, and always wanting more from me, us, and herself. She always reinforced the value of education, as she had been unable to complete hers when pulled out of the eighth grade. She yearned for education, and vicariously she was very happy with her children's education. I was so grateful that she did not push me into marriage at a young age. Although my first suitor came to our house in Aleppo when I was only twelve years old, my parents told him, "Our daughter is too young to marry; she needs to complete her education." It was my relatives rather than my parents who pressured me to marry my cousin.

Arranged Engagement

I had traveled to Aleppo to see my sister and her family, as well as my high school sweetheart there. While my high school friends and I cried the entire night before my engagement, my sweetheart, a twenty-two-year-old, was very sad, but unable to marry me at that time, as he was still studying. My Uncle Hovanness and other relatives planned this big, wonderful engagement with my first maternal cousin, who lived in Beirut, Lebanon. The engagement looked like a wedding, with a live band, dozens of arrangements of flower baskets, gifts, and poolside festivities. I was a lost teen, twenty-two but felt like sixteen years of age, and could not withstand the pressures of my family. I got engaged and returned to the USA. As soon as I returned, I knew this was not an engagement I wanted to keep; after all, we were first cousins. I wrote a long letter to my cousin and explained to him that I got engaged under extreme pressure, and that it is not healthy for us to stay engaged, as our children will have a high probability of being abnormal, and I apologized for ending it. I am sure he was relieved as well, as he himself was also pressured into the engagement, although we both liked each other as cousins. He had already been seeing someone else, whom his family did not approve of, so they went ahead and got married, and thankfully they are still very happy together; and I enjoy a great friendship with both of them.

Generational Transmission of Trauma

The most straightforward advice on awakening enlightened mind is this:
Practice not causing harm to anyone—yourself or others—and every day, do
what you can to be helpful.
~ Pema Chodron

20

History, despite its wrenching pain, cannot be unlived;
But if faced with courage, it need not be lived again!
~ Maya Angelou

One day when I came home from the elementary school in Aleppo, I noticed that my mother, along with a few female neighbors, was wearing all black, and they were all crying or looking very sad. Other times I noticed that men were gathered in sadness, looking through the daily Armenian newspapers, frantically looking, in vain, for long-lost relatives. When I inquired what they were sad about, they almost always denied they were sad and brushed me off by telling me to go focus on my homework. I understand that they were brushing me off to "protect" me, as I was too young, but in hindsight, if they had given me some response it would have been healthier—as I carried a lot of that sadness and pain in my body and it all lodged in my intestines. When children ask a question, no matter how hard, challenging or difficult it is, adults must give a short response to comfort the child, then reinforce that they care about and love them, and only then direct them to the next task or a distraction. When questions are left unanswered, children find other ways to get the answer, and most of the time it may not be the right answer and they will be in even more distress. Then children may shut down and start making up their own answers, distancing themselves further and further from reality.

At this same time in 1967, the Syrian and Israeli war was taking place and we had to run to our subbasements many times for protection. Or we had to smudge our windows with starch and blue powder so the Israeli military would think no one was living in our home. In the subbasement, I remember having a serious conversation with a mouse, which was not even afraid of me, and was standing on top of an empty Gigos aluminum milk can. Our windows were shattered many times because the Israeli military airplanes flew so low in our residential communities. I felt that adults were not only untrustworthy, but many actually behaved as though they were evil. I remember thinking about how to discern who is evil and who is not.

No matter what happened, war, rain or shine, Mom continued her strict rules of reading a verse from the Bible before even touching a piece of bread to her lips. Some days it was only bread and raisins that we had for lunch or dinner, as we were poor. There were three of us at home at this time: Kevork, Vasken, and me. Kevork, being the mischievous one, always wanted to skip lines from his Bible reading to get to breakfast faster. I took everything seriously then, and I reported it to Mom. Kevork was very upset with me and would then call me derogatory names, which truly hurt my feelings—and I even remember crying frequently. I cried because I did not mean to hurt him at all; I wanted us to all be truthful, I feared being deceitful before God, and fooling Mom. Fortunately, Mom and I still continue our praying rituals today (2017), at her golden age of ninety-four, as we pray daily before her bedtime, no matter if it is on the phone or in person.

Part II:

Self-Reflection Embracing Adulthood: Being the Change We Want to See

This section is about life changes and our initiatives. When did you feel a shift, and a transition from sad to happy? Did you feel a shift from victimhood to victorhood? Did you feel a shift from dissatisfaction to satisfaction? Or shifting from helplessness to empowerment? From illness to well-being? Was there a turning point in your life, and when was that?

1. What was the turning point for you? How old were you? Who was involved in this shift?
2. Describe your strengths, both scholastically and personally.
3. What are some of your special talents or skills that you feel proud of?
4. What would you like to start doing?
5. What would you like to stop doing?
6. How is your free time spent?
7. What kind of generational trauma do you feel you are carrying?
8. Were your ancestors involved in a war, genocide, or other mass trauma? How? What are the legacies that they have transmitted to you?
9. Reflect on the positive lessons you have learned from your ancestors.
10. What is the meaning of your existence?
11. What are you here to accomplish or fulfill?
12. How are you nurturing your passion in life?

Part III
Outreach to Families, Communities and the World

Workshop at the United Nations: World Congress of Women, Beijing, China

*There is nothing outside of yourself that can ever enable you
to get better, stronger, richer, quicker, or smarter.
Everything is within; everything exists inside of us,
seek nothing outside of yourself.*
~ Miyamoto Musashi

In 1988 I was invited to be a United Nations Representative for the World Federation for Mental Health. As part of my work at the UN, I was invited to conduct a workshop at the United Nations' International Women's Conference in Beijing, China, in 1995, on transforming violence against women. Ironically, I witnessed violence right at the conference between two Iranian women's groups, one group covered in black hijab, and the other group dressed in modern Western garments. It was apparent to me that the government of Iran had sent these women in hijab to Beijing to fight, as they chanted "Down with the West, down with the West, Islam is the best." It was sad to witness this violence, as the conference was all about human rights and women's rights. While I was videotaping this conflict, I was caught in the middle of their fight, pulling hair and hijabs—they even damaged the video camera I had borrowed from my brother-in-law.

I chose to stay away from the congress hotels and stayed in the infamous Tiananmen Square, so I could learn more from the authentic Chinese culture and the everyday residents. During one of my touristic visits I was followed and attacked by two what seemed to be police officers. I could not guess why. They were both trying to take my cameras away, yelling things in Chinese that I could not understand, and they seemed very angry. I was scared, but I knew somehow that

25

they would not hurt me and all they wanted was my camera. But I couldn't give them that, as it was a borrowed one. After five minutes of struggle, what seemed like hours, one of the men gave up and told the other officer in Chinese some things and left. I was left with one officer to fight with, and I felt confident that I could handle him. After all, I didn't do anything wrong. Imagine all this conflict is going on and everyone around me is ignoring us, they were not even looking at us. They were acting as if we did not exist. I was screaming for help, hundreds of people were walking by, many others were on bicycles or mopeds, but no one turned around or made eye contact with me. Finally I kicked the officer in the knee, jumped around a moped and ran into an alleyway, and from there I ran directly to my hotel. Locking my door twice, I kept looking out from the window to make sure that the officer had not followed me. At the hotel, I looked at the footage to find out what I had videotaped, but I could not find anything unusual.

I ended up returning home from China with a severe intestinal parasite. The United Nations' tropical physician put me on very strong antibiotics, yet despite that I was not getting any relief. I went to the hospital and underwent all sorts of exams: colonoscopy, endoscopy, and many other stool and blood tests—only to reveal nothing. As always, whenever medical doctors are frustrated regarding intestinal and gastric complications and cannot find anything conclusive, they surmise that you have irritable bowel syndrome (IBS) and that there is nothing they can do, except advising medications such as Prilosec, which has a list of negative side effects. I refused to take the medicine and continued my search for healing. Clearly, my anger and frustration were growing deeper.

Organize to Transform Global Traumas

People were created to be loved.
Things were created to be used.
The reason the world is in chaos is
Because things are being loved,
And people are being used.
~ Anonymous

In 1988, a few years after completing my doctoral degree at Columbia University, I invited a group of psychiatrists, psychologists, nurses, and social workers to start a new organization called the Armenian American Society for Studies on Stress and Genocide (AASSSG), a charitable, not-for-profit organization with a primary mission of studying the impact of genocides on individuals and communities, then studying the generational transmission, and then to work on prevention campaign. Our first project was to interview all the Armenian survivors of the Ottoman-Turkish Genocide of 1915 before they passed away. At that time, they were in their late seventies and early eighties. After that we interviewed the next generations. We interviewed close to fifty survivors. Their stories were depressing, and I was affected vicariously. Hearing of atrocities such as mass killings, mass burning of people while they were alive, gang rapes, slashing open the bellies of pregnant women, the nipples being cut off of young girls, was extremely difficult to endure. My frustration, disappointment in humanity, and distress grew deeper and deeper and transformed into raw anger.

Remember that anger is a secondary emotion, the result of other feelings such as sadness, frustration, disappointment, guilt, embarrassment, shame, hurt, jealousy, fear, anxiety, and worry, amongst others. If we do not identify and work on processing our feelings, then the anger and feelings of losing control take over, leaving us helpless in our rage, unable to control or manage our emotions.

At the end of 1988, a devastating earthquake struck in Armenia. (Armenia was under Soviet regime, it became independent in 1992). The quake caused more than 75,000 deaths and more than half a million internal displacements. We shifted our work to assist the traumatized communities in Armenia. I was the founder of the Mental Health Outreach Project to Armenia and sent more than fifty volunteer mental-health professionals over a two-year span, while also going there myself every six months. While we were working in Armenia, we came across many examples of the generational transmission of trauma: for example, the nightmares after the earthquake were not about the earthquake, they were about the Genocide. Survivors explained that their nightmares were about "Turkish Gendarmes, deserts of Arabia, and mass killings." The nightmares were all about the Genocide, even though these people had not witnessed the Genocide themselves, and some had not even heard it before. This was our very first scientific proof of the generational transmission of trauma. I had a big *AHA* moment, and then committed to continue this line of research.

Dialogue for Peace

In 1990 I started the Armenian Turkish Dialogue groups, which held monthly meetings with Armenian-Americans and Turkish-Americans (or those Turks who were studying in universities in New York area). We met bi-monthly, and once a year we had a public meeting at Fordham University, where I was teaching at the time. These public meetings had to have undercover New York Police officers present to prevent any undue aggression by denialists.

I continued the dialogue groups for a decade and concluded them in 2000. The last all-day dialogue involved both Turkish and Armenian scholars who acknowledged the Genocide: Professors Taner Akcam and Muge Gocek (Turks), and Professors Vahakn Dadrian and Richard Hovannisian (Armenians). We had two separate groups of processing. One group was composed of all Armenian-Americans, with an Armenian psychologist facilitating and a non-Armenian observer, and the other group had a Turkish psychologist facilitating and a non-Turkish observer. At the end of the day we shared our findings: The Turkish participants reported feeling humiliated and shocked, as they knew nothing about the Genocide. In fact, they believed just the opposite, as they had been taught that Armenians had killed the Turks, and not to trust Armenians (the Turkish government denialist agenda born out of fear of reparations)—while the Armenian participants expressed sadness and then anger when faced with the Turkish denial.

We concluded that the Turks and Armenians needed to process some of their unresolved emotions separately from one another, and then resume in a year or two. Unfortunately, in the meantime, the

Turkish participants concluded their studies and moved back to Turkey. I continued working with the Armenians, and I am still working with the Armenians as well as all who want to work on their ancestral trauma and who wish to transform that ancestral trauma into both lessons learned and ancestral wisdom.

Negative Impact of Anger

Anger is one letter away from **D**anger. I remember what Martin Luther King, Jr. said:

> *Darkness cannot drive out darkness;*
> *Only light can do that!*

As a secondary emotion, anger has many negative consequences to our physical body, to our emotional management, and to our spiritual connection. Anger constricts our lungs, preventing their expansion and constricting our breath. Breath (oxygen) is vital for our health, nurturing our cells and giving us a relaxed mind.

I invite you to refrain from gossip and any negative thought or comment about yourself, as well as about others. Stereotypes and negativity will block the creation of peaceful opportunities around us. Prejudice and negative attitudes will stop you from getting to know another fully and from embracing that person's strengths.

Remember that no two individuals respond the same way when facing a conflict or a problem. How you respond depends on your biological constitution, psychological characteristics, the social structure that you are in, your culture and religion, and your environment. Therefore, first disarm yourself and then listen mindfully and don't take anything personally. Always ask, "What can I do differently now?"

I recommend that we all disarm ourselves within, emotionally—to release our negative feelings that are restricting us and holding us hostage:

Let go of **A**nger
Let go of **N**egativity
Let go of **G**reed
Let go of **E**nvy
Let go of **R**age
ANGER

I invite us to focus on where the anger is coming from. What is underlying our anger? Looking at the Anger Wheel we can easily Identify, Describe, Express, and Let go—(IDEAL), an easy way to recall the acronym and to reinforce the concept.

Remember that anger is a poison. "Anger and resentment are like taking a poison and expecting and hoping that the enemy (or the other) will die" (Anonymous). Actually, the only person dying slowly is the one who has the anger or the outburst of resentment. In this way, the conflict continues. It's just as Martin Luther King, Jr. said:

"The ultimate weakness of violence is that it is a descending spiral, begetting the very thing it seeks to destroy. Instead of diminishing evil, it multiplies it. Through violence you may murder the liar, but you cannot murder the lie, nor establish the truth. Through violence you murder the hater, but you do not murder hate. In fact, violence merely increases hate... Returning violence for violence multiplies violence, adding deeper darkness to a night already devoid of stars. Hate cannot drive out hate: Only love can do that."

In order to release and let go of our negative emotions, we first need to learn about ourselves. What are our biases, perceptual filters, or blind spots? What are our personal triggers? Meaning, if we haven't slept and are not well rested, how do we usually respond to situations? Do we react? Or do we take it in and take it personally and still react with extreme frustration? Remember that attitude is everything. Remember also that while we may not consciously choose the difficult situations we find ourselves in, we can definitely choose our attitudes and our responses. Kindly see attachment 13, Elizabeth Lukas's diagram.

I invite you to approach challenges or problems with flexibility. I invite you to be more like an elastic band than a piece of metal. Life requires flexibility to cope with its multiple challenges. Remember that we cannot change others, or the circumstances around us. We can only change ourselves—and then we will, perhaps, attract more positive people and positive situations into our lives.

Then I invite us to take a listening stance. Remember that we have two eyes and two ears, but we have only one mouth! This is a reminder for us to be twice as observant and to double our listening while we speak less. As you already know what is on your mind, therefore, if you speak you will learn nothing new; while if you listen and are observant, you may learn new things.

7 Steps for Empathic Listening

~ Dr. Kalayjian

1. Listen with your ears: Listen fully; don't prepare what you have to say next.
2. Listen with your heart: Hear what is really meant, beyond the words, through heart-to-heart connection.
3. Listen with your mind: Listen to what they (opponent, the other) went through, where they came from, where they are going.
4. Listen with your entire body: As you listen, also observe the other person's entire body.
5. Listen with prayer: Pray to get help with difficulties.
6. Listen with love: After all, that is what bonds us as humans.
7. Listen with intention: Listen to be there for the other, to understand the other fully.

We could transform most of our frustrations and disappointments through assertiveness. Assertiveness is owning our observations and perceptions and expressing our desires in a non-judgmental way—that means without pointing the finger at and blaming the other, all while owning and being mindful of our own feelings, thoughts, and responsibilities.

Managing and figuring out our emotions is of primary importance. If we do not manage our negative emotions well, then we are vulnerable to reactions and outbursts that hurt us more than they hurt anyone else. After hurting ourselves, then we might transfer this to others who are near and dear to us. This is called Horizontal Violence.

Horizontal Violence

Original research on Horizontal Violence was conducted with oppressed groups of people such as women, African Americans, and other oppressed groups in America. The oppression and resulting frustrations are usually top down: Oppression goes down from governments to the people, from a boss at work to the employees, from parents to a child or children. When this oppression continues, the oppressed individual may make several attempts to cope with the resulting negative feelings, but he still grows continuously sad and mad, and at the end, he blows up on the very people who surround him, the very ones he loves. Therefore, those who will be impacted by this blowing-up negative behavior are the ones who love us most and who are innocently trying to help us in their own ways.

Crab in the Bucket Phenomenon: Southern African Americans call horizontal violence the "crab in the bucket" phenomenon. Have you ever observed a dozen crabs in a bucket? When one crab tries to crawl up and attempts to come out of the bucket, another crab pulls it down. A third crab tries to get out of the bucket, yet a fourth crab tries to pull it down. What is the outcome? None of the crabs are able to leave the bucket—and they all suffer in there together.

When we were conducting a postwar humanitarian mission in Sierra Leone in 2010, they called it "the pulling down syndrome." The Sierra Leoneans were pulling one another down with violence, using machetes and knives. This also happened in Haiti, as well as in Armenia. The people of small countries that were oppressed for generations by either colonizers or the Ottoman Empire (for Armenia) —countries that were finally gaining independence—were engaging in

Horizontal Violence, hurting the very people they care about, namely their communities and their families. We found that these communities were pulling one another down, through their jealousy, envy, comparisons, negative gossip, or outward physical and emotional violence. And when we brought it to their attention, they agreed with us fully that it was indeed an unconscious "pulling down syndrome."

When you are mindful of your reactions, you can then consciously choose peaceful actions. For example, before speaking out, think about the following: Is what you are planning to say positive? Is what you are thinking kind? Does it help uplift others from their darkness? Is what you are planning to say empathic? If the answer to any of these questions is no, then it is best that you say nothing at all. Instead, take a few moments to breathe deeply, and reflect on where did these negative thoughts came from. What are the roots of your negative thought patterns? Through the IDEAL process, you clarify your feelings and transform them into positive steppingstones that enable you to rise above the negativity, toward enlightenment. Reaffirm your compassionate self by repeating with visualization, faith, and commitment:

I am a positive healing light;

I am full of positive thoughts and uplifting intentions.

How many times have you observed your parents or friends who are so caring outside of their home, perhaps in their workplace or an organization, but when they come to their own homes, they behave in an abusive and demeaning way? I have observed this behavior many thousands of times, among my clients in my private practice and through firsthand observations of my own parents, as well as my friends, who have high positions at the United Nations, in government, or as independent CEOs or CFOs of large companies.

Of course, we are mostly unaware and unconscious of our Horizontal Violence behavior and its impact on others. I repeat again: Trauma and pain that are not transformed will be transferred to others around us. If, when we are mindful, when we notice, observe, and realize that we are hurting ourselves and that we are hurting our loved ones, then we need to stop and do something drastic to transform our behavior—and we always need to apologize. Always start by saying, "Oh, I am sorry," even if you have not caused any harm or ill feeling, but you know very well that your family member is in pain. Say "I am sorry you are in emotional pain." I think we could transform the world when we start saying "I am sorry" more often—and meaning it.

Part III

Self-Reflection Outreach to Families, Communities and the World

In this section, after nurturing yourself and caring compassionately for yourself, I invite you now to learn or discover the positive lessons.

1. Identify your support system; write about who they are, how they are supportive to you.
2. Identify and reflect on how you nurture your support system.
3. Have you found yourself losing control of your emotions and blowing up, or having an anger outburst? Identify three feelings that you felt from the Anger Wheel. Reflect on the negative consequences you had to endure due to this outburst.
4. Through the use of IDEAL, kindly identify, describe, express, and let go of all negative feelings one by one.
5. Identify and share about your friends; are they part of your support system? How so? If yes, describe how they are supportive.
6. How many long-term close friends do you have? Remember that Face Book and other social media friends do not count unless you see them in person; you can call on them when you need to, and you can rely on them when you're in a difficult situation.
7. I invite you to use the listening tool to improve your empathy, and to embrace your family and friends.
8. Who is in your community? Do you belong to a religious, cultural, social, professional, or spiritual community?? Please describe in detail who your community is and how you are benefiting from it.
9. If you don't have a family of origin (or they have been deceased or displaced), please share about how you are selecting and nurturing a new family of friends. As the old saying goes, "Show me your friends, and I will tell you who

you are," so kindly be mindful of the mirror reflection in your mindful new family.

10. What are the three main lessons from your past experiences? Remember that lessons are not negative, and they are about us and not others. Lessons are positive reflections that we discover from our experiences. Even the most tragic incident can have positive lessons to be discovered.

11. Were you subjected to the negative feelings of Horizontal Violence within your family and community? IDEAL.

12. I invite you to share your three lessons with a minimum of three people in your immediate circle, as well as in your larger social network.

Part IV

Making Meaning out of the Nonsense

Training in Logotherapy:

Forgiveness is the economy of the heart...
forgiveness saves the expense of anger,
the cost of hatred, the waste of spirits.
~ Hannah More

Around 1988 I had begun to study logotherapy, the meaning-oriented therapy founded by Viktor Frankl (1962). I was fortunate that Frankl was traveling to San Jose, California, in 1990, for the Logotherapy Congress and I took a course with him. I also presented our research on the post-earthquake meaning-making in Armenia.

Meeting Viktor Frankl was the highlight of my life. He was so personable, so humorous, so down to earth, and even at age ninety-four, when he was almost blind, he had just returned from a mountain-climbing expedition. I was amazed that I was sitting next to Frankl, the author of *Man's Search for Meaning* as well as additional forty-plus books on meaning-centered therapy. Frankl told us how he was friends and colleagues with both Freud and Adler. He was disenchanted by their theories, and he separated himself and began his own school of thought: the meaning-centered therapy. I was very impressed that although he went through the Holocaust and lost all his family members, including his wife, he was not only able to overcome his trauma and multiple losses, but he was also able to embrace a forgiving stance and share his views in his publications, which helped me and millions of others tremendously.

I asked for Frankl's guidance on what I should do with the anger/sadness of the Armenian-American survivors of the Ottoman-Turkish Genocide, and without a moment of contemplation, in his strong Viennese accent he said, "You have to help them forgive." I was shocked, as I thought that since the Turkish government continues denying the Genocide that we cannot forgive. Therefore, I automatically said, "But the Turkish government is denying!" and he asked me quickly, "And how long do you plan to wait?" It was another major *AHA* moment, and I felt in my gut that it's true: being and staying angry at the Turkish government is killing me slowly inside. Anger was messing up my delicate intestines. Only then did I understand that forgiveness has nothing to do with the Turks or anyone else; it is an inner state of being, bringing peace internally, which has nothing to do with others. It's just as Jesus said: "Father, forgive them, for they know not what they do." I think this is the first statement reinforcing the value of mindfulness. Creating peace inside, ending anger, retaliation, and revenge, and embracing gratitude are the keys to our emotional health. Frankl reinforced that we have the will to exercise to be human, transforming the pain into lessons learned, and reframing.

The Oxford English Dictionary defines forgiveness as "to grant free pardon and to give up all claim on account of an offence or debt." Although this is not our definition of forgiveness, as we see forgiveness as letting go of our negative feelings, while pursuing our human rights through due process. The concept and benefits of forgiveness have been explored in religious thought, the social sciences, and medicine. In some contexts, forgiveness may be granted without any expectation of restorative justice, and without any response on the part of the offender. (For example, one may forgive a person who is incommunicado, denialist, or dead,)

> *The weak can never forgive,*
> *Forgiveness is the attribute of the strong.*
> *~ Mahatma Gandhi*

Reframing is using another explanation, placing another frame on the same situation, on the same script that we have maintained for years, which makes us realize that the frame or the narrative we give to our situation changes when we consciously and mindfully reframe.

Our scientific research with the survivors of the Ottoman-Turkish Genocide revealed that there was continued suffering, even seventy-five years after the Genocide. Armenian survivors shared that the

Genocide had a devastating effect on their ability to live a normal life. They were burdened with sadness, and forced to live in the past (due to the Turkish government's denial). They shared that they were living in a continuous state of trauma and felt generalized helplessness, which was turning into anger.

Logotherapy Course with Viktor Frankl

Taking the logotherapy course with Frankl was transformative for me, and I was excited to share this with my family, friends, other survivors, and the Armenian-American community. But the community was not ready to receive the message of forgiveness; therefore, I received a lot of threats to my life from the Turkish-American community, as well as hate messages and hate articles published by the Armenian-American community. The Armenian-Americans called me a "traitor" and an "enemy lover," while the Turkish Americans, filled with shock and humiliation, were denying that the Genocide ever happened. They projected that on me, and on all Armenians, by presenting a denialist view: The Genocide did *not* happen! Neither side was ready. Even after a decade of dialogue groups between Armenians and Turks in New York, from 1990-2000, neither side was ready to discuss forgiveness. In the dialogue groups, I used the *principles* of forgiveness, without using the "F" word.

One Armenian newspaper published this headline: "Dr. Kalayjian gives the wrong diagnosis and the wrong prescription." Another newspaper published "Dr. Kalayjian is not a survivor, and has no right to forgive the Turks." And there were many more articles depicting the lack of understanding, as well as the unresolved generational pain and frustration revealed in their angry posts and articles.

The healing can occur through forgiveness
Even in the absence of the perpetrator's remorse,
and through finding a deeper meaning in even the worst experiences.
~ Kalayjian, 2008

Establishing a MeaningfulWorld

I realized that we are all traumatized, not just Armenians as survivors and Turks themselves as offspring of perpetrators—not only Jews who went through the tragic Holocaust, nor Cambodians and Rwandans who were also traumatized in genocides. We are all traumatized in one way or another. Our differences depend on how long we have been traumatized, and what kind of support system we had—who was there to assist us. In 1990 I started another organization, which was more general and focused on transforming trauma: the Association for Trauma Outreach and Prevention, which became Meaningfulworld in 2000. Meaningfulworld is dedicated to fostering a meaningful, peaceful, and just world in which every individual enjoys physical, mental, emotional, and spiritual health. A sense of meaning, peace, and justice, although unique to each individual, is achieved through a transformative journey that integrates knowledge and experience with a sense of responsibility and reflection. This transformative process is also attained through healthy relationships that nurture open, honest, and transparent communication, insight into forgiveness, love and spiritual connection, service to humanity, and active collaborations.

> *Forgiveness is shifting from the automatic ego reaction*
> *(anger/self-protection, hurting back),*
> *to a non-reactive conscious response of empathy;*
> *Considering that the other person is*
> *ALSO. a human being, perhaps not mindful.*
> *~ 2010 Forgiveness and Reconciliation*

Meaningfulworld facilitates this journey through providing information through lectures, workshops, opportunities for informal networking, humanitarian outreach programs, healing groups, research, and publications. Individual and collective opportunities for change, development, and transcendence are also provided through workshops, clinical interventions, and referrals. These services are provided in a peaceful atmosphere of acceptance, respect, and compassion. At Meaningfulworld, the ultimate goal is to prepare a generation of conscientious individuals who are guided by love, peace, passion, justice, and meaning.

In 1992, Hurricane Andrew devastated southern Florida, so I organized another Mental Health Outreach program for Florida. We continued this work, organized volunteer professionals, and conducted many outreach programs in other parts of the world: the 1994 Northridge (California) earthquake; the 1995 earthquake in Kobe, Japan, followed by outreach missions to Africa, the Middle East, the Caribbean, Europe, Asia, South America, and North America (Attachment 11: list of outreach programs).

As I wrote in my first book in 1995, disasters will increase in their frequency and severity and will cause an increase in the number of casualties, due not only to the Global Fever, but also due to humanity's reckless abuse of our environment as well as ourselves. Sure enough, we witnessed the increase of devastation before our eyes. The devastation came not only from natural disasters, but also in human-made disasters such as genocides in Rwanda, Burundi, and Democratic Republic of the Congo. Meanwhile, terrorism and political violence were multiplying in Kenya, the Caucasus, the Middle East (especially in Palestine and Syria), and South America.

Naturopathic Healing

My intestinal issue was worsening. I began exploring Ayurvedic healing, body energetic work, Reiki, and many other modalities for healing. Interestingly, my marriage of ten years was also ending at this time, although I had thought we were compatible: we both shared a good sense of humor, both believed in higher education, both believed in women's equality and in having a child or two to pass on our love, compassion, and quest for self-knowledge. Somehow after marriage, however, his sense of gender equality shifted. Even though he could not support us financially, he expected at the same time that I stay home instead of taking a position as a professor at a nearby university, and that I not travel anywhere for professional conferences for career advancement.

In 1999 I met a wonderful, intuitive, naturopathic healer, Sandra Del Cioppio, who placed me on digestive enzymes and probiotics. Miraculously, I started feeling so great—I had not felt better than that in ten years. Of course, I had also changed my lifestyle, decreasing my work hours, and practicing yoga more regularly (I was already going to the gym three to four times a week). Then I began an active healing journey, increasing my yoga practice from once a week to three times a week, which I highly recommend to you. I became certified YogaFit Teacher and created Soul-Surfing, which integrates breath, yoga, visualization, mindfulness of color vibrations of chakras (energy centers), and positive affirmations with mindful movements.

Part IV

Self-Reflection Making Meaning out of the Nonsense

1. What is your global meaning in your existence in this life?
2. How has your newly discovered meaning helped you with your life situations?
3. With how many people have you shared your positive meanings?
4. I invite you to use meaning-centered resolution for your daily stressors. After discharging your emotions through IDEAL, always ask yourself, "What did I learn from this challenging situation?"
5. What indigenous healing lessons have you learned from your ancestors?
6. How do you use Mother Earth's natural flowers and herbs to heal yourself?
7. Make a list of your challenges, in detail, and then I invite you to use the IDEAL model to identify, describe, express, and let go of all the negative impacts.
8. Only then (after completing step 7 above) should you reflect on the positive lessons you have learned.
9. What have your challenges been when attempting to forgive?
10. How do you overcome the darkness—the negative—and embrace mindful healing?
11. Practice the seven steps of forgiveness over and over. Also, be mindful to protect yourself from harm.
12. Forgiveness does not mean staying in abusive relationships. Evaluate your friendships one by one, and let go of those that are pulling you down.

Part V

Healing Myself and Sharing
This Knowledge with Others

Discovering the 7-Step Integrative Healing Model

The world around us will never be peaceful until we ourselves are at
PEACE WITHIN
If we are fighting and angry on the inside,
we will never experience the opposite on the outside.
~ Dali Lama

It took me several years of trial and error, several years of medical, non-medical, traditional and complementary approaches to establish an integrative healing modality that is holistic and inclusive to address all illnesses that are emotionally based—from individual trauma, as well as inherited trauma. Most of all, I wanted to come up with a preventive tool to help us stay away from illnesses, infections, inflammations, and hospitals. This journey was very interesting; it started in the mid-1990s when I got a severe parasite infection, which made my intestinal situation worsen.

During this process, I came across many people who were suffering from similar intestinal issues, and I was able to help them through my experience. Establishing the 7-Step Integrative Healing Model not only helped me heal my own unresolved intestinal issues, it also helped many people in my private practice in psychotherapy as well as many around the world through our volunteer Meaningfulworld Humanitarian Outreach projects.

Here are the seven steps of healing for our bodies, hearts, emotions, souls, and spirit. (Kindly see attachments 3 to 5 for the versions meant for children and adolescents, adults, and older adults.) The steps are amazingly intuitive and non-clinical, but if you wish to make the process clinical, you can. It is an integrative and transformative journey for healing. Healing starts with self-appraisal, self-knowledge—knowledge that comes from being our own doctors and our own healers or shamans.

Through these seven steps, various aspects of distress, conflict, trauma, or disagreement are assessed, identified, explored, processed, worked through, and reintegrated into our psyche with the lessons learned—therefore, we do not have to repeat nor attract similar traumas, as we have now learned the valuable lessons (Kalayjian, 2002).

Nothing will go away
until we learn the lessons!
~ Pema Chodron

This innovative and integrative model incorporates various theories. Here are the scientific steps of the model: psychodynamic (Freud, 1910); interpersonal (Sullivan, 1953); existential and humanistic (Frankl, 1962); Electromagnetic Field Balancing (EMF, Dubro & Lapierre, 2002); forgiveness and reconciliation (Kalayjian & Paloutzian, 2010); Learning Theory, flower essences, essential oils, physical release (van der Kolk, 1987); and mind-body-spirit chakra balancing, Soul-Surfing, prayers, and meditation. The following are the seven steps of the Integrative Healing Model:

Step I:
Identify and Assess Your Feelings

Assess your feelings and then measure

I am still learning.
~ Michelangelo, age eighty-seven

If using this model on an individual level, kindly refer to your anger wheel (attachment 1), and identify the feeling that's most dominant (around the wheel) that may result in the secondary emotion of anger. When you are successfully able to identify your feeling, then you are invited to measure it from one to ten, with ten being the most severe feeling. This is just like taking your temperature if you are feeling feverish, to find out the degree of your fever. Since we do not have thermometers to measure our emotions, you are empowered to use your inner connection and come up with a number. With anything under five, you may be able to manage easily. With anything over five, you need to work through by following the steps of this model.

If this model is used in a group setting, participants are given a written questionnaire to help them define the kind of distress or dispute, trauma, or issue they are working on and elicit the impact of this trauma or conflict. Formal assessment instruments may also be provided, such as the Harvard Trauma Checklist and the Forgiveness and Meaning Questionnaires. (Kindly see attachments 6-8.)

For example, if you realized that you are feeling frustrated, ask yourself: On a scale of one to ten, what level is my frustration at this moment? When you find out the level—let's say it's at eight—then ask yourself, "What makes me feel frustrated?" Never ask "Why am I feeling frustrated?" as our minds play tricks and then we start taking things personally and therefore judging ourselves and then blaming others, and we never get to discharge, nor learn the lessons. Even if a friend of yours is sharing that he or she is feeling frustrated, always ask the person, "What makes you feel frustrated?" In this way, we are not blaming anyone, or putting them on the spot, and instead focusing on the roots of the feeling—where it came from, how we perceived it, and how we could release it. Questions that start with "why" make us handicapped, as they take us to the past, where we felt vulnerable, frustrated, embarrassed, hurt or sad, or a host of other negative feelings, while questions that start with "What makes me…" bring us to the present, to the moment that we are in, and take us away from the painful past. They also may empower us to think rationally, and release the feeling more easily.

Questions starting with "why" make us feel guilty, embarrassed, or another negative feeling that we do not like, and then we either hurt ourselves unconsciously or try to hurt someone else. Questions starting with "why" are leading to a reason, and at many intervals or situations, we may not know why we are feeling what we are feeling. It is like asking why the sky is cloudy. Of course, there is a scientific reason for the cloud formation, but the fact remains that we cannot change the number of the clouds, nor the wind factor that changes their direction, but we could definitely rearrange our sails (if we are sailing), or our attitudes about the meaning of clouds. It means we could change our outlook, and our attitude, which are the only things we could change and manage.

Situation:

A sixteen-year-old adolescent male named Jess was having issues with his new supervisor, who was not paying him on time, and even when he did pay him he was not paying him the full hours that he worked as a lifeguard. Jess kept on repeating that his supervisor was an idiot, stingy, and a thief, as he was not paying him fully. He kept asking why his supervisor had not paid him fully. And therefore, he was coming up with assumptions that his supervisor was a thief, and that his supervisor was stingy, etc. which was making him louder, angrier, and more and more out of control. After he discussed this with me, I asked him to identify what was behind his anger. He said he felt frustrated and disappointed. He assumed that responsible behavior from an adult supervisor would not be to withhold payment, which made him even more "mad," as he described it. When I asked him, "What can you do about it now?" he took a deep breath and responded by saying, "I want him to be a responsible adult supervisor and be fair and pay me fully." I followed: "That is about him, we cannot change him, what can you do about it now?" He then said "I could assert myself and write him an e-mail indicating my needs." I responded with a positive affirmation.

The Anger Wheel is a helpful tool to use in this step (Attachment 1). Many clients identify with the secondary emotion of anger very easily, without noticing that anger is just the outcome and the secondary feeling, not the underlying roots of this feeling. Many clients have had *AHA* moments of realization when using the Anger Wheel, as they realize and identify the core issues underlying their negative feelings. When Jess used the Anger Wheel, he too had an *AHA* moment. He said he felt frustrated, and that his assumption that an adult should be more responsible elevated his levels of frustration and he became angry. As soon as he released the assumption and focused on the moment and what he could do about the situation, Jess felt empowered. He wrote an assertive e-mail to his supervisor, and the issue was resolved and he received his full payment within two weeks.

7-Step Model with Children

Knowledge is learning something every day.
Wisdom is letting go of something every day.
~ Zen Proverb

If the 7-Step Model is used with children, then the child's level of stress symptomatology and other distress is assessed through observations during play and art therapy. Parents' and other caretakers' levels of trauma and distress are assessed as well, as parents' unresolved stress and anxiety pass on to the child. On an individual level, the Anger Wheel is given to children, adolescents, and adults to help them identify their feeling and measure it on the scale of one to ten that indicates the severity of the feeling.

Each morning when you awaken, I recommend that you scan your emotions and ask yourself, "How am I feeling at this moment?" If we have difficulty identifying our feelings, then we can take a look at the

Anger Wheel and identify each feeling, or look at the longer list of feelings (Attachment 1a). After identifying our feeling, we then go on to measure it on a scale of one to ten. Just as you would use the thermometer to measure your body temperature, you can use this wheel to identify (measure), describe, express, and let go your emotions (IDEAL). Without going into our ego or judgment, we ask ourselves: "What can I do about it now?" It means we consciously bring our attention to the present—and what we could do (or not do)—instead of reinforcing our sense of helplessness and our self-judgment buried in the past trauma.

Situation:

A successful businessman in his late forties was experiencing severe anger outbursts in his marriage. He came to see me to resolve his anger issues, and after seeing the Anger Wheel, he realized that he was actually feeling extreme hurt, frustration, embarrassment, and disappointment—which were making him feel angry—and that he was losing control of his emotions and behaving irrationally or inappropriately. This was a big *AHA* moment for him. As soon as he made this realization, he began working on measuring the levels of his hurt, and then slowly he was able to talk about how hurt he felt, and what was making him feel hurt.

Situation:

A single mother in her late forties was extremely "angry," as she put it, regarding her teenage daughter, who smelled of marijuana smoke. The daughter was denying it vehemently. When I gave the Anger Wheel to the mother, she immediately said that she was extremely disappointed in her daughter. Feelings of anger were melting away as the mother began to understand that her reactions grew from feelings of disappointment, and only then was she able to manage her feelings step by step using the 7-steps of Integrative Healing Model.

Situation:

A young woman, Mary, twenty-two years of age, made an appointment to discuss and heal an eating disorder that she was suffering from. Although she had been suffering for a long time, since she was a teenager, she never knew the underlying reasons for her disorder. After the assessment, she was able to realize that she had distressing and conflictual relations with her father, starting when she was a preteen. After examining the Anger Wheel, Mary realized that although at first she identified with the secondary emotion of anger, it was actually sadness that she felt, resulting from her conflictual relations with her father. Although she had been to many psychotherapists before coming to me, she had never realized the source of her anger—the roots of her conflictual relations with her father—therefore, she'd been unable to manage the overwhelming anger she'd identified with at first.

Step II:
Express and Release Your Feelings

You are confined only by the walls
You build yourself.
Healing doesn't mean that the damage never existed.
It means the damage no longer controls our lives.
~ Anonymous

Express your feelings: If we are using this 7-Step Model in a group setting, one at a time, each participant in the group is encouraged to describe his or her feelings about the trauma, or the conflict from his or her perspective and express feelings in the "here and now" in relation to the trauma, dispute, or conflict that has been identified and measured in Step I.

Step II is a very important step. It is the clearing and cleansing process. While we may take daily showers (at least in Western countries, where water is freely available), we never think about washing our inner selves, and cleansing our hearts from our negative emotions. We wash our face and brush our teeth regularly, but what happens to our heart? What happens when our emotions are in havoc or we have cluttered minds? Who cleanses our mind, our heart, our soul, and all the negative emotions? Who will be responsible for releasing our negative emotions? We have, on an average, more than 60,000 thoughts per day, and each of these thoughts generates some kind of feeling, with differing levels of intensity, and when the feelings are sadness, hurt, and helplessness, we push them down, as we don't like them. We push such feelings down and want to push them out as fast as we can, to make them disappear. Why? Some say it's because it hurts to talk about our traumas; others are afraid that they will cry or have a flood of negative or sad emotions; still others say that they don't want to lose control. Therefore, as we often say, "We sweep it under the rug." We actually let those feelings cause us pain and suffering; we attach to and identify with our thoughts and feelings and therefore end up judging ourselves negatively. We think: "I was so

53

stupid," "I cannot believe I am such an idiot," "I am embarrassed by my actions," and on and on, with one negative judgment followed by another. We link our ego with our thoughts and feelings, and usually our ego is judgmental, selfish, and self-centered, focusing on "me, me, and me." We judge negatively, and reprimand ourselves. Talking about our feelings with a purpose of release helps us through this negative cycle.

In order to release our emotions in a healthy way, we select someone to talk with who is not judgmental, or someone who will not ask us to forget about it, to not think about it, to go out and get a drink or offer some other way of distracting us so we do not feel our negative feelings. We tend to push our feelings down deeper and deeper, until they are no longer available to us, while the painful impact is still haunting us.

So, what if you cannot find a non-judgmental and empathic person to talk with to help you release your negative emotions? Well then write it in your journal, release it and then burn the paper (if you feel it's too personal and you don't want anyone to find it and read it). Write all you can in longhand (cursive), hand written, and then have a small ritual of prayer and meditation, and bury it outside of your home, in a park, or outside your workplace. Then burn sage and cleanse your home. Or reach out to talk with a professional psychologist or a psychotherapist.

Whatever you do, please find a way to release your emotions, because if you don't release them they will haunt you, handicap you, and control your life. This issue or trauma will then be central in your life, and since you have pushed it so far down, you will need a skilled psychologist to help you release it. This is a very important step!

I'd like to remind you that you don't need to have a big problem to see a psychologist. You also don't need to be in a crisis to see a psychologist, as a friend of mine protested a few days ago when I recommended that she speak with a professional. She said to me, "I don't need to see a psychotherapist, as I am not in crisis, I am not having panic attacks, I am handling it," meanwhile, she was having issues managing her feelings; she had lost her house and her employment. Preventive psychotherapy is an important step for a healthy and a joyous life. Just as you are advised to get annual physical check-ups, you also need annual emotional and psychological check-ups. It's just like getting a massage—you don't need to wait for a back pain to schedule one. Massage is a preventive approach to physical health and healing. Psychotherapy is similar, in that it is a preventive method to achieve emotional health, to help you learn to manage your emotions in a healthier way, and learn to manage others' emotions as well by setting boundaries and protecting yourself from those who drain your energy.

Psychotherapy is a journey to help you heal, feel empowered, and grow through the processing and releasing of your anxieties, fears, and frustrations, and to establish inner happiness. By letting go of painful experiences, we allow positive energy to fill our hearts and we generate compassion, hope, and love first for ourselves, and then for others. After all, when we learn to practice forgiveness - embracing that which we cannot change and being the change we want to see- we bring peace into our lives. We then learn how to discover a meaning or a positive lesson, transforming the painful past into an insightful present.
(Kalayjian, 2010)

Psychotherapy helps us learn to practice Emotional Intelligence (EQ)—knowing how to manage your own feelings (by identifying, describing, expressing, and letting go = IDEAL). The research shows that EQ continues to develop as we learn throughout our life span—unlike IQ, which we are born with, and we cannot teach it nor improve it. We could teach EQ to older and younger individuals, even to those with learning disabilities, developmental disabilities, and those who are diagnosed with autistic spectrum.

In step II we express, release, and let go of our negative emotions. We establish a distance between our thoughts, feelings, and our identity of who we are. We establish our humanity, and move on to the next step. Imagine you eat three balanced meals per day (in privileged Western countries), and you do not release these by moving your bowels (at least twice a day)—of course you will become severely constipated. Therefore, when you witness someone yelling and losing control of their emotions and then their behavior, they are emotionally exploding (causing harm to others), or they may be imploding (causing harm to themselves). Either way, these buried emotions will come out to the surface, when you least expect them, and with the most severe intensity, impacting many people around you and jeopardizing your life.

Situation:

Alec, who had reached out for psychotherapy for his anger outbursts, was able to identify that he was feeling hurt, and then he was able to release his emotions and share his story. Through the genogram homework I gave him, he realized that both of his parents were alcoholics, and that he has attracted a wife who has the characteristics of both of his parents, including addiction and manipulation. Alec also realized that his wife's father was also an alcoholic and her mother had abandoned her while she was a child. Through the genogram, Alec realized that he had begun drinking as well, joining his wife in this behavior. When he made these realizations, he then decided to stop drinking, and the dynamics of the marriage soon began slowly shifting.

Situation:

Seth, a father of two adolescent daughters, realized that he was "losing control" when he came home from long day at work and a long commute from New York City to New Jersey. Although he came to therapy to work on his anger, he soon realized that he was suffering from extreme disappointment, as his stay-at-home wife was not managing the household bills, was ignoring important housekeeping chores, and was addicted to playing games on her new iPhone. Ironically, she was addicted to the FarmVille game, where she was growing flowers and vegetables and needed to water them in the game, while she was not even watering her own actual plants in her house. After the assessment, he then began sharing his feelings and discharging his disappointments, which were leading to his frustrations and to more outbursts of anger. After he expressed his feelings and discharged his frustrations, he then felt a release of negative feelings and felt empowered by controlling his emotions, and he began developing Emotional Intelligence.

Situation:

Jean, a woman in her late sixties, reached out to me with a history of depression (she'd been taking antidepressant medications for over fifteen years) and extreme anger. After examining the Anger Wheel, she identified that she was feeling extremely sad. Some of the sadness was from her father, who survived the Ottoman-Turkish Genocide of the Armenians. She remembered that she had spent a lot of time with her father, who was depressed and sad about losing his entire family at the hands of the Young Turks, and being the only one to survive. These newfound realizations gave her tremendous feelings of empowerment, as she had previously thought that she was "crazy" for having those negative feelings. The more she thought she was "crazy," the more she felt isolated, and she did not want to relate to or socialize with others. When she realized that her sadness was partially generational, and then learned how to release and manage it, she was relieved—and she began feeling empowered.

Step III:
Empathy and Validation

When love rules, power disappears.
When power rules, love disappears.
~ Paulo Coelho

Putting yourself in the other person's shoes: If this model is used in a group setting, each participant's feelings are validated by the mediator/group facilitator and group members. Emphasis is placed on understanding others and putting one's feet in the other's shoes. When disputes or traumas rupture an individual's link with their group, an intolerable sense of isolation, helplessness, and victimization may occur. Providing validation and empathy in such a group setting will transform these negative effects by reestablishing the mutual exchange between the individuals in conflict, while the presence of others in the group witnessing this process validates the experiences.

When this model is used on an individual level, Step III is about seeking and receiving acknowledgment and empathy. Many of our negative emotions can lead us into loneliness, abandonment, and isolation. Many of our feelings make us think that we may be going crazy; we may be alone in our emotions, or we may be alone in our thoughts, or we may think that no one understands us. Joining in with another and letting go of judgment of our emotions will help us receive validation. That which you endured may be a terrible experience; you may have done the best that you could (which you did). Perhaps you are courageous to express those feelings, and that you were held in the peaceful energy of being with the other. The importance of empathy and validation was reinforced by H. S. Sullivan in his Interpersonal Theory (1953). Acknowledgment and validation reinforce our humanness, our oneness, our legitimacy of feeling, and our connection to one another. This is the ultimate union for the purpose of support and love.

What is empathy, and how is it different from sympathy? Empathy is joining in with the other with the purpose of sharing sorrow (or other emotions). It's just like our Meaningfulworld mottos:

Our joys, when extended, will always increase, and
grief, when divided, is hushed into peace!
and
Shared sorrow is half sorrow, while shared joy is double joy!

Empathy is being non-judgmental, and it also means not sharing or comparing our trauma with those of others. Sympathy is feeling sad or bad for the other, and then sharing our sorrows and our losses as a response. Just a few weeks ago, at my elder brother Father Vertanes's wake, people kept on embracing me to express condolences and then telling me how their mother or their brother died in the same month, and I "should be" feeling lucky that my mother is still alive. There is no *"should"* in empathy. Others told me, "Sorry about your brother, *at least* he witnessed his son's ordination into the priesthood" and "At least he did not suffer for long." I understand that people are uncertain as to what to say when empathizing with grieving family members. I understand that it is not easy to comfort a grieving person. Even I, a seasoned integrative healer and therapist, experience challenges as well; but when in doubt, I say nothing. Or just say, "I don't know what to say, this is so sudden, and I cannot imagine how much pain you may be feeling." It seems we are often not mindful of what we say, and may cause more distress while trying to empathize. We also don't know how to grieve. Once again, we push our sadness, pain, and frustration down for the "sake of family, to appear strong." A dear friend just told me, a week after my brother died, "You are a psychologist, *you **should not** cry,* you have to stay strong (not cry) to help support your family." I know she was trying to be supportive in her own way, but she was oblivious of what she was saying, as well as how she was saying it, as I felt totally not supported.

Many people don't know how to express their feelings: we may put our feelings in a bottle, until there is no more room, and then we explode, or implode, or freeze up. That is why I prepared a list of self-care items to be mindful of while grieving. (Kindly see Attachment 9.) Grieving is both an art and a science. You could get as creative as you wish by painting or drawing your feelings or your memories of the deceased, or writing a poem, or sending a heartfelt expression through social media, blog, or e-mails.

Here are other ways of helping you discharge: singing in the shower, or outside the shower; talking with a non-judgmental friend, writing in a journal (either to keep or to burn and release), writing a poem and transforming your pain and sending it out for publishing. The important thing is to remember that we need to release, and let go- if we don't we will explode or get sick. While some of these aforementioned ways will help you to release, always remember that receiving validation is very important. Validation will help us achieve closure. We achieve closure from our trauma and humiliation, and from this, we begin the transformation process to the next level of healing.

Empathy is the most challenging practice, as socially we are not accustom to practicing empathy. Imagine this: Once I was in a car accident; someone hit my vehicle from behind while I was driving, and I hurt my knee. I shared this with a friend, and she said, "Oh, that is too bad, but it's nothing and at least you did not have to have surgery. I also had an accident last year, but I had to have surgery." Empathy does not contain the phrase "at least." When we compare our pain and hurt with another person's pain and hurt, and we bring our trauma into the conversation, then we are taking the attention away from empathy for the other and bringing ourselves into the conversation, and taking the focus away from joining with the person with whom we are trying to empathize.

In another situation, I called a friend to share about the issues I was experiencing at work in a university, where the chairperson was behaving combatively, and my friend said, "At least you have a job, many people don't have jobs." Yes, of course I am grateful for my employment, but I am distressed at this moment and I am sharing my feelings of frustration at work, measured at level eight (from one to ten), and was seeking an empathic person. Let me repeat myself once again—empathy does not include the phrase "at least." Therefore, I reached out and called someone else, someone more empathic, who said, "I am so sorry you are having such frustrations. Is there anything I could do for you?" Now this is an empathic expression. If I go on and on for several days and months, talking about the same accident or the same issue at work, yes, then an empathic friend could bring it to my attention that I may be stuck in the situation, and that I may need to speak with a professional.

Comparing Ourselves to Others

Comparing our traumas with those of others is not conducive to healing. We had coined this in the past as the "hierarchy of suffering": Victims compare themselves to one another, and have a hidden hierarchy or a measuring stick—always feeling their pain and suffering as more than that of others—"I suffered more than you did." We also see this phenomenon with large-scale genocides: Armenians call the Ottoman-Turkish Genocide the first genocide of the twentieth century, while the Jews refer to the Holocaust as the genocide with the largest number of people killed; the Rwandese identify their genocide as the largest number of people killed in 100 days, and on and on. Even in large-scale mass traumas, we compete and compare ourselves with another group. Suffering is suffering, and trauma is trauma—no matter how small or how big, it needs to be expressed and worked through, without comparisons. Suffering is also unique to each one of us. How I may feel when my pinky finger is fractured would be much different than how another person would feel with the same trauma. Trauma and pain need to be heard and "witnessed" by others with empathy, so we can continue our healing and move on to the next step of learning the positive lessons.

Remember that we cannot learn the lessons without first taking the time to express, release, and let go of our negative emotions. We need to make sure to take time to cry for our pain and suffering, to express our frustration with others, and to release our disappointments if others around us are not following our intentions or expectations. We also need to take time to release our feelings of hurt, betrayal, guilt, and sadness.

Situation:

John, a police officer who worked at Ground Zero (where the terror attack of two airplanes crashing into the Twin Towers happened in New York City) for six months nonstop, was wheeled into my office in a wheelchair, as he could not walk after he retired. Although John had consulted many orthopedic specialists, they could not find anything wrong with his physical ability to walk, and they referred him to a psychologist. John spent several sessions releasing and expressing his emotions that he had bottled up in the past six months. John described how he was part of the "clean-up" crew, and he worked overtime hours and benefited from the overtime that he earned. He then went into details of picking up parts of bodies of children and adults from the rubble. Although he experienced a lot of negative emotions and traumatic feelings, he had "no time" to process those feelings, as he had to get back to working six and sometimes seven days per week. He wanted to retire after this project and therefore benefit from a big check for his retirement. John reported that after he retired, he could not walk. His negative emotions were so severe that they had impacted his body and handicapped him. He spent several sessions crying, describing his experiences in that six-month-long term of service. He described his emotions as severe sadness and frustration with the system as well as disappointment with some of his colleagues, fellow police, and other officers. As he began releasing his negative emotions, John slowly regained his ability to walk. His negative emotions had lodged in his spine and legs, preventing him from walking.

When our bodies reach the point of neurochemical exhaustion, we call it adrenal fatigue. By neurochemical exhaustion, I mean that you've been pumping out so much of the stress chemicals adrenaline and noradrenaline that your body starts to secrete extra cortisol because cortisol is long acting (twenty-four hours long), as opposed to adrenaline, which only lasts a few minutes. This means that if you are constantly going into a stress response, then your body shifts to creating more cortisol to be efficient. (After all, why only secrete a two-minute acting stress chemical [adrenaline] when you can let one loose that'll last twenty-four hours!)

If you are burning the candle at both ends, if you have a history of early trauma, developmental trauma, abuse, adversity, and/or chronic stress in your current life, the trauma will eventually catch up to you, and it will immobilize you until you take the time to work at restoring your nervous system's health by discharging your negative emotions and resolving your trauma. By resolving your old, stored-up traumas and your body's fight/flight/freeze instincts that are running the show, you will ensure the transformation of the trauma into lessons learned.

Of course, not every stored and unexpressed trauma causes immobility. It may cause different symptoms in each person based on past experiences, one's physical and psychological characteristics, family constellation, childhood experiences, and available resources. For example, other outcomes of unresolved trauma and symptoms of a survival system are: a sluggish or poor immune health, sleep disturbances, anxiety, depression, digestive troubles (acid reflux, irritable bowel syndrome, ulcers, gas, and other woes), chronic fatigue, chronic pain, difficulty concentrating and learning, autoimmune illnesses, skin rashes and disorders, headaches (migraines, cluster headaches), etc. Unresolved traumas also negatively impact our social as well as romantic relationships. Unresolved trauma or distress also impacts our daily tasks, our motivation to change, and our ability to create, focus, and be a productive citizen. Therefore, the fight/flight/freeze instinct—which is the adrenaline and cortisol response system—must change for you to feel like a whole, healthy, happy, and productive human being with harmony and love.

When we're in our teens, twenties, and thirties, we can push through and keep going with chronic stress physiology, with constant high adrenaline that eventually turns into more cortisol being secreted. The signs and symptoms start to reveal as we reach our late thirties and into our forties and fifties. Cortisol, when left ON for too long, is toxic to our DNA and literally ages our cells and brain tissue, and also causes inflammation. If it is left too long, autoimmune disorders can set in and turn into illnesses such as cancer, MS, ALS, osteoarthritis, and so many more. Reproductive problems fall into this heading too, as do hormonal imbalances, it's kind of staggering.

Recently I've been noticing more young clients in their twenties and early thirties coming to me with a lot of stress-related ailments: weakened immune system, depression, anxiety, cystitis, GI problems, etc., low levels of testosterone, low libido, and some of them had "okay" childhoods. The pressure to perform is very high in our society, and it's also growing in other parts of the world such as Japan, India, China, and the Middle East. We are pressured to always smile and look pretty while stuck in two-career families beleaguered by economic stress, always working, and in addition facing challenges with career choices, the pressures of social media, the stress of "making it" in the world with the population as high as it is now and, well, our nervous systems just can't cope with these overwhelming stressors. We forget being, and focus on doing and having.

Situation:

Julie, a nineteen-year-old first-year college student, had failed all her midterm examinations and came to me in what she called "depression." She said she was extremely angry at her father for not providing her funding for her to stay in the dormitory. Although her college was only thirty minutes away from her home, she wanted to distance herself from her family, to be able to focus on her schoolwork. She felt that her father was unable to understand and empathize with her. After two sessions, Julie was able to identify what was underlying her feelings of anger, and she recalled a trauma from her childhood that she had buried. Although she resisted at first, indicating that it would make her cry and be unhappy while recalling her trauma, then, when she began releasing, she realized that she had held on to those negative emotions for too long, and that they were interfering with her concentration and her focus on her course work. This realization gave her more courage and energy to focus on the release of her traumatic past. As soon as she did that, she was able to concentrate much better, and slowly her grades improved dramatically.

Situation:

Josephine, a twenty-five-year-old who is completing her baccalaureate as well as working full time, complained of anxiety attacks, insomnia, constipation, and nightmares. She has seen her primary caregiver, a physician, who prescribed six medications for her: for sleeping, for constipation, for anxiety, for depression, for losing weight, and for pain. Imagine, she is only twenty-five years of age! Of course, Josephine had the good sense to make an appointment to see me, having heard about my practice through a friend. In two sessions, we were able to get her off the six medications, through the seven steps and through naturopathic healing. I was able to empathize with her childhood trauma of her father's abandonment and her mother's overly controlling behavior. I shared tools for assertiveness and self-confidence, recommending simple adjustments to her daily self-care, starting with physical exercise, developing the ability to observe, using her breath as a source of relaxation for sleep, cultivating mindfulness to decrease her anxiety, journaling her negative emotions, and seeking empathy. Josephine was also advised to take supplements such as natural magnesium complex for relaxation, stress reduction, and moving her bowels. Additionally, I recommended vitamin B6 before bedtime to relieve her nightmares by relieving her water retention, and Mustard Bach Flower Remedy to address her emptiness and depression. She then began working on Step IV, on meaning-making and transforming the emptiness that she felt.

Step IV:
Encourage Discovery and Expression of Positive Meaning

We delight in the beauty of the butterfly, but rarely admit the changes it
Has gone through to achieve that beauty.
~ Maya Angelou

Making Sense out of the Nonsense: In a group setting, participants are asked, "What lessons, meaning, or positive associations did you discover about yourself as a result of this difficulty or traumatic experience?" This Step IV is based on Viktor Frankl's (1963) logotherapeutic principles: that there may be a positive meaning discovered in the worst catastrophe. There are lessons to be learned from the most difficult conflicts and traumas. In an active crisis or conflict, the facilitator helps opposing parties discover creative ways to make meaning. Dr. Martin Luther King, Jr. has said that only light can transform darkness; therefore, we should appreciate and reconnect with light.

When this model is used with children, the adult facilitator/teacher or the parent helps the child focus on the strengths that they gained from the stories or drawings that they shared during play. Some of the positive lessons shared by children are: "I am stronger now," "I know how to be positive," "I can use words instead of hitting," "Thank God that Mommy and Daddy are alive, that is more important than the house and the car we lost," "It's better to love than to fight," "It's better to forgive than to hold a grudge," "When Mommy and Daddy are happy, they show me more love." Forgiveness is also reinforced here as a tool for self-care, and for letting go of resentments, revenge, and the resulting feelings of anger, which only reinforce the conflict—and then add dead weight for us to struggle with all day and all night long.

> *That which does not kill me*
> *Makes me stronger!*
> *~ F. Nietzsche*
> *Positive lessons transform us*
> *From a victim to a victor*
> *~ A. Kalayjian*

Step IV is the breaking point, where we are transformed from a victim to a victor: from the "Poor me, I suffered so much and I am a victim," to "I am a strong survivor, I learned to live life fully, and by integrating these positive concepts I learned many great lessons." You, therefore, are transformed by these lessons that you have learned by going through this awful experience. You may learn the lessons of strength, patience, love, empathy, and compassion and the lesson of unconditional love, toward yourself first and foremost, as well as toward others. We may learn that we are important; that we deserve self-protection and self-love and respect. We start by acknowledging ourselves rather than buying into the false belief that we live in an individualistic society in the West and think only of ourselves.

We start with self-care because we need to care for the engine that is helping us to serve others. Just as the flight attendant in the airplane guides us in case of emergency to place the oxygen mask *on ourselves first*, before attempting to help others (children or older people alike), life is exactly the same—we need to engage in self-care first, and then try to help others. Sean Covey in his book, *The 7 Habits of Highly Effective Teens* (1998), reinforces this point in Habit 7, "Sharpen the Saw." Just like taking care of and maintaining your car, you too need time for refueling (energetic balance), time for an oil change (releasing negative and painful feelings and connecting with positive ones), and time for tune-ups (physical, mental health, and spiritual checkups).

Growing up in Syria, I was always told that it would be selfish to care for myself. It would be self-centered to focus on the self. Especially as a girl child, I had to view everyone else as a priority— our father, our siblings—especially the male ones, and the elders. We need to evaluate this notion of self-care, and realize that just as our automobiles cannot move without gasoline, we cannot function without self-love, self-compassion, and self-care—it is as simple as that. As Jack Kornfield said in his *Buddha's Little Instruction Book*:

> *If your compassion does not include yourself,*
> *it is incomplete.*
> *~ Anonymous*

If we are asking and telling others that it is important for them to care for themselves, we first need to be good role models, and so we cannot go around with disheveled hair or attire, being overweight nor having skin rashes, sarcastic expressions, and negative and unhappy feelings while attempting to make others healthy and happy.

I often hear people respond by saying "I don't have time to care for myself." I have met many mothers who respond this way, as well as many caregivers. Many people share that they are the fourth on their priority list: Their children are first, their husband is second, work is the third, and they themselves are fourth. I am sure you can already predict the challenges that arise when we put ourselves last on our own lists.

Situation:

A mother in her forties with two sons (twenty-one and fifteen) shared in a session that she is so stressed from work, driving her fifteen-year-old around to his school and extracurricular activities and driving around her octogenarian in-laws that she has no time to care for herself. As a result, she drinks coffee to wake up and stay awake, and then she smokes cigarettes and eats sugary snacks to keep her energized during the day. When I asked her about her self-care, exercise, and relaxation, she said very quickly, "I don't have time for me." She actually did not even realize what she was saying, as the bad habits that she had begun practicing were already causing her more stress; her health was jeopardized, causing her to have more visits to physicians, scans of her lungs, a tragic mass growth in her breast, and ulcers in her stomach. When your body begins expressing symptoms of distress such as headaches, migraines, high blood pressure, intestinal complications, obesity, etc., it means you have ignored your emotions for so long that now that the emotional distress has invaded your physical body, and that means you have to stop and attend to your health and emotional issues or else you could actually drop dead.

The journey of change to embrace health and happiness starts with us, and that is what this book is all about. I encourage you to take this healing journey and make it your own, without blaming others, nor blaming yourselves, without carrying the negative past with you and traveling in compromised situations, carrying more than you can bear. I encourage you to refrain from making your journey heavier and heavier, more and more challenging and growing to be more and more negative and resentful while judging others and ourselves alike. The judge is at one extreme and the victim is at the other. People usually go from one extreme to another: we feel victimized, and go around and around, asking "Why me?" and attracting more suffering and more victimization. Or we may go to the other extreme of judging negatively, and we judge ourselves harshly and then judge others negatively as well. There is no escape from this roller coaster of two extremes; the only escape is to release both the victim and the judge, and embrace self-love while asking "What can I do about this now?"

> *You never know how strong you are*
> *Until being strong is the only choice you have.*
> *~ Anonymous*

In Step IV, the lessons learned will help you with the realization that you survived, and that you can survive. Now, learn how to thrive—to live fully present in health and happiness. You may learn that you are strong and confident as well as present and happy, that trauma doesn't define me nor does it define you; that suffering does not identify me nor does it identify us. Yes, trauma impacts me, and how that impact affects me is my choice; this is when I use my free will to focus on my choice of learning the lessons so that I do not repeat the same trauma, or attract the same dysfunctional relations. I am able to find meaning in my suffering, and make those meanings my lessons in life. I may want to hang them on my walls like precious university degrees or awards. Or I may envision them to be steppingstones to take me higher in the journey of self-discovery. These lessons are unique; although I cannot give you any prescriptions to follow, I will make some recommendations and share some examples. Learning a positive lesson and discovering a new meaning are shared by Viktor Frankl (1968), who has been my mentor and someone whom I've looked up to like a father figure.

Meeting and Studying with Viktor Frankl

I reached out to Frankl when I was down and out, overwhelmed by anger derived from frustration, disappointment, and sadness. My anger was toward the Turkish government, which not only sat on all the Armenian lands, the factories of my grandfathers and great-grandmothers, but which also for the last 102 years (as of 2017) still denies that the Ottoman-Turkish Genocide happened. They also lie in their Turkish history books, indicating that Armenians killed 350,000 Turks. The truth is that those Turks had died during WWI, while the Ottoman Empire was attempting to expand to Russia and Europe. Armenians were under the occupation of the Ottoman-Turkish Empire; they were not independent to wage war and were prohibited from bearing arms. I had also just concluded our research (in 1988-1990) with the survivors of the Genocide and learned the details of the tortures performed by the Ottoman Turks: all the killings, cutting the nipples off women (then putting them on a string to play with them), cutting pregnant women's bellies just to see if the fetus is a male or female, and so many more atrocities described by eyewitness survivors. I was overwhelmed with deep sadness, hopelessness, and vicarious trauma, which resulted in the secondary emotions of anger and rage.

I was intrigued and confused at the same time when Frankl guided me by saying that I need to help my Armenian community to forgive. I was perplexed as to how one could forgive when many nations have been denying the atrocity. There are only twenty-two nations that acknowledge the Ottoman-Turkish Genocide of Armenians, Greeks, and Assyrians (as of 2017). Self-healing through forgiveness is a process, a self-liberating process, a way to learn that forgiveness is not about forgiving the act of killing, or the act of Genocide itself. We are forgiving the ignorant people who were not mindful at the time, the Young Turks who thought that by killing Armenians they would be able to maintain the expansion of the Ottoman government. Because NO ONE in their right mind would kill millions of people and then deny it and blame the victim for another century. Frankl helped me to see that waiting for acknowledgment does not help—it doesn't work, nor does it heal our wounds. Instead, we would benefit by releasing our negative feelings and learning a positive lesson.

Warning: Please take enough time to express, release and let go of all the negative feelings before you start planning on forgiveness and leaning the positive lessons. If you rush through out of guilt or pressured by your religious beliefs, then the trauma gets infested and exacerbated, and your negative reaction would be eminent.

Here is another erroneous belief: "time heals." Time does not heal if you are continuing to deny your feelings and push them down under the rug. Time could just worsen the situation, and make the trauma pass on to other generations, while making your trauma a more complex one and thus much more challenging to heal. According to the Native American belief system, untransformed trauma will be passed on to seven generations. It all depends on what you do in that time; for example, Armenians (as Ottoman-Turkish Genocide survivors) have not healed their pain, and they still suffer from extreme anger and depression, sadness and frustration. While for Jews, despite receiving acknowledgment for the Holocaust from the German government as well as receiving reparations (and until today, some still receive reparations), many suffer from "destructive entitlement," a phenomenon seen a lot with traumatized populations in which they turn their past trauma into a commodity and want to be treated extra especially/differently in everything they do. They are extremely sensitive and reject constructive criticism while they continue displacing their unresolved pain and suffering onto another group of people, in this case, the Palestinians.

Situation:

Let me explain further with an example: As part of the Meaningfulworld Humanitarian Peace-Building efforts, we have been working in Israel and Palestine since 1998. During our 2015 Humanitarian Mission, we were staying in Camp Faraa and had just gone to sleep at 1:30 a. am. After a long day's work, and waiting at multiple checkpoints for hours and traveling on dilapidated roads, etc. At 2 a.m. we were awakened by a bomb, and more than twenty-five Israeli military personnel barging into the camp to take away a teenager who had burned a tire by the infamous wall earlier that day. All of the camp residents were traumatized, including our team. We were so fearful. The next morning, the Palestinians told us that these bombings were frequently occurring traumatic events in their lives. No one would know where that young man was taken to for at least three weeks, as the Israeli military does not follow the democratic procedure of giving Palestinians the right to make a phone call. His Palestinian parents would have to hire the most expensive lawyer to find out where their son has been imprisoned. In a democratic country such as Israel, why is it that human rights are not protected? These teens are imprisoned without education and without rehabilitation. If and when they are released, years later, they are illiterate, and therefore, unable to find suitable employment.

Now we are complaining about our American President, Donald Trump, and many call him crazy for his idea to build a wall around the U.S. to prevent Mexicans from entering the country. History has shown that walls are not the solution. Berlin's wall is an example— remember how joyously the entire world celebrated the fall of the wall? And the Israeli government spent more than $4 billion to build this separation (some call it apartheid) wall to separate the Palestinians. And 85 percent of the wall is within the Palestinians' land, and it costs about $260 million per year to maintain it (972.mag.com, by Haggai Matar, April 9, 2012). Now this wall-building behavior is one that creates more conflict and less resolution, more hatred and less love, more separation and less unity, more continued conflict causing more wars and more suffering of innocent people on both the Israeli and Palestinian sides. Many Israeli Jews we talked with were unhappy about the wall and admitted that the wall has created more conflict and separation among the two traumatized nations.

In this Step IV we ask people what positive lessons they have learned from their trauma, or what meaning have they discovered. Instead of identifying with the trauma and attracting more traumas in an attempt to resolve them, we identify, describe, and let go of the trauma (IDEAL). We focus on the lessons we have learned, and on how we have changed since the incident—how our strength and our endurance have stabilized our life, and how we make decisions differently now, after the trauma.

Meaning is not something you stumble across, like the answer to a riddle or the prize in a treasure hunt. Meaning is something you build, you create, and then you integrate into your life. You build it out of your own past, out of your affections and loyalties, out of the experience of humankind as it is passed on to you, out of your own talent and understanding, out of the things you believe in, out of the values for which you are willing to sacrifice something. The ingredients are the following three:

1. You are the ONLY one who can put them together into that unique pattern that will be your life.
2. Let it be a life that has dignity and meaning for you; if it does, then the particular balance of success or failure is of less importance.
3. Let it be a value, and not a material thing. For example, a value would be something like love, helping others, loyalty to human rights, etc.; an example of a material thing would be your house, your belongings, your bank account, and even your family.

In over the more than forty-five countries in which we've worked, as well as in more than twenty-five states in the United States of America, we always ask survivors this question: *What lessons and positive strengths have you gained as a result of this trauma or negative experience?* Of course, when the trauma is not Identified-Described-Expressed and Let Go (IDEAL), we may feel that we have learned nothing—or perhaps only negative lessons—such as "not to trust others," or that "people are violent," or "the world is a terrible place," or maybe "no one cares," or "no one understands us." These interpretations may result from holding on to our trauma and not being able to discharge and release, which puts us on the wrong (destructive) path. When we realize that we are still on a negative path, we need to recalculate and awaken our souls to embrace the healthier path, via the 7-Step Integrative Healing Model. The negative lessons are derived from being too attached to our suffering. We jump into a negative interpretation/meaning when we aren't able to let go of our pain and suffering, when we're not able to release the pain and humiliation. We're not able to acknowledge to ourselves that we did not contribute to the problem, and even if we did, we are a different person now, while in the past, we did the best we could.

Now is the time to transform and to take action in our self-care and self-love. Since we cannot change the past, we can only change this moment—and by approaching it one moment at a time we could co-create a beautiful, healthy, joyous, and peaceful life. No amount of worry will change this reality. As it has been well said by an anonymous author:

> *Worrying does not take away tomorrow's troubles,*
> *It takes away today's peace and joy!*

Self-love is our choice, and this is the moment to do it. Postponing does not help; it just creates more frustration and anger. Anger is a byproduct of a list of emotions such as sadness, guilt, frustration, disappointment, humiliation, worry, embarrassment, jealousy, hurt, anxiety, shame, and fear, and many more. (Kindly see Attachment 1, Anger Wheel.)

Situation:

A twenty-one-year-old man came to therapy expressing his feelings of hurt and pain in an angry outburst: "My girlfriend dumped me!" I expressed empathy and asked him to share his feelings. He continued with the angry outburst: "Well, I'll show her, I will go and slash all four tires of her car." When I asked, perplexed, "What is that going to change? How is that going to help your pain?" He quickly responded by saying, "Oh, she will feel the pain she has caused me." "I am not following you," I replied. "What if she in turn slashes your four tires?" and he replied by saying "I never thought about that!" He then exclaimed, "I cannot trust women or girls." This is not a positive lesson I am referring to; this is the outcome of unresolved feelings of betrayal, sadness, and hurt, and jumping to the wrong conclusion by generalizing from feelings of hurt and dumping them onto others.

If we continue externalizing our issues and finding blame in the other person, we are rewiring our brain circuitry, physically changing the brain itself to make it easier and more likely that the proper synapses will share the chemical link and thus spark together—in essence, making it easier for the thought to be triggered. Therefore, our thoughts reshape our brain, and thus they are changing a physical construct of reality. Think about this for a moment before you continue, because that's a seriously profound insight for us to pause, breathe, inhale, exhale, and pause again.

Situation:

I have a client who after three years of weekly therapy was finally able to share and let go of something that had happened to her over ten years ago. It was something that her sick, abused, and abusive mother had told her: "You are nothing, your life is not important, your brother is more important, you are stupid." This forty-five-year-old successful financial officer was in tears while she expressed this, telling me that she had been embarrassed to share this with me until now. Even in therapy, I see over and over that people are unable to share their most humiliating or embarrassing feelings until they work on all their other fears, traumas, and pain. Our emotions have layers, just like an onion, and we can only shed one layer at a time, as we are unable to see the layer beneath until we transform the outer layer first. When we are ready to finally release, we feel this inner freedom: as my client said: "I feel free now, I feel light as a feather, and I feel like I can fly." Indeed, she can, as she has finally let go of the chains of the horrific words that she had heard growing up—words that had disabled her. Her mother was a victim of abuse from her own mother and Mother-in-law. This is how pain and suffering are transmitted from one generation to another, from one family to another, and from one family member to another. We can transform this generational trauma by working on it, rather than passing it on to our children and grandchildren. When we heal ourselves, we then transform health, healing, and positive lessons learned to be able to establish our self-esteem and have a positive self-concept.

One way to work on this Step IV is to engage in our ancestral tree, or work on our emotional genogram (Attachment 11, sample genogram). This exercise is not only for determining our ancestral biological health, but also for establishing our ancestral emotional connections and relations. Who is relating to whom in my family? Who does not connect to whom? Who has cut relations with whom? This emotional relational genogram is a creative way to prevent future traumas while understanding our past family emotional dynamics and establishing our emotional health. In this genogram, we also focus on family secrets—who holds them? What are these about? Are there any suicides, affairs, emotional cut-offs, or addictions? And how were these issues addressed (or not) in our family?

The more we learn from our own past—as well as our collective historical past—the less we will repeat these issues in our lives. As my mentor, Maya Angelou put it so well:

History, despite its wrenching pain, cannot be unlived,
but if faced with courage, need not be lived again.
~ Maya Angelou

The more we understand the dynamics of the past, the more we can gain control of preventing the repetitions. It is a path to a healthier life. We engage with the elders in our family to discover the details of the emotional history in our genogram. My client, a forty-eight-year-old who has two grown sons in college is figuring out the dysfunctions in her family by reviewing her emotional genogram. She asked, "Why did Uncle Bob all of a sudden stop driving, and people had to give him a ride to his work?" After some searching and talking with elders in her family, she found out that Uncle Bob had a drinking problem and he had several DWIs (driving while intoxicated), and his license was suspended for several years.

A young twenty-one-year-old client had found out that one of his uncles had disappeared, and he could not see Uncle Richard, whom they called Dick. He then found out through the genogram that Uncle Richard had molested a young girl in his neighborhood and had to serve time in prison. He was away for a few years and then moved out of state because he was not able to face his family; meanwhile, his family tried to keep it a secret.

These and other family secrets are important lessons for us to learn from, as when we don't learn the positive lessons, then we are doomed to repeat them, over and over, through many generations. Human patterns of being mindful or not being mindful are just that: patterns. Patterns then turn into habits, habits then turn into our life script, and this turns into our life drama. In order to change this script, we need self-knowledge, self-love, and self-compassion, combined with the knowledge gained from our ancestors.

Educating is not the learning of facts,
But the training of the mind to think.
~ Albert Einstein

Educating the Mind
Without educating the Heart
Is no education at all.
~ Aristotle

Most often, our ancestors have so much baggage that we shun them away, and then we miss all the wisdom to be gained. We have the power to transform our present, and truly make it a PRESENT: a gift for ourselves, a gift from us to the generations to come, and to our planet. This knowledge is invaluable, indispensable, irreducible, special, and precious. The more we engage in this kind of mindful learning, the more we can transform and be in the moment, detached from materials, and connect to the true essence of being human.

Genograms will help us realize all the wrongdoings of our parents, and of our ancestors' shortcomings, faults, challenges, and dysfunctions. We cannot change what has happened. Therefore, by learning about the past, we could make a commitment to be conscious in our behaviors so that we do not unconsciously repeat our ancestors' mistakes over and over. We would avoid the trap, and the web of misery—the ongoing pain and suffering, the humiliation, the discontent. Many of us start playing the blame game and blame our ancestors, our parents, our siblings, and everyone around us. When we blame, we are pointing an emotional index finger at someone or something, without realizing that we have four fingers remaining that are pointing at us (Pointing the Finger: Attachment 12). Four fingers are pointing at ourselves, indicating that we could:

1. Identify, Describe, and Let go.
2. Express our feelings, share our stories, tell our point of view, and continue releasing.
3. We will then receive validation and empathy (hopefully when appropriate).
4. We also may receive reparations.

Step IV is the one that transforms us from a victim to a victor. We have grown from the ashes of suffering and pain to a place of strength and knowing within. This is an essential step, and I invite you to take as long as you need. These steps are fluid, and we could go back and forth sometimes—it is okay. Kindly make sure that you integrate it, and reinforce the positive lessons.

Situation:

Nicky, a nineteen-year-old college student, was sharing in one of our workshops. She was born in China and studied in New York. She felt she was not understood by her parents, as her parents in China were paying her high tuition for a private American university, and all they wanted to hear was that she had great grades. Nicky cried in pain and sadness sharing that her parents did not care about her life, her desires, and her aspirations. "All my parents care about is for me to get 100, the best grades. They don't want to hear that I have to read one paragraph three times to understand it, as English is a new language for me, and it may take me three hours to understand one page in English." Through the 7-Step Model we helped her identify her feelings and discharge them. We gave her tissues and made her feel safe, empathized with her, and encouraged her to let go and find a new meaning. Sure enough, on the following day, Nicky texted us to let us know that she had continued to discharge her sadness by writing in her journal and releasing that sadness. She now embraces us as her emotional family, and she knows the value of empathy. She has learned a new meaning in her life, which has changed her outlook, and it changed the self-conscious way she had kept herself away from her peers. Nicky now embraces those who express and show caring and compassion toward her, and feels happier and more connected than at any time prior to the workshop.

Lessons are like jewels, precious diamonds that are always within us. If you cannot feel, experience, or see your inner authentic healing gifts, engage yourself in the 7-Step Integrative Healing Model. You will help yourself transform the obstacles, obstructions, fears, and anxieties so that you can see, feel, and share your true brilliance—and you will shine. Your authentic healing abilities will surface, and you will not only become empowered, but you will also begin empowering others. Make a list of your lessons learned and keep it in your wallet. Make it the cover image or screen saver of your mobile phone, iPad, or computer. Make a list of your lessons, laminate it, and place it on your refrigerator, the mirror in your bathroom, or other places that you frequently visit and look at in your home, office, and vehicle.

Reinforcement is essential. There are many research studies showing that commercials use the same approach of repetition and reinforcement, and making you think, feel, and imagine that you cannot survive without their product. Therefore, create your own commercial for your self-growth. Chant it in the morning when you first wake up, such as: "I am beautiful, I am loved, I am grateful, I have abundance all around." Or create one that's specific for your issues: "I am strong, I am confident, I am love, and I express love all around." Once again, have this written and place it strategically, everywhere you frequent, for reinforcement play it or chant it seven times per day. The first time, you chant it twice when you first wake up; the second time, chant it right before your healthy breakfast; then again, reaffirm right before your lunch, when you give gratitude; then reaffirm again right before your dinner, and then twice more right before sleeping, totaling seven times.

Situation:

Remember Josephine and the situation from Step IV? She was suffering from emptiness and meaninglessness, due to the abandonment she felt from her father, who left her at age two—and then she had inconsistent visitations filled with disappointments, cancellations, and many lies. Josephine was able to come to a deeper understanding that her father had done the best that he knew how to do. He had no education, was an undocumented immigrant, and hustled to make ends meet, he was recruited by drug gangs, was imprisoned and finally deported. It was time for Josephine to heal her emotional childhood wounds and focus on the present, and on self-love and self-nurturance. Soon she was able to find a deeper meaning in her existence, renew her trust in herself, and discover a life full of joy.

Remember that we cannot find a deeper positive meaning in our lives and in our existence in this life form before we heal our emotional wounds. Rushing through will only complicate and extend the healing process. Our unresolved emotions will blow up in our face sooner or later, at the most inopportune time. Affirmations are one of the ways to promote mindfulness and to stay focused on positive messages within us as well as those that are energetically all around us.

Here are seven examples of affirmations you may use; one for each day of the week, or select one that is appropriate for you for each day.

1. I am in peace; the peace is in me, and peace is all around me.
2. I care, love, and accept myself more and more each day.
3. I send love and peace to those I am having most difficulty with, as they are my teachers.
4. I release my expectations from others, while focusing on myself.
5. I keep my thoughts positive, as I am mindful of how powerful they are.
6. I embrace each day as a gift or a present, always with gratitude.
7. I am in harmony: my head, hands, heart, and gut are aligned, creating inner and outer harmony.

Now that you have discovered or created your lessons, and you are working on reinforcing those lessons, let's go to the next step of the 7-Step Model.

Step V:
Provide and Gather Information

Provide Information: Information is empowering, and it's essential to our growth and healing. In this day and age, in the Western world, we could Google and find new information, or elaborate on our previous information, or create new information. If the 7-Step Model is used in a group setting, practical tools and information are given on how to gradually overcome fears, utilizing the systematic desensitization process. The importance of preparation especially concerning natural disasters such as earthquakes, hurricanes, and tornadoes will be reinforced and how to prepare will be role-played. As part of the preparation we also ask you to prepare your emergency duffle bag. Included in the bag are: water, blanket, dried fruits and canned protein, extra batteries for your flashlight, and important documents (or copies placed in multiple sites: in a bank deposit box, at work and at home, scanned and placed on cloud storage or a Google Doc).

To educate about mass trauma, resources are shared with teachers and prospective group leaders on how to conduct disaster-evacuation drills and create safe and accessible exits. Booklets are given to parents and teachers on how to listen and relate to their children's nightmares, fears, and disruptive behaviors. Assessment tools are given to psychologists, psychiatrists, and other healthcare professionals. Handouts are provided on grief as well as on how to take care of oneself as a caregiver to avoid secondary trauma or vicarious trauma. We also emphasize nonviolent communication, forgiveness, and empathy. Handouts will be given about feelings for those who are unable to identify their feelings.

Step V is meant to help us continue our education about the issues that we have identified in Step I. If it is about our pain and suffering coming from our ancestors through wars and genocide, then we need to work on forgiveness, for our ultimate release. Forgiveness is shifting from the ego reaction of hurting/hitting back to a conscious

83

choice of empathy, compassion, and understanding, that those people who killed my ancestors were not mindful, as no one in their right mind would pride themselves on killing others. This is what I had to learn while working with Frankl and getting deeper into what forgiveness is and what it is not. Forgiveness is not about justifying or forgiving the act of killing, the genocide, excusing the incest, the rape. It is very important to understand this, as many people have fought with me, argued with me, and written hateful articles in the newspapers indicating that "Dr. Kalayjian does not know what she is writing or talking about; we cannot forgive Genocide and the Turks, as they are denying." And that "Dr. Kalayjian is giving us the wrong diagnosis, as she may not be a child of survivors herself." In fact, my father is a survivor of Genocide, and my mother is a child of survivors. It was a very painful time for my grandparents on both sides, although they survived, they tragically lost beloved family, friends, employment, lands, homes, and treasures of art and jewelry while the remainder of their lives were riddled with fear and suffering.

We all need to be re-educated about what forgiveness is and is not. I frequently encounter people who are confused and uncertain as to the meaning of forgiveness, people often think forgiveness is justifying, and making the abuse okay and acceptable.

Here are some of the myths on forgiveness:

> If I forgive, I will forget.
> If I forgive, you will do it again.
> If I forgive, the enemy will be set free.
> If I forgive, I will hurt those who died.
> If I forgive, there will be no justice.
> If I forgive, I will no longer be a victim.
> I need the anger to survive.
> I have to wait for the enemy to acknowledge and ask for forgiveness first.
> Only survivors themselves can forgive; offspring should not forgive.
> Only God/Allah can forgive, not humans.

Situation:

After one of my lectures on the anniversary of the Ottoman-Turkish Genocide (April 24) in an Armenian church in Philadelphia, I remember a passionate mother came to me and told me, "Anger has kept me alive; anger has made me educate my children to be vigilant and to hate the Turks for what they did and what they are still doing by denying the Genocide. Who are you to take away my anger? I need the anger to survive." I understood what this mother was telling me; I had been in her situation myself not too long ago. I too was suffering from the anger that she was talking about. The anger will give you the impression that you are feeling empowered, but it is an artificial form of empowerment—it gave me the energy to fight, but then I was drained inside. The anger was eating my intestinal walls and making me more and more susceptible to many unattractive symptoms, such as gas, a bloated feeling and distended abdomen, and intermittent diarrhea.

Situation:

At another lecture in a community center, one gentleman who was around sixty years of age stood up and said, "Who are you to forgive the Turks? I guess none of your family members suffered? Only the survivors could forgive, and they are not here to do that; they are all dead. So mind your business." This is another myth in the forgiveness process, thinking that only the survivors could forgive and not the generations to come. Well, how about in the United States of America? Slaves are all dead, but do we not express our sorrow and apologies and ask for forgiveness from the subsequent generations of slaves who are carrying the post-traumatic slave syndrome (PTSS)? Very similar to post-traumatic stress disorder (PTSD), PTSS is a trauma, in this case one that's passed on generationally, and that is one of the reasons we still have discrimination and race issues in every state of the United States of America, the land of the free. Many young black men are killed at the hands of white police officers, which is a clear sign of unresolved trauma on both parts: on the part of white officers, and on the part of black teens or young men. How long are we going to be blinded by our fears and ignorance and continue the same old patterns—and then set the white police free by exonerating them? This just creates another wave of violence, to be transmitted all around in our American neighborhoods, as justice is not present. Violence does not stop the violence; it only fuels it. Martin Luther King, Jr., said it so poignantly:

Hatred does not drive out hatred, nor establish the truth. Hatred begets more hatred. Killing does not deter nor establish peace; it only fuels more killings.

Situation:

At another panel discussion at the United Nations, where I was the chairperson at a symposium I had organized on Preventing Genocide, during the Q&A a man raised his hand to ask a question. I pointed at him so he could ask his question. He was a middle-aged man and looked to be in distress and anger regarding the Ottoman-Turkish Genocide. He shared how his grandfather was killed and all his belongings and farms were taken away by Turks. Instead of asking a question, he was going on and on, talking about his family's suffering. At the United Nations, audience members are only permitted to ask questions. I redirected him and said, "I am sorry for all the pain you have endured. Kindly share your question." My statement must have triggered him, as he began yelling at me, turning his unresolved anger toward me and displacing it on me. In the end, I had to call security, as he was getting more and more agitated; he was unable to listen, be present, and take advantage of his position at the conference.

This is a clear example of how unresolved anger makes us act inappropriately, as the bottled-up negative emotions can cause an outburst at a most inappropriate time and make us look foolish in the presence of others. This man had to be asked to leave the conference room at the United Nations, as he was inappropriate and disruptive. Instead of making the best of the opportunity to participate at the United Nations, he made it all the worse for himself. Therefore, transforming one's anger is a necessity for improving self-care, cultivating emotional growth, and promoting forgiveness. Instead of using his time to ask a wonderful question, he humiliated himself and victimized himself once again, thereby continuing the cycle of trauma.

Forgiveness is shifting from the automatic ego reaction (anger/self-protection, hurting back) to a non-reactive
conscious response of empathy;
considering that the other person is ALSO a human being,
perhaps not mindful.
~ Ani Kalayjian, 2010 Forgiveness and Reconciliation

We often think of forgiveness as a favor to others, and not something we do for ourselves. I have often heard clients or friends say in response to forgiveness: "Oh no, I am not going to give that gift to him/her!" Somehow, they never perceive forgiveness as a gift to themselves, a way to bring peace and harmony into their own lives. They continue by saying, "I want her/him to come down on their knees and apologize; only then might I think about it." In fact, forgiveness is a gift to give to ourselves, so that we can stop the hurt, sadness, and betrayal and begin healing.

Emotions are like a vehicle;
In order to enjoy the ride fully and arrive safely
One can learn EQ, Emotional Intelligence:
Learning how to operate our emotions, control them,
Manage them, reframe them, and transform them,
Especially in challenging situations,
Always navigate with love and forgiveness.
~ Ani Kalayjian (2013)

Seven Steps of Forgiving

1. Select a grievance against someone, or yourself, and review it in complete detail.

2. Hold in your mind the image of whatever is to be forgiven and say: "I release you from the grip of my sadness, anger, disapproval, or condemnation."

3. Imagine for a while what your life will be like without this grievance that has haunted you.

4. Make amends with someone who has hurt you; tell a friend about your self-forgiveness.

5. Ask for spiritual (God, humanity, nature) guidance to overcome fear or resistance at any step.

6. Have patience—forgiveness is a healing process, not a destination.

7. Repeat steps 1 through 7 as often as needed, for life.

Fear

Another area to work on is our fears. Fear is a natural part of being human. Fear can protect us from harm by sending a rush of adrenaline to help us physically deal with a potential danger. While fear may be normal, and a natural self-protection, there are times when fear may keep us from participating fully in life, hindering us, handicapping us, and holding us hostage to our own self. Once we realize that fear is a state of mind, we can choose to face our fears, change our minds, and create harmony and inner peace.

I challenge you to approach your problems, or difficult and new situations, with curiosity—just like opening a well-wrapped surprise gift. Embrace your fears instead of denying them and pushing them down. Ask yourself, "What is the worst that could happen?" Begin to look at the worst-case outcome. When you make yourself face the worst outcome, which is highly unlikely to actually happen, then you are able to empower yourself with love and acceptance. I invite you to affirm, to repeat seven times with conviction and visualization: "This is a new situation, I have not done it before; I am a little anxious, but I am going to do the best that I can." Repeat this, if you feel the need, with each new situation that provokes fear for you.

Situation:

A client of mine named Alec, age fifty, he was abused both physically and emotionally by both of his parents. He was always called "stupid" or "idiot" and told disparaging things such as "You will never learn to drive a car…" "You will never get married…" "You will never be able to go to college." Alec's confidence was so far down in the gutter, thanks to his abusive parents (who were also abused by their own parents), that he did not have the strength to prove them wrong, and as many victims do, he joined them, and felt self-pity, thought he was stupid, and stayed home under his parents' abuse. One day in therapy, when I asked him what made him stay with the abuse for so long (until age forty-four), he turned his anger toward me (the therapist, which is therapeutic) and yelled in frustration that no one cares about him, no one loves him, and everyone blames him. This is a common phenomenon, a common occurrence: If we don't resolve our issues in time, they shock us without our knowledge. Or they make us act inappropriately, destructively, or abusively, especially toward ourselves. It is a vicious cycle, and we need to break through it. We go through a cycle of pain, suffering, sadness, and hurt, and then embarrassment, self-hate, and self-depreciation. After a year of therapy, Alec began driving a car, and he started college later in his life.

We are resilient and can heal from anything, if only we acknowledge the hurt, identify the feelings underlying it, and describe them, let them go, and then learn the positive lessons. There is no shortcut, there are no express lanes for healing, nor elevators, and we all have to experience and go through all the steps for a holistic, integrative, and lasting healing: engaging our body, mind, spirit, and ecology. Therefore, Step V is a step for us to gather information that is pertinent to our healing. It includes reading articles online or off line, searching the websites for products related to our issues, learning to forgive, and learning not to take things personally, even when we are told "You are stupid." We need to realize that those who label and defame others are the ones who are traumatized, and we could benefit if we send them lots of love energetically, as they are suffering a lot, and they are dumping their suffering and pain on others. Almost 90% of my clients received abusive labels from their parents that were and are extremely hurtful and embarrassing, and which ultimately put them down. Believe me, I understand that most parents love their children, and it's human to get frustrated—but oftentimes, these parents don't know how to manage their frustrations. Parents have their own traumas, both on the individual level and with unresolved generational traumas.

Situation:

One day a young mother came to my office for the first time and said, "Doc, you must help me. I am suffering extremely, as I've just had a child, and I am not sure how I told my two-year-old girl that she is 'stupid.' Although I promised myself and swore to God that I would not say this word to my child—this word, 'stupid,' which my mother used to say to me repeatedly. I am not sure how it came up, as I hated it when my mother labeled me 'stupid' in frustration." She went on to talk about her frustrations with her mother, the generational trauma that had been passed on to her, her mother's untreated depression, and her father's addiction. This young mother was coping with a lot. Most of all, she needed to be congratulated, as she finally realized the impact her past was having on her present. Not only did she acknowledge it, but she also reached out to do something about it by starting psychotherapy. I recommended a book for her to read, *My Mother/My Self* by Nancy Friday, which presents parallels between how we were parented and how we parent our children. Through the 7-Step Model she was able to release her trauma, learn the positive lessons, and continue educating herself holistically.

Situation:

In another case, David, a forty-eight-year-old man, came to me disenchanted and frustrated with his wife of two years (and a relationship totaling ten years). His wife was addicted to alcohol, food, and shopping and she alternated among the three. He came to therapy as he could not end the destructive patterns within his marriage, and he found himself acting inappropriately, just like his father. He was dismayed with himself one day, after throwing and breaking things in his step-daughter's room when she told him that she'd smoked marijuana with his brother. David completed a detailed inventory of his childhood and present problems, and it was transformational for him. He was able to realize that he was repeating his father's style of parenting by getting frustrated and lashing out. He realized this and was shocked at the realization, as he had always been considered the quietest, the most relaxed, and the most rational person. David could not understand his actions, where the anger came from, and how he could be acting so abusively. He had been exposed to extreme anger and acts of frustrated displacement by his father, who was abusive to his mother and to his own self. The father also had an alcohol addiction, as well as other addictions that David did not know about. At Step V, I recommended that David go to our Meaningfulworld website to read about the generational transmission of trauma, our research on the impact of terrorism after 9/11, and other pertinent topics.

Situation:

In another case, Tulle, a married woman in her mid-fifties, came to me with a severe trauma. Later on we found out that she was in fact not ready to work on her trauma, as she felt too embarrassed to share her parents' trauma with me. After a few sessions, Tulle felt more and more grounded and strong, and she was able to share that she had a father who drank at night and then would act in a belligerent way, hitting and getting angry at her, her brother, and her mother. She needed lots of support, as well as education, through reading materials to broaden her perspectives and help her realize that taking our parents' or other people's behavior personally will make us feel embarrassed, guilty, and humiliated. The major lesson here is that we ourselves could be the generation to break the chain, embrace with empathy and love, and commit to better behavior.

I invite you to observe your thoughts just like the clouds in the sky: with awe, detachment, and curiosity. Remember that everything is energy—our thoughts begin it, our emotions amplify it, and our actions reinforce it. This makes the exact thing that we don't like a habit—a bad habit, of course!

In this Step V we also teach about different modalities for mindfulness, breath work, meditation, and gratitude. We advise people to keep a gratitude journal and to make a list of things we are grateful about each morning and each night. I recommend hanging these lists in places of common reinforcement.

> *Let's welcome each day by morning pages.*
> *Writing down and letting go of the painful past,*
> *Embracing the present, and transforming our future.*
> *Holding a grudge, holding on to negative views of ourselves,*
> *and having negative thoughts will stunt our growth,*
> *impacting our mind, our body, our brain, and our spirit.*
> *Let us start our day by opening our heart, and*
> *sending love to ourselves, families, and friends,*
> *to all those who have hurt us, and to humanity at large.*
> *~ Ani Kalayjian*

Situation:

One day, Tom, a new client in his thirties, came in for a problem at work. He began his story this way: "Doc, you don't know all the bad things that happened to me today. My alarm clock did not work and so I slept late, and woke up with the phone ringing at nine a.m. and my boss yelling at me that I am late to work. I was so pissed that I threw my alarm out the window, and in the process, I broke the window, as I did not know it was closed. I then jumped out of bed in anger and tripped and hit my foot on the bedpost. I had to go to the hospital, as the pain was too severe, and I had to have a cast, as I fractured my toes." He then concluded that in his experience when one bad thing happens, there will be two other negative incidents following, to make it three—and he was not able to do anything about it, it just had to happen that way (expressing victimization). When I tried to ask him how and what he could have done differently, he was not mindful and could not come up with a solution, as he was completely blaming the alarm clock, and not the choices he made after the alarm's malfunction.

I then invited him to think about this: What if he expressed apology to his boss and offered to work an hour extra to compensate for the hour delay? He thought about it for a few minutes and said: "I guess I could have done that. I did not think about it." In this way, he would not feel as though he had to throw his alarm clock out the window and break his window, and then in an angry outburst trip and fracture his toes. More importantly, he was compelled to realize that the sooner we learn from our situation, the sooner the list of negative incidents shortens, or even ends. There is no magic in thinking that bad and negative events must happen in threes (or in sevens, or).... They can be looked at individually, and transformed into valuable lessons learned and new meanings discovered—so that we can enjoy life fully, without regrets. Tom learned to disconnect the myth of negative things happening in groups of threes. He also learned to assert himself and communicate transparently, and with apology, and that blaming others is not helping him any longer, as he cannot change others, and that is making him feel helpless.

Choose Gratitude

Gratitude is indeed like a gearshift that can move our mental mechanism from obsession to peacefulness, from stuckness to creativity, from fear to love. The ability to relax and be mindfully present in the moment comes naturally when we are grateful.
~ Joan Borysenko, Ph.D.

Transcendental Gratitude, however, goes beyond social conventions. Instead of feeling grateful to someone, we feel grateful for them—for God or Spirit working through them. We begin to feel grateful for everyone and everything that arises in our lives. The feeling uplifts us, embraces us, and helps us uplift and embrace others in the recognition that we are, ultimately, in this together.
~ Dan Millman

Nurturing gratitude is essential for our journey of forgiveness. Instead of flying into a rage, consider that there are so many other options that are more positive. Starting with gratitude and self-compassion, these show us the way to freedom of choice. Today I choose gratitude and appreciation. What is on your gratitude list? Here is what was on my gratitude list this morning:

1. I am grateful that I can see as I have vision.
2. I am grateful that I can hear, I hear the birds chirping and singing.
3. I am grateful that I can move my body as I have healthy extremities and can move my arms and legs and walk.
4. I am grateful I can taste, as I brush my teeth and feel the toothpaste on my gums and tongue.
5. I am grateful I can write while I write my list of things to be grateful for.
6. I am grateful that I can rush to go to work, that I have a job to go to.
7. I am grateful that I have a house to live in.
8. I am grateful that my work supports my expenses.
9. I am grateful that I can volunteer with Meaningfulworld.

These nine items were on my list even before I left my house in the morning to go to work and volunteer. This list makes me feel empowered, and strong, focused, and centered. I recommend that everyone engage in writing this gratitude list every morning—and at night, before going to sleep, to focus on another list of gratitude, and on lessons learned.

The common meaning of gratitude is to be thankful for benefits received. While this is important, I feel that the energy of gratitude is one of the most powerful attracting forces in the universe. A heart filled with Thanksgiving, even when appearances tell us that we are mired in scarcity, conflict, and affliction, moves us to a higher frequency in consciousness—and we soon witness reality shining through the illusion.
~ John Randolph Price

Step VI:
Connecting with Mother Earth

The Earth is 4.6 billion years old.
Let's scale that to 46 years.
We have been here for 4 hours.
Our industrial revolution began 1 minute ago.
In that time, we have destroyed
More than 50% of the world's forests.
This isn't sustainable!
~ Anonymous

Step VI is about connecting with Mother Earth. *Sshhh,* you may not be able to say this in some countries in Africa, or in Haiti, as they may interpret it as spirit, or voodoo, or something totally negative like "devil." What I mean when I say "Mother Earth" is the land, the air, the vegetation, the oxygen, and the nutrients that the Earth provides for us and with which it continues to nurture us unconditionally. Oh, well, how about when Mother Earth has a temper tantrum, and shakes to high levels of 6.5 or 7 on the Richter scale and causes harm to the world and all of its inhabitants, you may ask? Well, some of those dangerous tremors or hurricanes are natural in origin, but many times they are human-made. That is because we keep the Earth in bad shape; we don't take care of her well. For instance, we throw trash and dangerous chemicals into our oceans. These and all the other abuses of Mother Earth make the temper tantrums happen more frequently and more intensely. Since we also have a population explosion—more than 7 billion humans and growing—naturally more people will be negatively impacted by it.

Mother Earth is the provider of nurturance, food, nutrients, and unconditional love and support. For example, if you are depressed and hopeless, and you do not find any meaning in life, I recommend that you wake up early and watch the sunrise. The sun gives us energy, the power to survive in spite of troubles, traumas, and challenges that we feel we cannot endure. The sun is our caring brother; it gently warms our body, heart, and soul. The sun also nurtures our solar plexus energy center, filling us with self-esteem and inner will. It gives us enough energy to sustain ourselves, as well as the confidence that the sun will rise again tomorrow, despite the dark clouds. The sun will come through the dark clouds to give us hope and faith.

If you have felt violated, either personally through rape, incest, physical violence, or any other physical challenge, I recommend that you find a way to submerge yourself in water, whether it's in the ocean or sea, in a lake or river, or even in a bathtub. The water is cleansing to our soul and body, washing away the pain and suffering, rejuvenating us from the darkness and giving us a womb-like support, a familiar nurturance that we once felt in our mother's womb, during the first nine months of our inception.

If you feel stressed—highly stressed, to a degree that your blood pressure has risen—I invite you to sit under an almond tree, or any large, old, grounded tree with big branches to give you shade. It will serve to comfort your weary body, to relax your mind, and to nurture your soul. Relax and take deep breaths as you sit under this majestic shade tree, and embrace this healthy and protective place.

I also welcome you to hug or touch trees, to welcome yourself and talk with the tree. Release your emotions. Remember that trees and other aspects of nature are not judgmental like humans. They will not be able to respond in the way we may be accustomed, but they are a wonderful source of connection for warding off isolation and a sense of aloneness. I also recommend using the shaded tree to meditate, and to connect with your breath. Breath is the ultimate healing tool, and although many people say they cannot meditate and relax, one thing I know for sure is that we all breathe. What I am recommending is that you connect with your breath and follow your breath, even count your breath, so that you can fully concentrate on your breathing.

When you are feeling completely exhausted, I recommend that you focus on belly breathing, about fifty breaths in the morning, and another fifty breaths before going to sleep. During the day, whenever you might feel distress or exhaustion, come back to your breath and focus on an additional fifteen breaths during your breaks. Instead of going for another cup of coffee or another piece of chocolate, lie down somewhere, or simply sit still and focus on your belly breaths.

If you have experienced a traumatic loss of a relationship, or a loss through death, timely or untimely, I recommend that you focus on the sunset, reinforcing that no matter how deep and painful the loss is, the impact of what remains is beautiful, and it needs to be celebrated. Imagine how the sky looks after a storm, with a rainbow across the clouds. Imagine how after a stormy sunset the sky is so beautiful, painted in pinks, oranges, and yellows, and red. Yes indeed, our bodies and physical beings are temporary; we have leased these bodies to contain us while we are in this world, creating meanings and helping to lift one another up. After we transition, we then become detached from the body, while the body goes through its disintegration. Our souls finally feel the ultimate freedom and peace. Our souls will find a peaceful home.

We use flowers from Mother Earth to heal emotional as well as physical ailments. We also use essential oils for relaxation through our skin, our tactile sense, and our sense of smell. On August 5, 2016, my elder brother, godfather, and father figure transitioned from this world. I used Rescue Remedy at first to address the shock and disbelief. I then used Grief Relief for addressing the grief, the heart-wrenching pain. I also used Star of Bethlehem for loss and grief, and if you have persistence in those feelings or if you feel depression then you can use Mustard Remedy for anger and deep sadness. These work on the vibrational levels to address the seven main energy centers of our bodies.

If under stress and distress you tend to have muscular issues, such as knots in your shoulders, back, or legs, then I recommend the following:

Physical Level: Stretch twice daily, first when you wake up in the morning and again before going to sleep at night. You could use a positive affirmation to release the tension and allow you to focus on the area that needs attention. The musculoskeletal system has an immediate correlation with the emotional struggle. Everything has a balance. Any area under tension will create a lack of blood flow, and eventually this will change the alignment of one's vertebrae and trigger more disharmonies in other organs, thus perpetuating the cycle. At the initial stage I recommend therapeutic massage and body energetic work to minimize the reaction to the emotional challenge. Working on the emotions will decrease the physical symptoms.

Supplements: I recommend Magnesium complex, 500 mg, ingested orally before bedtime, and if you're highly stressed, another 500 mg in the morning. Magnesium complex releases stress and relaxes our tense muscles—it acts like a prescription muscle relaxant, but with no negative side effects. In addition, it helps us move our bowels fully and effortlessly. I recommend massaging the impacted areas with tiger balm/biofreeze three times a day. If you have an aversion to a particular smell, our senses are nurtured by our past experiences. These are your imprints, and you need to be mindful of them when using aromatherapy.

Essential Oil: I recommend peppermint (for headaches and tension aches) or anything mentholated to penetrate to the deeper muscles, and lavender for calming. If your kidneys are sensitive, lavender will calm the mind and allow your body to relax, and not create inner hostages. Most of us feel high levels of anxiety when distressed. In order to alleviate anxiety, I recommend essential oil of bergamot and deep-breathing exercises: inhaling for a count of four, holding for a count of four, exhaling for a count of four, and pausing for a count of four: 4-4-4-4.

Step VII:
Healing Through Breath and Movement

In this last step, we incorporate breath as a healing and centering element to create peace within. We incorporate breath, combined with movement and the colors of our energy centers, as well as affirmations to chant out loud, while being mindful of the impact of these measures on our regulatory system.

Soul-Surfing: Chakra Balancing with Affirmations, Mindfulness, Sound, Essential Oils, and Breath

There are major chakras, or energy centers, in our bodies, for which we can use movement, color, and affirmations to balance. Our thoughts create our reality, and by practicing positional chakra balancing, we can achieve a healthy flow of energy, and ultimately harmony.

All exercises are done while using deep, slow, and diaphragmatic breathing. All stretches or challenging movements are done during exhalation, as during exhalation our body and mind are in release mode, while during inhalation we are more tense. All inhalations and exhalations are recommended to take place through the nostrils (unless congested).

Mindfulness is the ever-important essence while practicing these movements; this is not gymnastics or a competitive sport, but rather an intentional act to bring peace and calmness to our physical being. Our cells, joints, and muscles have memory; they hold on to the painful memories of our lifetime, even some from other generations. The purpose of these exercises is to release the hostages that our bodies may hold for our lifetimes, bringing peace to our physical being, releasing the trauma that is lodged in our body, and restoring our health on mind-body-eco-spirit levels as well as assisting the Chi, the energy, to move easily and effortlessly, without blockages.

We start with a physical warm-up and massage starting from our arms, neck, shoulders, chest, back, sides, and legs. We massage our bodies by cupping our palm and patting firmly down our arms, chest, sides, back, belly, and legs, inside and outside. Then we form a circle and using the same method we begin massaging one another, and we express gratitude at the end.

After the warm-up, we are now ready to balance our energy system, our Chi, or our chakras. While balancing chakras, we repeat affirmations to ourselves, which correspond with the energy each chakra holds.

1. Root Chakra (first chakra): It is located at the base of the spine or coccyx. It's commonly related to primal survival instincts and our basic physical needs. This is the chakra that grounds us to the Earth, connecting us to our human form.

The color vibration is red, thus red clothing can be worn to enhance the vibration of this chakra. The organs/areas associated with this chakra are the bones, teeth, nails, gonads, anus, rectum, colon, prostate gland, blood, and blood cells. Simply wearing the color red enhances the vibration of this chakra.

If the root chakra is switched off we can become physically lethargic, and colon issues could develop. If, for example, we hold on to resentments, we may suffer from constipation or loose bowels, while if you are experiencing severe fear, or the inability to respond to a new situation, then you may suffer from diarrhea. When we release the fear of the unknown, or the fear of a particular traumatic situation, we then invite life lessons and our purpose on Earth.

Position: To open the root chakra, we start by placing our palms together at our heart and then slowly pulling our core in as we squat down to the Earth, opening the hips and knees, and embracing and connecting with Mother Earth. The soles of our feet are firmly grounded to the Earth, while our back is straight, and our chin is parallel to the ground. With each exhalation, we get deeper into our squatting position. We place our elbows inside our knees to open our hips gently through each exhalation. Taking deep diaphragmatic breaths, slowly, intentionally, peacefully, and quietly we maintain our straight back, facing one another in a circle. Breathing through our nostrils help us sustain our body heat. Grounding through squatting will help us maintain a strong and healthy back. We continue breathing deeply, slowly, diaphragmatically, and intentionally, three to seven breaths, repeating if needed!

Affirmations: "I trust myself and Mother Earth," "I love and nurture Mother Earth," and "I am grounded and connected to Mother Earth."

2. Sacral Chakra (second chakra): The sacral chakra is located at the lower abdomen, below the navel. The color vibration is orange. This is the center for our emotions: passion, creativity, and joy. This chakra corresponds with water, and when balanced, it helps with the free-flowing expression of emotions, the ability to experience pleasure and pain, and the ability to appreciate life and change of flow. The organs/areas associated with the sacral chakra are the reproductive system, kidneys, bladder, prostate, womb, circulatory system, and sacred liquids of the body: blood, lymph, sperm, and gastric juices.

The kidney is the major area for the fight-flight-freeze response. Our emotional reflexes will trigger our kidneys (knee-jerk reaction) based on our generational patterns and emotional wiring. When we identify our own personal style of reaction we then have proper information on how we can mindfully change our response to the trauma. Questions you may wish to ask yourself in order to identify reactions include; Are you quick to jump to conclusions? Do you feel the need to urinate frequently when under distress? Do you experience back pain which changes in intensity? I encourage you to notice and monitor your physical symptoms to give you a deeper understanding of yourself.

Position: To open the sacral chakra, we make circular movements with our hips as if we are turning a hula hoop. Inhaling, we thrust our hips to the front, then to the right, exhaling as we move to the left and back to center. Repeat three to seven times circling to the right and then three to seven times circling to the left and around. Taking deep breaths in and out, feel the hips opening.

Affirmations: "I am beautiful, passionate, creative and sexy, and I enjoy a healthy and passionate life."

3. Solar Plexus Chakra (third chakra). The Solar Plexus chakra is located at the solar plexus, above the navel and directly in the stomach area. The vibration color is golden sunlight yellow. The solar plexus chakra relates to courage, strength, and empowerment, and opening it increases self-assurance and self-esteem. It corresponds with the element of fire and relates to personal power, our place in the world, and energetic balance. The organs/areas associated with the solar plexus chakra are the lower back, digestive system, muscles, stomach, small intestine, liver, spleen, pancreas, gallbladder, and the production of insulin.

In order to relieve stress during emotional upheaval, and control the amount of stress on the pancreas, adrenals, liver, and gallbladder, you would choose your food intake carefully. Too much sugar will overload the pancreas and the adrenals. Reduce fatty foods in your diet to relieve the liver and gallbladder, and omit fried foods.

We recommend green juices with beets, ginger, lemon, and turmeric. If you are easily reactive, with overflowing emotions of extreme anger and reacting loudly and aggressively, then you are stressing your liver as well as distressing your pancreas.

Position:

a. To open the third chakra, key poses are Warrior poses. To begin with Warrior I pose, we take a step forward with the forward foot facing straight out in front and the back foot at a forty-five-degree angle. We bend the forward knee, not going farther than a ninety-degree angle, and making sure the knee is directly over the ankle and the hips face the front bent knee. We raise both arms above the head while keeping the shoulders relaxed and engaging our core.

b. Warrior II pose requires that we turn our hips toward the side and open our arms into a T shape, parallel with the ground. Our gaze rests above the middle finger of the front hand while we engage our core.

c. Side-Angle Pose: Bring the elbow down to the bent knee, and as you inhale, raise the opposite arm up toward the ceiling. Then, as you exhale, bring the arm over the ear, making a straight line from the heel to the fingertips, palms facing down, as we gaze up toward the hand of our extended arm. Keep the knee bent directly over the ankle, sink the hips down toward the floor, and reach the fingers of the extended arm away from the back foot. Breathe and hold for three to six breaths. If possible, circle the extended arm forward and back seven times.

During all Warrior poses, we switch to the other side as well, making sure to balance both sides before moving onto the next posture. In all postures, we take deep breaths, focusing on the activation and strength of all limbs and our core, embracing the feeling of empowerment.

Affirmation: "I am courageous and strong, and a peaceful warrior. I use my strength to create peace within me and all around me." "I use positive thoughts, words and actions, rather than my fists."

4. Heart Chakra (fourth chakra): The heart chakra is located in the center of the chest. The vibrational color is green, and either pink or green clothing can be worn to enhance this chakra. The function of this chakra is to energize the blood and the physical body with the life force. It anchors the life force from the higher self and represents divine and unconditional love. The organs/areas associated with this chakra are the heart, lungs, upper back, breasts, blood and air circulation, and part of the thymus gland (because of its effect on the immune system).

Trauma impacts the heart the most, through experiences of loss, frustration, fear, betrayal, disappointments, grief, and feelings of vulnerability. Therefore, we tend to close off our hearts to protect ourselves from further hurt, pain, and suffering. When that happens, we have divided our energy center into two split halves, without communication and without a healthy flow; as we have three energy centers above the heart, and another three energetic centers below the heart.

Position: To open the heart chakra, we recommend the following exercise:

A. Cow Face: Lifting our right arm up and over to the back, we try to scratch our back, then bring our left arm up and over, placing our left palm on our right elbow and gently (with exhalation) pushing the right hand further down our back to reach the lower part of our back. We then release our left hand and bring it behind our back from below to join with the right hand (or bring it as close as our body allows at that moment). Then we switch to the left side, and repeat the entire position. We breathe deep, slow, diaphragmatic intentional breaths, three to seven times, repeating if needed.

B. Cow Face: Using left arm, repeat as on right side.

Affirmations:

a. On the right side, for self-care, we affirm: "I am in peace," "I am opening my heart and embracing myself," and "I love, accept, and truly respect myself fully and unconditionally."
b. On the left side, we affirm: "I love, accept, and truly respect my family, friends, neighbors, community, country, humanity at large, and all living things, fully and unconditionally."

C. Secret Prayer: with our hands in prayer position behind our back, we open our heart and take deep breaths from the diaphragm and belly, slowly, intentionally, always through the nostrils. We close our eyes and breathe deep, slow, diaphragmatic intentional breaths, three to seven times, repeating if needed. This center is also the center for feeling loved; therefore, I recommend starting to mindfully increase your self-compassion.

Affirmations: "I open my heart and send love to all those who have hurt me, knowingly or unknowingly; because they are my best teachers, and life coaches." (They teach us patience, forgiveness, unconditional love, empathy, and compassion.)

If, or when you are under stress, you are prone to congestion in the chest, bronchial area, and lungs, then it is the heart energy center that has been impacted the most. I recommend the following:

Essential Oil: I recommend citrus (grapefruit, citrus, or rose) essential oils to clear the heart energy center.

Supplements: I recommend the HAS natural supplement that relieves bronchial congestion, as well as oregano oil for the release of congestion, and Wellness Formula, EmergenC, and probiotics.

5. Throat Chakra (fifth chakra): The fifth chakra is the throat chakra; the color is turquoise blue. The Throat chakra governs our ability to express and clearly communicate thoughts and ideas. It corresponds to truth, maturity, independence, and the ability to trust others. This throat chakra is associated with the throat, neck, thyroid and parathyroid glands, ears, windpipe, and the upper part of the lungs.

To open the throat chakra, the Fish yoga asana pose is wonderful, if we have an option to lie down on the floor. If we're in an upright position, we use the following instead: First we stand up straight, hips aligned with shoulders, and then as we exhale, we tuck our chin to our chest and gently place our fingertips on top of our head, pushing down to elongate the back of our neck and enhance the position. This position is intended to balance our throat chakra. Then we open the same chakra while standing up: hands are interlocked behind our back and away from our back, shoulder blades are tightened and squeezed close to each other, the head is dropped down behind our back and between our shoulders, and the eyes are gazing behind us, jaws (mouth) closed.

We breathe deep, slow, diaphragmatic and intentional breaths, three to seven times, repeating if needed!

Affirmation: "I express my true feelings easily and effortlessly," "I am in touch with my authentic self and express my needs and desires assertively," and "I am assertive, and able to communicate my true feelings easily, effortlessly and respectfully."

6. The Brow or Third Eye Chakra (sixth chakra): Located in the center of our forehead between our eyebrows, the third eye has a color vibration of indigo blue. The third eye chakra is associated with inner guidance and divine vision. It helps develop intuitive clarity, releasing repressed emotions and promoting the attainment of self-realization. Organs/areas associated with this chakra are the face, nose, sinuses, ears, eyes, and brain functions that include the pituitary gland, cerebellum, and central nervous system.

Position: To open the third eye (between the eyebrows) we wet our index finger (or put a drop of lavender essential oil) and gently massage the third eye clockwise and counterclockwise, seven times in each direction. Then we turn our head to the right, then the left, always being mindful of our third eye. Then we turn our head right center and then left, being mindful of the third eye.

We breathe deep, slow, diaphragmatic and intentional breaths, three to seven times, repeating if needed.

Affirmation: When turned right or left with closed eyes, we repeat: "Even with my eyes closed I see things clearly and effortlessly," "I am open and insightful," and "I feel, sense, and imagine peace within and all around."

If under stress you often feel nasal congestion and sinus congestion, then I recommend the following:

Essential Oil: I recommend using eucalyptus, thyme, and mint essential oils. Boil water in a pot, and after boiling, turn off the stove and add five drops of each essential oil to the hot water then cover your head with a towel and inhale the vapor slowly. If the vapor is too hot for you, then wait for a few minutes until it is more comfortable. Repeat this process, breathing ten deep diaphragmatic breaths, and then rest in bed. This can be repeated.

Affirmation: "I am clear; I am releasing negative thoughts and repeated anxiety-provoking thoughts from my mind." **Supplement:** I recommend a high dosage of vitamin C, as well as plenty of water to flush your system of the toxins. I also recommend the "Wellness Formula."

7. Crown Chakra (seventh chakra): Located at the top of our head, the crown chakra helps us connect with the universe and deity. It is concerned with the cerebrum and the pineal gland (which is sensitive to light levels), thus it affects the entire body. The color vibration is purple or amethyst. The crown chakra is associated with awakening consciousness, and attaining enlightenment, through the integration of the self into the one universal form of intelligence.

Position: To open and activate the seventh chakra, we visualize ourselves as a tree, which also is a great position for improving our balance. As we ground our left foot to the Earth, we imagine having roots extended seven feet below our left foot, which is anchoring us, while we place our right foot flat on our left inner thigh above the knee (or below if unable to maintain the above-the-knee position), pushing our right foot against the left thigh to maintain our balance, and focusing on one spot in front of us at our eye level. We activate our core, squeeze our gluteus maximus, and extend our arms up to the sky, lifting our rib cage and diaphragm up and out, reaching out to the stars, the universe, and deity. Once again, we take deep, slow, diaphragmatic intentional breaths, three to seven times, repeating if needed. Then we switch and work on the other side.

Affirmations: "I am connected to the universe," "I am in balance and harmony within me, with others, and with the universe," and "I am connected to both the universe and Mother Earth."

Essential Oils: I recommend lavender for this energy center.

Heart-to-Heart Connection, "Dr. Kalayjian's Circle of Gratitude and Love": While standing up in a circle, we hold hands, then take our right hand and place it on the heart of the person standing to our right. We stay in this position with eyes closed, and we feel, imagine, and connect through our heartbeats. While some hearts beat slower, faster, or even in some cases irregularly, we may soon enjoy a heartfelt synchronicity and peace when all hearts are beating in unison, in harmony, with strong, slow, and healthy beats. We do possess the power to influence and make our hearts beat in unison, in peace, in harmony, and in total synchrony.

There are many reasons a gathering of people in a circle is powerful. A circle is a shape that is found repeatedly throughout the natural world, and it is a symbol of perfection. We re-create this perfect shape when we join others to form a circle. Being in a circle allows us to experience one another as equals. Each person is the same distance apart from the next participant, and no one is seated higher than or stands apart from others in a circle. From tribal circles to the mythical round table of King Arthur, the circle has been the shape adopted by gatherings throughout history.

Affirmation: With our eyes closed, we look into our heart and feel the opening of our heart center. We then send love to the person to our right side, then to everyone in our group, then to our city, the country, and then the world. "I am grateful for our connection," "I am getting deeper and deeper into my connection with myself, and with others." We also express gratitude and love to everyone who has assisted in organizing the event.

Ubuntu Circle of Unity and Oneness: Ubuntu is a philosophy of African tribes that can be summed up as "I am because we are." This is our Unity and Oneness circle: We are arranged in a circle, our palms are facing up to the sky (to be open to receive the gifts of the universe, nature, and God). With thumbs connected to one another, we extend our palms up, parallel to the Earth and open in a circle, all palms touching one another through our thumbs and our pinkies. We come closer and closer to one another until this unity and connection are established. Our palms are open for abundance, and for being ready to be in the circle of giving and receiving. We close our eyes; we take three to seven deep breaths from the diaphragm; then we express to our circle any message that comes to us. We feel, imagine, or visualize a deeper feeling of joy and oneness with one another.

Affirmation: "I am connected to me, others, and the universe," "I am one with Mother Earth and the universe," and "I am loved and extend my love to others."

Healing Activity with Children: Heart, snap, clap (with a partner), and then heart-heart snap, clap, and then SHHHHHHHHHHH HHHHHHHHH. The message is to connect with your heart.

Then release with a snap, knowing when to let go and release without attachment, then connect with the other and celebrate, then have a moment of silence for reflection.

Prayer

Prayer is different from meditation. Although many religions may use meditation in their practices, prayer does not replace meditation. If you are a meditator, you also need time for praying, and vice versa. Prayer is very essential for our healing and health journey. Research conducted by Miller (Miller, 2011) indicates that those who pray and have a deep sense of faith will be healing from their physical and emotional challenges in a healthier way.

Pray for yourself, for your self-care, self-forgiveness, and self-healing. Pray for your ancestors, drawing up the lessons you've learned from them and letting go of the pain and suffering. Pray for your family, and your circle of well-chosen family and friends. Pray for your community, lifting one another up and out of misery. Pray for humanity and for all living things mindfully.

Meditation

Seeing that we are the sun,
we give up the candle's habit
of fearing the wind.
~ Thich Nhat Hanh

Our body rests at night, but not our mind. Meditation acts the way medicine does, by transforming agitation into peace, anxiety into joy, and anger into acceptance and gratitude. Meditation lessens suffering, transcends knowledge, and transforms pain and anxiety into lessons learned and discoveries of meaning. Meditation is focused on breath. Trauma causes a fight, freeze, or flight protection system. Breath links our bodies with our heart and mind, providing us an emotional self-mastery. Mindfulness helps us practice self-love.

Self-Love Through Hugging Ourselves, Then Giving Unconditional Heart-to-Heart Love to One Another

After releasing our physical bondage, releasing our inner hostages, then we are ready to meditate, for ultimate relaxation.

Meditation and Prayers

You are never more essentially, more deeply,
yourself than when you are still.
~ Eckhart Tolle

Meditation is a process that cleanses the mind of impurities. It cultivates such qualities as concentration, awareness, intelligence, and tranquility, leading finally to the attainment of the highest wisdom.
~ U Thant, Secretary-General of the United Nations, 1961-1971

"Meditation" in its modern sense refers to the yogic meditation that originated in India. In the late nineteenth century, theosophists adopted the word "meditation" to refer to various spiritual practices drawn from Eastern religions such as Hinduism, Buddhism, and Sikhism. Thus, the English word meditation does not exclusively translate into any single term or concept. Meditation has been helpful for reducing stress and reducing symptoms of post-traumatic stress disorder (PTSD), as well as anxiety and depression.

There are hundreds of research studies indicating the effectiveness and usefulness of meditation for relaxation, stress reduction, reversing cognitive decline, reducing anxiety, and PTSD-related disorders. Recent research was released from Wake Forest Baptist Medical Center in Winston-Salem, North Carolina. The study, conducted by Zaiden (2005), looked at how meditation impacted adults, age fifty-five to ninety. Results showed that eight weeks of meditation significantly improved the ability to retrieve memories, decreased atrophy in the hippocampus, and decreased anxiety and stress.

Meditate for Peace by David Wilcock (2013) indicated that fifty different scientific studies have confirmed that the Meditation Effect is real. About 7,000 people got together and meditated—and global terrorism went down by seventy-two percent. Similarly, dramatic decreases were seen in war, fatalities, and violent crime. Of course, there are always skeptics who want to argue about whether or not this is "real," but the fact is that they ruled out all other variables, such as weekends, weather, and holidays.

This positive impact of meditation has been documented in numerous peer-reviewed publications, including the Journal of Offender Rehabilitation (http://divinecosmos.com/start-here/davids-blog/1123-boston).

According to several research studies, mindfulness meditation—a practice that encourages focusing attention on the present moment—can ease emotional stress. And evidence is mounting that mindfulness may also have key benefits for physical health—from lowering blood pressure to helping to curb addiction. A new study conducted by researchers working in Wisconsin, Spain, and France shows that mindfulness can even affect our genes. Specifically, the study shows that mindfulness can limit the "expression" of genes associated with inflammation (http://m.huffpost.com/us/entry/4391871).

Meditation is an ancient practice that has been in existence for centuries, but only in the last two decades has scientific research supported its usefulness and effectiveness. A recent National Institutes of Health (NIH) grant proved meditation's effectiveness in generating alpha brain waves, which are relaxing and conducive to the sleep state. When our mind is tranquil and serene, our body then follows the mind's lead and relaxes, thereby releasing fears and creating a metabolic state that is tranquil and pure consciousness. This state is not only free of fear and pessimism, it's also a more optimistic state that heightens problem-solving skills and promotes an expanded view of the world in which we live and our role in it. A review of scientific studies identified relaxation, concentration, an altered state of awareness while suspending logical thought, and the maintenance of a self-observing attitude as the behavioral components of meditation; this mode is accompanied by a host of biochemical and physical changes in the body that alter metabolism and decrease heart rate, respiration, blood pressure, and brain chemistry. Meditation has been used in clinical settings as a method of stress and pain reduction. Meditation has also been studied specifically for its effects on stress, and studies have shown that it does in fact consistently reduce stress.

Seventy years ago, the United Nations was founded on the principles of dignity, peace, justice, and cooperation. UN Secretary-General Dag Hammarskjold stressed the relevance of these values, stating: "Unless there is a spiritual renaissance, the world will know no peace." There is a specially designated room for meditation at the United Nations, and Mr. Hammarskjold, delegates, ambassadors, and non-governmental organization representatives have frequented the meditation room, throughout the UN's history, before important meetings.

In June, 2007, the United States National Center for Complementary and Alternative Medicine published an independent peer-reviewed meta-analysis of the state of meditation research, conducted by researchers at the University of Alberta Evidence-Based Practice Center. The report reviewed 813 studies in five broad categories of meditation: mantra meditation, mindfulness meditation, yoga, tai chi, and qi gong. The report concluded that further research is warranted.

There has been research conducted with veterans to address their levels of PTSD. Interventions included yoga (Kearney, McDermott, Malta, Martinez, & Simpson, 2012) and meditation and mindfulness–

based cognitive therapy (Rosenthal, Grosswald, Ross, & Rosenthal, 2011). Results indicated a statistically significant reduction in stress and anxiety (Stoller et al. 2012), daytime dysfunction and hyperarousal, and decrease of depression (Kearney et al. 2012).

Meditation has been integral in all deliberations in the Association for Trauma Outreach and Prevention (ATOP) Meaningfulworld. Meditation is utilized at the beginning and end of all our monthly training and empowerment programs, as well as at all of our humanitarian global outreach projects in more than forty-five countries. Although most religions incorporate some form of meditation, at ATOP Meaningfulworld we focus on the healing and integrative aspects of meditation and its mind-body-eco-spirit effect, and therefore, it is not based on any religious foundation.

We use meditation to reduce stress in the central nervous system (CNS) and to strengthen the immune system. Our mind wanders and moves inward and outward like a pendulum, also known as the "monkey mind." Whenever we are able to relax the CNS, we are relaxing our mind. Of course, relaxation is challenging for many individuals, since we live in a culture that over-identifies with production and volume of doing, rather than being mindful and conscious.

Breath is the foundation and center of any meditation. This is very essential for traumatized people, when they experience shallow chest breathing and shortness of breath. Based on the fight-freeze-flight protection system, our past traumatic history may have inhibited complete expression of our breath. When we start breathing deeply, diaphragmatically, or through our belly, we are able to heal the remaining suffering of old trauma, and we are empowered—we establish a healthy distance between the traumatic memory and its effect.

Through breath, meditation links our body with our heart and mind, providing emotional self-mastery and mindfulness. Mindfulness helps us practice self-love. Love is the center of the pendulum of duality, swinging back and forth from positive/negative, masculine/feminine, light/darkness, yin/yang... Remember, throughout the course of existence, we have swung farther and farther into the realm of polarities.

All religions incorporate some form of meditation. Meditative quiescence is said to have a quality of healing and of enhancing creativity. The Prophet Muhammad spent sustained periods in contemplation and meditation. It was during one such period that he began to receive the revelations of the Quran.

Meditation also helps us ignite the fire within, activating our passion and love for humanity and Mother Earth. In order to create fire, we need two things: oxygen and fuel. Oxygen intake and distribution improves with meditation. Oxygen helps us expand our thoughts, concentrate on what's important, and relax the joints, muscles, and all of our internal organs. The fuel is our passion and commitment to serve ourselves, our families, and the human family at large.

Trust yourself and be patient

Don't rush to arrive,
Take time to enjoy the journey!
~ Dr. Kalayjian

Meditation helps us regain our control and have patience. If we are not mindful, we could be driven by our ego, which is selfish and self-centered, wants to see things happen yesterday, and has no patience. As a result, we will experience a vicious cycle of impatience, frustration, and disappointment, and then anger takes over. But meditation helps us accept setbacks and learn from them. We then realize that what hurts us is resistance. We need to nurture patience, most of all with ourselves, for if we are not mindful, we could be our worst judge and jury.

On August 5, 2016, my elder brother, godfather, and father figure transitioned from this world. He looked to be at peace already. I had asked a Haitian Spiritual Guide about him last year, and he said "Your brother is a deeply spiritual man (I had not told him that he was an Armenian Arch-Priest), he has concluded his spiritual journey here, his physical body is suffering, and he cannot withstand it too much longer.

But he is okay; he has done all that he could do. He is waiting for one important thing for him to witness before he leaves; please don't attach to his body." This was totally accurate, as my brother died right after his son's inauguration into the priesthood.

Meditation also helps us surrender, as we cannot control life or death. It takes wisdom and strength to surrender to our own helplessness and to accept that we, just like every other human being, have limitations. The gifts of surrender are numerous. We discover humility, gratitude, and a deepening understanding of the human experience that enables us to be that much more compassionate and surrendered in the world.

Here are the 7 important agreements for health and happiness

1. Transforming our beliefs and identifying our ethical values
2. Exercising our will and perseverance
3. Maintaining continuity and consistency in practicing our healthy habits
4. Using SMART goals and revising them as we evaluate our goals
5. Being mindful of our attitudes and interpretations: positive, kind, loving, non-assumptive, non-judgmental, loving, and forgiving
6. Thinking critically and creatively: seeing all the colors between black and white, good or bad, and seeing it from outside the box
7. Finding our global meaning in life and the specific meaning in our goals

SMART Goals are: Specific, Measurable, Attainable, Realistic, and Timely. We at Meaningfulworld use this among the interns, staff, and coordinators with great success. It helps us to be specific as well as realistic with our expectations, and it helps us to easily evaluate ourselves and one another in a timely fashion, minimizing frustrations. I recommend daily SMART Goal setting for yourself, as well as for your family. Start when your children are young, and you will see how organized, focused, and meaningful your life will become.

In addition to the SMART Goals, we also use a set of principles to guide our life. We call them our vows. Kindly review our Meaningfulworld Vows that I prepared, and see if it fits your life purposes:

1. I vow to take good care of myself with compassion and love on mind-body and eco-spirit levels.
2. I vow to be present in the moment, to be responsive, assertive, and aligned.
3. I vow to have empathy for others with understanding, love and refraining from judgment.
4. I vow to adhere to our core values: love, compassion, empathy, acceptance, letting go of attachments, embracing oneness, and serving humanity.
5. I vow to care and serve my family, community, country, humanity, and the planet fully and unconditionally.
6. I vow to uphold the *Declaration of Human Rights* (1945), read it, teach it, practice it, and disseminate it.
7. I vow to learn the *7-step Integrative Healing Model*, commit to practice it, teach it, and disseminate it.
8. I vow to practice forgiveness, shifting from the ego reaction, to an empathic, mindful and loving response.
9. I vow to commit to a life-time journey of self-knowledge, and continue my growth on mind body eco-spirit levels, to promote unity, oneness and energetic interconnectedness around the world.

Surrender

Surrender is coping with powerlessness or helplessness, and nurturing the ability to accept what cannot be changed or controlled. I recommend building and sustaining trusting relationships, at a minimum four close relationships, as well as seeking out support groups. I also recommend being receptive to the help offered by others, and being grateful for this help.

Co-Creating Our Future

Together, we could co-create a wonderful future. The future is not what happens to us; it is what we co-create, a new narrative of conscious evolution by:

1. Commitment to self-care, self-compassion, and self-forgiveness
2. Building a global community and creating a culture of peace
3. Restoring ecological balance to nourish all life, and mitigating the effects of climate change
4. Engaging in social and political transformation by calling for a conscious and mindful democracy and conscientious leadership
5. Promoting health and healing by acknowledging the profound mind-body-eco-spirit connection
6. Supporting research and education that optimize human capacities
7. Encouraging integrity in business and conscious media

Commitment to Service and Helping Others

Remember that you are helping and serving humanity by taking care of yourself. Do not undermine self-care, or downgrade it. I have heard many times mothers of small children who are working full time and overtime in their homes tell me or others, "I don't work." Well, let me share with you that of course you are working, but perhaps not receiving acknowledgment? You are working as hard as you can, I am sure. When you have mastered caring for yourself, then it's time to start sharing your lessons with others.

Focus on also protecting yourself, and being proactive. If you can spare an hour, start teaching your family the 7-Steps for Healing that you've just learned. We start first with our family, then we share with our neighbors, creating a community. Then we expand to our larger community through faith-based or religious groups, or through community centers, as well as professional organizations. Knowledge that is not shared is no knowledge at all. When knowledge is shared, it may be transformed into wisdom.

> *When we commit ourselves to the service of others,*
> *we transcend the problems we have.*
> *When we reach out to a survivor who is suffering emotional pain*
> *from a trauma and share our own experiences,*
> *that person is more likely to realize that his or her reactions*
> *are perfectly normal and acceptable.*
> *~ Horn, 1990*

> *You give but little when you*
> *Give of your possessions.*
> *It is when you give of your heart*
> *That you truly give.*
> *~ Kahlil Gibran*

Part VI

Reflections

1. How has your healing journey been? Describe it in detail.
2. What are your challenges at this time?
3. What are your strengths, both personal as well as professional?
4. How have you used empathy to improve your relationships?
5. What are the lessons you have learned from your most difficult relationships?
6. What are your continued challenges at this time?
7. Have you practiced the seven steps of forgiveness? Continue practicing whenever the opportunity presents itself. Remember that there are many layers in forgiveness, and it is not a onetime exercise.
8. Tell us about your healing practice: on the physical, emotional, ecological, and spiritual levels. Strive to have a schedule and a list, and place reminders all around you.
9. Tell us about your prayer practices.
10. Tell us about your meditation practices; if you're not yet meditating, perhaps deep breathing? I recommend you start with ten breaths at a time, ten in the morning and ten in the evening. Then increase by adding five additional breaths each week.
11. Tell us about how you service others and humanity. If you are still focusing on yourself, I understand—take your time! You are the most important one to focus on at first, then others.
12. Kindly share what you learned with a minimum of three people from your inner circle; then ask them to share it with three additional people each.

Part VII Handouts and Support Attachments

Attachment 1: Anger Wheel, Managing Your Emotions
Attachment 1a: List of Feelings
Attachment 2: COPE Model of Empathic and Assertive Communication
Attachment 3: 7-Step Integrative Healing Model
Attachment 4: 7-Step Integrative Healing Model for Children and Adolescents
Attachment 5: 7-Step Integrative Healing Model for Older Adults
Attachment 6: Harvard Trauma Questionnaire
Attachment 7: Forgiveness Questionnaire
Attachment 8: Meaning Questionnaire
Attachment 9: Grieving
Attachment 10: List of Humanitarian Outreach Projects
Attachment 11: Genogram
Attachment 12: Pointing the finger
Attachment 13: Our Response Is Our Choice

Attachment 1: Anger Wheel, Managing Your Emotions

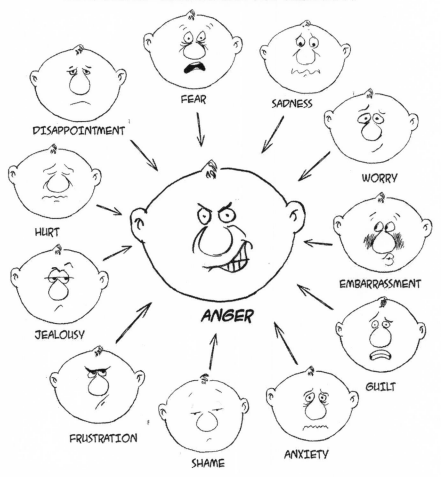

MANAGING YOUR EMOTIONS

NURTURING EMOTIONAL INTELLIGENCE

DISAPPOINTMENT

FEAR

SADNESS

WORRY

HURT

EMBARRASSMENT

JEALOUSY

ANGER

GUILT

FRUSTRATION

SHAME

ANXIETY

IDEAL: Identify, Describe, Express, and Release   www.meaningfulworld.com

Attachment 2: COPE Model of Empathic and Assertive Communication Spiritually Guided and Peacefully Asserted Communication Model

COPE

By Dr. Ani Kalayjian

Communication is an integral part of our energetic, spiritual, physical, and emotional connection. Although we may have different values, assumptions, life experiences, and emotions, COPE, the four steps below can enhance our connection and improve our communication so that we understand others first before trying to make others understand us (S. R. Covey, *The Seven Habits of Highly Effective People*: Free Press, 1989). Communication is challenging because we often create our assumptions from our own centers: The center of your world is *you*, and the center of my world is *me*. Communication is also influenced by old unresolved traumatic/negative experiences, familial-cultural-religious-ecological-and-spiritual values, current emotions, and awareness. Therefore, it is essential to nurture your forgiveness practice (Kalayjian, 2010).

It is important to keep Miguel A. Ruiz's *Four Agreements (*M. A. Ruiz, *The Four Agreements: A Practical Guide to Personal Wisdom*: Amber-Allen Publishing, 1997) alive in our hearts: 1. Be impeccable with your words; 2. Don't take anything personally; 3. Don't make assumptions (since it is challenging not to make assumptions, my revision here is "Be mindful of your assumptions and familiarize yourself with the assumptions of others"); and 4. Always do your best.

The COPE Model has four mindful steps toward spiritually guided and peacefully asserted communication:

1. ***Connect with compassion, compliment, and gratitude***: Connect with the other by finding something positive in the other to be grateful about, to be reinforced, or a simple compliment to bring

you on a horizontal level transformed from a top down, or a me-against-you position. For instance, "Thank you for that thoughtful question…" or "I am very grateful for your contribution to…" or "I appreciate your passion and involvement…" etc. Think of something positive to connect with your "adversary," or the one you're having difficulty communicating with or getting your thoughts across to, instead of simply reacting.

2. ***Open your perspective and share what you see***: Issues involving human beings always have multiple perspectives. It is imperative to review all sides of an issue without judgment. Try to present your side as neutrally as possible, much the way journalists share what they have seen during a conflict or disaster. For example, 1. "I appreciate your passion and involvement." 2. "From my perspective, I noticed that you missed the last two EC meetings but we did not receive any notification…."

3. ***Present your feelings:*** Identify and describe your feelings clearly. How does the presenting story, picture, or situation make you feel? Express your feelings in a clear but not accusatory manner using an "I" statement, such as: 1. "I appreciate your passion and involvement." 2. "From my perspective, I noticed that you missed the last two EC meetings without notifying us." 3. "I feel disappointed that you were unable to attend the meetings, as we missed your vital contribution, creative input, and passion…" (Kalayjian, 2009 the Biopsychosocial, and Eco-spiritual Model, www.meaningfulworld.com)

4. ***Express your recommendation:*** Clearly state your recommendation to change and improve the situation at hand. State your point of view as to how this problem could be resolved. Relate to your child, or the person you are having problems with, how this challenge could be transformed and how the situation could be improved. Stay on the issue (missing the meeting without notification) and not on the person or their character; do not globalize nor generalize the issue at hand (i.e.: "You're always absent").

Unless you have a lesson to share from the past, do not bring the past into your present. For instance: 1. "I appreciate your passion and involvement..." 2. "From my perspective, I noticed you missed the last two EC meetings without any notification..." 3. "I feel disappointed, as we are missing your vital contribution, your creative input, and your passion..." 4. "Therefore, I suggest calling us if you anticipate being absent so we can find alternate ways for you to connect with us, such as a teleconference..."

These four steps can create a way for you to cope (COPE) with the difficulty assertively, constructively, proactively, spiritually, and most of all peacefully. The best cure is prevention, and with these small steps we can transform conflicts peacefully.

Attachment 3: List of Feelings

1) Fulfilled Feelings

AFFECTIONATE

Compassionate
Fond
Friendly
Loving
Openhearted
Tender
Warm

SELF-CONNECTED

Centered
Open
Relaxed

INSPIRED

Amazed
Awed
Enthused
Moved
Stirred
Wonder

ENGAGED

Absorbed
Curious
Engrossed
Enchanted
Entranced
Fascinated
Interested
Intrigued
Involved
Spellbound
Stimulated

REFRESHED

Enlivened
Recharged
Rejuvenated
Renwed
Rested
Restored
Revived

GRATEFUL

Appreciative
Moved

Attachment 4: 7-Step Integrative Healing Model

7-Step Integrative Healing Model
(The Biopsychosocial & Eco-Spiritual Model)
For Healing, Transforming Disputes, Conflict
Transformation, Peace-Building, and Forgiveness

Dr. Ani Kalayjian

The Meaningfulworld Humanitarian Outreach Program developed by Dr. Ani Kalayjian utilizes the 7-Step Biopsychosocial & Eco-Spiritual Model, through which various aspects of dispute, conflict, or disagreement are assessed, identified, explored, processed, worked through, and reintegrated with the lessons learned from the process. The 7-Step model is at the core of all workshops (Kalayjian, 2002).

This innovative and integrative model incorporates various theories, including: psychodynamic (Freud, 1910), interpersonal (Sullivan, 1953); existential and humanistic (Frankl, 1962); Electromagnetic Field Balancing (EMF, Dubro & Lapierre, 2002); forgiveness and reconciliation (Kalayjian & Paloutzian, 2010); Learning Theory, flower essences, essential oils, physical release (van der Kolk, 1987); and mind-body-spirit chakra balancing, prayers, and meditation. The following are the seven steps of the 7-Step Integrative Healing Model:

I ***Assess Levels of Distress, Disagreement, or Conflict:*** Participants are given a written questionnaire that helps them define the kind of dispute they are working on, and elicits the impact of this dispute or conflict. Formal assessment instruments may also be provided, such as the Harvard Trauma Checklist and the Forgiveness and Meaning Scales.

II ***Encourage Expression of Feelings:*** One at a time, each participant in the group is encouraged to describe his or her feelings about the trauma or conflict, from his or her perspective, and to express feelings in the "here and now" in relation to the trauma, dispute, or conflict that has been identified and described.

III *__Provide Empathy and Validation:__* Each participant's feelings are validated by the mediator, group facilitator, and group members. Emphasis is placed on understanding others and putting one's feet in the opponent's shoes. When disputes rupture an individual's link with the group, an intolerable sense of isolation, helplessness, and victimization may occur. Providing validation and empathy in such a group setting will transform these negative effects by reestablishing the mutual exchange between the individuals in conflict, while the presence of others in the group witnessing this process validates the experiences.

IV *__Encourage Discovery and Expression of Meaning:__* Participants are asked, "What lessons, meaning, or positive associations did you discover about yourself as a result of this dispute?" This question is based on Viktor Frankl's logotherapeutic principles: There may be a positive meaning discovered in the worst catastrophe, and there are lessons to be learned from the most difficult conflicts and traumas. The facilitator helps opposing parties discover creative ways to make meaning. Dr. Martin Luther King, Jr. has said that only light can transform darkness. Participants are invited to focus on individual and collective growth, strength, and meanings that naturally arise out of any trauma, dispute, or conflict. Forgiveness is also reinforced here as a tool for self-care and letting go of resentments, revenge, and anger, which only reinforce the conflict or dispute, poison the individuals involved, and hinder the process of healing and peace-making.

V *__Provide Information:__* Practical tools and information are shared on how to gradually integrate the conflict-resolution information that has been provided, and care for oneself as a caregiver/mediator. Information is also shared on the steps of practicing forgiveness, and ways to transform the dispute, as well as how violence begets more violence and is transmitted through seven generations. Information on assertiveness (COPE Model, Kalayjian), anger management, and mindfulness is also shared, as well as the UN Declaration for Human Rights. The ancestral healing CD is introduced (Kalayjian, 2011).

VI ***Instill Eco-Centered Healing:*** Practical tools for helping participants connect with Mother Earth are shared, as well as ways to care for one's environment. An emphasis is placed on starting with the care of one's environment through neighborhood associations, and expanding to the larger globe, as well as being mindful of a systems perspective. Participants learn how we impact our environment and how our environment impacts us. Peace and Forgiveness Gardens are introduced as a sacred space.

Breathing, Movement-Centered Healing, and Meditation: Breath is used as a natural medicine and healing tool. Since no one can control nature, other people, or what happens outside of one's self, participants are assisted in being mindful of how they can respond to the dispute instead of reacting to it. Participants are guided on how to use breath toward self-empowerment, creating peace within, and engendering gratitude, compassion, faith, strength, and forgiveness in response to conflicts. Energetic Balancing movements will be practiced, in combination with diaphragmatic breathing and reciting uplifting affirmations. Integrative tools are also introduced, such as Flower Essences, essential oils, chakra alignment, Electromagnetic Field Balancing, meditation, compassionate listening, prayers, etc.

Attachment 5: 7-Step Integrative Healing Model for Children and Adolescents

7-Step Integrative Healing Model (The Biopsychosocial & Eco-Spiritual Model) For Children and Adolescents

Dr. Ani Kalayjian

The Mental Health Outreach Program, developed by Dr. Kalayjian, utilizes this 7-Step Integrative Healing Model. Through it, various aspects of feeling are assessed, identified, explored, processed, worked through, and reintegrated.

This innovative and integrative model incorporates various theories, including: psychodynamic (Freud, 1910), interpersonal (Sullivan, 1953), existential and humanistic (Frankl, 1962), Electromagnetic Field Balancing (EMF, Dubro & Lapierre, 2002), Forgiveness and Reconciliation (Kalayjian & Paloutzian, 2010), Learning Theory, Flower Essences, essential oils, physical release (van der Kolk, 1987), as well as mind-body-spirit chakra balancing, prayers, and meditation.

The following are the seven steps of the Biopsychosocial, and Eco-Spiritual Model, focused on working with children and their families.

Step I: Assess Levels of Post-Traumatic Stress: The child's level of stress symptomatology and other distress is assessed through observations during play and art therapy. Parents and other caretakers' levels of trauma and distress are assessed through the Harvard Trauma Questionnaire. On an individual level, the Anger Wheel is provided so that children and adolescents can identify their feeling, and measure its severity, on a scale of zero to ten.

Step II: Encourage Expression of Feelings: Children are encouraged to express their feelings through art and play therapy, or through role-play. In post-natural as well as human-made disasters, the predominant feelings expressed in children are fear, anger, and sadness, and they may exhibit disruptive and avoidant behaviors and/or have sleep disturbances and nightmares.

Step III: Provide Empathy and Validation: Children's feelings will be validated using statements such as "I can understand…" or "It makes sense to me…" and that it is a normal feeling, and that it will get better after talking about it and finding the best activities for release. Also used is intentional therapeutic touch, such as holding a child's hand. Here it will be reinforced that the child's feelings of grief, fear, or anger, as well as the joy of surviving, are all natural responses to the disaster, and that they all need to be expressed. When trauma ruptures the child's links with the group, an intolerable sense of isolation and helplessness may occur. Providing validation and empathy will correct these effects by reestablishing the mutual exchange between the child and others. Family therapy is provided in this setting to help parents and caretakers overcome their own trauma, so as to aid their children in a healthy way.

Step IV: Encourage Discovery and Expression of Meaning: Children will be asked, "What lessons, meaning, or positive lessons did you discover as a result of this experience?" This question is based on Viktor Frankl's logotherapeutic principles, that there could be a positive meaning discovered in the worst catastrophe, as well as the Buddhist assertions that it takes darkness to appreciate and reconnect with light. The child will be invited to focus on his or her strengths from the stories that they shared. Some of the positive lessons shared by children are: I am stronger now, I know how to be positive, I can use words instead of hitting, Mommy and Daddy are alive—that is most important than the house or car, it's better to love than to fight, it's better to forgive than to hold a grudge, and when Mommy and Daddy are happy, they show their love to me more.

Step V: Provide Information: Practical tools and information are given on how to gradually overcome fears, utilizing the systematic desensitization process. The importance of preparation will be reinforced, and how to prepare will be role-played. Handouts will be given, with lists of feelings for those who are unable to identify their feelings. Resources are also shared with teachers and prospective group leaders on how to conduct disaster-evacuation drills and create safe and accessible exits. Booklets will be given to parents and teachers on how to listen to and relate to their children's nightmares, fears, and disruptive behaviors. Assessment tools will be given to psychologists and psychiatrists. Handouts will be provided on grief, as well as on how to take care of oneself as a caregiver. In this area we emphasize nonviolent communication, forgiveness, and empathy.

Step VI: Connecting with Mother Earth: Practical tools are shared to connect with Mother Earth. Discussions and exercises are conducted around environmental connections. Ways to care for one's environment are shared. We start right in the classroom, then in the children's homes, and then we expand to the larger globe, explaining how we can impact our environment, and how the environment in turn impacts us. A list of mindful acts is shared to help us co-create an emerald-green world. Children are encouraged to engage in tasks centered on caring for their surroundings and making their environment beautiful through chores such as cleaning, gardening, organizing, recycling, color coding, etc. We empower children to engage in playing in the parks, hiding around trees, playing hide-and-seek, watching sunsets, and enjoying moonlight.

Step VII: Healing through deep breaths and being present: Breath is used as a natural medicine and a healing tool. Since no one can control nature, other people or what happens outside of oneself, children are assisted in controlling how they respond to fear and disaster. This will be an experiential section of the model. Children are provided with instructions on how to move their body to release fear, uncertainty and anger. In addition, children are instructed on how to use breath toward self-empowerment, as well as to engender gratitude, compassion, faith, strength, and forgiveness. Children are engaged in enjoyable exercises to allow for physical release and chakra balancing.

Attachment 6: 7-Step Integrative Healing Model for Older Adults

7-Step Integrative Healing Model
For Older Adults: *"Old is Gold"*
For Healing, Forgiving, Reminiscing, and Passing Wisdom to Younger Generations

Dr. Ani Kalayjian

The Meaningfulworld healing and empowering for older individuals, by Dr. Ani Kalayjian, utilizes the 7-Step Biopsychosocial & Eco-Spiritual Model, through which various aspects of life accomplishments and challenges are identified, processed, released, and reintegrated with the lessons learned. The seven-step model is flexible, and it can be tailored to meet individual needs (Kalayjian, 2002).

This innovative and integrative model incorporates various theories, including: psychodynamic (Freud, 1910), interpersonal (Sullivan, 1953); existential and humanistic (Frankl, 1962); Electromagnetic Field Balancing (EMF, Dubro & Lapierre, 2002); forgiveness and reconciliation (Kalayjian & Paloutzian, 2010); Learning Theory, Flower Essences (Bach, 1930), essential oils, physical release (van der Kolk, 1987); and mind-body-spirit chakra balancing, prayers, and meditation. The following are the seven steps of the 7-Step Integrative Healing Model:

I ***Assess Levels of Distress, Disagreement, or Conflict:*** Participants are given a written questionnaire that helps them define their feelings, coping styles, and levels of trauma. Formal assessment instruments may also be provided, such as the Harvard Trauma Questionnaire and the Forgiveness and Meaning-Making Questionnaires.

II ***Encourage Expression of Feelings:*** One at a time, each participant in the group is encouraged to describe his or her feelings, in the "here and now," in relation to the stress, trauma, or conflict that has been identified and described. Catharsis is essential to be able to transform our pain and suffering.

III ***Provide Empathy and Validation:*** Each participant's feelings are validated by the group facilitator and other group members. Emphasis is placed on understanding others and putting one's own feet in the opponent's shoes. Stress, dispute, or trauma ruptures the individual's link with the group, and an intolerable sense of isolation, helplessness, and victimization may occur. Providing validation and empathy in such a group setting will transform these negative effects by reestablishing the mutual exchange between the individuals, while the presence of others in the group witnessing this process validates the experiences.

IV ***Encourage Discovery and Expression of Meaning:*** Participants are asked, "What lessons, meaning, or positive associations did you discover about yourself as a result of this stress/situation?" This question is based on Viktor Frankl's logotherapeutic principles: There may be a positive meaning discovered in the worst catastrophe, and there are lessons to be learned from the most difficult conflicts and traumas. The facilitator helps in achieving the discovery of meaning. Dr. Martin Luther King, Jr. has said that only light can transform darkness. Participants are invited to focus on individual and collective growth, strength, and meanings that naturally arise out of any trauma or conflict. Forgiveness is also reinforced here as a tool for self-care and letting go of resentments, revenge, and anger, which only reinforce negative feelings, poison the individuals involved, and hinder the process of healing and the transmission of wisdom to the next generations.

V ***Provide Information:*** Practical tools and information are shared on how to gradually integrate the healing information that has been provided. Information is also shared on the steps of practicing forgiveness and how to transform inner conflicts, as well as how violence begets more violence and is transmitted through seven generations. The following will be shared: assertiveness (COPE Model, Kalayjian), mindfulness, EQ, and how to write one's autobiography or a short story about oneself. In this stage, we experience Ego Integrity vs. Despair, in which wisdom is the basic virtue developed (E. Erikson, 1959). Therefore, suggestions will be shared on how to transform the past, focus on the present, and share one's gifts and wisdom with the next generation.

VI ***Connect with Mother Earth:*** Practical tools for helping participants connect with Mother Earth are shared, as well as ways to care for one's environment. Participants learn how we impact our environment and how our environment impacts us. Benefits of starting Peace and Forgiveness Gardens, and gardening in general, are communicated.

VII ***Breath, Body, Movement, Meditation, and Prayer:*** Breath is used as a natural medicine and healing tool. Since no one can control nature, other people, or what happens outside of oneself, participants are assisted in being mindful of how they can respond instead of reacting. Participants are guided on how to use breath toward self-empowerment, creating peace within, and engendering gratitude, compassion, faith, strength, and forgiveness. We distinguish among self-forgiveness, forgiveness of others, and forgiveness toward physical challenges. Integrative tools are also introduced, such as Flower Essences, essential oils, chakra alignment, Electromagnetic Field Balancing, meditation, compassionate listening, prayers, and emotional freedom technique.

Attachment 7: Harvard Trauma Questionnaire

Harvard Trauma Questionnaire

"The following are symptoms that people sometimes have after experiencing hurtful or terrifying events in their lives. Please listen to each one carefully and decide how much the symptoms bothered you in the past week." Kindly write in what these terrifying or challenging events were:

	"In the past week, how much were you distressed by..."	(1) Not at all	(2) A little	(3) Quite a lot	(4) Extremely
1	Recurrent thoughts or memories of the most hurtful or terrifying events	☐	☐	☐	☐
2	Feeling as though the event is happening again	☐	☐	☐	☐
3	Recurrent nightmares	☐	☐	☐	☐
4	Feeling detached or withdrawn from people	☐	☐	☐	☐
5	Unable to feel emotions	☐	☐	☐	☐
6	Feeling jumpy, easily startled	☐	☐	☐	☐
7	Difficulty concentrating	☐	☐	☐	☐
8	Trouble sleeping	☐	☐	☐	☐
9	Feeling on guard	☐	☐	☐	☐
10	Feeling irritable or having outbursts of anger	☐	☐	☐	☐
11	Avoiding activities that remind you of the traumatic or hurtful event	☐	☐	☐	☐

12	Inability to remember parts of the most traumatic or hurtful events	☐	☐	☐	☐
13	Less interest in daily activities	☐	☐	☐	☐
14	Feeling as if you don't have a future	☐	☐	☐	☐
15	Avoiding thoughts or feelings associated with the traumatic or hurtful events	☐	☐	☐	☐
16	Sudden emotional or physical reaction when reminded of the most hurtful or traumatic events	☐	☐	☐	☐

Demographics			
Age:		Gender:	
Marital Status:		Education:	
Nationality:		Religion:	

Attachment 8: Forgiveness Questionnaire

Forgiveness

Because of my religious or spiritual beliefs:

	Always almost always	Often	Seldom	Never
I have forgiven myself for things that I have done wrong	1	2	3	4
I have forgiven those who hurt me	1	2	3	4
I know that God forgives me	1	2	3	4

Attachment 8: Meaning-Making Questionnaire MLQ

Please take a moment to think about what makes your life and existence feel important and significant to you. Please respond to the following statements as truthfully and accurately as you can, and also please remember that these are very subjective questions and that there are no right or wrong answers. Please answer according to the scale below:

Absolutely Untrue	Mostly Untrue	Somewhat Untrue	Can't Say If True or False	Somewhat True	Mostly True	Absolutely True
1	2	3	4	5	6	7

1. I understand my life's meaning.
2. I am looking for something that makes my life feel meaningful.
3. I am always looking to find my life's purpose.
4. My life has a clear sense of purpose.
5. I have a good sense of what makes my life meaningful.
6. I have discovered a satisfying life purpose.

7. I am always searching for something that makes my life feel significant.
8. I am seeking a purpose or mission for my life.
9. My life has no clear purpose.
10. I am searching for meaning in my life.

Attachment 10: Mindful Grieving

WHAT WE NEED DURING GRIEF

Dr. Ani Kalayjian

Our joys, when extended, will always increase,
and grief, when divided, is hushed into peace!
~ Anonymous

1. *ACCEPTING:* Recognize and accept that which you cannot change.
2. *MOURNING:* It's healthier to do your mourning **now**—don't hold back the tears.
3. *CARING:* Accept expressions of caring from others, and care for yourself.
4. *GIVING YOURSELF TIME:* Give yourself time alone as well as with others whom you trust, and in whom you find comfort.
5. *CRYING:* Acknowledge the pain and cry. It is necessary to cry as soon as you can, and for as long as you feel you need to. Remember, men cry too.
6. *RECOGNIZING THAT YOU ARE NOT ALONE:* It may feel as though you are alone, but you are not alone. Connect with others to share and ease the pain.
7. *RESTING, RELAXING, EXERCISING, AND NOURISHING:* You may need extra rest and relaxation to replenish yourself physically, emotionally, and spiritually.
8. *STICKING TO YOUR SCHEDULE:* Try not to add new and difficult situations to your life. Maintain your routine as much as possible, and keep decision-making to a minimum.
9. *REAFFIRMING YOUR BELIEFS:* Reaffirm your belief in life, in yourself, in others, and especially in the loved one who has transitioned.
10. *HOPING:* Keep hope and faith alive. Seek those who help you reestablish hope.

11. ***VALUING SMALL PLEASURES:*** Do not underestimate the importance of little things such as walking in a park or in the snow, watching sunsets or sunrises, smelling a rose, etc.

12. ***PERFORMING YOUR RITUALS:*** Perform the rituals that exist in your belief system. Engaging in rituals will help you process the pain and help you heal by changing your relationship with the object of loss.

13. ***IDENTIFYING HARD DAYS:*** Remember that Sundays, holidays, birthdays, and anniversaries are difficult times—surround yourself with loved ones.

14. ***AVOIDING DRUGS, ALCOHOL, AND SLEEPING MEDICATIONS:*** Substances may prolong and delay the grieving process, plus inflame the wound. Take the following natural remedies: Rescue, Star of Bethlehem, and Grief Relief.

15. ***INFORMING PEOPLE OF YOUR LOSS:*** Grieving can make it harder to concentrate, focus, make decisions, etc. People around you need to know about your loss. **"Shared sorrow is half sorrow, while shared joy is double joy."**

16. ***PERMITTING YOURSELF TO BACKSLIDE:*** There is no set formula for grieving. After feeling good for a while, you might find yourself angry, sad, and in despair all over again. This is okay; just continue processing and healing.

17. ***REAFFIRMING YOUR GOALS:*** You might find it difficult to pursue your goals, since they will lose their potency. Focus on one little step, one foot at a time.

18. ***BEING GENTLE WITH YOURSELF:*** Remember that grieving and mourning is hard work, so be gentle with yourself and pamper yourself.

19. ***CELEBRATING YOUR LOSS:*** Celebrate the life and achievements of your deceased loved one through rituals, stories, commemorations, and anniversaries.

20. ***DISCOVER A POSITIVE MEANING IN YOUR LOSS:*** As per Viktor Frankl, find a positive lesson in your experience of loss— something you learned about **yourself.**

Attachment 11: List of Meaningfulworld Humanitarian Outreach Projects in Forty-five Countries and Twenty-five States in the USA

Meaningfulworld List of Humanitarian Outreach Projects

1. Soviet Republic of Armenia, earthquake 1989-92
2. Florida, USA, Hurricane Andrew, 1992
3. One-year follow-up for Hurricane Andrew, 1993
4. Former Yugoslavia, ethnic cleansing, 1993
5. California, Northridge earthquake, 1994
6. Kobe, Japan, earthquake, 1995
7. Kuwait, NYC, DC, Gulf War, 1995
8. Former Yugoslavia, ethnic cleansing, 1996
9. Dominican Republic, Hurricane George, 1998
10. Armenian-Turkish Reconciliation, 1998-2010
11. 9-11 Terrorism in New York, 2001 (Six months of outreach)
12. Sri Lanka, post-tsunami, 2004 (Six months)
13. Texas, USA, Hurricanes Katrina and Rita, 2005
14. New Orleans, Hurricane Katrina, one-year follow-up, 2006
15. Pakistan, earthquake, 2005-06
16. Lebanon and Syria, postwar 2007 and 2013
17. Bosnia, Sarajevo, postwar 2007
18. Armenia, postwar 1995, 1998, 2000, 2004, 2007, 2008, 2010, 2013
19. Sierra Leone, West Africa, 2009
20. Saudi Arabia, 2009
21. Haiti, 2010-2015 (Nine teams)
22. Kenya, 2010-2013 (Four teams)
23. Rwanda and Democratic Republic of the Congo, 2011-2013 (Two teams)
24. Palestine and Israel, 1998, 2012, 2013, 2015
25. Burundi, post-genocide, 2013

26. Jordan, 2014
27. Lebanon, 2014
28. Palestine, 2014
29. Israel, 2014
30. Haiti, 2014
31. Armenia, Syrian Refugees, and Suicide Hotline, 2014
32. Palestine, 2015
33. Israel, 2015
34. Haiti, 2016
35. Armenia, Syrian Refugees, and Suicide Hotline, 2017
36. Haiti, 12th Mission, 2017

Attachment 12: Emotional Genogram

Sample: Eugene O'Neill Family

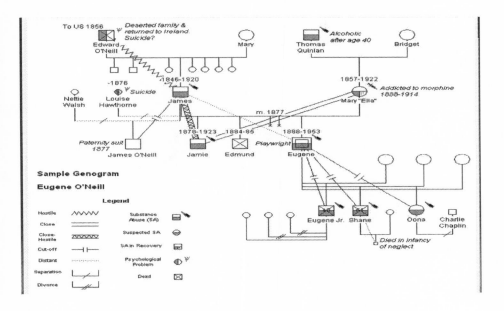

Attachment 13: Pointing the finger

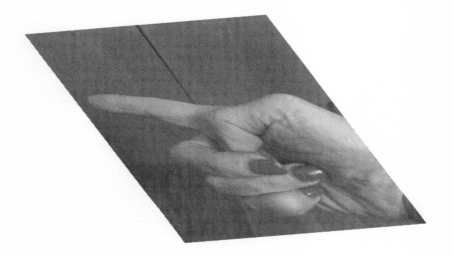

Attachment 14: Our Response Is Our Choice

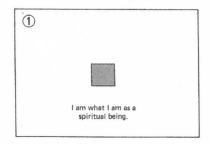

① I am what I am as a
spiritual being.

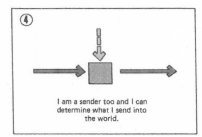

② I can't determine what
I receive from the world.

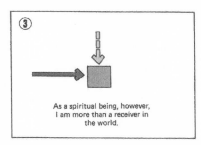

③ As a spiritual being, however,
I am more than a receiver in
the world.

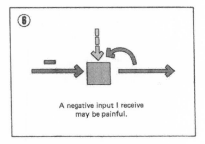

④ I am a sender too and I can
determine what I send into
the world.

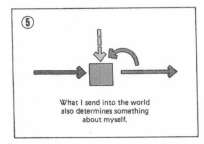

⑤ What I send into the world
also determines something
about myself.

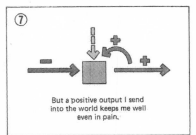

⑥ A negative input I receive
may be painful.

⑦ But a positive output I send
into the world keeps me well
even in pain.

8th World Congress of
Logotherapy
June 26–30 1991

With compliments

References

Angelou, M. (1993). *On the pulse of morning.* Poem performed at the first inauguration of President Bill Clinton on January 20, 1993. Retrieved from http://www.nytimes.com/1993/01/21/us/the-inauguration-maya-angelou-on-the-pulse-of-morning.html

Covey, S. R. (1989). *The seven habits of highly effective people.* New York, NY: Free Press.

Dubrow, P. P., & Lapierre, D. (2002). *Elegant empowerment: Evolution of consciousness.* New York: Platinum Publishing House.

Erickson, E. (1959). Identity and the life cycle: Selected papers. *Psychological Issues, 1(*1), 133-134.

Frankl, V. (1962). *Man's search for meaning.* New York: Vintage Books.

Freud, S. (1910). The origin and development of psychoanalysis. *The American Journal of Psychology, 21*(2), 181-218.

Howard, J. (2013, December 9). "Mindfulness" meditation alters gene expression, study suggests. *The Huffington Post.* Retrieved from http://m.huffpost.com/us/entry/4391871

Journal of Offender Rehabilitation http://divinecosmos.com/start-here/davids-blog/1123-boston).

Kalayjian, A. (1995). *Disaster & mass trauma: Global perspectives in post disaster mental health management.* Long Beach, NJ: Vista Publishing.

Kalayjian, A. (1999). Forgiveness and transcendence. *Clio's Psyche, 6* (3), 116-119.

Kalayjian, A. (2002). Biopsychosocial and spiritual treatment of trauma. In R. & S. Massey (Eds.), *Comprehensive handbook of psychotherapy: Vol. 3, interpersonal/humanistic/existential* (pp. 615-637). New York, NY: John Wiley & Sons.

Kalayjian, A., & Eugene, D. (2010). *Mass trauma and emotional healing around the world: Rituals and practices for resilience and meaning-making.* New York: Praeger, ABC-CLIO.

Kalayjian, A., & Paloutzian, R. (2010). *Forgiveness and reconciliation: Psychological pathways to conflict transformation and peace building.* New York, NY: Springer Publishing.

Kalayjian, A., & Sofletea, G. (2012). Victim, perpetrator, or BOTH?: A child soldier's journey into healing wounds of war in Sierra Leone. In S. Poyrazli & C. E. Thompson (Eds.), *International case studies in mental health* (pp. 33-52). Washington, DC: Sage Publishing.

Kalayjian, A. S., Shahinian, S. P., Gergerian, E. L., & Saraydarian, L. (1996). Coping with Ottoman Turkish Genocide: An exploration of the experience of Armenian survivors. *Journal of Traumatic Stress, 9*(1), 87-97.

Kearney, D. J., McDermott, K., Malte, C., Martinez, M., & Simpson, T. L. (2012). Association of participation in a mindfulness program with measures of PTSD, depression and quality of life in a veteran sample. *Journal of Clinical Psychology, 68*, 101-116

Nietzsche, F. (1998). *Twilight of the idols, or how to philosophize with a hammer* (D. Large, Trans.). New York, NY: Oxford University Press. (Original work published 1889)

Rosenthal, J. Z., Grosswald, S., Ross, R., & Rosenthal, N. (2011). Effects of transcendental meditation in veterans of Operation Enduring Freedom and Operation Iraqi Freedom with posttraumatic stress disorder: A pilot study. *Military Medicine, 176*, 626-630. Retrieved from http://m.huffpost.com/us/entry/4391871

Ruiz, M. G. (1997). *The four agreements: A practical guide to personal wisdom.* New York: Amber-Allen Publishing.

Sullivan, H. S. (1953). *Interpersonal theory of psychiatry.* New York: W. W. Norton.

Van der Kolk, B. (1987). The psychobiology of the trauma response: Hyperarousal constriction and addition. In B. A. Van der Kolk (Ed.), *Psychological trauma* (pp. xxx). Washington, DC: American Psychiatric Press.

Van der Kolk, B. (2004, January/February). The limits of talk. *Psychotherapy Networker.*

Wilcock, D. (2013, April 15). Boston Marathon: Meditate for Peace. *Divine Cosmos.*

Gratitude to my family, friends, colleagues and clients for all their insight and support. Gratitude to all readers and supporters. Special gratitude to the following editors: Prof. Ray Paloutzian, Seta Papazian, Zarmine Boghosian, Daria Diakonova-Curtis, Prof. Takooshian and Lorraine Walker-Simmons

Author's previous books, CD and films

1. Kalayjian, A. S. (1995). Disaster & Mass Trauma: Global Perspectives on Post Disaster Mental Health Management. Vista Publishers, Inc., Long Branch, NJ.
2. Kalayjian, A., & Eugene, D. (2010). Mass Trauma & Emotional Healing Around the World: Rituals and Practices for Resilience and Meaning-making. II Volumes: Vol. I Natural Disasters and
3. Vol. II Human Made Disasters. New York: NY: Greenwood Publishing Group, ABC-CLIO Inc.
4. Kalayjian, A. and Paloutzian, R. (2010). Forgiveness & reconciliation: Psychological Pathways to Conflict Transformation and Peace Building. Springer Publishing: New York: NY.
5. Kalayjian, A. (2010). From War to Peace, Transforming Ancestral and Generational Trauma into Healing and Meaning-Making, Meditation CD.
6. Kalayjian, A. (2017). Soul-Surfing: Mindful integration of yoga, energetic release, positive affirmation, breath, color consciousness, and movement. A DVD.
7. Over 18 films on Meaningfulworld Humanitarian Outreach Programs around the world in Africa, Asia, the Caribbean, the Caucuses, The Middle East, and North and South Americas:

Related links and films

1. United Nations, Commission on Status of Women (CSW) Parallel event 23 March 2017
   http://voiceofarmenians.com/programs/atop-meaningful-world-symposium-on-the-un-day-of-commission-on-the-status-of-women
2. Meaningfulworld Humanitarian Mission to Haiti, an overview 2016
   https://www.youtube.com/watch?v=x9_WTq6PoJs
3. Meaningfulworld Humanitarian Mission to Haiti 2015
   https://www.youtube.com/watch?v=mka8-PWn398
4. **ATOP Meaningful World celebrates the International Day of Peace.** 2015
5. Meaningfulworld symposium on the UN day of Commission on the Status of Women 23 March 2017
6. Interview on Haitian National TV, TV Metropol
   http://www.metropolehaiti.com/metropole/lepoint.php
7. Humanitarian Mission to Armenia, 2014
   https://www.youtube.com/watch?v=sN6KlUtIOw0&list=UU9r9k4e53c8acKjm-Bj8Mpw
8. Humanitarian Mission to the Middle East 2014
   https://www.youtube.com/watch?v=dh1-juQNbEI&feature=youtube_gdata
9. Meaningfulworld Humanitarian Mission to Haiti, 2014
   http://youtu.be/GrWVkRESKGk
10. Meaningfulworld at the United Nations, Commission of Status of Women (2014)
    https://www.youtube.com/watch?v=BnV0y6hzuHM
11. Transforming trauma into Healing and Meaning-Making
    https://www.youtube.com/watch?v=zBA-qI8uAA4
12. Meaningfulworld Mission to Haiti, 2010
    https://vimeo.com/18053846
13. Meaningfulworld Humanitarian Mission in Sierra Leone
    http://www.youtube.com/watch?v=Iam-DpsTbWI

(or visit You Tube and type in <u>Meaningfulworld.com</u> Smile for Sierra Leone).

14. Dr. Kalayjian presents at ICERM Conference in NYC
    https://www.youtube.com/watch?v=3oC5ixJoAo8&index=6&list=PLYE8rrwZqMsfgEQsdmtL56UotY436VZM7

15. Dr. Kalayjian on ABC TV Channel 7, Facial Transplant with Kimberly Richardson
    http://youtu.be/72_Gjawn6zE

16. Dr. Kalayjian Chairing a panel discussion at the United Nations. Committee on Spirituality, Values and Global Concern. CONGO. 66th Anniversary of the UN. Visionary Leaders in Times of Crises.
    http://youtu.be/wGch1z9GORM

17. Dr. Kalayjian Chairing International Day of Peace, Honoring Patch Adams.
    https://www.youtube.com/watch?v=p0lZ6kQIlus

18. Dr Kalayjian chairing a panel at the United Nations, on Preventing G

25241445R00099

Made in the USA
Middletown, DE
22 December 2018

Executive Sexism

How Men Treat Women at the Highest Levels,
Why Law Does Not Protect Them,
and What Should Change

Elizabeth C. Wolfe

 PRAEGER™

An Imprint of ABC-CLIO, LLC

Santa Barbara, California • Denver, Colorado

Library of Congress Cataloging-in-Publication Data

Names: Wolfe, Elizabeth C., author.
Title: Executive sexism : how men treat women at the highest levels, why law
    does not protect them, and what should change / Elizabeth C. Wolfe.
Description: Santa Barbara, California : Praeger, [2019] | Includes
    bibliographical references and index.
Identifiers: LCCN 2018060676 (print) | LCCN 2019004072 (ebook) |
    ISBN 9781440859571 (ebook) | ISBN 9781440859564 (hard copy : alk. paper)
Subjects: LCSH: Women executives. | Sexism. | Glass ceiling (Employment
    discrimination) | Discrimination in employment.
Classification: LCC HD6054.3 (ebook) | LCC HD6054.3 .W625 2019 (print) |
    DDC 331.4/133—dc23
LC record available at https://lccn.loc.gov/2018060676

ISBN: 978-1-4408-5956-4 (print)
       978-1-4408-5957-1 (ebook)

23 22 21 20 19   1 2 3 4 5

This book is also available as an eBook.

Praeger
An Imprint of ABC-CLIO, LLC

ABC-CLIO, LLC
147 Castilian Drive
Santa Barbara, California 93117
www.abc-clio.com

This book is printed on acid-free paper ∞

Manufactured in the United States of America

This book is for Charlene.

My mother has six daughters. We grew up using food stamps. She took a minimum-wage food service job to put all six of us through college. Free tuition was a benefit of her union contract. She worked at that job for 18 miserable years, being degraded by her male boss, and performing count-less other selfless acts along the way to ensure her daughters became quality people. I don't know anyone else with character or perseverance like hers. Something being hard or out of reach was never an excuse to stop pursuing it.

Her quiet and persistent example always modeled through her actions that character matters. The quality of who you are, and the quality of self you put into the world, matters. My mother reminds me each day never to underestimate the effect you have on other people. Having just one person who really sees you for who you are is invaluable to the soul. This book was emotionally taxing, and it would not have happened were it not for her presence in my life.

Contents

Acknowledgments   ix

Part One   Facing Gradual and Sudden Sexism

Chapter 1   It's Not Just You   3

Chapter 2   Systematizing Culture and Structure   22

Chapter 3   Verbal Messages and Social Cues   36

Chapter 4   Sexualization   55

Chapter 5   Why Women Remain Silent   65

Chapter 6   The Role of Pornography   84

Part Two   Why Bystanders Don't Speak Up

Chapter 7   Cultural Gaslighting: The Double Standard   107

Chapter 8   Not a Sexist, He Says   123

Chapter 9   How Women Try to Control Sexism   142

Chapter 10   It Isn't about a Particular Woman   157

Chapter 11   How Women Are Pitted against Each Other   173

Chapter 12   The Double Bind of Advancement   196

Part Three   Intervention Strategies to Activate Bystanders

Chapter 13   Speaking Up   217

Chapter 14   Naming the Behavior   224

Contents

Chapter 15   Addressing the Behavior   234

Chapter 16   Destabilizing Sexist Environments   247

References   273

Index   279

Acknowledgments

If the subject of this book resonates with you, you may be in a difficult place, like I was when I proposed this book—in a professional environment that made no sense, being treated in ways not reflective of your professional abilities or stature, and told by media and other people who have no idea about it, how you should feel.

I would like to acknowledge Debbie, my editor. Thank you for your patience, and thank you for wanting this book to happen. That was a sentiment I desperately needed to hear, and at the exact moment you said it. Because of your support and flexibility, a new generation is now armed with knowledge to do guerrilla warfare against sexism. I appreciate so much the role you played.

In this book, we address sexism that occurs at the highest professional levels. Levels that you, we, fought to attain. Levels that we struggled and suffered and sacrificed to reach. As you try to understand who you are in this problem and how to navigate through it, go to the balcony. Look at the people who have made your life particularly difficult, and those doing it now. Whose decisions have most impeded your progress. Whose lack of character allowed disgraceful conditions to thrive and persist, to your detriment.

Now imagine those people had been instructed differently.

This is what power you hold. Someone is always watching your example. Recognize things for what they are, not what you have been told they should be. Discern what has worth to you and why. Help where you can. You have been placed where you are for a reason.

PART 1

Facing Gradual and Sudden Sexism

CHAPTER ONE

It's Not Just You

"The greatest trick the devil ever pulled is convincing the world he didn't exist."

—The Usual Suspects

"Don't take yourself so seriously. It was a joke. You have no sense of humor."

You know the script. We all know the script.

The most important thing to know is that you are not alone. You are not the only one. Isolation and gaslighting are the biggest allies of sexism. I wrote this book to show you that the sexism you are living has played out time and again, across different countries, industries, and languages. It's not just you.

How many times have you had a "work introduction" and the man acted like you were on a date? It's not just you. How many times have you looked at a man's face, twisted in confusion, as if you lacked the ability to communicate adequately? It's not just you.

Changing your hair, dark clothes, no makeup, painstakingly choosing your accessories so as not to give the "wrong impression," only to be sexualized anyway? It's not just you. Being caught off guard by a vile comment, asked to fetch everyone coffee even though you hold a senior position? It's not just you. Knowing that snide comment was not a joke, that it was a status move to make you look bad? It's not just you.

Telling your professional credentials to someone who acts like you are lying, or making up your work history? It's not just you. Getting grilled on your qualifications as if you are incompetent, by a man who *is* incompetent? It's not just you.

I interviewed women from nine countries. Their narratives all complemented the perspectives of the others, even though they spoke different languages and have never met. In a multinational corporate world, women in executive positions experience the same elements of sexism. Executive sexism brings to mind an office setting with a male superior chasing his female colleague around a desk. That is one possible scenario, but some men are smarter than to be so overt. Sexism just blends into every aspect of life. Delineating it as its own entity is difficult.

Oh, you are not being too sensitive. Communication training fails to address inequality. While you are being coached on your executive presence, that middle ground you are encouraged to find, it does not exist. You go from silent to aggressive, from zero to bitch. Ask a question and you are emotional. Ask a follow-up question and you are hysterical. Again, it's not just you. Research for 60 years has concluded decisively that whatever women do or say will be relegated to a lower status than a man saying or doing the exact same thing. It was not your imagination when you thought it was happening. You were never intended to win.

The reason you cannot win where you are is because sexism is socialized and reinforced by messages everywhere in culture and society. Isolation and gaslighting help you stay unaware. So do media and politics. By the time men hit the executive level, many have been conditioned to disrespect you and consider your place at the table as less legitimate than their own.

As each of the interview participants pointed out, the dynamics at the executive level look the same as they do at every level, beginning in high school. Sexism is a result of culture, which does not switch itself off when you enter work space. That deck is stacked against you at more levels than you realize. Playing by men's rules will never yield a woman the results those rules yield other men. Women do not win playing by sexist rules.

What This Book Is About

As a woman, by the time you fight your way to the executive level, men are already hardwired to disrespect and undermine you. This book describes the stealthy expressions of sexism and how naturally they meld into our professional interactions, our personal relationships, and our social activities. That was the purpose of the interviews. After organizing the data, I chose the most useful way to present the information to accomplish the following three goals:

1. **Create visibility**: *Open and articulate the world of sexism, in which women are "other."*

    The greatest strength of sexist culture is its invisibility. Each of the women I interviewed had an idea about what executive sexism was, but none of them had anywhere close to a full understanding of how sexism manifests in daily life. I find this with myself, and every other woman I know. If we want to address sexism on a meaningful level, we need to know what it looks like.

2. **Compare similarities in experiences**: *Expose the myths that women have been socialized to accept.*

   This book is not *making the case* that sexism exists in all levels of society. That evidence has been theorized and proved by brilliant minds for over a century. The case has been made. Instead, we are focused on what sexism looks like, how it creeps into our psyche, and how to transmute it.

3. **Create new pathways to success**: *Replace old scripts and ideas with new scripts and ideas.*

   For professional women, sexism is an enormous waste of time. Once we see how the same tactics are tried over and over, with no success, we can redirect our energy to lines of effort that will yield better results. To accomplish this, we needed solid data from which to derive practical perspective.

SEXISM

1. Prejudice or discrimination based on sex, especially: discrimination against women.
2. Behavior, conditions, or attitudes that foster stereotypes of social roles based on sex.

(Merriam-Webster, 2018)

Women Define Sexism Differently

Sexism is so pervasive that we experience it like breathing; it becomes such a fixture in our daily existence that we rarely identify it as an independent entity. This includes our work life.

Some interviews felt like the participants were resisting and challenging me about the existence of sexism. They identified it in their work and personal lives during the interview, but they just did not think in terms of sexism. In fact, few women explained their situations as sexist, and only one realized it at the time it was happening. Two women I interviewed were adamant that they had not experienced it, and then went on to describe it. Women live it, but do not assign the same terms to what they experience.

How can it be that such prevalent dynamics are experienced and understood so differently among women? The answers lie in how sexism is discussed, the common cultural scripts that women and men are fed through media and politics, and the corresponding beliefs men and women internalize about themselves based on these external messages.

Sexism in the News

Media and political discussion of sexism is not useful in the context of this book. How a reporter or commentator angles issues about sexism serves their purposes, and those industries tend to relegate sexism to a very narrow field. An older white man, well past his prime, has committed some sexual act with a woman much younger. Or they were all young and attractive, but he was well liked in the media, so he got a pass. Reporting tells us what someone wants us to hear about sexism, but the perspective of individuals describing someone else's experience to gain ratings or elicit voting behavior is not direct information.

Politics

Politics intentionally highlights volatile points. As an industry, the purpose of political messaging is to make you angry. The primary tool used to exchange information is debate, where people engage in one-upping, interrupting, disrespect, and manipulation of issues. Anger is an intention tool. The creator of a political message is eliciting behavior. They want you to *feel* a certain way so that you *vote* a certain way. The rest of your life, to them, is inconsequential. As an industry, politics thrives on sexism.

Media

Media, too, functions so you will consume their product. When it comes to sexism, news reports center around the most salacious details, a few powerful people who are interesting to readers, and the sense that talking about something is the same as taking action. Media itself is a big problem,

---

SEXISM IS HARD TO IDENTIFY WHEN YOU ARE IMMERSED

"In my corporate career, even before that, if I think back, I've known nothing but executive sexism. The difference is that I have constantly been in a position whereby I've been immersed in it, so I hadn't seen it from the outside. Now for the first time in my career, I'm working with a company that is extremely gender equal and I can look back on some of my experiences in a different way, with a different lens. You get a different perspective from the outside."

—Mila, *Aviation and Philanthropy*

and it does not come close to attacking the structures that ingrain those attitudes in the first place—how things like violent pornography constitute free speech, the largely sexist structures on which the media industry is based, and the prospect of risking advertising dollars.

Speaking about Sexism the Way Women Experience It

Sexism is a set of beliefs embedded in politics, law, culture, and economics. This book discusses how sexism impedes the advancement of executive-level women, and in that examination, you will see how sexism cannot be relegated to any particular social space.

The purpose of this work is to understand how executive women understand sexism and experience it in their lives, so we can interrupt sexist dynamics. Methodology provides a way to map women's experiences, but not define them. When describing the experiences, I frame them according to corresponding theory and behavioral definitions. In this way, you can identify what information corresponds with your own experience and frame it accordingly.

Although they are typically dichotomized between the private (street harassment) and professional (sexual harassment) realms, they are indeed reflections of each other. Sexist dynamics are perpetuated, reinforced, and reified by behaviors learned and repeated in public and private situations, so sexism in professional settings simply reflects the attitudes and dynamics found in social settings. The sexism reported by women interviewed was often subtle and informal, embedded in everyday dynamics, behaviors, and language.

Sexism manifests as interpersonal violence in the form of assaults, domestic violence, murder, and rape. Less known are the institutional violence of sexism manifested in unpaid household labor (performed by women globally and considered normal); lower wages for the same work performed by a man; standards of beauty and fashion that cause lifelong depression, anorexia, and other disorders; and asymmetrical standards of parenthood (French, 1992; MacKinnon, 1979; Rich, 1976, 1980; Roth, 1999; B. Thompson, 1994; Wolf, 1991). Women discussed these issues as well as other health-related problems due to the stress of sexist behavior.

Framing provides an initial schema to organize mentally, to map your landscape into cities and towns and blocks, so you can recognize the dynamics, name the behavior, and choose what course of action you want to take. To intervene in sexism where we can, we need a clear picture of exactly what is happening. Material in the public realm only provides a skewed and self-interested view, but we require accurate and unbiased material from which to gain a fresh perspective.

Use as Primary Material for Research and Training

My approach for this book is to provide primary material for future examination, further study, and practical application. As students, teachers, trainers, and HR professionals, you will read this material with different eyes. The issue of how to confront sexism in our professional lives is critically important and woefully understudied. Certainly, part of that is a lack of available executives for research studies. As such, the information contained herein is valuable primary material for researchers. In addition, trainers and human resource departments can use these narratives to create realistic ways of dealing with sexism. My hope is that their collective experiences will enhance our abilities as professionals and scholars to intervene and interrupt sexism at interpersonal and institutional levels more aggressively.

Conflict Analysis and Resolution Perspective

Current discourse on sexism is not useful in a way that women and men can conceptualize it and interact with each other differently. We are led to believe that women on the whole feel the same about sexism: *enraged*. When you inquire directly and without an agenda, you get different answers. In the midst of it happening, women do not always realize they are being sexualized by their employer, and so they may not voice strong feelings about that. On the other hand, that same woman may experience strong negative feelings about being asked to bring in the coffee. I assumed that losing your job would be the primary factor in why women remain silent. Just as big a factor is the fact that women are more concerned with other people's feelings. Men routinely belittle women in large meetings with key company stakeholders, and women do not speak up for fear of embarrassing *him*. The invisible enemy is stealthy, so unbiased inquiry matters.

Clear Information

To see the issue clearly, information (data) is obtained through academic inquiry, and put through a rigorous methodological process. Women were asked about their experiences with executive sexism, and then asked clarifying questions so the information would be precise and accounted in the appropriate context. The narratives in this book are divided into chapters, and each chapter into subjects. The subjects are variations of how women experienced a certain aspect of sexism.

Accurate Context

In addition to clear data, conflict analysis also takes into strong account the peripheral issues, the context of the problem. Context helps us understand how individuals are situated in the problem, which affects how each of us might handle it. Context also provides a shared understanding, as well as a variation of understandings, of how different concepts can be applied when seeking solutions.

Terms like dominance and oppression feel very fixed, finite, decided, as if they are inevitable and immovable. My perspective is conflict analysis and resolution. As a discipline, conflict is quite mercenary. We borrow from all disciplines and have allegiance to none. We use what is useful in a specific conflict, and for only as long as it is useful. The theories we employ in conflict are reflective of the factors involved in a specific situation.

If the Socially Dominant Shoe Fits . . .

In this case, the most useful way to explain the problem as the women described it was social dominance. This section provides an overview of social dominance, and how it works in a cultural context.

The Function of Culture

Culture itself is derivative of complied individual experiences, which become norms and traditions. Ideological culture ensures individuals that they are part of a larger group. Social culture is expressed through family, friends, and networks, and ultimately through economic and political structures. Individuals derive a sense of value and belonging through culture.

Social Dominance Orientation

Some populations within a culture demonstrate a desire for their group to have higher status and want to achieve that by dominating other groups. Those who want to dominate others have a high *social dominance orientation* (SDO), and support ideologies that adhere to group-based hierarchies. High SDO is the notion that someone has to be in charge and not everybody is meant to succeed. These groups tend toward political and economic ideologies that support group inequality and are not in favor of equal rights for women. "Somebody has to be in charge" is a common saying among high SDO people. Conversely, reading this book, if you reverse the scenario and think, "I would never do that to someone," it is because you rate as low SDO. The values are different. Men generally rate high, while women rate low (Sidanius and Pratto, 1999; Waller, 2002, p. 1985).

How Dominance Works

Differentiating Traits and Assigning Value. Social dominance begins by differentiating a group based on a characteristic such as color, ethnicity, or gender. Once a group is differentiated, it can be defined as having certain characteristics. When a group is famed as having specific qualities, the dominant group can assign worth based on the differentiated traits. Individuals within that culture become socially constructed to view themselves and behave toward others, either in with the positive or negative characteristics assigned to members of the group (Durkheim, 1895; Simmel, 1907; Caputi, 1989; Faludi, 1991; Riger and Krieglstein, 2000; Barak, 2003; Waller, 2002).

Internalizing Traits and Internalizing Value. Regardless of whether the perceptions and behaviors assigned by a dominant group are positive or negative, the recipient generally *internalizes* them as truth. As time goes on, both the giver and receiver of these perceptions and behaviors subscribe more deeply to their social roles, and further internalize their socially prescribed feeling of either relative importance or insignificance. These socially constructed ideologies become a frame of reference for how people interact with one another. These ideologies also become the basis for a dominant group's ability to maintain power in political and economic structures. To them, the ideologies justify the control they have over other people's lives. Men with high SDO enacted sexism as an ideology, and it was set up long before we were born (Hardiman and Jackson, 1997; Durkheim, 1895; Simmel, 1907; Caputi, 1989; Faludi, 1991; Riger and Krieglstein, 2000; Barak, 2003; Waller, 2002).

Rethinking Bystanders

Bystanders are those who witness something and have the opportunity to intervene. When it comes to sexism, we need to activate bystanders. This means you. Yes, you. Even when it's uncomfortable. Even when you will get called the "f" word (*a feminist!*). Even when people oppose you, which they will. If you want to fight sexism, you have to fight sexism. You. This is not the responsibility of somebody else.

Because we all have the ability to interact with society and culture, we can use the same tools and invent new meanings. People are taught by the people around them, so if one has the ability to teach sexism, you have the ability to teach something else. If a man does not support sexism, he can change his behaviors that propagate it.

Sociocultural Concept of Mediated Action

Planning your attack on sexism is no small task. You face the concurrent task of understanding the enormity of the problem, while figuring out how to enact your personal agency. Approaching sexism from a structural perspective creates mental distance and unclear immediate benefits. You also run the risk of abstraction, with no foreseeable intervention. Depressing.

On the other hand, approaching sexism as a psychological flaw of the individual makes it too easily dismissible. Trying to think about sexism as interpersonal conflict with a single man will make you a basket case. Each man's behavior would be an anomaly, rather than a standard form of communication to convey superiority. You would always be taken off guard, thinking that each remark is a one-off, and that would render you unable to operationalize your thinking and devise a solid response. It also fails to address the fact that men have a whole system that supports their behavior and rewards their dominant attitudes.

Mediated Action

We learn culture, we practice culture. Things and activities have no inherent meaning, we assign them meaning. In that way, our relationship with society and culture is dynamic and interrelated. In confronting sexism, men and women have a choice in how we understand the situation and respond. Our individual choices and actions comprise society, and society does not change without the alteration of our individual behavior.

Mediated action accounts for both the systemic and the individual components of sexism. Combining the social (individual) and the cultural (collective), mediated action is the interplay between individuals and society. Mediated action works with the combination of two elements of *individual choice* and the *cultural tools* individuals use to accomplish their goals (Rogoff, 1995).

Cultural Tools. We interactively give and derive meaning through culture. Cultural tools are the items we use, such as scripts (names, stereotypes, prejudice), images, words, jokes, phrases, and movies. They teach us about culture and society, our place in it, and other people's places relative to ours. The way we use cultural tools symbolically transmits and reifies status. So, how we use cultural tools conveys a symbolic interaction of how we perceive ourselves and others. We are taught how to use cultural tools by media, parents, sibling, peers, teachers, coworkers, groups, and others with whom we interact (Manis and Meltzer, 1978; Rogoff, 1995).

Individual Choice. As autonomous agents, everyone has a choice of how to use cultural tools. We choose who we are and what we want to communicate. If we do not subscribe to a conventional use of a cultural tool, we can choose to stop using it or change its meaning. The person you become is ultimately your own choice. We are always in the *process of becoming* who we are, and we all have the ability to communicate our intention in innumerable ways.

Nothing is fixed. Things are as we make them. "That's just the way things are" is something said by people with high SDO (Sidanius and Pratto, 1999; Manis and Meltzer, 1978; Rogoff, 1995).

Why Women Experience Sexism Differently

Citations: How Our Experience Builds on Itself

My first round with professional sexism was in political campaigning. I was 18. Men who were much older (wealthy business owners) began sexualizing me in a way I was not prepared for. I could not name the behavior because it was new to me, and I did not feel right setting firm boundaries since I was working on behalf of a political candidate. The men who were sexualizing me contributed large sums of money to the party, and I was expendable. If I wanted to keep working in politics (which I did, then), my choices were either to accept sexist treatment or to keep silent.

After a few years of this, I finally did tell people. They were friends. They asked me what I said to turn the conversation sexual. "He wouldn't have just come out with that. He wouldn't have said that out of nowhere." I know those words now to be a script. At the time they felt like a punch to the throat. Hearing that, feeling that just a few times, made me silent for the next 10 years. I started wondering what I said, what I did, how I acted to *make* the men say sexual things, even though I knew I had done nothing except talk about politics.

This was my experience with being repeatedly sexualized, and my experience when I disclosed it. And I kept experiencing it. Sometimes I felt powerless, and other times not. It depended on the man, the power I felt, the setting, how badly I needed the work, many things. In counseling I would tell the psychologist, "It's not all men, it's just *some* men."

Some men reduced me in ways I did not understand until much later.

The origins of oppression are in our conversations. My personal experiences are my *citations*. They were my reference points for how people responded to me. When situations repeated themselves, my citations were my baseline points of reference for what to expect. We internalize people's reactions and learn to feel about ourselves how people direct us to feel over time. That looks different for women, so women experience sexism differently (Kumashiro 2002, p. 38). If I respected the opinion of the person who responds negatively toward me, that citation evokes strong feelings of failure or wrongdoing. One way we can intervene immediately in sexism is by responding to women with support instead of judgment.

When I became an executive at a philanthropic organization, making six figures, my boss told me he was in love with me. He fired me when I got a boyfriend. His actions were not illegal, and I had no recourse. From the outside it looked like there was a problem with me, to have lost my position so suddenly. And again, I was told by professionals and psychologists that this was the way of things. It was my own fault; I took a calculated risk by accepting the job in the first place. I should have played along; what would it have hurt?

Explanations like that are given for lack of understanding how sexism actually impacts your life should you be targeted. People who respond in such a way sometimes cannot fathom the level of outright injustice that occurs. In this case, you can be fired and blackballed from an industry because you did not reciprocate a man's romantic interest. End of story. Sexualization is just one expression of sexism, but these career-altering decisions are made by men every day. Those decisions and consequences are invisible to others but enormously costly to the women subjected to them.

So, what does it really cost? It depends on your industry. For me, $560,000 in five years, base salary alone. That is based on my starting salary, not including benefits or investments. My credibility, my employment and salary history, my physical health, and my ability to gain employment in the sector were also directly affected. Where you might have been, versus where you are, is not an easy thing to calculate, and thus not an easy thing to prove; nonetheless, sexism is expensive.

Critical Consciousness Raising

Within a larger dynamic that I cannot control (sexism), I do have the power to show other women that they are not alone. In reading this work,

I hope you find new ways to understand what is happening around you, and ways to intervene in a problem that is bigger than any one of us. To guide your thinking, we examine *critical consciousness raising* applied to the three goals of this book.

1. **Create visibility**: *Open and articulate the world of sexism, in which women are "other."*

   Much of this book is firsthand accounts of executive sexism as told by the women who experience it. We hear in their own words feelings of being ignored, disregarded, less than, lower status. These are high-achieving, intelligent women. No matter their level, they get treated the same. And every one of them felt like there was nothing they could do to gain the respect of the men around them.

2. **Compare similarities in experiences**: *Expose the myths that women have been socialized to accept.*

   Men who do not respect women do not respect women. Men who buy women do not respect women. Women are a utility, a commodified means of communicating a man's social stature. Men use women at the expense of women's reputations, time, and careers. There is no way to change your hairstyle, or wear certain clothes, to make a man respect you. If he feels you are not equal to him, he will not respect you regardless of your appearance. He may give you the guise of respect, but only if you serve some purpose for him.

   Women's communication and emotions are constantly defined by men. Women are treated as if they have no range of emotion and accused of going from zero to bitch. Her level of diplomacy is irrelevant. If a woman objects to a man's treatment, she is the problem for having spoken up about it. We will expose these myths and no longer be constrained by them.

3. **Create new pathways to success**: *Replace old scripts and ideas with new scripts and ideas.*

   Women do not talk more than men, and women are not more emotional than men. These are fallacies that have been disproved through decades of research. Important here is the fact that these false notions had to be *disproved*, rather than proved in the first place. That itself is indicative of men's ability to invent a cultural narrative. This narrative is called a *script*, and it is invented. Men create a cultural lens in which women will never be enough, because in the eyes of a sexist man, women are never enough. Many individuals working in unison can shatter that lens.

Myths about women have been conclusively invalidated. After being disposed and disproved, we as men and women who oppose sexism have the power to change our behaviors to create new scripts. This book names, defines, and categorizes sexist behaviors, and offers communication strategies to expand your current options to change sexist scripts into respectful and accurate discourse.

Research Methodology

Phenomenography

For this study I used a qualitative method called *phenomenography*, which is the study of discovering the various ways in which people experience the same phenomenon and understand how they are situated in the midst of it. The purpose of phenomenographic studies is to discern the layers of meaning and interpretations that individuals apply to their experiences with a particular phenomenon. Rather than creating a description of the phenomenon itself, phenomenographic findings reflect how participants understand the phenomenon and their place in it. Phenomenography is the world as it is understood, rather than the world as it is. Key in this work is how women understand sexism and how they interact with it in their daily lives (Marton, 1981; Ornek, 2008; Larsson and Holmstrom, 2007; Soon and Barnard, 2001).

Research Questions

The goals of this research study were to gain a greater understanding of what sexism looks like from the perspective of women working in executive-level positions, and to understand what aspects of sexism they find problematic. The research questions were asked of each participant to answer as she understood it:

RQ #1: How do women understand sexism in their professional workspace?

RQ #2: How do women experience sexism in communication with their colleagues and adjacent professional people with whom they interact?

RQ #3: How does sexism impede the professional success and advancement of women?

Sample: Purposive Snowball Sample

This study included a *purposive snowball sample* (Babbie, 1998) of women who work in executive-level positions in their respective fields. Women recommended other women. Largely due to inaccessibility, there is a noted lack of involvement of elite participants in academic research studies. Studies that require research participants outside of academic settings require between two and six participants, and an acceptable sample in a phenomenographic study is three (Welch, Marschan-Piekkari, Penttinen, and Tahvanainen, 2002; Cope, 2005; Soon and Barnard, 2001; McCosker, Barnard, and Gerber, 2003; Joosa and Berthelson, 2006; Yates, Partridge, and Bruce, 2012).

This study had 17 participants. They lived in nine different countries and worked in various fields.

Instrument: Semi-Structured Interviews

Interviews as the sole source of information. Literature and discussion about sexism are generated by various industries that reflect the interests of the industry that produced the material. The purpose of this research was to ascertain individual points of view from the participants, and then find the interconnectedness among the data. This did not include comparing or "testing" the individual data against other sources of information. For that reason, I intentionally did not research the literature, professional field, or websites of those who agreed to participate in this study. Additionally, not having preconceived notions about the interviewees allowed me to enter the interviews without the bias that might have accompanied examining any existing information and influenced the direction of the interview. In sum, each woman's story is hers to tell. The academic approach to inquiry is a distinctly different approach than that of media.

New understandings emerge during interviews. People typically have constructed conceptual understandings of their lives, their work, and their experiences; however, the level at which people consciously reflect on their experiences varies. Presenting new questions in a conversational manner makes the subject of the interview actually come into being. This research method is noted for interviewees adjusting their perspective as they reflect on the subject of the interview, and the results of a good interview will elicit new insights. What you will notice while reading some accounts is the changing and evolving of that person's perspective (Marton, 1994; Dortins, 2002; Gray, 2004).

Data Analysis

Research poses an interesting dilemma when you already have the book contract, under which you have agreed to certain subjects. In my case, the data looked different than my preconceived chapter, and the subjects needed to be revised. What you will read in the coming chapters are the organized data. Here is a methodological explanation of why the material is organized as it is:

Categories of Description. The categories were reviewed for consistency and then were reviewed for inclusion of new insights, and then again for internal consistency. Finally, the categories of description were refined, checked against the initial data, readjusted, and then retested. This process produced a decreasing rate of modification, until eventually the categories were accurately defined, and the internal classification of meanings became stabilized (Larsson and Holmstron, 2007, p. 57; Marton, 1986).

Collective Meaning. Phenomenography is not concerned with the psychological reduction of data. Rather, the research in phenomenographic studies is to understand a phenomenon as the participant understands it. Findings are then synthesized to group the variation of ways in which a single phenomenon is understood. Knowledge lies not in the ascertaining of a single meaning among participants, but in the various ways that participants make meaning of the same phenomenon (Soon and Barnard, 2001).

Summary

I explored the subject of executive sexism by asking participants about their experiences and provided an open and anonymous forum for them to speak. They talked about what was relevant to them and how they understood what was happening. They also discussed the personal, social, professional, and economic consequences they face having sexism in their lives.

Participants

Being the recipient of sexist behavior has nothing to do with a woman's level of professional competence, her position or status, or her list of accomplishments. The participants of this study are described below with pseudonyms. Their ages range from 35 to 44. Professional status was sought as a study qualification, age was not. Most work globally, and their nations of residence are Dubai, Germany, Sweden, United States, Netherlands, Spain, Libya, Russia, and England.

Anonymity is standard practice in academic research projects, and it was especially necessary for this study so the women could speak candidly without fear of social or professional repercussions. When asked about their professional life, most provided a rich history of their career path, and noted how their industries were male dominated.

Here are the women who generously offered their perspective to inform this research:

Natalya, Corporate Energy Lawyer. Natalya is an equity partner in a law firm, and her specialization is oil and gas and corporate transactional work. She negotiates on behalf of private interests and governments of emerging markets in the Balkans, China, and former Soviet bloc countries.

Mila, CEO of Helicopter and Boat Manufacturing and Charter Company. Mila's current work is in aviation and yachting. Previously in her career, Mila focused across humanitarian, philanthropic, and new business development in the Middle East.

Mara, Senior Associate of Public Affairs. Mara began her career working for the prime minister and top-level politicians. Next, she wrote editorials for one of the biggest papers in the Nordic countries and became a TV political commentator. She worked in the cultural sector as a CEO, and now works as a senior consultant at a public affairs company.

Alicia, Federal Bureau of Investigation Anti-Terrorism Agent. Alicia served on a National Security Council's hostage and personnel recovery working group, getting people out of captivity and getting them home. She had a very distinguished and decorated career handling controversial investigations like Blackwater in Iraq, and high-profile cases of international war criminals.

Allison, Director of Marketing for Political Party. Allison is responsible for the political campaign messaging for the current party in power of a European nation. She interviewed right after a successful national election.

Catherine, Tech CEO and Land Developer. Catherine began her career as a middle school and high school teacher, then a department head, then a principal, and then founded a network of 16 schools in three years. She opened a financial services business, develops land, and then became the CEO of a tech and green space company that supports startups and entrepreneurial ventures. She holds a PhD.

Sarah, Criminal Defense Lawyer. Sarah started her legal profession as a public defender and went on to found her own law firm. She does mostly felony-level criminal defense work. She also holds a master's degree.

Sophia, Senior Manager of Global Brand Communications at Tech Company. Sophia oversees global brand communications at an $8 billion technology company. Prior to this role, she spent her career in technology marketing, mostly in professional audio gear for musicians, stadiums, and high-end studios. "I've been in this line of work for fifteen years and it's an incredibly male dominated industry. I have often been the only woman on the team, in the room, to the point that I don't think about it a whole lot."

Emma, CEO of International Casting Company. Emma runs an international casting agency, working with companies like Netflix, Showtime, and HBO.

Avery, VP of Marketing for Pharmaceutical Company. As an executive in a health-care corporation, Avery worked on the Executive Committee. "I was the only female and the conversation would often become crude, racist, sexist, whatever. I remember vividly after Hurricane Katrina, multiple comments by two or three of the white—well, they were all white—men, talking about how it was God's retribution on the black criminal element in New Orleans."

Janni, Executive Manager of Human Resources for National Transportation Company. Janni oversees 7,000 employees at a transportation company for a European country. She has also worked in the airline industry and as a negotiator for the national labor unions, which represent 95 percent of the labor force in her country.

Lauren, Criminology Professor and Board Member of an International Organization. Lauren's career has been in social justice and humanitarian work. She works as a professor, writes books, raises money, and serves as a board member for nonprofit organizations dealing with domestic violence, human trafficking, gender equity, and humanitarian issues.

Julia, Director of Marketing for Cosmetics Company. Julia leads the creative direction for marketing and branding for a global cosmetics company.

Rebecca, Senior Scientist for Military Special Forces Curriculum Development. Rebecca's work entails the scientific development of curriculum to counter violent extremism. Her work supports Special Operations Forces Civil-Military Affairs and Psychological Operations. Prior to her current role, Rebecca worked in political campaigning, fund-raising, press relations, and philanthropy. She holds a PhD.

Olivia, Marketing for Record Label. Olivia recruits and promotes music talent for a major record label. She began her career as a political operative.

Maryam, Founder of Personal Branding Company. Maryam began her career in marketing and went on to start an international personal branding company. She holds a PhD, works with businesses and private clients, and delivers keynote addresses.

Isabella, Barrister in a European Country. As a barrister, Isabella presents cases in court. Her role is different from that of a solicitor (a standard lawyer), in that she has less contact with clients, and the entirety of her role is conducting litigation.

Layout of the Chapters

The chapters in this book are arranged into categories, and each category provides a depth and context in explaining how different women experience aspects of sexism. Chapters contain brief pieces of narratives that describe the subjects being discussed. Not all women are present in all chapters, but dividing the book into chapters and subjects was necessary to capture relevant themes.

The book is divided into three parts. Part One discusses the ways sexism manifests, the social and organizational structures that support it, and the sexual-social context in which sexism occurs. Chapter 1 has outlined the need for a new approach and unbiased information to work from so readers can identify and name behaviors and dynamics they are also experiencing.

Chapter 2 discusses how systems support executive sexism by maintaining structures that are biased against women and considered to be normal. Chapter 3 details social cues and verbal messages men use to communicate their superior status and women's lower status.

Chapter 4 begins to describe how sexist men continuously sexualize women as a means of communicating domination. Despite how frequently women deal with sexism, they remain silent for different reasons, material and personal, which we detail in Chapter 5. Chapter 6 begins the discussion on pornography and the highly sexualized social context that fosters sexism and misogyny.

In Part Two, we move on to the issues adjacent to executive sexism and how those factors all influence women's work life. Chapter 7 outlines the double standard of conduct that women face under male rules. Chapter 8 describes male gender expectations, and how men cannot seem to get their head around strong, ambitious women, which is a problem for professional women.

Chapter 9 describes how women try to control sexist reactions and behaviors by *defeminizing* themselves, altering their appearance and manner. Commodification is discussed in Chapter 10, and how men collapse the identity of women. To sexist men, you have no dimension; you are all the same woman. Chapter 11 talks about internalized domination and women who try to exercise dominant, demeaning, and destructive behavior toward other women. Chapter 12 discusses the double-bind of advancement, the situation women find themselves in under gendered expectations. They are viewed as "cold" for being ambitious, and penalized by men and women alike for a perceived lack of social skills.

Part Three addresses the way men and women can address sexism when legal action is not a viable option. The law does not protect against sexism because much of sexism is not illegal, and because the law itself is inherently sexist. Different ways women speak up is the topic of Chapter 13. Chapter 14 gives names to the behavior dynamics to promote healthy intervention. Chapter 15 Identifies personal ways to intervene in sexism in systems and organizations. Chapter 16 discusses how the FBI and other agencies treat women who report harassment and concludes with personal changes we can make in our lives that will further undermine sexist culture.

You are not reading my analysis of what women talked about, you are reading what *they* thought was important, in the context of how they described it. I found pieces of my own story scattered throughout the interviews. Perhaps you will, too. I hope this information helps you direct your energy productively.

CHAPTER TWO

Systematizing Culture and Structure

MAN AS SUBJECT—WOMAN AS "OTHER"
In male dominant cultures, "man represents both the positive and the neutral, as indicated by the common use of man to designate human beings in general; whereas woman represents only the negative, defined by limiting criteria, without reciprocity. . . . Thus humanity is male and man defines woman not in herself but as relative to him; she is not regarded as an autonomous being . . . she is the incidental, the inessential, as opposed to the essential.

He is the Subject, he is the absolute, she is the Other."
—Simone de Beauvoir, *The Second Sex*

Introduction

Executive sexism manifests and reinforces itself through three distinct channels. The first is systemizing culture and structure. This chapter describes male-oriented work structures that seem natural—"the way things are." Because so much of our everyday life is male centered, nothing seems amiss. The following narratives show the ways in which men convey their ownership of executive space to women.

The first account is of a woman who is told she does not belong at the company. The remaining stories concern women being told they do not belong in the discussion, they do not belong in the decision making, they do not even belong in the room. Sometimes these messages are conveyed outright, sometimes through job assignment and structure. If men who are in charge wanted it to be a different way, they would change it. These stories should be familiar.

We begin with a historical overview of how modern male-dominated culture came to exist as we know it.

Historical Context of Male-Dominated Society

Have you ever taken a moment to wonder why we live in a male-dominated culture? Is our culture in fact male dominated? Has it always been like this? And finally, why does male-dominated culture seem to be so persistent? Anthropologists speculate that patriarchy, the social structure that places males-as-fathers in the homes into males-as-social-leaders in society and business, was not always the way of the world. In the earliest recorded human past, male-female roles appeared to be balanced in and out of the home. Females fought, hunted, foraged, and constructed shelter and life alongside males. So, what changed?

Transition from Tribal Clan to Towns and Cities

Likely, what changed was social construction that moved from family-clan-tribe to larger social constructions of towns and cities. Larger social constructions required alternative organizations that mass-produced goods, services, and orderly social relationships such as marriage, child-rearing, and family organization. Social practice was later encapsulated within religious and legal tradition.

Excess labor in premodern societies meant that only the most efficacious would bring in a good price. In the mass market of premodern labor, the division of male and female roles would change from an egalitarian system to one that measured each gender's role according to marketplace value dictated by supply and demand. This meant that what was good enough in the gender role marketplace was suddenly insufficient. A female member of a family could not compete in the open labor market.

Creation of Gender Roles

We don't have to guess how this story ended. Males became the primary external (of the home) actors due to the premodern emphasis on physical strength and endurance that most occupations required. Females became the primary internal (of the home) actors due to the premodern emphasis on procreation in sufficiently high numbers to overcome infant mortality.

As the male-female roles of premodern towns and villages separated into distinct gender patterns, archetypes of male masculine and female feminine identity structures evolved into ever-deepening divisions. The archetypal ideals of male masculine identity solidified into roles of warrior-as-protector, brute strength as savior, strength and speed as the personification of gender perfection. The archetypal ideals of female feminine identity solidified into roles of fertility-to-procreate, and beauty-to-allure the greatest warrior-protector and savior from the disorganized community of lawless town and city. The fastest, strongest males attracted the most fertile, beautiful females, assuring the continuation of a desirable line of human physical turned social life. Consider the images that permeate our modern existence, for example, models, actors, and athletes. Strong males and beautiful females continue to be held in extraordinarily high social regard.

Origin of Male Domination

In all of the following chapters and sections, the outlines of this premodern social structure that evolved within early towns and cities can be easily observed. This early experimental practice quickly became law and religion. New classes of males, freed of their labors through mass-organized labor redistribution, found work as philosophers, scholars, and religious seers ordained on their own say-so. It should be no surprise that these early males quickly justified their gender roles using divine ordering from a fatherly male god, imaged using male gender and social role division. One of the earliest unitary god-figures to appear in social construction was the God of Abraham, who is revered and followed by Jews, Christians, and Muslims.

But the Jewish god has no name, no face, and no genitalia. Jews (then and now) are not supposed to speak his/her Name, so they refer to this entity as "YaWaH." Is the God of Abraham a male or a female? Or is YaWaH supposed to be gender neutral? If the latter, then why do Christians and Muslims refer to God as *Him; His* word, *His* will, or *His* benevolence? Because males got to write the books, since they were the first gender freed from labor by the mass-production marketplace. Just ask yourself, who are the Jewish, Christian, Muslim, Buddhist, and Hindu priests? Mostly women? Mostly men?

Codification of Male Gender Rule

The truth is that the God of Abraham did not create a world dominated by male culture. The God of Abraham did not direct that "men run things" or that the male archetype dominate medicine, law, business, and leadership. The first gender to have surplus labor created the new social roles of lawyer, scholar, priest, and social leader.

The earliest towns and cities created labor marketplaces that produced surplus male labor from mass organization based on physical attributes. These same crowded marketplaces increased instances of disease and accidents, which maintained high incidences of infant mortality. Infant mortality in turn drove the near enslavement of females to interior spaces of the home to dramatically increase baby production and maintain population density.

Thus, for 30 centuries or more, human social life has been a construction of male gender rule that originated in premodern cities, where disease forced females into perpetual roles of procreation necessary to replace losses. Around this reality, law, religion, and social order built a powerful self-reinforcing narrative that this organized division of labor was divinely mandated and part of a natural order of all things human.

Male scholars, lawyers, priests, and social leaders have written their roles into laws and history in a way that creates a monopoly over social order. Females, only recently freed from childbearing labor by advances in medicine and receding disease vectors, have begun advocating for a rebalance of social roles.

Women Do Not Belong in Male Culture

This section highlights that being a woman is of note. Women's presence is something different than what was expected, and not in a good way. As you read the accounts, reverse the script. Would you ever say the same things to or about a man?

Woman Won't Fit In with Culture

I interviewed at this firm, which is Texas based, like a real hitter in the oil and gas sector. And they have an office here in London. And it was really interesting—they're all, everyone's white, every single one of them is in his early 50s minimum. I mean, there's a guy that he's like, eighty-six. So, they're all men, they're all white, they're all quite old.

And I interviewed with them, because one of my clients, actually it's *my* client that this firm really wants, and they approached him. And he said, "Well, if you want me, you better hire her." So that's how the conversation came about. And one of the partners in the firm, he was very open with me. I don't know intentionally or not, but he was saying to me, like, "We—you're not someone that we would ordinarily be talking to."

And I said to him, "Why, why is that?" And he was like, "Well, I didn't think you fit into the culture of the firm." And I said to him, "Okay."

And he's like, "Look, we understand that we need to change the culture. We understand that we have to do it because it's being driven by external factors. But that is not what our current culture is."

And I said to him, "Is it because, you know, in order to enter the partnership, you need to have like, a $5 million book of clients? Is it because my book is less than that, is that the issue?"

He said, "Partially, but don't make me say it. Look around."

I could see this really painful process, which was like a Jekyll and Hyde, where you could see that they really wanted me, because they wanted the client, and also because they understood that the world around them is changing. And they need to have a woman in partnership, right? Maybe not in Houston, maybe in London, but they couldn't do it. They just couldn't bring themselves to do it to the end. They were really struggling, presenting it as a part of their firm's culture. And they were saying to me, "We know you would feel isolated here."

I said, "Why? Because I won't have other girls to talk to? I wouldn't have anyone to go to the toilet with? What are you talking about?"

He said, "You're being factitious." I said, "And you're being a bit out of date. Which I'm guessing, you know, because otherwise we wouldn't be having this conversation.

I don't want to be part of a firm . . . where I, I feel like I'm the black sheep. You know, when you are the odd one out. When you're there as a token female. Because that's really disheartening. Because then you know, you come in, and you're really excited. And you want to seize the day. And you actually realize that you're actually there to look pretty, because that's what people expect from you.

(Natalya, *Law*)

That You Are a Woman Is of Note

My previous work I was running a communications agency and it was me and another woman who ran it. And we were both quite young and we were both looking quite similar. And in every single article that was written about our agency they mention the fact that it was run by two young women. And I'm just thinking out of the thousands of agencies in Sweden, I've never seen one where it said, "Oh and it's run by a man by the way."

(Julia, *Marketing*)

Conflicting Messages: Christian Culture That Diminished Females

I started out as a consultant, which was great, and I probably should have stayed that way. I had seen what had happened to many of their newer employees who were brought on because they had special skills, but then they didn't buy into the corporate culture. . . . At the same time the CEO was Christian . . . corporate culture of saying a prayer at meetings or thanking God for our successes . . . there is this, you know, pervasive patriarchal culture that diminished females. So, they are clearly two cultures that should be in conflict.

(Avery, *Marketing*)

I Wanted a Lawyer and You Bring Me a Girl

I give you an example. I was acting for the government of (Eastern European company) . . . and the reason I was on the deal is because, obviously you know I'm native Russian speaker, and they were very concerned about confidentiality so they didn't want to hire an interpreter. What they wanted was a lawyer who could negotiate in both languages. And I never forget it, I walked into the room, because I arrived a little later and everyone's already sitting at the table.

The president of (the client country) and the Prime Minister were there, so it started on a very high level. And the Prime Minister turned around to my partner, so to my boss, and to the guy from the investment bank who was acting for them, and he said, "I told you to bring me a lawyer and you bring me girl."

He said it in Russian, in front of everybody. It was the most humiliating experience of my life to this day. It was just awful. I wanted the ground to just swallow me and just never be there.

(Natalya, *Law*)

Be Grateful You Are Getting Attention

And this is such a terrible example but unfortunately the way the culture is—in this case it was an airline—where the men are pilots and of course the commanders of the flights. And the cabin crew members are women and supposed to say, "Yes Captain, no Captain" in the workplace.

And when this happens it became clear to us that this is an issue of structure and culture. Because in so many years this has happened thousands of times where pilots had grabbed cabin crew members, have sexist comments and harassment and they just laughed it away, *because the culture was that you should never say no to a captain* (italics mine).

"They're the boss, and they're men, and they're flying the plane, so you should be grateful that the captain gives you this attention." That got me really thinking about how company culture can be feeding this sexism structure and it's almost invisible because everybody thinks it's normal. Until it goes too far. When you push the boundaries, and you push and push and finally someone gets really hurt by it, then you realize we should have done something much sooner.

(Janni, *Transportation*)

Men Own Things

Not all people are aware of this, but there exist unwritten "rules" of certain industries. The first story discusses how this applies to real estate. This business owner had to pay a man to pretend he was the buyer, because the owner would not sell to a woman. Had she not been privy to the rules, she would have been blocked from the purchase. These industry secrets are subtle ways of men maintaining ownership of land and industry, and thus economic power.

Not Going to Sell to a Woman

I wouldn't have got my building if I didn't have an attorney go in and broker the deal, because there's a rule on the block that I own on. They weren't going to sell to a black person and they weren't going to sell to a woman. The entire block is owned by men. The entire block, white men, old school white men. I'm being real candid, older like in their 70s, 80s, like older. And they just, they were very clear. We're talking about in a modern city.

Like this has been my experience here, and listen I'm not attached to it. I run a business, and in business we make money. That is the vehicle of whether you're successful or not. It's not a lot of room for feelings. I got to pay extra people so that cuts into my bottom line, right, that their company doesn't need to pay.

And I'm the CEO, so they can't always speak like me. They try, but they may miss a point because I got to teach them what to say. So that's my time, which also costs money. So my ability to grow and leverage climb to the heights that the person next to me, with *half* the background, half the standard, half the anything I can do, it's unparallel.

(Catherine, *Land Development*)

Expect a Male Owner

When a woman wants to be a good CEO, they need to have a good straw man. That's how I'm here, because I'm okay having a straw man. In many business meetings with men, I got to have people talk for me. It's just the way it works in the South.

Okay my first business in Miami, I put a guy's picture up on the wall. Maybe I didn't put his name, but his name was Chris Gonzales. In Miami that's everything, right? He's white, Jewish, blue eyed, with a Spanish name. I'm just being candid. I put his picture up on the wall. He was handsome. He come to the office, once every two weeks, to get his check, for having his picture up on my wall.

And, myself and my business partner, two black women, ran a financial services firm. Did everything, hired everybody, ran the business and when people came in and had any questions about who owns it, we just said, "Oh that's the owner right there on the wall." We just pointed to a picture. And everybody was cool with that. We learned the hard way that we had to do that from the beginning.

(Catherine, *Financial Services*)

Catherine understood the being a woman would be a problem for some people and cause her business to suffer. Nobody ever needed to meet the "owner"; they just needed to know he was a man to feel comfortable using the financial services.

Men Run Things

These women are describing their business dealings with men, and they have different results. Just because a woman is in the room does not mean she will be heard. You will see that repeatedly in this book. Watch the ways women are treated when they offer input, and note how the most successful strategy is for women to pretend that the men are in charge. For men of high social dominance orientation, being in charge is the important part.

Why Are You Still Talking?

Almost sort of, like almost in a pitiful way—and it's different, because when you have an open conversation, you know, people gesticulate, people relax, they kind of relax in their chairs. And it's a conversation and they will say, you know, that's an interesting point of view, or can we discuss it later, or that's a little bit off track of what we're discussing. But interesting point we can pick it up later.

Here, you know, it's a, it's a complete deafening silence, there's no engagement and what you're saying, you feel like you're having a monologue . . . where you have like, these eyes looking back at you, which are completely glassy, completely not engaged and looking at you as if to say, "Why are you still talking? You are supposed to nod, or best, just turn up."

It's just, just in this really disengaged way. But also, it's this—if I can describe it, it's sort of almost [a] pitiful look. Like this particular guy that I think of, he's just looking at me as if he knows—you start to squint, and you're like, really *focusing* on what somebody is saying, because they don't enunciate or because you don't understand them, or because they're speaking a foreign language or with a really difficult accent? So really like *furrowing* your brow, you know, really like *concentrating*.

And I always, I find that really puzzling because I just think, "Why are you concentrating so hard on what I'm saying? I'm not speaking Russian, or in riddles."

And this is really off putting actually. It's really off putting to have somebody who's on the other end of the conversation and he's just looking like he's really struggling to understand, you know, what is happening. He's not really engaging in the conversation. He's, he's almost confused by what's happening. The fact that I dared to speak up.

(Natalya, *Law*)

Women Should Be Silent While Men Handle Business

I'm going into a city meeting with the city manager to handle a dispute over another property. In the meeting there is, on their side, four men—attorney, building official, you know, four men. On my side I had my black middle-age manager for my company, my Latin Colombian contractor, and my Jewish attorney.

Now I want you to understand that this is my contract, my business, my building. I'm the CEO. I pay everybody on my side—and I say nothing until the end of the meeting.

I said nothing the whole meeting and I promise you it is the only reason the meeting moved forward and I learned to do that. I just blend one of each color, right in the position they expect them to be in, the Jewish attorney, the Latin contractor, and the black manager, right? And we sat across from the table from these four city men, and they handled business.

We walked out in time for everybody to shake hands, right, this tense moment, their high moment. I just sit back, I say nothing the entire meeting. At the end of the meeting I walk out, I shake hands with the city Mayor and I said, "You know what, I'm the granddaughter of a WWI veteran, the daughter of a Vietnam vet. I like to follow the rules. Just give us the rules and we're going to follow them."

(Catherine, *Land Development*)

Male Networks Override Women's Authority

Some of them would always intervene in my area. They would try to interfere, and they would go the president of my board, he was officially my manager, he was the one I was reporting to. But he got his position from the CEO of the lottery, so he couldn't be against the one who gave him his position.

So the managers went to their CEO, who went to my chairman, who went to me saying, "You cannot do this." Instead of my chairman supporting me, "Okay we're leaving this culture foundation with decisions we should make." So they always rounded me.

(Mara, *Culture and Politics*)

Enforcing Male-Oriented Work Norms

This section describes male-dominated business structures, in which jobs and responsibilities are assigned by gender. It also describes work expectations by gender, such as the idea that a single woman has "nothing better to do" than work; if she is not married with children, work must be the only thing in her life. Finally, it addresses business and legal structures that dictate what type of work a *woman* can depend on whether or not she has children.

Assign Jobs According to Gender

What I meant when I talked about different responsibilities. Women get communications and HR and men get all the hard stuff like IT and security and selling. Plus when you are in the team, you are just assigned different tasks. If you are doing a big event, it is the women who are responsible for ordering refreshments, making sure the localities look good, and the men are responsible for security and IT. That very sharp division of coded responsibilities between male and female workers.

(Leah, *Politics*)

Single Women Have Nothing Better to Do

This might be a little bit of a non sequitur but I do remember quite frequently in this first job being very grateful that I had a long-term steady boyfriend because I felt like it protected me from—I'll get into that next—but I really felt like I needed a champion quite frequently to somehow validate me as a woman in the workplace.

That has two layers for me. One is that, as a single female not going home to a husband or to kids, which was on the other side with some of my female colleagues, who they had this—they had this excuse to go home. They had this excuse to leave the office early. It was like, "oh, she has kids.' But when you didn't have kids and you didn't have a husband it was very much, "well what better do you have to do than to focus on this?"

What better thing do you have to do just get on the private jet and just fly to this thing without any spare clothing or whatever else. And I felt bullied quite a lot as well, in certain elements of my time being really—like I was owned one hundred percent by the company, I was fully owned by them. And I'm a quite empathetic, sensitive being; When I'm asked to do something, I want to do it to the best of my ability and I want to smooth things over and keep everybody happy and do a good job.

I also understand everybody else's viewpoint of oh you know, she doesn't have kids. Oh but he does have to get home. I'll do it for them, I completely understand. And I was always in that position of being the one who was expected to kind of get into that role and go above and beyond. And I remember in all the times, again, feeling quite bullied.

And this, layered, a woman in this position—you must be hired because you're tall blonde and female and he likes having you around, in terms of my boss.

I remember feeling that at least I had this strong character and boyfriend to come home to say, you know, almost, they were mean to me. And knowing I would be able to say, Well, you know, I have to go home because I have to get home to my boyfriend, as well. Being my own person wasn't enough of an excuse.

(Mila, *Philanthropy and Business Development*)

Women's Profession Is Relegated by Child Care

You know, it's not all about maternity leave, it's not all about allowing people to go back into the workplace. You know, stop talking about it, that you're doing them a favor, that you are such a flexible employer. You are obliged to do this, by law, so you're doing the bare minimum, you know. You're not really this progressive company that you think you are, allowing people with children to work more flexible hours, that's a great idea. But we all know that in certain teams, with certain partners with certain clients, that doesn't always work. There that has to be a degree of flexibility on both ends.

(Isabella, *Law*)

Exposing Sexist Scripts and Thought Patterns

The subject topics serve as a guide to walk us through prevailing scripts and thought patterns of sexism. In Chapters 2–12, a subject outline is included for the reader's quick reference, and the remainder of each chapter focuses on integrated analysis of the topics, and questions to generate new scripts and thought patterns.

I.   Women Do Not Belong in Male Culture
   A.   Woman Won't Fit In with Culture
   B.   That You Are a Woman Is of Note
   C.   Conflicting Messages: Christian Culture That Diminished Females
   D.   I Wanted a Lawyer and You Bring Me a Girl
   E.   Be Grateful You Are Getting Attention

II. Men Own Things
   A. Not Going to Sell to a Woman
   B. Expect a Male Owner

III. Men Run Things
   A. Why Are You Still Talking?
   B. Women Should Be Silent While Men Handle Business
   C. Male Networks Override Women's Authority

IV. Enforcing Male-Oriented Work Norms
   A. Assign Jobs According to Gender
   B. Single Women Have Nothing Better to Do
   C. Women's Profession Is Relegated by Child Care

Analysis

Sarah, a criminal attorney, talks about the male networks evident in the justice system. In a system that is supposed to be based on blind justice, relationships matter. More specifically, male relationships matter.

Judicial System: The Power of Male Relationships

There's still very much a good old boy network and those networks are still very much alive and very much kicking. It's very obvious. You can tell when you walk into the courtroom.

The white male will call the judge by the first name. "Hey Bobby." I think this is kind of their way of professionally peeing and marking their territory like "Look, I've got this because I'm on a first name basis with this judge."

There is a sense of backdoor dealings that happen. I have nothing I can threaten them with, just me saying over and over again, "Hey, listen, if you give Johnny white boy lawyer over here a better deal than you gave me, when I did all of this work, we're going to have a problem because that's not fair." That's completely disparate treatment, but it doesn't really matter. They don't really care. I guess they have a problem with the black girl, because black girls give problems and attitudes.

But the other network is very much, I can't put my finger on it or say, "Oh, they meet at this place or that place." Or that they do backroom deals and I overheard them, but the way things play out in court, it's very obvious that there are connections and networks that I'm just not going to be fully a part of. And that is what gets things done. It's not how justice should be, but it is how justice is done, unfortunately. At least until something changes.

(Sarah, *Criminal Law*)

Sarah's description is how activity and social cues in the courtrooms reflect that male dominance is the norm, and male networks are functioning in a way that excludes women from informal power structures.

Natalya, an international energy attorney, describes the male-dominated culture of her law partnership. Though she made it into the decision-making room, she spoke at length about the nonverbal social cues she received that conveyed the men did not want her there or care what she had to say. Her experience demonstrates how women are excluded at a different level in the law firm, but the dynamics of exclusion are the same. Her contributions are relegated to stereotypical feminine subjects, and female-related business.

Diversifying Because They Have To, Not Because They Want To

There's all this training on unconscious bias that everybody goes to, and everybody nods their head But of course nobody's going to put up their hands and say, "Well I am biased!" Nobody's going to be like, "I'm really racist" or "I'm really homophobic." (laughing)

I feel like men have been told that you need to employ more women, because it looks good. And because a lot of your clients can be women and they will be looking for diversity. They're diversifying because they have to, not because they want to or because they understand it.

Without anyone saying it out loud, but with their body language and the way that they conduct and hold themselves in your presence, they make it very clear to you that you are not an equal. You are not here to participate, or share your opinions, unless those opinions relate to the female associates initiative, or what color cups we're going to have or what hairstyle we're going to implement.

(Natalya, *Oil and Gas Law*)

Conclusion

Institutions did not just come to be. They were set up and run by certain people due to certain circumstances. The introduction provided a brief historical overview of how men wrote themselves into an elevated place in history. Of important note are the circumstances. In a contemporary setting, women are fully capable of performing the same cognitive functions as men. Neither gender is superior to the other in that regard.

In examining why men are in more prominent positions, consider the social and historical context in which women were situated. The result of many historical disparities, including access to education and a child-free life, has created a significant advantage for men. While the past cannot be redone, noting the historical context is important when interpreting the present.

In current high-level work settings, as experienced by many women and depicted in this study, men convey a pervasive attitude that suggests that they are meant to run things and women are not. Silent rules exist that perpetuate female exclusion of property ownership. In the same way, formal and informal male networks function to dissuade women from being present in decision-making bodies by exhibiting communication and social cues that indicate that they do not want the woman there, nor do they value her input.

In short, if men were not sexist, the presence of women would not be of significance. In fact, more women would be present, and women not be treated with such striking disrespect and shown such disregard for their professional capabilities. Women being treated as "other" indicates that men consider themselves the norm, and as such male leadership is the norm. That perceived norm is sexism.

Creating New Scripts and Thought Patterns

- Have you ever thought about why certain people had a more prominent demographic showing for certain positions?
- What did you attribute that to? Why do you think it was?
- Do you ever find yourself in conversation about the formation of institutions?
- What explanations have teachers or parents or religious leaders given you for who holds the leadership positions in certain institutions?

CHAPTER THREE

Verbal Messages and Social Cues

Introduction

Spoiler alert—All those times you wondered if you were overreacting? You weren't.

Did you read too much into it? Probably not.

Language and words are the communicator of a woman's status relative to his. "Can you get me some coffee?" is not about the coffee. If you are alone in the office, it might be about coffee. If you are in large meeting, it is about status. Sexism is communicated verbally and nonverbally through the scripts and stereotypes that men have created for women. That is why, when you refuse to get the coffee, you are chastised as being overly sensitive. You take yourself so seriously. That's not what I meant. Man hater. Feminist. What happened is, the men wrote you a script, and you refused to play your part. Bitch. When you refuse, you get a label, or worse. Those are the rules of social dominance (Hardiman and Jackson, 1997; Tannen, 1990; Feldman, 1992).

Internalized Domination

Gender communication differences are best explained through high and low social dominance orientation (Sidanius and Pratto, 1999). Having *internalized domination*, men "learn to think and act in ways that express internalized notions of entitlement and privilege" (Hardiman and Jackson, 1997, p. 21).

> "Examples of internalized domination include men talking over women while simultaneously labeling women as chatty. There is an absence of feeling that one has to prove oneself, or that one's status, talent, and qualifications would be questioned in any situation."
>
> (Hardiman and Jackson, 1997, p. 21)

Communication research also acknowledges that men communicate to achieve status and interpret women's communication as lesser status. The item of note is interpretation. No matter what you say, he will find a way to interpret it as less (Tannen, 1990; Feldman, 1992). Sexism is communicated with intention, and that intention is to elevate men and reduce women.

Let's Both Agree That You're Really Stupid

Sexist men do not question why they are in a dominant social position. They feel they deserve it and the status quo is perfectly normal (Griffin, 1997, p. 76; Hardiman and Jackson, 1997). Because it seems the natural order of things, women also tend not to question too deeply and thus internalize oppression. Socially dominant behaviors become a dance. Men project their superiority and women respond. This is the interplay between individuals and society. What we do, how we think, how we speak, how we treat each other, it all creates our culture.

Q 1: How Long Have You Been Beating Your Wife?

A popular joke in political circles, this is an accusatory statement in question form. Merely asking the question asserts its validity. The person being asked is in fact being accused and is put in the position of having to defend himself against the accusation.

Q 2: Why Do You Think Women Are So Emotional?

Imagine five women and five men are discussing this question. The women cite certain reasons why women are emotional. The men cite different reasons entirely.

The reasons do not matter. What matters is the shared frame of reference. Men and women answered the question *as if there was validity to it*. This is a shared framework, also known as consensual ideology.

Consensual Ideology: Sharing a Conceptual Framework

In explaining how dominant groups operate to stabilize society, operating within shared framework is key (Sidanius and Pratto, 1999). The current shared framework under which we live is rife with stereotypes and prescribed gender roles; loaded with inherent expectation; and reinforced by how our economic, political, and family institutions are set up. Until we realize differently, our social structure seems perfectly normal and we go along with it. Maybe we dislike certain components of it, but we all agree on the structure.

Imagine I am hosting a party. The topic of discussion is what type of gloves we wear to strangle the neighborhood pets. I wear leather. Someone else suggests a cloth fabric. Another says to skip the gloves altogether. We are consensual on the topic. We express variation in our answers (consensual disagreement), but we all buy into the framework of murdering pets (consensual ideology).

Another example, in proper context for our subject: Strip clubs have become a lunch venue for tech people in San Francisco. *Forbes* published an article debating the merits of several strip clubs in deciding where to go for lunch (Mac, 2015). Several people weighed in on their preference (consensual disagreement), while one respondent said it was not an inclusive environment for work colleagues (dissensual disagreement). All except one person agreed on the framework of strip clubs being an acceptable lunch venue for professional colleagues. The dissenting person said it was not an appropriate venue for work colleagues because there existed such high potential for someone to feel uncomfortable, and thus be excluded (dissensual ideology).

As we proceed in exploring this and subsequent chapters, I ask that you consider whether you agree on the prescribed framework of sexism, and with it, the invented scripts constructed to maintain power for men at the expense of others.

Men Assign Expert Status and Authority to Other Men

Women described many situations where men assumed expert knowledge. They acted and asserted that they had knowledge that they did not have. On the other hand, they acted and asserted that women did not possess knowledge that women did indeed possess. Men said they knew things when they did not, and men said women did not know things when the women had significant knowledge on a subject. Participants talked about men actively ignoring them in meetings when the woman was running the meeting. Also, while actively ignoring women, men directed their questions to men. Even upon learning the men did not have the information, men continued to direct their questions to the men, who did not have the answers, rather than the women who did have the answers.

Men Assume Other Men Are Experts—Including Themselves

Recently, I have someone who came to me. They reached out to me because they wanted to buy a license in the North Sea, a petroleum license. Someone in the sector said they should come and talk to me. There were two of them coming, so I brought one of my male partners with me.

My male partner, by the way, knows nothing about the sector, nothing. Both of the guys who came in to see *me*, they would ask questions to my male colleague, who couldn't answer them. I would answer them. They would then reluctantly look at me and watch me answer them, and then engage him in the conversation on the follow-up points.

I was just like, no. I will just not work with you. I'm in that position in my career that I can just say no thanks. Secondly, when we left the room I said to my partner, "Well that was a bit weird." He said, "Well what do you mean? Oh, yeah, I didn't think they know what they want."

I said, "That may be, but that's not what I was referring to. If I was in that situation, don't you think it would have been appropriate, rather than you facilitating whatever the fuck was going on in the room, to make it very clear that actually I am the expert in this field? Rather than sitting there basking in the glory of them so wanting you to be the expert, because they thought somehow that was the right thing to do."

It did not occur to him, and he was pissed off with me for bringing it up. "Well I didn't think that was appropriate. I think that you're being overly sensitive."

(Natalya, *Law*)

Men Directing Their Questions to the Man

When you're in a meeting with subcontractors, even though you go around the table and everyone introduces themselves, and I say, "I'm the manager," you feel like they are still constantly directing their questions toward the man. Basically acting as if they don't think that I'm really in charge.

(Allison, *Politics*)

Woman Is Not Credible unless a Man Says She Is

Ignoring me, meetings with men, especially meetings when the men do not know who I am or why I am in the room. They ignore me, they don't take me seriously, they don't listen. Not until a man kind of lifts me up and tells them who I am and why they should listen to me, do they do it. It's happened several times during my whole career.

(Julia, *Global Marketing*)

Man Asserting Knowledge He Did Not Have

The fact they thought they knew more than me about things I was hired for. We were setting up a meeting between me, the CEO of the (company), and the Minister of Culture. I was trying to give the communications manager an idea of what that meeting should be, what it should revolve around. He just told me, "This is not the way you do meetings with Ministers."

I asked him, "Have you ever worked in the governmental offices or with a Minister?"

"No, but I know."

I said, 'Well I have worked with the Prime Minister and with several other Ministers, so I do know—the way you think is not the way."

And he was startled, "Oh have you? I didn't know." Suddenly he started respecting me.

Never occurs to them to check, and it never occurs to them that they could be wrong. It had to take that round before he understood that, "she knows something that I do not know, and I have to act like a douchebag until she tells me what she knows."

(Mara, *Culture and Politics*)

Man Assuming a Female CEO Did Not Know Technicalities of Her Business

You're on a need to know basis. This is between us boys. Now being the CEO of an aviation company, I was just told—I was sitting in a meeting with one of the partners in my firm who is a male helicopter pilot and engineer, and another woman who is in marketing, and another man who is in aviation brokerage. The man who was in aviation brokerage said, "Why don't the two of you girls speak about the marketing bit and I'll speak to the helicopter pilot about helicopter stuff."

I said, "With all due respect, we're in a meeting regarding helicopters in my office, which is a helicopter company. Anything that you have to say about helicopters should be spoken amongst the table."

And he said, "Well it's an operational point so I should probably talk to technicalities."

I said, "I'm the CEO of the company so anything that you speak about regarding the company, you say at the table. This is not a sideline conversation of 'us boys are going to talk about the helicopters and moving parts, and you girls can talk about the pretty colors that you're going to design for the brochure.'" That happens a lot in aviation, which is incredible.

(Mila, *Aviation*)

Man Actively Ignored the Woman

I was at a business meeting where the entire meeting—there was me, a male colleague, and a man who owned one of our biggest American customer organizations. He looked at my colleague the whole time, to the extent that my colleague noticed and was really uncomfortable with it. He would never look at me. I tried to engage. He was talking about fishing, I've fished my whole life. I was trying to add to the conversation and he was just not interested. (Laughs) You know he did have a more established relationship with my colleague, but the imbalance of like eye contact and stuff was extreme. It was odd.

(Sophia, *Global Marketing*)

You Misunderstood—We Were Not Soliciting Your Opinion

Natalya described the active ignoring of her in a partners meeting when she speaks, and the strong nonverbal social cues of exclusion that men give her.

When you start speaking—sometimes I catch myself, "Am I speaking a foreign language? Am I saying something really outrageous? Why are you looking at me this way?" You're asking me about something that is directly within my line of work. It's my practice. I'm not commenting on medicine.

I'll give you an example from a partner meeting. When you're sitting around the room, and there's 30 guys and you. You are discussing matters which affect you as a group. You might say, "Well I don't really agree with that, have you thought about X, have you considered Y?" All of a sudden you have thirty eyes looking up at you like, "Oh my god, the monkey speaks?"

Individually they're all perfectly fine with you. Nobody's rude—I mean, nobody actively seeks your opinion—but in that forum, when you do speak up, then people just *look* at you.

I can think particularly about a couple of senior partners who are from an era gone by, they look at you, and they're like, "Oh, my God, this is really embarrassing *for you*. And for everyone in the room, because you really misunderstood. When we said, 'What do you think about it' we were not soliciting your opinion. Stop talking, please just stop it."

You may disagree with me, but don't look at me, not the way that I would look at my *dog* if he started talking. I find that so strange. I have actually pointed it out to another female partner. I told her, "Do you notice that? Because if you look at when a male partner speaks, how this particular individual looks, and what happens when *you* speak."

(Natalya, *International Energy Law*)

Men Treating Women as Incompetent and Illegitimate

In this section, the narratives are describing situations when men actively assign women low-status positions. Men assume women lack technical knowledge, regardless of their credentials or position. When they are corrected, the men do not acknowledge their biased assumption and apologize. Instead, they challenge the woman's credentials and make her prove her legitimacy, as if she was making it up or trying to deceive them. Even in situations where the woman owns the company or clearly demonstrates technical competency, the men assume that is not really the case.

> "You're not a doctor, you're an aunt. You can pretend you're a doctor."
>
> —Lana, my niece, age 4

"Doctor" Could Never Be a Woman

People call me Dr. Gibson. When I go into meetings, people will look around the room and say, "Oh, Mr. Gibson, are you here? Is there a Mr. Gibson?" It's because "doctor" could never be a woman, right? That's not possible. It's just not humanly possible.

That is a regular thing. . . . I mean, down to the mayor's office where you think they would have some sense, or someone of power's office where you think they would have had some sensitivity training. Again, these are *women* who are doing this.

(Catherine, *Tech*)

Are You the Victim?

Courtroom personnel, that's always fun. If I am unknown in a courtroom, the person has never had an interaction with me or I have never been in that courtroom before, I am asked always, 100% of the time, if I am the victim, and that's actually the best of the questions.

Are you an attorney? I usually am happy I get that question.

Because otherwise I normally get, Are you the girlfriend? Are you the defendant? Are you the victim? Are you the probation officer? Are you the court clerk? Are you the interpreter?

And I've had judges do that, too. At least once a day, at least once a courtroom appearance. It's like, why do I have to do this?

"Who are you?"

"I'm the attorney of record, Judge."

"I'm sorry I didn't realize you're a lawyer."

A white man sitting here in a suit, you're going to think he's a lawyer before anything else.

That's before I start to talk. Literally upon sight. It's terrible.

(Sarah, *Law*)

What Could You Possibly Know?

I'm not a pilot and I work with a lot of men on the business side who aren't pilots. When a man's not a pilot, it's not a big deal. He can still know about helicopters. But for a woman, "What would you know about helicopters? You're not a pilot, you weren't in the Navy. Why is this woman involved in helicopters? What could you possibly know?" Well, people are car salesmen and they didn't build the car. Unbelievable.

(Mila, *Aviation*)

The Inmate's Girlfriend

Recently I had an encounter with a courtroom deputy, a bailiff. I walked into the courtroom. My time was set for 1:30 to do a plea with the judge. The judge hasn't entered the room yet. The state attorneys are there. State attorneys on misdemeanors are normally brand new, fresh out of law school. They don't know anybody yet.

I see my client sitting in the jury box, which is where they keep the inmates in court. He's sitting there with a sheriff's deputy and a court deputy. I walk in and say, good afternoon, everybody. I put my things down. I'm like, let me just go talk to my client.

I approach. The (sheriff's) deputy has no problem. The court deputy says, "Who are you?"

I have interacted with him before. I jokingly go, "I'm (name)!" and try to laugh it off and talk to my client, and he goes, "No ma'am, who *are* you?"

"I'm sorry. I'm (name). I'm the attorney."

He goes, "I don't know that you're an attorney, I have never seen you as an attorney in here before."

"Fine, okay. Noted, but I am the attorney."

"I don't know you're not this guy's girlfriend."

"Excuse me?'

"Step away from the inmate. You can't talk to him. I need to see some ID."

And at that point I got angry because it was 13 years I've been practicing. I've never been asked to show my ID in a courtroom. To prove that I'm an attorney. Never once.

"I will not show you my identification. I will not show you my bar card. If I was a white male, you would not be asking me that question. Even if you never laid eyes on it before in your life. I refuse."

He says, "Well, I'm going to call my supervisor."

"Call your supervisor because you're not getting me to show you my ID. Not this day."

I was really emboldened because I had defended the supervisor's grandson. "Get her down here!"

She comes into the courtroom and says. "This is the lawyer that you called me about?" That guy got reamed out by his supervisor and got put on administrative leave. They almost fired him.

The way he came at me was unreal. Never have I had anyone demand my identification. Never.

There were other male attorneys that came in that he had never interacted with in the courtroom. He didn't know any of those other people, and he didn't ask them any questions.

(Sarah, *Law*)

Regulating Gender Roles and Femininity

Much like an accusation in the form of a question, men regulate women's appearance in the form of compliments. Men also communicate their higher status and women's lower status by requesting that the women perform menial tasks. These tasks are communal in nature, usually having to do with food and drink, much in the way some women serve men in the home. Women's interpersonal traits are also regulated according to communal gender roles. The use of names also emerges in this section. Men use diminutive and intimate names that strip a woman of her identity and reduce her from her professional status.

Evaluating Appearance

Compliments Are Judgments

(Compliments) They're *judgments*! "I'm a man who is passing opinion on how you look, and you should be absolutely thrilled that I told you that you look nice. I could have told you that you didn't look nice. I could have not commented on your appearance at all. You would be wondering, 'Does he think I'm pretty?' I did you a favor by telling you that."

(Olivia, *Politics*)

Like Your Hair

Always, especially if it's a male client I will get a comment on how I look. First and foremost. They never want to address me as an attorney. It's like, "Oh I like your hair, I like that dress. I like your heels."

(Isabella, *Law*)

Hair Too Short

Not my client but someone on the other side commented that my hair was too short. I said, "Well, I'm not Samson so it doesn't affect my strength, it's fine." Because I had a haircut! It was just, really bizarre.

(Maryam, *Branding*)

Ordering Menial Tasks as Public Status

How That Looks Externally

I was a little confused, and I have a pretty strong self-confidence. I remember thinking to myself, I got a master's degree for this? I don't know how I feel about making coffee. And then I talked myself into a "It's not a big deal. People make each other cups of coffee and it is my meeting." And then it got to the stage a couple years later, especially more important projects, I was actually quite bitchy about it.

Thinking about it, how that looks externally—this is not just for the boss but also male colleagues saying, "You'll go make me a cup of coffee won't you? Be a dear, we need coffee." Or someone at the table would say, "Should we grab some coffee?" and they would all look at me, even though they didn't know what my role was. And there were a couple times I said, "With all due respect I'm not a barista. I'm sure you can find someone to bring the coffee in."

(Emma, *Casting*)

Reduce Me to the One with Long Legs

"Oh, you're so young and beautiful, could you please go get the coffee?" And I was a negotiator for an employee's organization and I had a good profession with my education and everything but he—this boss just tried to reduce me into the one with the long legs and the young face who could get coffee. And he did that in front of board members.

(Janni, *Transportation*)

Male Counterparts Would Not Have Been Asked That

I was working on a project in Iraq, and fully engaged in it 24/7 to make it happen. Regardless of my seniority or rank, I was asked to make coffee and bring the coffee because I was the only woman in the room. I was also very frequently asked questions of, why I also haven't provided the catering. I would not have ever expected to hear of male counterparts in my role, dealing with the senior executives and members of government that I was dealing with, with full authority—I don't think they would have the same thing.

At this point in our interview I tell her that getting coffee and menial task requests are a status communication, in this case deliberately asked to indicate lower status on her part.

That's interesting and thank you because sometimes I thought, "Should I have just done that, or should I have just done this?" But I noticed that as a pattern because I started getting that again with my last job.

(Mila, *Business Development*)

Put That in My Diary and Fetch the Drinks

She indicates in this passage being aware of the status by avoiding talking about him as her superior, yet he still treated her like a
subordinate.

> I never called him *my* boss because I was very particular about working *with*
> him and not *for* him. People would say "oh your boss" and I would say "he's
> not my boss" because I didn't respect him. I didn't want somebody to be
> my boss, *you're not the boss of me*, that kind of a thing.
>
> There were a couple of times where he would say "You didn't put that in
> my diary" or "why don't you call and do this or do that." They were things
> that he easily could have done himself and there was no reason for me to
> do it. I didn't have time, and he would stand around and smoke cigars while
> I was doing all the work. Then he would ask me to do something that was
> just so ridiculous.
>
> "I'll give you the money and you can go out and fetch the drinks" kind
> of thing. I would say, "*Or*, when the waitress comes over, we can order
> from *her*. That makes a lot more sense." Or you can have somebody else
> do that because my time is more valuable. I don't actually have time to do
> that.
>
> That's interesting that it is kind of a typical thing, not just something that
> I experienced.
>
> (Mila, *Business Development*)

Using Diminutive Names

Thank You, Little Girl

> (In the context of being gradually sexualized over years,) the bigger issues
> were being asked to make a cup of coffee for these top execs and govern-
> ment people. I had been working on their project. I was senior, I had
> been there, I was a member of the team and it was like a "thank you,
> little girl" for your contribution. "Us men will be in the board room," door
> shut.
>
> (Mara, *Politics*)

You Don't Know What You're Talking about, Little Girl

> I got called "little girl" several times, especially "little girl" in negotiation. "You
> don't know what you're talking about, little girl." Again, speaking with gov-
> ernment agencies and government channels, I definitely got treated very
> differently than I think I would have as a man.
>
> (Janni, *Labor Negotiation*)

Isn't She a Firecracker, and a Little Girl

There are certain things I would be called, like "little girl." I've also been told, "Isn't she a firecracker. I can see why you hired her." Like it's out of the norm and I'm thinking, "Would you say that to a man?"

(Olivia, *Politics*)

Intimate Names That You Wouldn't Call a Man

I get called babe, I get called gorgeous, I get called beautiful. I have to "course correct" to say what if my male colleague was here you wouldn't be calling him—I don't know what the equivalent of gorgeous or beautiful or babe is for the men, but they would not be getting that. I always have to "course correct" when they start that way and remind them this is a professional relationship.

(Natalya, *Law*)

Forgot My Name Because I'm a Woman

The reason that the guy felt like he could call me out my name or do whatever. Or call me sweetie, or to, you know, just those kinds of things, "Oh, it's because I'm a woman." Like, all of a sudden you forgot my name when—it's just like little little things like that.

(Natalya, *Law*)

Regulating Feminine Traits

Polite, But Not Sunny and Happy

This participant describes how colleagues have critiqued her interpersonal traits. Rather than being focused and efficient, she is perceived as difficult and aggressive.

Absolutely! Tone that down. A lot of the word aggressive. I use that about myself, but I think I use it about myself because I've heard it so many times in talking about a woman trying to get what she wants in the office. She becomes aggressive rather than just doing your job. With a man it would be doing his job, but with a woman she's aggressive. I have been told that I come across as difficult and aggressive. So yeah, I've been told to "tone it down" or "soften it."

Q: What made you "difficult"?

That's a good question! I think "difficult" is standing my ground and asking for something and not doing it in a cheerful friendly happy way. Rather than saying, "Oh hiya, morning, so happy we work together, it's amazing! Do you mind doing this and that and the other?"

Getting right to the point, I think it's very corporate and professional and sometimes it's quite cold, but I need to get the job done. Unless I have that really fun atmosphere I say, "Hi, can you have that on my desk by that time." Being polite about it but not necessarily sunny and happy.

I experienced that yesterday. I just said, "Hi, I don't have the time to dwell. Can you get this to me by that time? Thank you very much." I got a very, "Wow that was harsh."

I have been told that I am overly formal by communicating in that way. That is my corporate upbringing of being formal. It's a job, it's not social hour.

(Rebecca, *Politics and Philanthropy*)

This is a double standard of gender communication. Not only is it her job to communicate content, as a woman it is also incumbent upon her to foster a happy and upbeat atmosphere. Efficient communication is not challenged when a man does it, but women are made to feel like not making people feel happy is a personal deficiency.

Men Using Male Privilege to Suppress Female Contribution

In demonstrating their high status, men exclude and block women from contributing and being part of the decision-making process. They employ several strategies, including talking over and interrupting women. Women reported men making decisions before meetings were held, so contributing was impossible. Other times their input was blocked by men prior to the meeting. An important item to note is that the ideas presented by these women did get implemented, but being blocked by the men took extra time and effort to reach the original point.

Exclusion of Women in Decision Making

From managers and directors . . . foul language, maybe far often glances and looks. And even more common I think, decision making. Without including women, who would be included if they were men. When you say sexism, it has to deal with the harassment—that is part of it—but I think it begins a lot earlier. It begins with an exclusion of women in decision making.

(Allison, *Politics*)

Withholding Information

I sent an email to one of them asking, "I heard that you have been in contact with this person that I am having a process with to donate money to this organization. What kind of contacts have you had with him? It's good for me to know." The question would be, "Who is asking?" Well, I am asking. Who do you think is asking?

(Mara, Culture and Politics)

Interrupting or Talking over You

Q: Have you experienced men interrupting, or talking over you?

That happened a lot. . . . All the managers, all the men managers. Just, during all kinds of meetings, really. Yes. Yes, to all them. Yes, yes, yes. Ignoring me, meetings with men, especially meetings when the men do not know who I am or why I am in the room.

All the time. Literally all day, almost all day every day.

That feels more like an everyday kind of thing. (Laughs)

Q: Ignoring your suggestions or presence.

That one is every day, all the time. Always.

Q: Being asked personal questions about personal subjects?

Every day, all the time. In almost every conversation.

(Olivia, Music Industry)

Man: "I Just Did What I Usually Do"

It comes in different expressions. It's more abstract and it's harder to define since it's not physical things. more like suppression . . . from a male point of view, "No, I just did what I usually do." And they don't see the gender perspective and hierarchies being affected by their acts.

(Mara, Politics)

"Perhaps You Are on Your Period"

At a negotiation table we were trying to—they were selling a refinery and my client was buying a refinery. And I just kept saying "No." He said, "You don't understand." I said to him, "I'm saying no, not because I don't understand, because it's a shit deal and I don't agree." Not like that, but that was the gist. And he said to me, he was just like "You're being very dramatic and very unreasonable. Perhaps it's one of your critical days." He's Russian, so in Russia that means that you're having your period.

(Natalya, Law)

Men Already Decided on What They Wanted

We had meetings where we were about to brainstorm on a new thing or a new idea. It was very hard to speak in those meetings.

We, the two females, we knew that they had already decided on what they wanted. And if we started questioning that, they would just say, "That is not the right way to start the discussion. No, no, you're doing it the wrong way."

He gave us all these comments and critiques that did not involve the issue itself. Only the *way* we spoke, and the *order* in which we brought up things. They had already decided so there was nothing for us to talk about.

(Lauren, *Professor*)

They Just Did Not Listen

I came to the management team and I tried to explain something to them. They just did not listen to me, it was about the law. We have to comply with the law, so it was really important to me, for the company's sake, that they listened and understood and took action on it. The feeling when I presented this, and they just started talking about something else. I think part of this was because I was a woman in a room full of men.

Q: Did anybody react?

One of the strong voices in that management team is no longer in this company, he didn't agree with me. He had prepped the group before I came in, so they were very soon to take his side. I can't remember if that was that meeting or after, I came again and some people in the group repeated what I said. And questioning him on his point of view. That got the discussion going and I got a bit more air time and it ended well. They ended up doing what I thought they should be doing in the first place. But it was just so unnecessary. It took a few weeks longer just because it came to a halt.

(Janni, *Transportation*)

Analysis

Woman's Ideas Are Disregarded by Men

Mara describes a conference in which she met her regional colleagues at the public policy firm where she works. They did not know her background and assumed she was in the public relations instead of public policy area, and that she was a junior staff member instead of senior associate.

They also disregarded her idea, which was the same idea that won the competition of the conference.

> I was at a conference with my new job. I'm highly respected since they know who I am. I have been a public figure for more than ten years. But the Nordic—we have offices in Helsinki, Oslo, Denmark in Norway, in Belgium in Brussels, and Estonia, and so on. No one else from the other countries knows who I am. I'm new to the organization so they haven't met me before.
>
> We had this competition where we were assigned a case and making a pitch to these clients. On my own team, the colleagues from the other countries did not take me seriously. This is my perception and (that of) the male colleague who was with me. He's twenty-four, much younger than I am. I am almost forty. They did not really listen. They discarded my ideas. Straightaway, "No no no no no. We can *never* give that advice to a client. *No* way. You juniors working with PR might have other ideas but" blah blah.
>
> In that meeting I did not say "I'm a Senior working with Public Affairs, I'm not a Junior working with PR." I just let them be.
>
> Then when we were presenting our cause for the jury, they were also discarding some of the things I was saying. "Do you *really mean* that we should focus on that *dialog* in this process?" while making me feel stupid in front of everyone else . . . They were colleagues acting as representatives for the company we were pitching a case on.
>
> The other team won this contest because they had the best pitch. It was a colleague of mine, an older man around sixty. I'm his favorite colleague. He's my favorite colleague. We're so different. He's from the right party, I'm from the left and we work really good together. And he really respects me.
>
> I told him about this when we came back after the conference. "What was your idea? Why did they discard it?" I described it and he was, "Well, that's the idea that we presented, and we won the contest." I said, "Yes. But that was *you*. That was not *me*. And we're *different*." That is a recent example of things that you have to endure.

Exposing Sexist Scripts and Thought Patterns

I.   Let's Both Agree That You're Really Stupid
  A.   Internalized Domination
  B.   Consensual Ideology: Sharing a Conceptual Framework

II. Men Assign Expert Status and Authority to Other Men
  A.   Men Assume Other Men Are Experts—Including Themselves
  B.   Men Directing Their Questions to the Man

    C.   Woman Is Not Credible unless a Man Says She Is

    D.   Man Asserting Knowledge He Did Not Have

    E.   Man Assuming a Female CEO Did Not Know Technicalities of Her Business

    F.   Man Actively Ignored the Woman

    G.   You Misunderstood—We Were Not Soliciting Your Opinion

III. Men Treating Women as Incompetent and Illegitimate

    A   "Doctor" Could Never Be a Woman

    B.   Are You the Victim?

    C.   The Inmate's Girlfriend

    D.   What Could You Possibly Know?

IV. Regulating Gender Roles and Femininity

    A.   Evaluating Appearance

        1.   Compliments Are Judgments

        2.   Like Your Hair

        3.   Hair Too Short

    B.   Ordering Menial Tasks as Public Status

        1.   How That Looks Externally

        2.   Reduce Me to the One with Long Legs

        3.   Male Counterparts Would Not Have Been Asked That

        4.   Put That in My Diary and Fetch the Drinks

    C.   Using Diminutive Names

        1.   Thank You, Little Girl

        2.   You Don't Know What You're Talking about, Little Girl

        3.   Intimate Names That You Wouldn't Call a Man

        4.   Forgot My Name Because I'm a Woman

    D.   Regulating Feminine Traits

        1.   Polite, But Not Sunny and Happy

V. Men Using Male Privilege to Suppress Female Contribution

    A.   Exclusion of Women in Decision Making

    B.   Withholding Information

    C.   Interrupting or Talking Over You

    D.   Man: "I Just Did What I Usually Do"

E. "Perhaps You Are on Your Period"
F. Men Already Decided on What They Wanted
G. They Just Did Not Listen

Conclusion

Throughout this chapter, women have described everything from seemingly minuscule situations to overt and crass instances. The emphasis of men has been to communicate their power. The emphasis for women is to do work and contribute to their work effort.

Men make status claims about themselves in these narratives that are not validated. Conversely, men make low-status claims against women that also are not validated. In these instances, men claim to have knowledge they do not have, and never questions themselves. They do question women, to the point of forcing the woman to prove her credentials. The fact that she is in the position is not adequate to justify her abilities. However, men do make that same assumption about other men. They assume a man is the expert by virtue of his presence.

This bias comes at a price to the organizations for which these executives work. When men are so blinded with bias that they cannot recognize the merit of solid thinking, the company suffers. The woman suffers professionally because her work cannot come to fruition if she is not heard, but that is only a problem for her; however, simply because a problem exists does not mean it will be addressed. If the company continues to make money, it feels no loss and therefore is not incentivized to enable women's voices to be heard. The problem is hers alone, and that is the trap.

Creating New Scripts and Thought Patterns

- What consensual ideology do you feel subjected to?
  - What issues?
  - What makes you disagree with the conceptual framework?
- Have you ever had your intelligence or experience assumed as less?
  - Upon sight, by merit of assumption?
  - Still after you spoke?
- Have you witnessed this happening to somebody, in a work or personal setting?
  - Did you address it for yourself, or correct on behalf of the other person?
  - Why or why not?

- Have you been subjected to the communication patterns mentioned in this chapter?
  - What happened?
  - Was there a consequence?
- Knowing what you do now, would you intervene in the future?
  - On behalf of yourself? What would you say?
  - In defense of someone else? How would you handle it?

CHAPTER FOUR

Sexualization

Introduction

Executive sexism conjures images of men behaving in a sexual manner toward women. Roger Ailes and Harvey Weinstein spring to mind. Due largely to media, people narrowly relegate their ideas about sexism to assault or quid pro quo situations. While those situations exist at staggering and disgraceful rates, men sexualize women in many ways. In this context, sexualization communicates power. This chapter describes those scenarios.

Sexualization

Sex is the ever-present specter of male-female interactions, and the executive work space is no different. The Psychological Association Task force on the Sexualization of Girls (2007) conducted a study in which they determined that boys begin sexualizing the girls around them by the age of 12. Two subsequent chapters in this book are devoted to the role of pornography and the commodification of women, both of which help to shape the behavior you are about to encounter. This chapter describes situations experienced by our interviewees, but first we will define and explain sexualization.

1. A person's value comes only from his or her sexual appeal or behavior, to the exclusion of other characteristics. Your value comes only from your perceived sexual appeal or sexual behavior. You are something men want to have sex with, and to them there is nothing more to you than sex. Your identity is collapsed, and you possess no other characteristics worthy of being acknowledged. We will address the collapse of identity further in Chapter 10 when we discuss commodification.

2. A person is held to a standard that equates physical attractiveness (narrowly defined) with being sexy. Your appearance is compared to the narrowly defined, compartmentalized social ideal of what is considered sexy, and men remind you of that in various way. What men claim are compliments are substitutes, euphemisms for what they really seem to want to say. The words "You look really nice today" have a completely different inference with the highly sexualized nonverbals attached. When dismissing or minimizing sexualization, people often forgo the context when recounting the event (another way of making a woman seem like she is overreacting).

3. A person is sexually objectified—that is, made into a thing for others' sexual use, rather than being seen as a person with the capacity for independent action and decision making. You equate to a thing for men's use and enjoyment. Subsequent chapters talk about how men use women for entertainment and try to "pimp them out" in business contexts. Unfortunately this dynamic is alive and well, and regularly used.

4. Sexuality is inappropriately imposed upon a person. You know when you are suddenly in the midst of a sexual conversation, or when some anatomical reference gets inserted into the conversation? That is inappropriately imposed, and men do this quite frequently. Quite frequently. Ironically, when men turn a conversation sexual in a one-on-one setting, they turn it around and accuse the woman of having done so. Several participants noted this, and one also mentions how men include their wives and children in the conversation. This woman says that when she shuts down their advances, the men accuse *her* of being inappropriate because they have a family. As proof they refer to back to the conversation.

Its extreme prevalence makes defining and delineating sexualization a challenge. Although they often are, not all these conditions need be present. Even one factor signifies sexualization (American Psychological Association, 2007; Wolf, 1991). The categories overlap, indicative of the insidious nature of sexualization. Following are accounts of how our participants experienced sexualization, passages about different types of sexualization women are subjected to by colleagues, clients, and bosses.

Quid Pro Quo

The first two accounts are straight-up requests to exchange sex for some good—in the first case a monetary contribution, and in the second, legal expertise.

For a Charitable Donation

My friend (name) as leader of (U.S. nonprofit), for a while got sizable dona-tions from (a man), who is the owner of the (NFL team). And so he was going to re-up that donation and he asked if she would come up and meet with him in (his city) and just talk a little about the organization. And she said yeah, sure. That's a reasonable request. She gets there and he was prop-ositioning her, "If you don't sleep with me I'm not going to give you the money." She was shocked. She was like well, this is not the kind of person I want to take money from anyway. She said "Keep your money" and she left.

It did affect the organization because we lost the $50,000 this guy was going to give us that we couldn't replace. I support her in responding the way she did, but this had *huge* effect because this guy thought they needed some type of exchange in order to do the philanthropic thing he'd been doing the previous two years.

(Lauren, *Nonprofit Board Member*)

For Help with Legal Work

I have colleagues who have men literally do the quid pro quo thing with them. She would go to them, "Hey, I need your help. I'm writing this motion."

"Okay well, you give me a blow job first."

Basically her entire career has been that. They've been older white men who want to take her under their wing and show her the ropes and teach her. "Yeah, if he's going to show me or teach me how to write this motion or show me pointers on how to make this argument or that argument, it just comes with, 'Well can I touch you here, or can you give me a blow job or at least let me jack off in your face.'"

When the whole MeToo thing was happening, one of the guys was running for some elected position, and he kept calling her, "Hey are we okay?" He wanted to make sure she wasn't going to come out and say, "Well, let me tell you what he used to do to me." The power had shifted a little bit, so she wanted to let him sweat it out.

I always—mouth open listening to her because—this stuff is real! (It shocks her to hear this.) I mean, I know it happens. I didn't know anybody it actually happened *to*. But she has a million of those stories.

(Sarah, *Law*)

Humiliating Sexual References

These women discuss being called humiliating names in executive work settings and being subjected to sexualized talk. Several narratives include bosses feigning sexual proximity to female employees and colleagues; that is, pretending they were a couple in work/social settings. Because of the power imbalance, women did not feel they could correct the behavior.

Referring to Executive Employees as Commodities ("Stripper Names")

I was standing with my colleague, a former Federal Elections Commissioner, at the Mayfair Hotel in Washington. This was my first job as a PhD. We were in town to discuss anti–human trafficking efforts with other philanthropists. Our boss was the president of the philanthropic foundation we worked for, he was ahead of us in line checking into his suite. He's standing at the counter and makes this large gesture with his arm referring back to us, "And I will joined by Trixie and Bubbles." My coworker looked at her feet. A male guest in line made a face and looked away. The receptionist looked as if she'd been slapped. My face burned. I wished he would die.

(Rebecca, *Philanthropy*)

Women's Bodies

I had this boss who would comment every time a cab or bus went by that had a strip club ad on it. He would read the ad out loud, the place, the name, when she was performing, and then say really slowly, "My, my." Just to bring everyone's attention to it to make us as uncomfortable and sick as possible.

(Olivia, *Music Industry*)

Sexual Jokes

It was a social job so we were out quite often and he had this very grotesque joke, "I like my women like I like my wine, young and cheap." The servers cringed every time he put his nasty hands on them. I was so mortified to be associated with that man.

(Julia, *Marketing*)

Sexual Proximity Reference

The other staff members, women, thought it was a joke. He would call us "Wives of (Foundation name)" and "(President's) Angels." They thought it was okay. I said it's not good policy to be referred to as if we're his harem. We don't wear black leather catsuits. That's good for his ego, but it can't be good for our images. What I didn't say but we all thought is, this man resembles a living toad. Sexual reference between any of us with him was a repulsive thought.

(Rebecca, *Philanthropy*)

Sex Acts

The client was an older male and my colleague was very young. They were joking about her age and that she was quite pretty. And then she said—it's a Swedish saying—"Oh, I'm just going to swallow that one. Can we move on with the meeting?" He was like, "Oh, so you like swallowing then?" Everyone in the room was just laughing. She said, "I just felt so mortified."

(Allison, *Advertising*)

Unwelcome Sexual Contact

These women experienced men touching them. One had men just touch her at the office when they felt like it, and the other had a man force himself on her.

Men Touching Her Leg

Men both internally and externally put their hand on my leg. That happened all the time, from my boss to my CFO, to meetings that I was in, inappropriate touching absolutely. Which to me at the time would sound ridiculous because it wasn't anything either sexual or behind closed doors but definitely uninvited. And actually quite sudden, inappropriate, and bizarre.

(Mila, *Middle East Business Development*)

President Pinned Her against a Car

The executive from this private research firm that was contracted with the House of Representatives to conduct the research came to my state for a site visit and took me to dinner. I wasn't 25 at this point, and he was an older, portly person. . . . after dinner, I was walking him to his car and telling them how to get back to his hotel. And he swung me around and pressed me against his rental car and stuck his knee between my legs and his tongue down my throat. Over dinner, he had suggested that there was a stunning place for me in the organization. After I pushed him away and told him to fuck off, there was no longer a stunning place for me in the organization.

(Avery, *Pharmaceutical Marketing*)

Sexualizing Business Relationship

This section talks about how men attempt to transition women from the work space into the social sexual space. Many women tell stories about older men exploiting their inexperience and coercing them to be in places alone with them.

Exploiting Inexperience

I heard several times, "Why don't we meet in my hotel room." I was quite young during this time, so I didn't know that that was an inappropriate question. I thought, oh well we're traveling and that makes sense. I'm going to go to that hotel room, because it's this important individual. I didn't really understand, like I do now, being invited to a hotel room because they have a suite and a comfortable place to talk quietly and privately is not appropriate. Or to offer a glass of champagne when you're talking about business in a suite in a hotel is not appropriate.

(Emma, *Casting Agency*)

Fair Game

So often there was a look at my hand for a wedding ring and again, "Why don't we meet, at 10 PM over drinks in the hotel and we'll talk about it."

(Olivia, *Politics*)

Show Piece

This woman refers to men closing the door on her to exclude her from meetings, but not when her boss was there.

And when my main boss was there that rarely ever happened. I think he liked carting me out for various reasons. I did work with this individual for almost ten years, I don't remember all the instances. Some of that just gets blocked out when you're trying to do your job.

(Maryam, *Marketing*)

Inappropriate Initiations

There were a few times that that boss had invited me for a week in his chateau. Or a week away—he had private jet—somewhere tropical just for the two of us to get away, that kind of conversation. I remember thinking how inappropriate, and then how sad because I was in a very happy loving relationship and had no interest in this guy at all.

And I knew what his intention was, and the way he phrased it was oh we were such strong colleagues and I was his right-hand woman and we were working on so many things together and we really enjoyed each other's time. I mean, he was a brilliant guy and we talked about everything . . . we would talk about business, we would talk about the project we were doing in Iraq, things like that. So there was a business aspect to it but then he would say something like, "Why don't we just go to my chateau. I need some time off. My family's not around, they're in the Middle East. The two of us can work and take some time off and go skiing and it would be such great fun."

And at the time I didn't allow my brain to sexualize it, it was more like, "This is so weird, why would he invite me?" I knew subconsciously what the invitation was for and why he was inviting me, but I also knew about the girl who worked with him in Paris who had nice handbags and there were a lot of rumors around her.

I did think at the time, that hand on my knee was not just a hand on my knee. It was representative of making that choice. Going down that path with him. So I was aware of the fact that I was maybe allowing him to think that at some point I might soften if I let him keep his hand on my knee thirty seconds before moving it, that at some point while we were working for so long that he might get me drunk enough or to break down enough for things to go further.

You can rationalize or in a court of law, in an interview or whatever else, you can all explain our mindsets around the time of why we did this or why we did that, but it doesn't make it right.

(Mila, Middle East Business Development)

Exposing Sexist Scripts and Thought Patterns

I.   Quid Pro Quo
  A.   For a Charitable Donation
  B.   For Help with Legal Work

II.   Humiliating Sexual References
  A.   Referring to Executive Employees as Commodities ("Stripper Names")
  B.   Women's Bodies
  C.   Sexual Jokes
  D.   Sexual Proximity Reference
  E.   Sex Acts

III.   Unwelcome Sexual Contact
  A.   Men Touching Her Leg
  B.   President Pinned Her against a Car

IV.   Sexualizing Business Relationship
  A.   Fair Game
  B.   Show Piece

C. Exploiting Inexperience

D. Inappropriate Initiations

Analysis

In this section we examine two stories. The first comes from Mila, who talks about the progression of a relationship in which her male counterpart continuously sexualized and degraded her over a period of four years. The question that prompted this portion of her interview was how she would respond to the idea that her colleague can do what he wants with his company.

It's His Company, He Can Do What He Wants

I had that feeling, too. If you don't like it get out. If you can't handle the heat get out of the kitchen. If you're that bothered by it get out. Now what's interesting, if I worked for somebody who was racist, I probably would have left. I probably would have said, I cannot work with somebody who has this mentality and speaks that way. And somehow it never really occurred to me speaking from a female perspective about the treatment of women it never really felt the same, but I did think that way, if it's his company he can do whatever he wants.

Interesting that she mentions if the man were overtly racist, she would identify his mentality and not work with him. Women, and men, should equate the two because there is an evident parallel of inequality.

Then it goes through everything. Payment structures and bonuses, any kind of compensation. Project focus, getting frustrated and saying "Well he did entirely the wrong thing" or "He doesn't know what I'm trying to do here, why didn't he approve this or that?" Well, it's his company. It never felt like black and white, with right or wrong, there are so many shapes and colors.

Next she talks about the vagueness of sexism, and how it slips into dynamics gradually and then suddenly you're immersed in it.

It's a slippery slope, right? When you lose an inch of ground as a female and you think "Well that wasn't right" and then all of a sudden you see the things that you're putting up with and that language you're dealing with. At the beginning you thought "Well that was a little weird or suspect" and by the time you're knee deep in it, you're already so entrenched.

I probably would have agreed with that back early on. Now I would say that any employer has the responsibility for their employees. And so, if you're making your employees uncomfortable, and this is not looking at what the law says, but if you're making your employees uncomfortable physically, psychologically or otherwise, then you're responsible for that. The CEO is responsible for the health of their employees and the health of the company. Private or not, you can't do whatever you want with your employees. I would definitely disagree with that. Now.

The second story is told by Rebecca. She worked at a private philanthropic foundation with only seven staff members. Although hired to do serious work, she became aware that in reality, her function in the eyes of her boss was to be his fake girlfriend.

It's His Company, and I Paid the Price

He was the president of a philanthropic foundation. I was a Director of Special Projects. I knew this man for months before he hired me. He knew how I felt about sexist behavior. We had discussed it at length, and I never saw it until he hired me. After he began signing my paychecks, his true self emerged. The staff, all women, called him "old school." They told me I should lighten up.

He had no boundaries when it came to me, between personal life and private life, so I was an employee and I was expected to be his fake girlfriend. His behavior at public events suggested we were a couple. I understood that having a boyfriend would be the end of my employment. If I said he creeped me out, please don't touch me, that also would result in the end of my position. My employment was at his pleasure. I could be fired at any moment, for any reason. Politics is like that, too. It gets complicated.

The work I was doing was fascinating. I traveled and met people. I loved that part. I did not love the blinding stress headaches I got each afternoon. I did not love it when my hair began falling out. My body was expressing what my words could not. Project wise, I had nothing to show for my time. He would assign me something and pull the plug right before its completion. The leash was strangling me, but exiting this job now posed a bigger problem.

Since he felt such a strong personal connection to me (people said he was in love), leaving would be the equivalent of me rejecting him. Philanthropy is a highly relational field. They take recommendations of who to hire, who to fund, and who to disregard. So with one word I could be blackballed from the entire industry. And eventually that is what happened. I got a boyfriend and then I got a letter. It was my last day, effective immediately.

I called an attorney after the fact, who said I had a clear-cut sexual harassment case, but they cannot be prosecuted (because) the organization has fewer than 15 employees. By some details I gave about the organization, the attorney said, "Oh he's smart. Sounds like he's done this before. He knew how to cover that." Had I been able to move forward, I do not know if I would have. At that point I did not realize that I did get blackballed. I got the message over a few months. Right then, immediately after, I still had hope.

Interviews went nowhere. One was very hostile, and then nobody returned my call. No person who worked for a nonprofit would even connect with me on LinkedIn, let alone speak to me. The contracts I had evaporated. And by then I had an employment gap in my resume. You get how this works? I have been dealing with sexism for 20 years. They always fall in love, and I always lose my job.

Conclusion

As a dominant group, men sexualize women as a way of communicating their superior status. They say and do things because they can. During the interviews, women talked about sexism *in the same way* at each progressive level of their careers. Sexist men communicate and exercise their power through talk and behavior that degrades women.

Women blame themselves and each other when men sexualize them. The reality is it has nothing to do with the women, and everything to do with men. If you have been sexualized, it was not about you. Sexist men do not care about your status and credentials. They care about letting you know they are in charge.

Creating New Scripts and Thought Patterns

- Have you ever sexualized someone?
    - What happened?
    - Are you aware how it affected him or her?
- Have you ever been sexualized?
    - What happened and who was involved?
    - How did it affect you?
    - How did you feel about yourself and whoever else was involved?
- If the situation was reversed, would you treat your colleagues the ways described here?
- How do you think a person's character affects business?
- What kind of person are you, and how does that reflect in life?
    - Your language and what you say to others.
    - What activities are you involved with, and what aspects of you does each activity satisfy?

CHAPTER FIVE

Why Women Remain Silent

Introduction

The Social Context of Silence

When a woman chooses to be silent about sexist behavior at any level, she is calculating.

When a woman chooses to be silent about sexism, it is not because she failed to notice, not because she was unaffected, and not because she thought it unimportant to speak, but because she is doing math in her head and the price of speaking up will not justify the price she will pay for having done so. While that reads like a typographical error, it is not. Let me explain.

The long and short of it is, at this moment in time, there is rarely any benefit to speaking up. Telling someone means you get both the unwanted behavior and some level of punitive social or financial punishment. The question is not if you will suffer fallout, the question is how bad it will be. That unknown quotient is what a woman works out in her head every time sexism enters her psyche.

Our understanding changes over time, and how we feel about it evolves as we understand it differently. These issues are never fixed. You are situated within them, and the elements are constantly changing.

Why Women Don't Report Rape on College Campuses

Speaking with a professor who helps students who have experienced sexual assault, she offered insight as to why women do not report it. A lot of them are involved with drinking, and they fear the legal repercussions of drinking underage. Most often an acquaintance assaulted them, and the woman feels like she has done something to precipitate the attack. She feels partially responsible, like someone raping her was her fault. She blames herself and suffers internally.

When it comes to reporting, the places she would go are public. Anyone seen going into certain offices is known to have a problem. On her campus, for example, public safety and student counseling are in the middle of the student union. The woman dreads the rumors and gossip, and what social repercussion may follow. They have no expectation of follow-up by authorities. If she does go through with it, the future looks uncertain and likely filled with more difficulty.

Why Women Remain Silent about Sexism

Reasons college women do not report rapes strongly resemble the information in this chapter, why women remain silent about sexism. Consider the similarities:

Women know the perpetrator. Sexism happens in public and private settings. Sometimes drinking is involved. Women blame themselves when a man violates their boundaries. Women feel they put themselves in the situation. They feel responsible, like they should have seen it coming. They feel shame for what happened. There is nobody to tell. Confidentiality is an issue. Rumor and gossip will damage their career. Realistically, they cannot ensure privacy if they report it. Reporting they have no expectation of privacy. Worse, the perpetrator is often a respected man of position. They have no expectation that anyone will take their report seriously. They have no expectation that anything will come of their time, effort, embarrassment.

This chapter cites the reasons that women say they do not speak out against sexism. The reasons and the situations are all different, but certain categories emerged, as follows.

Consequences of Hurting a Man's Ego

These women talk about the men sexualizing women. When the women stop them or reject their advances, the men take it personally and strike against them. In all cases, it ruins whatever working relationship had been there.

They Never Forget You Hurt Their Ego

There's this false notion that you can demand respect, and you have to say something if a man gives you less respect than you think you should command. But it's a trap. What you have created is—instead of somebody who's sexist and feeling somewhat in favor of you, you've created someone who's sexist and now you've hurt his ego. That is a pain that never goes away.

(Rebecca, *Senior Scientist*)

You Stand to Lose a Lot

So scenarios call on women to be hyper aware of who they are interacting with to make a split second judgment call really on how they want to address an offensive statement or comment or some sort of micro aggression like you have to just kind of figure out is this going to be worth it. What do I have to lose here in this situation versus what I have to gain and a lot of times professionally unfortunately, especially with what I do, what I have to lose doesn't just affect me. It affects my clients and I don't want to adversely affect my clients.

(Isabella, *Law*)

Ruins Your Business Relationship

They would apologize, but it would definitely chill interactions with that individual going forward. Even like I said with that gentleman this morning with the negotiation. He came across, he was a black male, but he came across as somebody who, if I called him out on the 'baby girls' thing, that all of a sudden everything would go south with the negotiations and trying to get my client's money back.

(Sarah, *Law*)

Nervous about Repercussions

I hate myself a little bit more every time I take it. But I do because I am nervous about what the repercussions might be, not for me necessarily but for my clients. I'm hoping that we will have a generation of women who would never have to think that way.

(Maryam, *Marketing and Branding*)

Rejecting a Man Becomes a Problem for You

In situations like that, people don't understand once you hurt that ego, what you've done is reject their sexual advances and they never forgive you for that. Then they hate you for it. Then the problem is on you, and you deal with that problem for the rest of the time you deal with them.

(Emma, *Casting*)

He Did It at His Own House

We all went out on the boat earlier that day, we went diving. When we were back at his house, his wife and some other executives were there. He and I were outside for a second. I don't remember why, we had been drinking all day. He like, it wasn't really dancing but he like danced with me, and I pushed it off. I'm like, "Oh I'm not a good dancer. I'm terrible," and laughed it off and pretended like I didn't realize—I played stupid—that's what I thought I had to do.

Then he started talking to me. He would "love to have me around more but you know (his wife) gets really jealous." Started saying some other stuff and then like got kind of close again. I don't know if he was going to kiss me, but I got in and I made it an awkward hug. I said, "Oh well I guess it's time for me to go. It's getting pretty late. Let me just get out of here." And then I just left.

Q: How was he to you after that in the office?

Well he tried to take me on his boat the next day, just me and him. He called me *relentlessly* the next day. I said, "Oh I'm really hung over." I wasn't but you know again, making excuses.

I have some memories, but I tried to block it. I wasn't supposed to tell his wife if we went on the boat, "Oh she gets jealous, you know how she is."

The next day was even worse than that night because at night I could have passed it off as drunk and inappropriate because we had been drinking a *lot*. And what, the next day when you sobered up, and you're still trying to—after that like I ignored him. I didn't interact much except when he comes up to me and I'm extremely fake. Noticeably fake. So it's never a question, if I'm being personal with you. He never said anything overtly but behind the scenes, he's fucked me over a couple times.

She describes coworkers telling her about a closed meeting where he changed her position and cut her pay. She got demoted and was making 30 percent less than her male coworkers who did the same job, and over whom she had several years' seniority. I observed that the retaliation of her boss was against the law.

Q: That's illegal.

Yeah well, I didn't sue, did I?

(Olivia, *Music Industry*)

At that point in her life, she could not switch jobs, nor could she afford to be unemployed during a lawsuit.

In all of the interviews, the head of the company was the problem. Sometimes the company leader was himself the perpetrator. Other times, company leadership was either overly sexist or complicit in it. One participant discussed a former coworker who filed a complaint with HR. HR then asked the complainant, who was her superior, what the problem was. He said there was no problem and gave the woman enough stress to miscarry her child before firing her a few months later.

More Concerned with Other People's Feelings

A dynamic that emerged in the research was women remining silent because they were concerned for the feelings and comfort of other people. In some cases, it was family, other times it was other colleagues or the man who perpetrated the offense.

Did Not Want People to Feel Embarrassed

They looked embarrassed, on my behalf, and I didn't want them to feel embarrassed, so I pretended like that was just normal and, "Of course I can get coffee, and he could have asked any one of you, too, but I'll do it." So yeah, kind of embarrassed on my behalf I'd say. But they didn't say anything. They didn't step in or correct him or anything like that. Although they could have because—we both worked for them.

(Janni, *Transportation*)

He's Just Lonely

I remember one time being in Paris with my boss and we went to dinner. He said, "Come and we'll talk about this project." I mean, he's a billionaire so we went after hours, after the restaurant had closed and we had I think three bottles of wine. Very expensive wine. Talked throughout the meal and he kept getting closer and closer to me and he put his hand on my leg and started to make very suggestive comments.

I started rationalizing for him. "Oh he's so lonely and he hasn't seen his family. They're out of the country and he hasn't seen them in a month. He's just trying to make a friend. he's just sad, he's just drunk. I can console him because I'm that kind of person. People can talk to me. They want my opinion, and I'm just going to be there for him." But I knew inside it was not right. I knew that he should not have his hand on my leg.

I was probably twenty-four and drunk and with my boss and wanted to keep my job. I thought to myself, I know what I'm doing, this is not that big of a deal. He has his hand on my leg and not crossing any boundaries. Obviously I'm not interested.

(Mila, *Middle East Business Development*)

Mindful of the Power Imbalance

There's a different power dynamic with my clients than there is with my colleagues and so I kind of try differently. If I do call them out on the "baby girls" or the "gorgeous"' or whatever else that they come at me with, then they kind of they will shrink back a little bit because they're thinking, "Okay but this woman, she's going to hold my fate in her hands and I don't want to piss (her) off cause if she's mad I might go to prison."

. . . I don't want to be wielding that kind of power over a client. I don't want them to think that if they piss me off I'm going to sell them up the river because that's not the type of person I am, but it kind of helps that they think that because in that case I get a little bit more respect than I do from colleagues.

(Sarah, *Law*)

Would Have Been Embarrassing for Him

Because that would have been embarrassing for him. Partly I think it's just Swedish culture that you don't take conflict in the big room. You take it one to one. Also surprise shock. You don't think about it. When something like this happens, you don't know how to act. And did I misunderstand? Of course, I contributed because I acted as if it was normal. So if I didn't react negatively then why should they? That's what I think they thought.

(Allison, *Marketing*)

Feel Bad, and Hate Having to Correct

I hate having to correct people. In all honesty, there's a part of me that feels bad when I have to do that. Then I hate that I feel bad, that I have to correct someone who is in a professional relationship with me about how they address me. It's a layered thing because I know they shouldn't address me with such intimacy—but I feel bad about correcting them for it. Like that's somehow my fault.

(Lauren, *Professor*)

Nothing Would Be Done about It Anyway

Women remain silent because they think after their effort of reporting, nothing will be done and nothing will change.

The Path Is Traumatizing

I find that this is common with a lot of women, like you know, to kind of "come forth, do the right thing, take legal action," comes at like a really great personal cost. And it was so anxiety inducing I was like, I don't want to spend anymore of my life on this. Like him being fired, that's enough. And I can't traumatize myself further by going down this path and so it's, it's a horrible thing because then this continues to impact other people.

(Sophia, *Global Marketing*)

Get Gaslighted

When I do call them out, I usually get the gaslighting. "Man, what are you talking about? You're crazy, come on." Yeah, yeah. Yeah. "I'm sorry." They gaslight me and pretend that what I was perceiving is not actually—"Ah man's" and "Oh no, you know me, I would never do something like that." And "I don't mean it like that," or "You're being too sensitive." Blah blah blah with the gaslighting.

(Olivia, *Music Industry*)

Women Decide to Leave

They are being treated the way I was treated, not being respected. Being frustrated by it but moving on. "It's just not worth it. I'm just going to do my job and that's it." Not putting up a fight. That's another way of navigating through it. Just deciding you're going to accept it and not let it get to you, just do your job.

(Mara, *Politics*)

Nothing Will Happen

I'm sure somewhere in some HR guide about if your employee is feeling sexually harassed or something. Certainly not widely disseminated. Certainly not a priority like a training component for faculty or for students so it seems to be flippant, like it really doesn't matter that much. Like it's not gonna happen. You know we'll put some boilerplate shit on paper, possibly, and have some policy but we're not really going to actively take action on it.

(Lauren, *Professor*)

Everyone Else Was Laughing

It was a colleague of mine. . . . They were joking about her age and that she was quite pretty. And then she said . . . it's a Swedish saying—"Oh, I'm just going to swallow that one. . . . And then he was like, "Oh, so you like swallowing then?" Everyone was just laughing in the room. And no one stood up for her. . . . She told me, "You know I didn't realize at the time, but now I see that was so out of line." There are so many things that women have taken over the years . . . you haven't until a lot later realize, I didn't have to take this, this was completely out of line.

(Allison, *Marketing*)

They May Side with the Perpetrator

The other thing that I really just thought of is once we figured out who it was, this guy was like a, he was a pretty valued member of the team and a pretty high performer and I was kind of afraid that my boss might take a side or not want to lose him. I remember those feelings. I haven't thought about that in a long time, but this feeling like okay this person is clearly in the wrong but, you know if it came down to it . . . would someone choose him over me? Would they? I don't know.

(Sophia, *Music Industry*)

Executive Committee Makes Fun of Their Own Policy

On the executive, I was able to at least put forth some suggestions for sexual harassment training. They actually did finally start sexual harassment training. Then they joked about it at the executive committee meetings. They joked about it, just undermining its meaningfulness and necessity by diminishing it in crude jokes.

(Avery, *Pharmaceutical Marketing*)

He Doesn't Care, the Point Wouldn't Matter

I just let certain things go. I don't ever anticipate calling out somebody for their racial comment or their sexist comment, and that person have a complete *come to Jesus* moment:

"Oh you opened my eyes and I can see the error of my ways. I can't believe I think that way. Thank you let me go forward!" No, I don't see that happening.

(Isabella, *Law*)

Just Want It to Be Over

Sophia discusses a situation in a previous position in which she was stalked by a coworker:

It was pretty bad. It went on for a long time. I remember traveling. I had a trade show that I went to, and making sure that I didn't list my name. Then coming back to work and getting emails from this guy about how he had been there and been in my hotel room and rifled through my underwear. It really was designed to make me feel violated and unsafe wherever I was. I mean I really did, for months.

It was like an interesting balance of "Fuck you, I am not going to be pushed out of this." I worked hard for my job, I've worked hard to be here like, how dare you try to scare me off.

I could have tried to get the cops to take legal action—I can't remember the technicality of how it works but usually they're the ones who bring the cases before a judge. But my dad's a lawyer and informed me, "They usually take cases that they think are going to be successful." Even though we traced this guy's home IP address, he kicked up some fuss about how it wasn't his, like someone using his IP spoofed him, and it was this whole thing and he denied denied denied.

He's someone I worked with very closely. I hung out with him outside of work, I knew his wife. My day to day work involved this guy. And his wife emailed me afterwards and was like, "Oh, this was a misunderstanding. Please don't take legal action against my husband." . . . So it was just like the whole thing kind of kept going.

(Sophia, *Music Industry*)

Social Consequences

It's not just having the laws on your side or not, depending upon for whom you work. It's does your organization's culture allow you to pursue a formal complaint or not. Now, some women, you know, once encouraged, will come forward. But many women without encouragement, even if the law's on their side, will not come forward, because despite the law, they still fear the repercussions of filing a complaint and I understand that . . . it's going to take more targeted employees challenging that kind of behavior. Without a group of people backing them up to really affect change in terms of organizational culture, I think.

(Janni, *Transportation*)

Avoid Becoming the Stereotype

These women were fighting what is called 'stereotype threat.' In order to avoid becoming the stereotype, they act against their own self-interest.

Not Wanting to Be One of "Those Women"

I've never been in that atmosphere. I also didn't feel empowered to tell anybody, I felt maybe I was being overly sensitive. I'm an ambitious person, I always wanted to get ahead at work. I would have never tried to get ahead in any other way than the boardroom.

I always felt it would be looked at like a snitch, or like I was trying to get special treatment by complaining and being one of "those women" because at the time, I had this feeling that women who utilize these arguments against men or sexism are looking for a fast track to be promoted to stop any sexual harassment suit. Or were overly sensitive.

(Mila, *Business Development*)

Don't Want to Appear to Be "Overreacting"

Sarah refers here to the occasions when clients masturbate in meetings. Despite their behavior, she is careful not to seem like she is overreacting:

Immediately I want to withdraw. I want to recoil and leave the meeting, is really what I want to do, but . . . I try to remain professional in that moment. I don't over quote unquote "over react." It will be showing an overreaction, maybe other than just to say, "Listen, you need to stop that. Hands on the table. If you cannot keep your hands on the table then I'm going to end the meeting. I don't want you to get charged. Let's just end that."

In court also, I had a guy masturbate in court. I've had to stop them and (say) "Please don't do that."

(Sarah, *Law*)

Avoid Being the Angry Black Female

I try to meet it with grace. I'll say I'm the lead and they'll say, "Oh, I'm sorry." And I say it's okay, but we know it's not okay. This is ridiculous. But I never really, it's very rare that I actually challenge on it.

In part because I'm already a female. When females are assertive, they are thought to be a bitch or bossy or some negative term associated with female assertiveness. And I'm black, so I know if I say something, I'm immediately the angry black female. Somebody's going to describe this event and have my finger in the air, my neck rolling. That is not how I address anyone ever. Ever.

I'm trying so hard to buck against the stereotype, so I swallow things. Injustices and micro aggressions and all that. I shouldn't. But I take it because I just refused to be the stereotype that you think I'm going to be in this moment.

(Sarah, *Law*)

Always Making a Fuss

Frustration is the biggest feeling. It's very hard to change. You many times find yourself standing alone in this change. Pushing them, but still not becoming the hard person, the person that is perceived as—I don't know, rowdy—is that a good word? Always making a fuss, always bringing up these uncomfortable issues to the table, that are hard to bring up. When you do, you are risking your own position, you are risking your own relations. That's a very frustrating position to be in.

(Mara, *Culture and Politics*)

Angry, Hostile, Man-Hating Bitch

It was one of those situations where he was being persistent to the point that she got uncomfortable and reported it. But at the executive committee level, she was faulted for *enticing* his interest in her. Seducing him, by the way she looked and dressed, and spoke sweetly to him. Of course, if she did not speak sweetly to him, she would have been criticized for being another quote, "angry bitch." Or "hostile bitch" or "man-hating bitch" or whatever the term of the day. The attitude there was sort of the classic, you have to be both a mother and a seductress to be a good woman. But if you pull either role at the wrong time, you are punished for it.

(Avery, *Pharmaceutical Marketing*)

Did Not Know How to Handle It

Women talked about themselves and women they knew who, for different reasons, were unsure how to handle the situation. Some chose to wait, and others chose to abandon it.

Until There Comes a Tipping Point

I actually have a friend who's named in the Les Moonves resignation. I know she's getting pressured for tons of interviews, but all in all I think she was able to get through it a way that didn't affect her life too severely.

It's hard because I hear the male perspective of "Oh yeah, Me Too, it's gone too far blah blah blah. Why would she come forth so many years later?" I get that. I'm not saying I automatically believe every woman who comes forward with an allegation because people lie. But I understand why someone might wait, or why they might choose to until there's a circumstantial tipping point.

Like for me it was, "Oh my god, I learned that this person had done this so many times." And that led me to say something so many years later. For someone else, it might be they reached a level of profits or have an opportunity or someone puts them in a position of power that they probably shouldn't have, or whatever it is. I get there might be a tipping point later that makes them do it. That might damage their credibility in the eyes of people who don't understand or can't really relate to circumstances like this.

(Sophia, *Global Marketing*)

Don't See How Damaging While Immersed in It

You just don't realize how prevalent it is or how much it will affect you. Does affect you, and will affect your future, too, unless you're out of it. That's like everything else. Being deep in the trenches for so long, for so many years, I can only wish that I had been out of it and in a company where I am now. To have seen it for what it was, because I would never go back to that. I would never ever in a million years go back to that environment. I never knew anything outside of that environment. That for me is the biggest thing, that there are so many women who are in that role, who just put up with stuff and they don't know any better. I can't believe I was that person making excuses for someone over so many years.

(Mila, *Aviation*)

Unprepared to Respond

I think I would have felt okay because I was still okay saying it to his face. I think I was just—I mean the shock of having that thrown at me—I think it just took me back a little bit.

(Allison, *Politics*)

I'm Strong, I Can Handle It

I pride myself on being a strong, resourceful—the word that keeps coming to mind is a survivor mentality. "Okay, it's fine. It's not changing who I am. They can say what they want to say, I'm tough. It doesn't bother me, I'm so tough. It doesn't affect me. Let the boys be boys. It's not going to bother me." I don't think I considered reporting it. Now looking back, if I could advise myself, I would say, "Hey why don't you tell someone." My point before, it starts from the top is the real problem.

(Natalya, *Law*)

Feels Responsible for Being in That Position

Unaware that sexism is not their choice, some women felt self-blame. They thought they were responsible for putting themselves into a siltation where a man would sexualize them. This dynamic is a feeling that results from internalized oppression. Sexualizing a work colleague was the man's decision, and sexism thrives on the woman feeling responsible when she is not the one who enacted predatory behavior.

Company Owner Is the Perpetrator

In companies that have HR you can report to HR, but a lot of times, if you're working in a corporate environment or you're working where I've worked—huge companies but solely owned by a founder—they're the ones at the root of the problem.

I remember talking to my boyfriend about going to dinner with my boss and I think he had said, "Just the two of you went to dinner?" And I said, yeah of course. He said, "Isn't that a little weird? You were out to dinner just the two of you until 2 AM?"

And I got very defensive about it, and "Well yeah! Do you know who he is, how important he is? How important he is going to be for my career? Do you know the things we're working on?"

I think I knew throughout those years of working with this boss that I wasn't always entirely honest with my boyfriend at the time of certain things of the way I was treated or the way I was made to feel. He would have gone crazy. He probably would have gone there and beat my boss up. He also would have lost some respect for me and I didn't want him to do that. I thought I was on top of it, I thought I knew what I was doing.

(Rebecca, *Philanthropy*)

Ashamed to Be in That Position

For the most part I told no one, because I was ashamed to be honest. Ashamed to put myself in that position. Ashamed it had gotten so far down that road. Being my own worst critic there are so many times that—"I should have done this differently. I should have done that differently." It always came onto my own shoulders.

I also just thought, well there's no answer to this. A couple times I was advised by people around me who could see that I was struggling, and also people that I had worked with in the past, they could see that my credit cards were getting declined. They started saying "You need out. Whatever you're doing is wrong. Are you being compensated? How much is this guy paying you? It can't be enough."

Being told that you're on the wrong path when you have conviction that you're on the right path, I didn't want to involve anybody because I felt the more I talked to anyone the more they would say, you need to get out, you're doing the wrong thing. Whereas I felt strongly about sticking to my guns about building this company regardless of anything around me because I felt like I could handle it. And I also felt like I would be compensated in the end.

I really did not believe that I could get so screwed over, and I just kept my pedal to the metal on that. I have really strong girlfriends and really deep relationships but I never brought it up because it was always, "This guy's a chauvinist fucking asshole" basically. "He's such a pig, I don't know how you work with that guy." Or "Have you seen his Instagram page recently? He's slobbering on women all over. It's disgusting, how do you work with this guy?" So at that point there really wasn't too much that I could say.

(Mila, *Aviation*)

It's Just This Industry, Things Are Probably Better Somewhere Else

I mean that is, this is probably not a great attitude on my part but—I mean if it's directed at me then that's a different matter. But if it's just joking around about things that are not generally safe for work, that's something I know is part of the environment. I don't mind, and will kind of be complicit—and you're right I think it is a weird thing to say, like "Oh I'm working with musicians so therefore there shouldn't be any standards," but . . .

Q: People say the same thing about people of wealth, they say the same thing about creative people, about chefs. So, it's not just musicians. But this is something widely done, "Well, I work in this environment, so therefore I must accept X."

I don't feel like I must accept, but I do choose to accept.

Q: If you didn't, what would be the other choice?

I mean, I could go work in a different industry, right?

Q: Do you think it would be different?

Yeah maybe, yes and no. Like I think certain professions still probably are a little bit different. I mean look, I'm sure there is sexism everywhere, but in terms of a very loose casual culture where people are routinely talking about things that are fairly obscene and using profanity, I don't think you'll get that in most legal offices. Maybe I have some misperceptions here. I do think it's kind of a cop-out for me to say, "Oh yeah, it's just the way it is."

(Sophia, *International Marketing*)

I confirmed her misconceptions and told her about the interviews with women in the legal field. They are asked for sexual favors and are sexualized on a consistent basis. Sexism is not different somewhere else.

She says she *chooses* to accept, not that she *must* accept. That is a delusion of her having control.

Exposing Sexist Scripts and Thought Patterns

I. Consequences of Hurting a Man's Ego
   A. They Never Forget You Hurt Their Ego
   B. You Stand to Lose a Lot

    C.   Ruins Your Business Relationship

    D.   Nervous about Repercussions

    E.   Rejecting a Man Becomes a Problem for You

    F.   He Did It at His Own House

II.   More Concerned with Other People's Feelings

    A.   Did Not Want People to Feel Embarrassed

    B.   He's Just Lonely

    C.   Mindful of the Power imbalance

    D.   Would Have Been Embarrassing for Him

    E.   Feel Bad, and Hate, Having to Correct

III.   Nothing Would Be Done about It Anyway

    A.   The Path Is Traumatizing

    B.   Get Gaslighted

    C.   Women Decide to Leave

    D.   Nothing Will Happen

    E.   Everyone Else Was Laughing

    F.   They May Side with the Perpetrator

    G.   Executive Committee Makes Fun of Their Own Policy

    H.   He Doesn't Care, the Point Wouldn't Matter

    I.   Just Want It to Be Over

    J.   Social Consequences

IV. Avoid Becoming the Stereotype

    A.   Not Wanting to Be One of "Those Women"

    B.   Don't Want to Appear to Be "Overreacting"

    C.   Avoid Being the Angry Black Female

    D.   Always Making A Fuss

    E.   Angry Hostile Man-Hating Bitch

V.   Did Not Know How to Handle It

    A.   Until There Comes a Tipping Point

    B.   Don't See How Damaging While Immersed in It

    C.   Unprepared to Respond

    D.   I'm Strong, I Can Handle It

VI. Feels Responsible for Being in That Position
    A.   Company Owner Is the Perpetrator
    B.   Ashamed to Be in That Position
    C.   It's Just This Industry, Things Are Probably Better Somewhere Else

Analysis

Not Wanting to Make the Men Uncomfortable

Janni explained how her executive team has an outing every year. The tradition involved using a sauna, where everyone is together naked. Her story embodies many themes of this chapter, and is a strong illustration of the social pressure women feel.

> Every year we go away with the management team and I am the only woman in the management team nowadays. We stay overnight and there is also a sauna. It got said when I came into the management team "the sauna is mandatory because we continue the meeting down there by the lake" and "Oh it's so special, we get to drink wine and beers and it's so fun and every-body takes their clothes off to go into the sauna and go swim." I'm like "I do not want to take my clothes off in front of you." Again, because I have my armor and I don't want to get naked or even half naked with my male colleagues. This is something that I haven't spoke up about. If I did speak up about it, I know that my managing director would feel really embarrassed. He would think, "oh my god, I didn't even think about that." But I just get around it. I keep my clothes on and I sit in the relax room outside and there are always a few other people who don't want to go into the sauna, so they don't want to take their clothes off either. So I haven't had to deal with it up front but it's something I'm avoiding to do, because I don't want them to feel embarrassed. I also don't want them to stop their fun tradition of being in the sauna together because they're fine with it. I put it on myself. Even though if I stand aside and look at it I think they should just realize that I'm the only woman, I'm twenty years younger than the rest of the guys. I'm not comfortable in that situation. They should think of that. But they don't.

Q: What would be the consequence of you speaking up about that? (Laughing) Because that's what we're talking about.

> (Also laughs) The consequence if I spoke up about it would probably be that they would keep going with their tradition. At worst because I can sit in the relax room while they're in the sauna. We never get much work done anyway because we start drinking wine and it's all fun and play. But they

would be a little more uncomfortable knowing so I take that uncomfortableness and put it all on me and then I package it and put it away somewhere inside me and ignore it. So the consequence would be that they would be uncomfortable and I wouldn't want to put them in that position. I can carry it! (Laughing) It's funny you ask. I never thought about it.

Q: Do you mind—it's a parallel to what you said about the situation that was 20 years prior—about you and the coffee. (I am referencing her earlier story this chapter about being asked to fetch coffee in front of the board of directors.) And you took that situation as well, because you didn't want your male colleagues to be embarrassed.

Yeah, exactly. You are so right. I haven't thought about it. (Laughs again)

Q: So your male colleagues sound very friendly, like they're happy that you're there, they actually enjoy you, and that you are invited—so while it seems really absurd that you have to say I don't wish to be naked around you because that's—

—Yeah!—

Q:—Crazy shit! You shouldn't have to say that—

I know!—

Q:—We're in these weird positions of like "Are you serious?"

So right. (Both laughing)

Q: Your people are nice, and they invite you. But then other situations, they do carry on the business in those closed spaces and that's where the relationships are. So that's where your opportunities for advancement are. In these spaces that you just don't want to go. For good reason.

And it also depends on the company. We are a big company and we go away only once a year as a management team. The rest of the year we're office hours and no play, no fun. Never a golf tournament on company time. It's just work work work and meetings and everything. So it's also a bit about the company culture. I think if you have other companies where you have to interact with customers or clients, it can be even more obvious the kinds of situations and places that are chosen for these customer meetings or client meetings. I guess also it's about the kind of business I'm in.

Q: May I—may I ask you one more time?

Sure.

Q: Why do you swallow it? Why don't you say something?

I deal with things in proportion. Principled proportion. That is, I weigh things. How important is it for me to change this situation and how important is it for them not to change it? And in this case, I know them. I don't even have to wonder if they speak about me when I'm not there. I don't suspect any of that. I feel completely safe in this environment with this group, and I know that they mean one hundred percent well. So for me to gain—it's unnecessary because it wouldn't help or destroy me in my career or as a person. It would be a feminist statement, which is important. I think if we had one more woman in the management team, then I would do it because then I'd be doing it for someone else. But for me, it's just not worth it. Why should I put them in an uncomfortable situation when it's not that bad for me? It would be worse for them to know than it would be for me to bear it myself.

Conclusion

The Silence of Shame

Another line of thinking is that we don't fail to report sexism from colleagues because we feel guilt over drinking, being at the wrong place, or because we do not want to cause other people distress. We sometimes fail to speak up because we understand that their sexism signals that to them, we are not worthy to be in their presence. We are not worthy to be in their circles of dignity, respect, collegiality, or psychological, emotional, and social equality. We feel guilt when *we make* a mistake. But we feel shame when *we are* a mistake, when our very existence is a false echo of something wonderful that others are but we are not. Imagine in this scenario, speaking up and nobody cared. Saying explicitly that,you felt excluded and having people you thought respected you show they do not actually respect you.

Throughout her interview, this woman emphasized the need to make their 7,000-person multicultural organization as inclusive as possible, and it was part of their core values to do so. She cited language, food, events, and several other ways that people can feel either included or excluded. She said many times how important it was for the company. Yet she felt excluded by the leadership team and had no confidence that anything would be done differently if she told them, by their own standards, that she was being excluded. In a sense, if she does not ask, the team cannot reject her. As long as it is not a definitive no, the answer might still be yes, they do respect her enough to include her. She can maintain a semblance of control in her situation by not asking, and not receiving confirmation one way or the other. In our own lives, as men and women we have the decision to behave in a way that communicates our values. Sometimes we shy away from the real questions we fear being answered.

Creating New Scripts and Thought Patterns

- How might reporting sexism affect your life?
- What do you consider a supportive response?
    - How would you know whether you were being supported or not?
- In the context of sexism, what overlap is there between your personal and private life?
    - What would be the responses of the people around you?
    - How does your partner react?
    - What would be the personal implications if your partner did not support you?
- What would it mean to you if your colleagues did not support you?
    - Do you feel like they would?
    - What makes you think so?

CHAPTER SIX

The Role of Pornography

"Don't lie, during whatever sports you are watching, there's a halftime. That's porn time."

—Forbes article, (Silver, 2018)

Introduction

Executive sexism is behavior that occurs among high-achieving professional men, and these men live in a sexualized social environment. Interviewees who network, entertain clients, travel, and conduct work out of an office all mentioned the prevalence of strip clubs in professional life. Women who only work in executive offices discussed how, at the office and in executive meetings, graphic videos and images are passed among men on a regular basis.

Typically, studies and news stories about sexism may mention the highly sexualized social context in which this sexist behavior is taught, learned, and nurtured, but fail to take it seriously, but we should. This chapter provides accounts of those situations, further demonstrating the hazy line that exists between professional and personal life. Before delving into those, we will take a closer look at pornography and its effects on sexism, rape, and bystander intervention.

Leaving Women to Buy Women: Strip Bars

Here women talked about when their male colleagues intentionally split off to go to strip bars or male-only venues.

Male-Only Invitation

There are actually a few gentlemen's clubs that are not strip clubs in London, so choosing specifically those clubs are male only. Strip clubs as well. Meeting at a strip club to talk business. I suppose a woman could go but given the fact that a woman would not want to go and *this* woman did not want to go, it definitely was a male-only invitation. Like "so-and-so is in town and he wants to talk at this upscale gentleman's club where women take their clothes off so we're going to go there."

(Mila, *Aviation*)

Strip Club as Soon as the Woman Is Gone

It's not uncommon for guys going out with solicitors ending up in a strip bar. What the hell am I going to do in a strip bar? There's a feeling that obviously the minute a woman's not there they can go off and do whatever they want to do, go to a casino, go to a strip bar.

(Isabella, *Law*)

One issue is exclusion and the exercise of dismissing a woman. To the woman this is a message the she only has a place as long as men let her have a place. A second issue here is that you are talking to male colleagues and their next move is to go watch a large room of naked women dance on poles and pay women for attention in time increments of 10–15 minutes. Or pay a higher amount and be alone in a room with a naked woman.

Men are thinking about that while in the presence of their female colleague and transition their night to renting a women's sexuality. The naturalness of this dynamic is better contextualized through the startlingly pervasive use of pornography.

Pornography Consumption

The numbers are astounding. *Forbes* magazine published an article entitled "Pornhub 2017 Year in Review Insights Report Reveals Statistical Proof We Love Porn" (Silver, 2018). The author cites research from the website PornHub.com about statistics from 20 countries, including the United States, United Kingdom, India, France, Russia, Canada, Germany, Brazil, and Japan. Fifty thousand searches per minute, 800 searches *per second*, was the average for PornHub.com consumption in 2017, averaging 81 million viewers per day (Silver, 2018; Pornhub.com, 2018).

The United States ranked first in the world for consumption, and 76 percent of searches were conducted on portable devices, 67 percent on phones (Silver, 2018; Pornhub, 2018). Every five minutes, Pornhub claims to transmit data in excess of the "entire contents of the New York Public Library's 50 million books" (Silver, 2018). Fifty million books' worth of pornography every five minutes.

Silver writes, "It's impossible to ignore" such notable statistics, and he is right. We certainly must not ignore those statistics, since boys 11–12 years of age begin watching pornography. When young boys look up pornography on the Internet, what they find look more like torture scenes; gagging, choking, and other forms of abuse (Dines, 2010). Twelve years of age is also when boys begin sexualizing the girls around them (American Psychological Association, 2007). Just a few years later, by college, heightened exposure to violent pornography increases the likelihood that men will commit rape and decreases the chances that they will intervene to stop rape (Foubert, Brosi, and Bannon, 2011).

In this work we are discussing sexism but consider the impact of men who are socially conditioned to perpetrate and validate violence against women. Do you imagine they would think twice about how they speak to you, or whether they discriminate against women at work or in an interview? Or speak crudely or sexualize women at a networking event? It would be foolish to expect differently. Understanding this mindset and its implications are essential to understanding sexism, especially when so many women have men feeling free to sexualize them in a work space. The following entry demonstrates that the process of sexualizing is a script that men use. Women reported it nearly verbatim.

The Script: Process Men Use to Sexualize Women at Work

Mila describes a dynamic that occurred so often and so consistently that she could name the steps of how men approached her at work and attempted to sexualize the relationship.

1. **Inquiry Made about Sexual Relationships in Your Personal Life.** Usually it starts with the "oh your boyfriend must be home waiting, or your husband." Kind of slide it in there and try to figure it out, "I'm not taking this social too quickly."

   Next, they ask her about other men, and whether she is single.

2. **Questions and Suggestions about Sexual Relationships at Work.** "Oh well, any office romances going on or anything else happening?" When that part is out of the way, "Oh you're not banging the boss kind of scenario?"

3. **He Makes a Vulgar Sexual Proposition.** The next kind of questions in there, subtle or not, would be quite vulgar or graphic. I felt like it was always,

"Oh sorry, I'm drinking too much. Never mind me, forget what I just said.'" Because then it just devolves into this final push of some kind. "I'm gonna just throw it all out there and see how she reacts," once they realize they've gone too far.

4. **Then Makes It Your Fault the Conversation Turned Sexual**. Then they kind of recoil and make it feel like you were the one who lowered it to that line of thinking or that place and twisting it around. I remember every time I've been in this position thinking about how this strategy must have been used on so many different women and wondering if the wives knew. It must have worked in the past because otherwise they wouldn't keep trying with new blood.

An example of a cultural script, this very recognizable formula of sexualizing work situations makes evident that men shape culture together. Other participants discussed these dynamics, and said men also talked about their wives and children while simultaneously making sexual advances.

"We at Pure Filth know exactly what you want. Chicks being ass f**ed till their sphincters are pink, puffy, and totally blown out. Adult diapers might just be in store for these whores when their work is done."
—Promotional copy for video *Anally Ripped Whores*
(TED Talks, 2015)

Pornography and Sexism

Gail Dines, author of *Pornland: How Porn Has Hijacked Our Sexuality*, makes the valid point that we must use the language of the industry to understand the ethos of the industry (Dines, 2010). In the field of conflict resolution, we also use industry-specific language when examining an organization or industry, for exactly the same reason. In the social sciences, this is narrative analysis. While graphic and violent, use of this exact promotional copy is necessary to set the stage.

A debate exists among the academic community, the political realm, and the pornography industry as to whether pornography influences attitudes and behaviors. Men consume images and videos of women being degraded and sexually abusing women, while calling them whores, cum-guzzling sluts, and so forth, and they sexualize every imaginable scenario—from boss/employee to father/daughter (Dines, 2010; TED Talks, 2015). Every five minutes, this material is consumed in the same volume as the entirety of the New York Public Library. Some discussions are purely absurd. I await the day when credible material disproving that link passes peer review.

Pimping Out Female Colleagues

Isabella describes a dynamic in her professional circles. Essentially men arrange drinks for women, under the guise that the women are receiving a professional introduction. In fact, the men setting it up and the men hosting the drink are intentionally deceiving the woman. She is meant to be the entertainment and possibly a sexual exploit.

> I heard of and saw situations where female barristers were almost being marketed by older people in chambers with good contacts with solicitors as being, almost being pimped. So "She's a really good-looking girl, she's also this and that, but she's also a really good-looking girl. I'll invite her round for a drink." That is obviously horrendous.

Q: Just to clarify, was that to get her business or was that to get—

—No, that was to get—what was happening was the elder person in the set had a good contact with the solicitor and wanted to maintain the good contact with the solicitor and was obviously taking them all out for drinks and the rest of it. A part of the good contact with the solicitor, he was saying, "Look, there's a really good-looking girl in my chambers, why don't I arrange a drink." The female barrister would be told, "There's a really good contact I think you should meet. He's a really great solicitor, he gives me great work."

So it was being sold to the female barristers, "This is a great contact, why don't you join us for a drink." And it was being sold to the solicitors, "She's a really good-looking girl and I think she likes a good time." With the idea that the person in the middle will get the currency from the solicitor of getting exposure to a good-looking girl and then who knows what may flow from that.

Q: So the girl is the currency; she's to get nothing from it?

Yes. What she thinks she's getting is an introduction to a great solicitor, who she thinks, "If I go out for drinks with him maybe he'll give me work" . . . But what's really happening is that she's being used, in the best-case scenario eye candy for the solicitor. And in the worst-case scenario maybe see how she does after a few drinks, who knows what may happen.

Q: How does that affect her career?

Well it gets out. If she does anything with the solicitor, it gets out that she puts out. Then that's the thing—the only reason she got that case is because she's flirting outrageously with the solicitor . . . (The idea is) That's how she gets the work. Of course, the person who is responsible for that information is the very point of contact who put them together.

Q: How can you tell the difference between a solid introduction for work versus a superficial introduction because you are a commodity?

That's a good question. Experience. What I did is, I stopped going for drinks after work. I stopped doing it because I was no longer sure why I was really there.

Women often find themselves in this situation: although you are a professional, men treat you as a commodity. Among the women interviewed, almost all of them mentioned in some way how groups of men behave as if the woman is their entertainment. Women see themselves as professional and know they are worthy of being heard and deserving of work., Yet the message continuously received from sexist men is that women are interchangeable. Also that they are there at the man's will, as a thing to amuse him. You are invited and go under the guise of a lie, that professional benefit might result.

Increased Pornography Means Diminished Effect on Bystander Intervention

A study about bystander intervention in sexual assault sought to understand which elements men and women considered when deciding whether to intervene. What researchers found is akin to what we are discussing: Bystander intervention depended on factors such as women's experiences, and how they understood misogyny and sexism. That is, how much men and women buy into the notion that women contribute to sexual assault. The role of alcohol was a factor in perceived responsibility in sexual conduct and bystander intervention, and participants were not clear on the lines of consent and entitlement. They believed "the myth that rape is falsely reported" and were hesitant to get in the way of someone's "good time" (DeMaria, et al, 2018). All of these factors strongly mirror the reasons women remain silent about sexism. In the context of cultural participation, men are honing their dominance.

These are college age-men with a permissiveness toward violence against women, an increased likelihood to commit rape, and a low chance of intervening if they witnessed a sexual assault occurring. This is our upcoming workforce. Following are examples of how a sexualized culture permeates the professional space. To men, you also happen to be a professional, but you are foremost a commodity for them to enjoy.

Men Using Women as Entertainment

Women often mentioned about being single and considered "fair game." You are never just going to work; their sex life is always of interest and considered a suitable topic of conversation.

They'll Like You

That's kind of a big one of "Oh they'll like you. Great, I'm so glad you're coming." Because I'm going to put on a dress and I'm going to charm the men. "This is going to be so good that you're here. It's going to be all men but so-and-so is single . . . everyone's going to go out and it will be great." Or, "You're easy to look at." Yeah, definitely it's always been part of conversation.

(Rebecca, *Philanthropy*)

Several women discussed being the entertainment for men in a professional setting:

You Are the Entertainment

Male solicitors would be taking colleagues out for drinks. Those colleagues would all be male, you would be the only female. There was a definite atmosphere where this was somewhere—you were almost the entertainment. Know what I mean? That you are the female here amongst a group of guys who are all wanting to have a good drink.

(Isabella, *Law*)

You'll Change the Dynamics

I have been at business dinners throughout my career whereby the fact that I am there is going to change dynamics and it's been discussed. It's always been discussed, but always in advance, in terms of is it appropriate for me to be at that dinner. Over time I have even felt that. Is it appropriate for me to be at that dinner? How is it going to change the dynamic if I'm there and the only woman?

(Mila, *Middle East Business Development*)

Sexualizing the Sales Process

There was a lot of sexual activity within the sales operation. It was a sales-driven corporation. They're often in the field and the CEO would often meet up with a sales rep in various parts of the country to try to close a big deal. There were lots of opportunity to be alone in the field with either the CEO or one of the other sales executives and a sales rep. And they tended to hire more female sales reps who were very attractive. So they could sexualize the sales process.

As in other industries, women are isolated and sexualized by men who hold power over their job.

So, not only in an organization do you have just this permissive attitude for sexual harassment to occur'; when you intentionally hire women perceived to be physically and sexually attractive and alluring, in order to sell more, you're setting that female employee up as a target for harassment from either other employees or from their potential customers. I don't think that's unique in the world of sales.

(Avery, *Pharmaceutical Marketing*)

A key point she makes here regarding sexism and harassment—if your job is to be sexually appealing, and then customers sexualize you, what would you expect your company or the law to do to assist you? This is an example of structural/systemic sexism, how a woman is situated and facing situations that a man does not face. It is also a perfect example of how male privilege expresses itself. Men would never find themselves in a position like that.

Social Dominance Orientation

Elsewhere in this work we discuss how the internalization of culture affects women. Here we examine the use of pornography and how it affects men when it comes to bystander intervention in sexual assault. The use of violent and degrading pornography is linked to a cultural acceptance of violence toward women.

Increased use of violent and degrading pornography decreased a willingness and intent to intervene in sexual assault. Further, participants demonstrated higher attitudes of permissiveness of violence against women. These are all traits of a high orientation to social dominance (Sidanius and Pratto, 1999; Barak, 2003; Bem, 1993; Foubert and Bridges, 2017; DeMaria et al., 2018; French, 1992).

Sexual References and Graphic Images of Women

Sexual References to Make a Business Point

Men together in the workplace. I know there's been a lot of discussion about how far it can go for men to be able to speak freely, make jokes. I've been in so many different scenarios where men say highly inappropriate phrases in a business environment that they think is getting their message across. Things that unfortunately I can't even say in an interview, but the way they do it, they say sexual phrases and then they look at me and "oh sorry." Right, like "Oh there's a lady present." But I can see when men kind of joking and getting sexual and they kind of get to that point and they're playing off it.

(Lauren, *Nonprofit Board Member*)

Permissive Environment Builds on Itself

If it's letting aviators speak about women in certain terms or seeing a photo of a woman and sharing it or sharing video in the workplace in your off time. This one came up—a video of a woman collecting ping pong balls in her boobs, because there's a guy hitting a ping pong and it's landing in her cleavage, and they're sharing that around the office. Then you're going to get more of that environment. And you know, if you're a woman there, they've been staring at a woman on their phones and sharing videos. I remember having a work group chat on WhatsApp and a colleague sent a graphic naked video of a woman and then had to say, "Sorry, I sent it to the wrong chat group." How do you become just another person in the workplace, especially if you're one of the few women and trying to fight for respect when that's what is being shared?

(Mila, *Aviation*)

Passing Sexual Images

It wasn't, it wasn't a universal attitude, but it came from the CEO and at least two of the other men on the committee. It was a small committee, we just think about six or seven, I guess, three or four of the men on the committee participated with the CEO. I remember this specifically, they were sharing some kind of a supposedly humor post or something, sharing it around from Blackberry. And I didn't get it. I said, "What are you all looking at?" Because they were all looking at it and hooting kind of thing and no one would tell me and the CEO just told me to bug off essentially, and stop asking. So I went to the two men with whom I was more aligned after the fact and said, "What was that?" And he said, "I deleted it. It was disgusting." It was a sexual joke with a visual about a woman's crotch. So it was being passed around the committee meeting with only one woman on the committee.

(Avery, *Pharmaceutical Marketing*)

Female Vantage Point of Men Sexualizing Them

Feels Like You Are Sitting Undressed

I definitely have been in that position quite a lot when men are speaking very sexually in the workplace. Especially if you're the only woman there, naturally all the men look to you to see your reaction and it feels very much like you're sitting undressed at a table, regardless of what you're wearing. When the conversation turns sexual and you're the only woman, it is really uncomfortable. And I've been there many times. I've felt very defensive and embarrassed and I've felt very exposed. A feeling that you're sitting at a boardroom table and all of a sudden, all the men are undressing you with their eyes because it's gone to a sexual place and their minds are in a sexual place, and you're a woman there so they are looking at you in a different way.

(Rebecca, *Politics and Private Practice*)

Business Potential, or Just Guys Having Drinks?

There are a lot of normal reactions, kicking aside any of the implications of "well I don't really want to go to that dinner, I'm happy to go home and get some sleep." Or "I don't want to be the only woman there, I don't want to deal with that" or "I don't want to go out tonight and I have a feeling it's going to end up in that kind of environment" or "I don't see any business potential here coming from me, I think it's going to be a bunch of dudes having drinks." Or "Maybe I'm going to charm them because I'm actually a really nice charming person and I get along with a lot of people. What does that have to do with me being a woman?" They can be bros, but what's hold back for me actually furthering a business relationship by me being there? There's of course a lot of client entertaining and also partnerships that are developed by strengthening relationships. Sometimes you need to go to dinner and not talk business. But I think there always has been for me—you know I do consider it before I accept the invitation.

(Julia, *Global Marketing*)

A Woman Will Never Be One of the Guys

There was very much a time when I remember thinking "I'm one of the guys, I don't care." You know, "I don't speak that way but it doesn't make a difference to me." But what I notice when I have that kind of exterior, the conversation become this whole talking about degrading women. When I was in that mode I kind of turned a blind eye to it. I wouldn't laugh and I wouldn't join in, of course, but I kind of went "Oh boys will be boys." Now I am very like, "That's inappropriate, doesn't belong in the workplace. Mind your manners." It doesn't matter if there's a woman present or if it's just men present, it doesn't belong in a workplace.

(Emma, *Casting*)

Will Never Be Uncovered in Front of Colleagues

I've been in that environment too, on work trips where colleagues have gotten into bathing suits in travel around the world. And I never will because of these experiences. I just will not do it, I will not be in a bikini in front of any colleagues, whether I'm in Monaco or Nice or Cyprus or anywhere else. Because I can see that change. I can see that sexualization and objectification of me. And I am highly sensitive to it, but it has been that kind of feeling when things take that kind of turn.

Q: Right, because how do you transition from a girl in a bikini back to a colleague again?

Yes, exactly. Part of that comes from listening to these men when we are in the workplace when they're very male dominated and they're not checking their language amongst each other and I do think a lot of this has to do with the corporate culture trickling down. It starts at the top with what the person at the top allows or treasures or holds in higher regard than other things.

(Olivia, *Music Industry*)

The Overlap of Sex and Business, and Why Women Pay Again

This section discusses women who had to leave their job or risk material consequences because of men overlapping sex and business.

Public Image

"I know you are sexual—have been sexually active with your employees in the past, and this company's public image is based on integrity. So I need you to confirm that you're no longer fucking your staff before we run this campaign."

We started a new advertising campaign that featured him as the face of the company. Because he was very popular in his industry, or very threatening to people in other organizations who we actually wanted him to be threatening to. So we made him the face of the corporation and this ad campaign. But before, when I first broached the concept with him, and I had a private meeting with him. . . . We did talk like that to each other. . . . That was when I was still fairly new there. And he laughed and said, "No, no, no, I'm an adult now. I gave that up."

Well, two years later, and clearly well into this campaign, I learned from one of his other sales executives that he was still boinking one of the sales reps and had actually set her up in a household near the corporate headquarters. Egads.

I came up with a new campaign and I had a private meeting with him. And I said, "We're killing this campaign because you lied to me. So now we're going to focus on this other aspect for the next two years." And it really pissed him off. But he also had a little boy guilty thing happening. But that was probably the death nail, *the* death nail, of our relationship. And it just went downhill from there.

(Avery, Pharmaceutical Marketing)

She Stands to Lose the Client

This woman describes a typical situation that involves female nudity and lying to other women, situations in which male attorneys and clients regularly share as relationship building. Because she does not wish to be a part of it, this woman is excluded and risks losing her clients to men, simply because they are men:

> Excluded from sporting events. Definitely dinners, because they get absolutely shit faced in those dinners and they know I don't do that in client settings, so I don't get invited to that. Going out. When you're doing a deal abroad, people are going out all the time, you know, they go to strip clubs and do all this kind of things and I don't get invited. Usually I'm the only woman there. I guess they don't want my judgment.
>
> I don't really love the idea of come and have dinner with me and my wife, and then go to a club with me and my girlfriend. . . . I actually think some of those clients wish I wasn't a woman because then they could really show me a good time. . . .
>
> I think that it goes to my point, if I was a guy I think I would have better relationships with certain clients. Or I would have more repeat (business) from him, from them. Purely because I'm good at what I do, not because I'm their buddy.
>
> Well I think I have to work twice as hard. The reason I would take a male colleague is because I would like to have skin in the game. I want to have somebody who my client feels they can engage with and who's one of the boys. But at the same time you have to be really careful because you don't want that—the boys, he's still my subordinate, you know what I mean. So me, who's the boss, I feel like I'm constantly having to establish my authority or my thinking . . . you always feel uncertain and you always feel like you always have to read the situation battle and make it up as you go along.
>
> (Natalya, Law)

She stands to suffer material consequences (loss of the client) due to not participating in adultery and strip clubs, activities in which women are undermined and commodified.

She Leaves Her Job

He did not appreciate strong females who challenged him. And again, he had some very challenge-worthy behaviors both you know, intimate interpersonal behaviors and corporate behaviors. He, we, ran an advertising campaign on the integrity of our distribution system. Yet he would take back specialty pharmaceutical products that had been left out in the sun and recycle them into the distribution channel, claiming that they never did that. So there were some really unethical things going on, as well as inappropriate interactions with female staff.

So it just wasn't a place I wanted to be anymore, where I could not affect the changes to protect staff from those kinds of behaviors. And I certainly couldn't protect our clients. I mean, I battled, I did bloody battle over the recycling products that had not been properly refrigerated back into the distribution system.

And that was another strike against me. I mean, I vividly recall saying, "This is just not right." And again, being yelled at in front of the rest of the executive committee that, "This is right, because it's good business, it's a good business decision." . . . It was probably, you know, a couple hundred thousand dollars' worth of product because the products we distributed were very special, very expensive pharmaceutical products.

So anyway, so I knew they would let me go, because the stage was already set for a Parting of the Ways and I knew because we had been through several sexual inappropriate sexual behavior issues on the executive committee, you know, happening at lower levels of the organization. Because of the way the people had responded to that, I knew that my concerns about the other female employees and how this VP was treating them would not be taken seriously. And I would be the angry bitch, and then that would be the thing that we boot me out the door. But because they were asking me to leave, I would get booted out the door with my final bonus.

(Avery, *Pharmaceutical Marketing*)

Exposing Sexist Scripts and Thought Patterns

I.   The Script: Process Men Use to Sexualize Women at Work
   A.   Inquiry Made about Sexual Relationships in Your Personal Life
   B.   Questions and Suggestions about Sexual Relationships at Work
   C.   He Makes a Vulgar Sexual Proposition
   D.   Then Makes It Your Fault the Conversation Turned Sexual
   E.   Pornography and Sexism

II.   Pimping Out Female Colleagues
   A.   Increased Pornography Means Diminished Effect on Bystander Intervention

III. Men Using Women as Entertainment
    A. They'll Like You
    B. You Are the Entertainment
    C. You'll Change the Dynamics
    D. Sexualizing the Sales Process

IV. Sexual References and Graphic Images of Women
    A. Sexual References to Make a Business Point
    B. Permissive Environment Builds on Itself
    C. Passing Sexual Images

V. Female Vantage Point of Men Sexualizing Them
    A. Feels Like You Are Sitting Undressed
    B. Business Potential, or Just Guys Having Drinks?
    C. A Woman Will Never Be One of the Guys
    D. Will Never Be Uncovered in Front of Colleagues

VI. The Overlap of Sex and Business, and Why Women Pay Again
    A. Public Image
    B. She Stands to Lose the Client
    C. She Leaves Her Job

Analysis

Sexual Possession in a Relationship

Establishment of the Business Relationship

Mila describes her introduction to a new project and work colleague:

> The founder of this aviation company asked me to have a look at his company and see if there is anything that I could add or contribute to his company. I identified an opportunity to start and build a new branch of this company in (city) and I brought the company over to (city) and opened the branch to the company.

The relationship began respectfully. She talked about deliberately setting equal status with him, so she was not his subordinate. She worked *with* him, not *for* him. Verbally he acknowledged her expertise in meetings and referred to her as his business partner.

Initially, probably the first place that I saw sexism for me—and this is within and outside of the boardroom—because the founder is probably 5'4" and fifty-five and quite rotund, and I'm about 5'8" and at the time was in my mid-thirties, the first question was, "Oh you guys are business partners. So does that mean you're married?" You know, "You must be sleeping together as well."

Perceived as Being Coupled with Her Boss

I would go to a business meeting and people would say, "Oh so you brought your wife." Or we would step out of a cab together to go to an event and it would be, "Oh that's so nice you have a new girlfriend." Constantly pairing us together as a couple. And of course, rather than it being the other way around, it was that this older guy had brought his younger girlfriend . . .

In the ultra-high net worth individual (UHNWI) space, a very regular dynamic is wealthy men have young, attractive women. The men are much older, sometimes *much* older, and the couples are quite conspicuous. This speaker works in private aviation, so she is describing the perception of her having that type of relationship with colleague. For a professional woman, this is beyond humiliating. I have operated in those circles for years. As an attractive woman, the assumption made about you is that you are materially benefiting from the relationship with the older, unattractive man. Wife is a polite assumption; "girlfriend" is a euphemism for escort. In any case, an attractive woman is the equivalent of a talking accessory. This is the social dynamic she is dealing with, and the problem is hers alone.

Like She Was Not an Independent Entity

Rather than it being my business, they would always say, "And what do you do?" And I would say, "We work together." It was looked at like I didn't have a job and I was in a supportive role. Even in places that were having cocktails or business events. . . . Conferences, outreach, events, and with clients. That really struck me and I felt really embarrassed. I always had to defend myself that I did not have a relationship with this man.

The repetitive assumptions of lower professional status makes her appear inferior in the business relationship. It negatively impacts her ability to network, since she has to spend time dispelling assumptions rather than talking business. It also becomes personally embarrassing because this is not a man she would choose to be with, and yet she has to be polite and delicate about it. For the man it is completely the opposite. He gets the dual benefit of professional status and the social status of having an attractive girlfriend.

He Enhanced the Perception That They Were a Couple, Which Only Affected Her

Now this is also compounded by the fact that he was a very handsy person. . . . What I noticed over time is when we had had a couple of drinks was that the founder would end up putting his arm around my waist, or shepherd me through doors, or in a group he would try to order for me and things like that. So this was not helping the appearance that there was a relationship. I started getting more and more defensive. I would have to say, "You do not touch me," several times and he would be a bit drunk and smile and wave it off. And I could see that the attitude from him was like, "Frigid bitch, it's not that big of a deal, I'm just putting my hand around my friend." I would say, "We work together, and this is giving the wrong idea."

This portion demonstrates his entitlement to have his hands on another person, as well as a blatant disregard for respecting boundaries. One can only repeat so many times the desire not to be touched and remain calm while you are repeatedly violated. The request should have to be made zero times, because they had a business relationship, not an intimate relationship. From the conventional point of view of what "frigid bitches" say in these situations, she would be the one considered out of line for overreacting.

Feeling Like She Can Be Assertive and Preserve the Working Relationship

And I felt like that was an important thing to say, whereas now looking back, if a man puts his hand around me uninvited, I smack him. I don't know why I felt like I had to excuse myself by saying we work together. I was not interested on any level and I did not want to be touched, and it didn't matter that we were in a social environment. I can only imagine what it's like for women working. Like a concierge or on a yacht, or even more in the hospitality industry.

Here she refers to the entitlement of men to touch women in service positions, who are required to be polite to them. She references industries that cater to wealthy men, who are the subjects of this inquiry. Her comparison, like in other interviews, shows the pervasiveness of social expectations and attitudes. What men do and expect, and how women are conditioned to cater to men or lose their jobs. On the executive level, men do not suddenly abandon their social habits. Men who do not respect women demonstrate that by violating their boundaries.

He Also Had Ambiguous Boundaries in His Personal Life

I just really felt on guard with that scenario, very on guard working with someone who had divorced his wife but not divorced her—I guess they were separated. And sometimes he was living at home with his wife and kids and sometimes he wasn't. There were always other women around.

She was in the position of having her physical boundaries violated by a man she found physically sickening, who may or may not be married, and who touched her in public settings as if they were intimate partners. And the perception of her being in a relationship with him made it also look like she was participating in his adultery. Despite all of this, *she* also bore the responsibility, the gendered social expectation of remaining "polite" to maintain the business relationship.

Trying to Ignore a Sexist Environment

His boundaries with women and relationships were vague at best, but without question he was a man who commodifies women. She describes how his sexism infiltrated his business.

It was just a really womanizing environment. Now this didn't affect me as much in the beginning because I turned a blind eye to it, thinking "well what he does on his private time, he does on his private time. It doesn't involve me, we are working on business together. Of course, now being out of that environment I would never again work with somebody like that because I think it's a huge red flag. If they're womanizing, they don't respect women. And from my side, if somebody is cheating on their wife, I don't want to do business with them. I don't like what they stand for. I like working with people who are true to their word.

She Ceased Being of Use to Him

What I noticed is when I stopped going out to these social events and I stopped being a valuable plus one, I realized that the relationship changed quite a lot. And then I realized there was a lot of plus one happening, regardless of how much I was bringing in or what I was contributing to the company.

When he could no longer have her as a fake girlfriend, he tried utilizing her from a different approach.

Trying to Loan and Pimp Her as Entertainment for Other Men

My value being able to bring people in, based on something that he didn't have, and it very much became, "Why don't I send you to that meeting because they'll probably like you." And "You're single, right? I'm sure he's available. Maybe you can have a talk over eggs tomorrow morning" type of conversation. And that was something that I was very uncomfortable with.

If any question existed prior to this point, this man is clearly using her to sexualize the business process. A real estate developer I knew had escorts at his house, as a regular fixture, as entertainment for his male business associates. This may sound shocking if it is your first time hearing such a thing. But consider the wider context of men doing business in strip clubs, and women losing clients because they do not wish to be at places where men buy women. Consider the deliberate deception of leading women to believe a business opportunity was available to them when in fact they were being put into a position of drinking with men who were trying to get them to have sex; and on top of it, ruining her professional reputation if she did what they wanted her to do. Sex is regularly integrated into business settings as entertainment for men and at the expense of women.

She Tries to Continue with the Partnership by Distancing Herself

In the face of being used as a sexual pawn, she continues to attempt moving forward in the business relationship by distancing herself personally. She notes this was in the context of not understanding the entire picture.

And I think I started actually reacting becoming more and more closed off, by becoming more so than the first job. And I started becoming the bitch, to be honest. I started, "Hey let's get to the point here, let's just do business." I don't want to talk, I don't want to make friends, I don't want to smile at you from across the table. I just want to do my job and go home. I think that came from a placing concept that I didn't know was happening.

After the fact, she realizes that the conduct of her male colleague was meant to position her into a lesser position in the company (she refers to a "placing concept"). While it was happening, though, she did not realize his intentions to demean her.

Her Lack of Sexual Utility Translates into Material Losses, for Her

She describes here the process of coming to realize that he only saw her as a "play toy" and consequent to her lack of participating as such, she received pay cuts and was pushed out of projects.

On another side of things was the feeling around that I was having, I noticed there were men being brought into the company on a different level, that again, treated me with the little girl attitude. And I have to tell you, I checked myself along the way: "Is this something you're being overly sensitive about, is this happening, are you imagining this? Or is this the way things are?" I would talk to a few of my girlfriends because I was waking up to this whole environment.

Being Overlooked for Projects

It was about that time that I was being overlooked for certain projects, or even in regards to my pay, because of the fact that I was not respected. A lot of people from the outside would say to me, "Oh he's lost his play toy," and, "You've lost any kind of relevance within the company." And this is while I was doing everyone else's job and structuring things and building a business and all of these other things. I realized that that was the case.

Having Her Contributions Be Attributed to a Man

I would say something and as soon as a man said it, then he was the one who had said it. I really wish that I didn't think that any of this had to do with the fact that I was a woman, but knowing now the partner I was working with, the head of the company—now realizing how chauvinistic he was and how sexist and how he actually did use women. I feel like I lost a few years and being held back working with someone like that and I wish I had recognized it at the time.

Conclusion

This story illustrates the slow progression of what occurs when sexism is present in a working relationship. Regardless of her abilities, the woman is perceived as lesser status. The man can use her for any number of reasons. Here it was for social access to other men he could have as clients, social capital for having perceived sexual access to young attractive woman and using her contacts and expertise to set up his business.

On her end, she suffers from the low status of being personally affiliated with a man who was physically unattractive and morally objectionable to her, who was portraying that they were together. Relationally she suffered the professional repercussions of lower esteem among clients because she was assumed to be affiliated with him for a sexual relationship from which she was presumably benefitting financially.

She brought to the table global knowledge and contacts of demographic that are inaccessible to most of the world, ultra-high net worth individuals (UHNWIs). The material losses she suffered were the time she spent building a business for a man who used her expertise while never intending to pay her. In time and earnings she was set back four years. None of this is illegal.

Creating New Scripts and Thought Patterns

- How do you distinguish when someone has crossed the line at work when they incorporate sex in any way?
    - What is the line?
    - How do you recognize it?
    - What specific things are said or observed?
- What are some ways you can see to intervene, either during or after the fact?
- What could you do as a man?
    - How would you approach it?
    - Who would you talk to?
    - What would you say?
- What could you do as a woman?
    - How would you approach it?
    - Who would you talk to?
    - What would you say?
- What outcome are you trying to achieve?
    - What will that change?
    - Why will it matter?
    - What effect will that change have on the people it touches?

PART 2

Why Bystanders Don't Speak Up

CHAPTER SEVEN

Cultural Gaslighting: The Double Standard

Introduction

Impossible to Get It Right

I remember my boss saying to me, "My advice to you is, find your own professional personality, be yourself. It's really important, because you shouldn't try to be a man because you're a woman, and you're good at what you do, and you're good at what you do, partially because you are a woman."

To a woman, this advice reads like a quote from the Mad Hatter. He presents a puzzle to which there is no solution. Looking through a sexist frame, women are perceived as permanently in limbo, a state never assigned to men. Why?

For example, adhering to gender expectations of appearance does not make a man respect a woman. In fact, her attempt to positively manipulate her appearance is seen as a flaw. To him, looking sharp seems like she is overcompensating. The same goes for work performance, reputation, and advancement. No matter what she does, it is never quite enough.

The False Pretense of Assimilation

We have discussed SDO, that men rate high and women rate low. The dominant group will differentiate other groups and assign them negative and lesser characteristics, and groups internalize their level of importance relevant to others. This structure must be maintained to preserve the power of the dominant group.

The most effective nonviolent method for a dominant group to maintain its control is under the guise of assimilation. The dominant group (men) gives the pretense that members of the subordinated group (women) can be accepted, but only if women abandon their defining characteristics and take on characteristics of the dominant group (men). The dominant group will uphold an exceptional few to exemplify what success *could* look like for the women, if only they abandon their defining traits and become like men (Waller, 2002).

Social Gaslighting

While trying to fit into structures that do not fit, they are subjected to different rules. The dominant group refuses to acknowledge that women have different rules, thus denying women's reality. Following are examples shared by the women interviewed. They explain how women are subjected to rules that men are not expected to follow, especially when it comes to reputation, personal conduct, assertion, work performance. Gaslighting is used in this chapter as a framing concept because women are told we are all operating under the same rules, which is not the reality.

INTERNALIZED DOMINATION

"There is an absence of feeling that one has to prove oneself, or that one's status, talent, and qualifications would be questioned in any situation."
(Hardiman and Jackson, 1997, p. 21)

Bravado Is Rewarded, Her Quality Is Disregarded

Men communicate their internalized social dominance to one another. The next few sections show what that sounds like to a woman. Here Natalya discusses how men respond positively to another man's boasting. On the other hand, a competent woman is disregarded, and it is always attributed to a substandard characteristic she has.

Not That Good, But He Is Loud

Let's say that you have to be a certain personality type to go into law in the first place. It's not really a place for a shrinking violet. Men in particular blow their trumpets all the time. You and I would be like, "Oh my god just *shut up*! You're not actually that good. I had to redo everything that you've done."

Female associates in my experience are considerably more diligent, more ambitious. But it's almost like those ambitions. . . . I believed in meritocracy, that you will be judged by your merits, as opposed to how loudly you talk by the water cooler, how little you've slept, or how amazing you are, which men are really good at doing. Especially male lawyers.

But men, because he's saying it to other men—by nature of the fact that there are mainly men who are in the partnership. They understand him, they were him, they are him. They get it, they get the bravado, "Oh, he's such an ambitious guy."

(Natalya, *Law*)

Brassy, Arrogant, Mediocre Men Advanced Ahead of Women

It's easier to be an average man in my profession—an average lawyer who's a man, rather than being the most talented female lawyer you can be. I'm not saying that (to be) mean, but you don't only have to be technically good . . . you also have to be some kind of a social chameleon, rather than this hammer ax guy who's pounding his fists on the table and everybody's in awe of him because he's so fucking awesome.

I've seen so many women who are technically very good. Great personalities, who to you and I, would have it all. They're good at what they do, they understand their client's needs, they meet those needs—quite frankly what else do you need in order to be a successful partner—and who are constantly overlooked. Brassy, arrogant, mediocre lawyers who are men are advanced ahead of them. I don't understand why.

(Isabella, *Law*)

Challenging Her Qualifications, He Can Just Walk In

It's those personal and inappropriate questions that are asked in the workplace. But there are so many times that I just thought, "You didn't ask the man that! Why are you asking me my full CV and I have to give you my full background and experience in this? You didn't ask him."

(Olivia, *Music Industry*)

Drinking and Reputation

Men and women have different rules when it comes to drinking and socializing. While these never hurt a man's reputation, a woman's character will get assassinated should she give the "wrong impression."

Rules for Herself That Men Do Not Have to Make

I have found myself restraining from perhaps having another drink because I don't want to give the wrong impression, not staying out very late, in a way that was completely different from my male colleagues. My male colleagues could go out for drinks until 10:30/11:00 at night. But I got the impression that if I were to do that, once a week or every couple of weeks with the solicitors, they would form a negative impression about me—the kind of woman I was, let alone the kind of professional I was, in a way that was different from my male counterparts.

(Isabella, *Law*)

More Than Two Drinks Gives the Wrong Impression

I have a rule of going out. A rule no man would have. But if I go with my male clients, whether it's one on one or two on one, I will never have more than two drinks. Because it's not a social gathering. I never want to be drunk in front of my clients. Even if you can hold your drink, there's still a certain calculus when you have two drinks in a professional setting. More than that creates an impression that it's something more. That's been my experience. And this is something that would not be the case in a group of men.

(Rebecca, *Private Practice Consulting*)

He's Fun, She's a Whore

Men don't seem to have that problem. I've seen them get completely, completely shit-faced—one of my colleagues, diabolically and embarrassing so—in front of clients. Does not affect his reputation. At all. In fact, they say, "That guy, he's a bit of a firecracker. That guy knows how to drink." What would happen if I did? Oh my god they would think I was having some sort of a mental breakdown. They would think that I was completely unprofessional. A loose cannon. Easy as well, because they would judge me as a woman. They'd say, "Well she probably sleeps around." That's the natural conclusion to jump to.

(Natalya, *Law*)

Her Perfection vs. His Mediocrity

The quality of work men and women are expected to produce differs drastically. Men can be average or worse, while women must do beyond perfect work. At worst it evens out, but either way the man will get promoted.

Men Can Be Crap, You Can't Be

As far as women are concerned there's also a double standard of men can be crap, men can make mistakes, but you can't be. I felt that there was also that judgment for women, where male counterparts seem to get away with being a lot less careful, a lot more—a bit looser in what they said and how they said it and how they did it. Women are expected to be on point, precise, know the detail about everything. If you didn't do that, you weren't on top of the case. That's from both male and female but I think I felt it more from certain female judges.

(Sarah, *Law*)

Have to Be Better

You learn to be better than them.

Q: Not on par with them, not equal to them, you have to be better?

You have to be better than them. It's something that you learn to do. I'm also mixed race so that also played a part for me in so much that I felt like I didn't want to be, "She's just there because she's mixed race and they had to make up the numbers," I was in a lesser class . . . that I didn't really know what I was doing that I was sort of one of those brown girls who thinks they want to be a barrister but doesn't really know what they're doing. I really felt like I was representing my race as well as my gender.

(Isabella, *Law*)

Always Need to Be on Point

In my mind what it tells me is I always must bring my A game. I cannot slip. I cannot in any way be even the slightest bit unprepared or underprepared in this setting with these people because they are looking for a chink in my armor. And I can't let them find it. And so it puts extra stress and anxiety and all that on me, because I've got to be—I really do have to be doubly smart, doubly articulate, doubly prepared. Triple in some cases, because I already know what the bias is when you look at me.

(Maryam, *Branding and Marketing*)

Act Like I Really Don't Belong There

Every profession has its procedures and their policies and so on. We have rules procedures that we have, documents to file, time frames for things to get done. I know a lot of times a lot of judges wink their eyes of that. A lot of attorneys don't necessarily follow all the rules to the letter, but most judges don't enforce the letter. I know for me, I have to make sure that I do every-thing to the letter because those are the things that they'll use against me in a courtroom to indicate that I don't know what I'm doing, and I really don't belong there.

(Sarah, *Law*)

He Gets Respect, She Has to Prove Something

Women noted how men garnered respect simply by showing up, while women had to prove themselves over years just to be considered competent. Regardless of age or knowledge, men just assume that other men know more than women. The collective experiences and sentiment among the women are that they just were not respected, while their male counterparts were.

Men were also regarded and treated as important, while women were regarded and treated as less important. People also get personal with women, extending comments on their appearance that men never seem to receive, apparently due to a higher perceived status.

Defer to the Man

This is interesting. I had a partner once in the PD's office. He was young, young like I just—I was like a mama bear for him because he was a baby attorney and I took him under my wing, I was going to teach him all this stuff, I'm going to bring him to trial on all my cases. Every time we would interact with opposing counsel, especially with a white male, they would always address him as the lead attorney.

Jeffrey just permanently looks like a deer caught in headlights. He's got big doe eyes and he looks like a 12-year-old that dressed up to go to court with his father that day.

But every single time if they're talking to attorneys and it's Jeffrey and me, they will look at Jeffrey and they will address everything to Jeffrey. And Jeffrey rarely speaks. He'll do this little weak point—she's the lead attorney. Because he feels bad to have to say it.

I'm like, "You're looking at both of us and really, this boy looks like a 12-year-old and you're addressing him as the lead attorney because I'm a black female so I must be the assistant or I must be the intern?" Come on!

(Sarah, *Law*)

Men Don't Get Compliments, They Get Respect

They don't get the compliments on their ties or anything like that. They just don't get that. It's always a really professional relationship, which I've never been able to witness personally and when I talk to colleagues they're like, no, guys, don't ever guys, or the women, none of their clients, male or female ever really say to them? "Hey, I like your hair. I like your suit." It's always just "Yes, sir. No, sir. Whatever you say, sir."

(Allison, Politics)

Assumed You Are Unknowledgeable and Incompetent

Sarah discusses handing over a case. Rather than inquire about the case itself, the new male attorney belittles what he thinks is her lack of experience compared to his.

> As I'm talking to you, I'm thinking all these things are like recently, it's not even like talking about 10 years ago when I first started practicing. . . . I went to meet with this new lawyer and he looked at me, "So basically you don't really have that much experience, right? You've just been a PD for most of your career."
>
> I was like, "Excuse me?" He said, "I'm not saying you don't know what you're doing. I mean, I'm sure you have some clue as to what's going on. But you haven't done as much as I have."
>
> Wow, is this what you would have done to a male whose case you were taking over? Doubtful. Most times when an attorney is taking over a case from another attorney they have questions like "Okay, what have you done? What does this case look like? Is this case really worth taking over?" These are the things that normal people ask each other but no, I mean I guess I wasn't given due deference of a normal attorney I suppose.

(Sarah, Law)

Takes Years to Prove Herself, He Just Walks in the Door

> Fifty percent of my clients are complete chauvinistic pigs and it takes a really long time to establish yourself and your street creds. A guy would command respect just from walking into the room, whereas you will really have to prove yourself.
>
> You have that market rep that draws them to you, so they come to you because you're good. Then they're disappointed that you are a woman, and you have to work really hard at it, and they get over it.
>
> I did another deal with the same people, and the prime minister . . . said, "Actually no, wait. We don't start discussions until my lawyer is here." That's right! And it only took us 10 years to get here.

(Natalya, Law)

She Is Assumed Inarticulate

When I start to talk, I get the "Oh wow, you're so articulate." I just laugh now. I used to get really angry about it but now I just laugh. That's my entire life. I had a court reporter in federal court once ask me if I grew up in the church. I said why? And she said, "because you're so articulate." She didn't say "you people," but basically she was saying that black people that come into the court that can speak well usually grew up in the church and spoke in front of their congregation. "That why they talk good!"

(Sarah, *Law*)

She Is Assumed Ignorant

Two women talked about male counterparts "mansplaining" the law. Here Isabella describes treatment of female barristers by older male judges, who assume the women do not know what they are doing.

I've also seen male judges being almost grandfatherly to young female barristers because they felt like they just didn't quite know what they were doing. "Let me just explain that to you" sort of attitude of "There there love."

(Isabella, *Law*)

Men Assume They Go First

If I have a co-defendant case and there's white males that are on the case, we're getting together to do a joint deposition, they always assume that they're going to talk first and they're going to do their questions first. They always assume.

(Isabella, *Law*)

Men Are More Important Than You

Colleagues, referring again to the older white males, never see me as an attorney. They never see me as an equal. I used to have to say I passed the bar just like you did. Then they would think I'm being rude because—only because I stood up for myself.

One guy, I wouldn't let him cut in the line. He had to be somewhere else, but my client had to get to work and it's not fair to my client. You have to be somewhere else, but so does my client. So I wouldn't let him cut me in the line. I was called a bitch for that and . . . "better hope you never run for judge." Because I wouldn't let you cut in the line? Excuse me? Wow. Okay.

(Sarah, *Law*)

Advancement: Him over Her

The advancement of men over women was a prominent theme, and many examples from all industries were shared. Here again, women had to prove themselves and perform at a vastly superior rate, but always some personality reason was cited for women not being the best candidate. In women's experiences, men did not have to demonstrate their performance, while women had to detail the entirety of their work history. Regardless of how impressive and accomplished her work history, a man's word was always preferred.

Skeptical of Her, But Bring Him In

If I turn up and I say to them all this is my practice, this is what I do, everybody gets out their skeptic glasses and they're like, "Well, can we have some client references, somebody to back up your revenue stream?" Or, "Well how is that possible, you're so young. Can you tell us about the origin of your clients? How long have you known them, where have they come from?"

All reasonable questions, but I know for a fact because I have sat in on interviews where we are interviewing a man, those questions are not asked. His word was taken as gospel. He's always able to walk in, flash a smile, talk some bullshit and everybody's like, "Well that sounds good to me. Bring him in." Which is—I find that fascinating.

(Natalya, *Law*)

Men Defend Their Choices to Advance Men

I think if you were to pose that question to, ultimately men, who are in charge of that advancement and you say to them, why do you do this? Why did you make this decision? They will make a number of justifications for it, and none of them are going to be like, "Oh because he's a guy and we really like him," it's not going to be that.

You know, they will find a number of reasons to character assassinate the woman. "Oh she's too meek" or "I just don't feel that she's ready for it." Or "I don't feel like she has the same level of experience."

(Natalya, *Law*)

Challenging Your Right to Be There

I'll hear the comment, "Well, you know why she's got that don't you?" The inference being, the implication being it is because she's a woman and they need to fill the quotas. Or she's a woman of color in particular, "Well you know why she's got that don't you?"

Her success is attributable to a quota rather than because she's really good at her job. You never hear that about a white man. It makes you think that, well it completely undermines the validity of your position . . . it's another way of challenging your right to be there . . . completely suggesting that you are there illegitimately, your appointment is invalid.

(Isabella, *Law*)

He Is Ambitious and Really Wants It, She Is Aggressive and Not Ready for That Level

When it comes from a woman, unless you are prepared to burn the place down and take some clients with you, you are perceived as *aggressive.* "You're a little bit, biting more than you can chew . . . are you really sure that you are at that level?"

If it comes to reviews and a guy walks in, and he's like, I want this and I want that, and I think I deserve it." They say, "Oh, he's actually really driven and he's really ambitious."

His behavior of "Jack the lad" being perceived as that of an ambitious guy who is burning the candle at both ends, therefore, he *really* wants it; as opposed to somebody who actually *does* the work and does it well?

(Natalya, *Law*)

Ignored until a Man Validates You

They ignore me, they don't take me seriously, they don't listen. Not until a man kind of lifts me up and tells them who I am and why they should listen to me, do they do it. It's happened several times during my whole career.

(Mara, *Politics*)

Assumed Her Incompetent

I have to beat them in court and then I get the respect that I need. Generally, once I've beaten them in trial or at a hearing or something like that, then all of a sudden, "Oh, well, you are a formidable opponent." Yeah, of course, I am. But you shouldn't have assumed I wouldn't be.

(Isabella, *Law*)

I Love When You Challenge Me. Now Stop It

Women reported beginning positions where men initially found them engaging. The male superior voiced enjoyment at having the women challenge him. Inevitably, the man tired of being challenged, and the women did not remain long in their positions. What women thought of as a professional relationship was more of a contrast situation: The boss liked to be challenged because it reminds him he is in charge.

After a period of time, these men changed their mind and women experienced professional repercussions. Instead of challenging, men characterized them as difficult. Women chose to leave those professions, or else they were fired.

Fuck Up Anything, Just Don't Challenge Him

And that's the kind of thing that the CEO would do. So if you challenge him in a way that he believed was inappropriate, you would be publicly punished for it, which is damaging to both psyche and career. And if you could stay in his favor, the benefits were great. The people who did not stay in his favor didn't last.

Q: What would cause a person to lose favor?

Incompetence was not the primary thing. Yeah, because if you adored him, which many of his employees did and probably still do, you could pretty much fuck up *anything* and he would keep you are because you were one of his beloved. It's really amazing to me.

(Avery, *Pharmaceutical Marketing*)

Liked Her Challenges at First

He adored me as a consultant because I would challenge him, but once you're an employee you are not allowed to challenge him anymore. I shouldn't have accepted the job, but typical in his style—he was one of those California CEOs who wear shorts and sneaks to work—very charismatic and also just happened to be very sexist.

We were at a sales conference and I was walking through the lobby and he was standing there with one of our biggest hospital chain customers and he said, "Hey, I want you to meet our new VP of Marketing." I was a consultant so that was how he offered me the job, and I admittedly got kind of swept up in this whole "Wow, great and I'm going to make all this money."

I took the job knowing that it could be problematic and I told him why I was resistant to taking it and he said, "Well just keep challenging me."

The upshot was that as a female, you know, I had the wrong body parts to continue challenging him. When he was paying a consultant rate I think the money somehow validated my right to challenge him. Although I have to say I made a lot more money as his VP.

I've left. That's what I've done. . . . And the thing is they shouldn't—or I shouldn't—have to reflect upon my or their reactions or actions. It's the men in power who should reflect on their actions, and they don't. And we're back to that spiral, where they can continue the way they've always been and some women just accept it and some women leave and everything continues as normal. Yeah, and I'm not very good at shutting up. So they usually end up just stepping on me, and I leave.

(Avery, *Pharmaceutical Marketing*)

Woman Can Challenge, until She Challenges His Status

It goes from you being cool, smart, embraced and listened to, to becoming the one that makes too much fuss. And challenging other managers, male managers, too much and they cannot handle it. I'm not the one just sitting there and accepting things, so both times it just ended with me saying, "Okay, why should I fight for your company or your organization if you don't want my ideas, if you don't want to develop, if you're content with how things are. Because you can just sit there and have the power and money."

(Mara, *Culture and Politics*)

Seriously, That's Enough

They like it at first when you challenge them, because they can think about things a little differently and feel like they have accomplished something. But then they get sick of hearing it and you risk your job every time you open your mouth. So it becomes a balance of losing your job or being sick from having to keep it all in.

(Rebecca, *Senior Scientist*)

His Need for Deference

What would get you fired is if you did not show deference to him. I was let go because I continued to challenge him. I challenged his business decisions, which he did not like. He believed he was the primary expert in his industry, so to have a subordinate, much less a female subordinate, challenge him was really uncomfortable for him. And he was not into tolerating discomfort.

Q: You didn't feel the need to smooth things out and make him feel okay about everything?

I was not gonna mother this fucker.

(Avery, *Pharmaceutical Marketing*)

Exposing Sexist Scripts and Thought Patterns

I. Bravado Is Rewarded, Her Quality Is Disregarded
    A. Not That Good, But He Is Loud
    B. Brassy, Arrogant, Mediocre Men Advanced Ahead of Women
    C. Challenging Her Qualifications, He Can Just Walk In

II. Drinking and Reputation
    A. Rules for Herself That Men Do Not Have to Make
    B. More Than Two Drinks Gives the Wrong Impression
    C. He's Fun, She's a Whore

III. Her Perfection vs. His Mediocrity
    A. Men Can Be Crap, You Can't Be
    B. Have to Be Better
    C. Always Need to Be on Point
    D. Act Like I Really Don't Belong There

IV. He Gets Respect, She Has to Prove Something
    A. Defer to the Man
    B. Men Don't Get Compliments, They Get Respect
    C. Assumed You Are Unknowledgeable and Incompetent
    D. Takes Years to Prove Herself, He Just Walks in the Door
    E. She Is Assumed Inarticulate
    F. She Is Assumed Ignorant
    G. Men Assume They Go First
    H. Men Are More Important Than You

V. Advancement: Him over Her
    A. Skeptical of Her, But Bring Him In
    B. Men Defend Their Choices to Advance men
    C. Challenging Your Right to Be There
    D. He Is Ambitious and Really Wants It, She Is Aggressive and Not Ready for That Level
    E. Ignored until a Man Validates You
    F. Assumed Her Incompetent

VI. I Love When You Challenge Me. Now Stop It
    A.   Fuck Up Anything, Just Don't Challenge Him
    B.   Liked Her Challenges at First
    C.   Woman Can Challenge, until She Challenges His Status
    D.   Seriously, That's Enough
    E.   His Need for Deference

Analysis

Natalya talks about a recent work introduction she had when looking to switch law firms. Her friend makes a professional introduction, and the man she meets with about a job treats the introduction like a romantic meeting.

Sexualized Professional Introduction, Pinned against a Wall

"If you are remotely attractive, everybody thinks it's open season. and that's not a good place to be in. I'll give you an example. This guy is the head of oil and gas of an international law firm.

A friend of mine, a very good friend and a client of mine, knows him very well and she said to me, I think you should meet him. Maybe go for a coffee because he knows the market, he knows the marketplace—this is in the context of me moving, looking for a new position.

Note that she was introduced by a good friend, who knows this man well, but may not know how he behaves.

I reached out to him, I suggested a coffee, he said, "Well, why don't we have a drink at five o'clock?" Five o'clock is early, it's not like I'm meeting him at nine.

She is cognizant of the time and the appearance of what a later time might indicate.

We have a glass of wine and we talk about work. I talk about where I'm at, he's telling me where he's at. Then we had something—a bite to eat—and then had another glass of wine. And we spent about two and a half hours together, so let's say by eight o'clock we're leaving.

Nothing about the encounter should suggests what follows.

We leave the restaurant to step outside. He pins me against the wall and he like, shoves his tongue down my throat. I literally was like, "No, no, no, no, no." At some point, I had my laptop in my, in my handbag, and I just kind of hit him with it.

Note that he does not stop when she resists, verbally says "No" several times. She has to physically hit him with her laptop.

"Whoa, what is happening?" And he said, "I don't understand."
    I said, "What are you doing?" He said, "Well I thought we were just talking. Did I just totally misread the situation?"

This is a frequent and painful moment for women. She must state the obvious, as if the facts of context of their meeting require explanation, as if there was somehow room for misinterpretation.

I said, "We were talking about work, we weren't talking about anything else. This isn't a date. I've never met you before. What are you thinking?"

He is a professional male, the head of oil and gas at a major law firm. The idea that he lacks the basic social skills to "misread" a professional conversation is ridiculous.

Then of course he massively tried to backtrack, "Oh I'm sorry I misread the situation—I understand and of course—why don't you come in tomorrow, into the office and we'll talk about it because I think you'll be a great addition to the team."
    I said to him, "I will never work in that firm as long as you're there. Never."
    Because this is a person who does this all the time. This isn't the first time.

Conclusion

Gaslighting! Gaslighting! Gaslighting! Gaslighting! Gaslighting!

As a woman speaking to someone interviewing her on sexism, she shares in the final sentence the knowledge that this behavior is repetitive and recognizable. It occurs so frequently that women see it as a regular thing. Its *lack* of presence is what women usually discuss, because this happens so often. When a man does not try to sexualize the interaction, that is noteworthy and rare.

The ludicrous idea that he misread the situation happens so regularly, too, that finding a response becomes difficult. For the woman to respond, it is like she is agreeing with the man's version of events, which is not reality.

Recall the script in Chapter 5, how men sexualize women in the office. I have never met the men Mila referred to, who all did the same thing, and yet I knew the script because so many men have done the same thing with me. With this scenario as well, it has happened so many times that I could have told the story.

From a harsher angle, men seem to lie often and easily. Women brush that off, too, as just something men do. Like this man, they put women in the position of having conversation that is entirely nonsensical on their end. The woman finds herself in the position of arguing reality while the man challenges what *obviously* just happened. This is a psychological technique called gaslighting, and it is a fixture that pervades gender dynamics.

Creating New Scripts and Thought Patterns

- How can a man or woman bring attention to a rule or expectation having a double standard of conduct?
- What information was requested of you in a job interview?
- How should a woman respond when a man sexualizes her and acts like it was a natural thing to do, even though their meeting or introduction was clearly about work?
- Why do you think a woman is challenged to prove her credentials and worth, while a man's word is enough?

CHAPTER EIGHT

Not a Sexist, He Says

Introduction

Gender expectations are a problem for women because women are judged by interpersonal characteristics and held to standards that men have created about them. In this chapter, we begin by some comparisons of women's experiences for which there is no male equivalent. Women discuss fearing for their personal safely and being sexualized, but men do not have relatable experiences.

Socialization and gender expectations are highlighted in this chapter as well. Women are socialized among men who mean well but clearly exhibit benevolent sexism. Professional sexism comes at a personal level because families are mixed genders, and the gender roles in families translate to male expectations of women in the boardroom. While fathers are supportive in a professional sense of their daughters, the participants mention here how that equitable support does not extend into family life. This sends her mixed signals about equality because her father is communicating confusion about equality.

How men perceive women, and perceive them as different, further becomes a problem in the hiring process. Aware of this, women talk about the gender expectations men place upon them that just do not fit. Once again, the invented male expectations for women become a problem for women. Also, and in addition to being misunderstood and categorized as "other," men tend to stay in their networks and hire other men. The inability to break into male networks in a male-dominated workforce puts women at a severe disadvantage. No matter how good they are in their profession, an average man gets hired instead of them.

No Male Equivalent to Sexism

The truest test of inequality is whether the opposite is plausible. Speaking with a woman, I can ask her to put herself in my situation. She can empathize in a way a man cannot, because he has never been subjected to a man who sexualizes him, makes him uncomfortable, or threatens his job or physical safely.

> "What men fear most about prison is what women fear most about walking down the sidewalk."
>
> *(Facebook meme)*

Fearing for Your Personal Safety

During her interview, Sophia discussed being stalked by a coworker for months. The stalker knew her movements, tried to get her to believe his identity was one of her friends, and sent messages to her all day at work so she knew he was in her midst. In trying to relate to her male coworkers, none of them could relate to fearing for their physical safety.

> One part that was challenging was this. Like there were a few people that I did tell what was going on. I told my boss, which I think I would have done regardless. There was someone in a different department who I knew personally, who was a friend in my personal life. And I told him, you know I just wanted to tell a few people (who) could have their eyes and ears out and kind of like for a little safety. And like, as much as these are very sweet, caring, emotionally intelligent men, when I did talk about it I never really felt like—like they just didn't know that experience of being in their workplace and feeling like *their* safety could be completely violated.

A woman friend tells her about a similar experience, having had someone try to rape her, and then telling a male friend who did not seem to understand.

> It felt like it wasn't a relatable experience for them so I kind of got responses like, "Oh gosh, wow, that's so terrible"—and I was actually talking to a girlfriend about that this weekend, relating to her because she was telling me she had gone through an attempted rape, like nothing to do with the workplace, just a horrible experience. She had told a male friend and it really, it wasn't a great experience for her. I can identify with that, I've kind of had that experience as well. Like it didn't ever seem to land with men the same

as it did with women so friends knew, people in my personal life knew . . .
but it didn't really motivate me to tell a lot of my coworkers who were male
because it just didn't really seem like they got it, or really struck them as
being as awful as it was.

(Sophia, International Marketing)

Having a Man Masturbate to You in a Meeting

Sarah discussed when she told her male colleagues about a client masturbating to her in a meeting, they could not even fathom that scenario. I asked
how she thought they might respond to a man doing the same thing to them.

I would imagine the males would act aggressively and try to assert themselves in that situation to try and shut it down. Some show of male aggression is probably what a man would have done if it was a woman. Who
knows? I have no idea. But they never get faced with it.

I've actually asked my male colleague. But they always—when I bring
that up, especially the masturbation, they are always shocked because they
can't fathom the idea of a client just, in the middle of an attorney meeting,
or in the middle of court much less, just whipping it out and just going to
town on themselves. They don't understand that.

And they have no counterpart for it, with the women. None of my male
colleagues have ever experienced that. A couple have joked "man I wish one
of my clients would masturbate in front of me." They're always shocked
when I saw these things happen.

(Sarah, Law)

Notice the disparity yet again, how the reverse situation—a woman masturbating to a man in a meeting—would be either amusing or arousing.
Reverse scenarios ("What if this happened to you?") are not applicable
with gender.

What Men Think Women Should Be

Women Not Being How Men Perceive Gets Their Backs Up

This participant observed that men perceive women a certain way, and
violating that expectation is psychologically uncomfortable.

And I think it's because men understand men, whereas women understand women a little better. And I think that men recognize they don't
understand women. So when they see those male traits in women, they're

put off by them, because it's almost, it gets their backs up, because it's not what they expect. It's not how they perceive, maybe even on some subconscious level, how women to be.

(Isabella, *Law*)

You Are an Equal and You Are the Weaker Sex

Conflicting messages are common in women's socialization. Natalya provides an example from her father, how he disregards her time and how differently he would treat a son in her same situation.

I give you an example of my father, right, I'm an only child, my father ran an oil company for many years, he was a very successful manager. He's won lots of awards and he's a great leader. . . . He always told me from a very early age that you know, I had to be independent and make my way, that I have to be strong, take the high road. . . . Don't be dramatic, think clearly. Yes, you've chosen a difficult industry, but you know you are a leader, you can be a better leader—you know all these things, that all the right things. . . . You are an equal and behave like an equal, all that kind of stuff, right?

But then it comes down to it, my dad as a man who perceives—when you ask him are the women the weaker sex? He'd be like, absolutely. . . .

Find Time or Find a Man

He said to me—I needed to change the batteries in my smoke alarm. Quite frankly, I just couldn't be bothered. My dad came over and was like, what's that flashing light? I said I need to change the battery and I just can't be bothered.

Her father: "Either you need to find time for these things or you need a man." I don't need a man, I need another 24 hours in a day. That's what it means. It's not a question that I'm incapable of getting a ladder or going to the shop and buying some batteries. Or that I'm confused by the wide range of batteries which are available out there. I just can't be bothered.

And I think my father himself is a conflicted animal. He wants the best for me. And he believes that I can achieve great leadership and laurels and everything.

Double Standard for Being Busy

But at the same time, you know, he's not particularly respectful of my time. Like if I say to him, you know, I can't do this because I'm in the meeting, because he wants to chat about something, he'll be like, "What do you mean? You're not saving the world, you know. You don't have time for your family?"

I'm telling you if anyone said that to my father when he was working, I mean nobody would *dare* to say it to him. But I'm pretty sure that if I was his son, he'd be like "Leave him alone he's too busy." I see that with my friends who have brothers.

You know, it's just a very different. I don't know, you know, I'm expected— you're expected to of course be also a baker, homemaker, all those things. . . . My home is expected to be tidy or you know, furnished in a certain way because I'm a woman.

And if I am, I'm too busy, I'm traveling, whatever, my father—I'm 38, I'm not sure on what basis he feels that he can say that to me. My mother as well, I would have a lecture, well you need to find more time, you need to be neater, you need to make more money, you can hire people who do this for you because you know, you can't live like this. And I think my god, if I had a brother and he had like hookers swinging from his chandelier, I bet you won't say anything to him because "Well he's just a guy, he needs to blow some steam, he's very successful, you know. He's *very* busy."

(Natalya, *Law*)

She Is an Equal at Work But Not in Personal Life

You know, I see that it's really funny because when you come to them with a work problem, they're really on it. Like, "You are the best of the best and you must push and you are an equal to any man if not better than most of the men that you work with."

Okay, but *you* don't see me as an equal in the social setting or outside of the work environment.

(Natalya, *Law*)

This encapsulates the problem with confronting sexism. The attitudes are so ingrained that many people do not think about it, men and women. For women, confronting sexism in your personal life is especially challenging.

He Looks at You and Thinks of His Daughter

The problem of men not seeing women as equal is that women are not entities in and of themselves. Here a woman confronts a long-term client who humiliated her during their first meeting.

I remind him to this day about that, I'm just like, "Do you remember what you said to me?" And he was like, "What did you expect me to say?" He's like, "I have a daughter your age, I wouldn't get my daughter to advise me on a $30 billion transaction."

I'm like, "yeah, but did your daughter go to fucking law school and work as a lawyer for five years before that?"

"Well, no, you know, she's a personal shopper."

"So there we go. I wouldn't be asking her to advise me on a $30 billion transaction, either."

(Natalya, *Law*)

Men Do Not Understand Strong Women

Natalya also discussed how men do not "get" strong, ambitious women, women who are similar in ambition to the men who do not understand them.

And I do think that that generally comes down to, as I said, you know, conditioning. Most of these partners, they're married, they have daughters at home, you know, and I'm sure that they will go home and they will tell their daughters that you must be independent, you know, you must pursue your goals, you know, you must strive to be equal, but not lose your femininity, and all those things that, you know, my father told me.

But when it actually gets to working with strong women, and working with strong women, because if they were not strong, they would never get to those positions in the first place.

There are a lot of average men, average lawyers who are male, who are promoted over much more talented and technically better lawyers who are females. And that's just a fact. If you look at the sort of facts in front of you, most of lawyers who start out so if you look at an intake of let's say, 60 lawyers, or 60 law students at a law firm in the UK would take for a two-year training contract, about 60 percent of them will be girls.

(Natalya, *Law*)

Less Intimidated When They Understand You

Olivia talks about how men favor their friends, who they have things in common with, usually other men. She discusses how men do not understand her because she is an ambitious woman, not married with children, and different from their wives.

I think that in a work environment, men are less intimidated by a woman. Or they're less wary of you or more accepting of you if they understand you. If you either come from a similar background or you have shared touch points. So I'm single, I'm not I don't go around going, Oh, you know, don't worry, I'm not a lesbian. No, no, no, I'm not, you know, in it, which is what I think they're just like, Oh, my, you know, she's ambitious, speaks up her mind. You know, whatever, she's good at what she does, and she's single, like, who knows what's going on there . . . she could be, like, drowning kittens in her spare time because she just comes across as really sharp around the edges, for example.

Half of the time I feel like I need to make up a boyfriend, I feel like I need to make up like some, you know, obviously I didn't sit and tell people about my non-existent boyfriend. But there are times when I just think people would actually be like, 'Oh, she's normal. She's like one of us,' because all of them are married. A vast majority of their wives don't work, they look after children . . . the husband is the main breadwinner.

I think a single woman is perceived as a bit of a threat because they're like, "Oh, my God, what if I say something that's inappropriate, or I look at her inappropriately?" Or, I don't know, "What if she's a sex maniac because she's single?" I don't know, I'm just making all of this up. But the fact is, you are—they don't get you. And if you don't get someone you don't really want to spend time with them.

I think that people help their friends and help the people that they like, and the people they feel engaged with whom they have built rapport with. . . .

Will you help your friend at work, or would you help someone who you don't really have any relationship with. If there is a lifeline, who are you going to throw it to? And also given the fact that we are talking about an incredibly male-dominated industry, you know, it is already like a white men middle-aged club. You already feel like an outsider before you even turned up.

(Olivia, *Music Industry*)

Being "an outsider before you turned up" indicates that, as a woman she is perceived as "other." Somehow the men are unable to connect with her as a human, and their inability to understand her becomes a problem *for her*, because men will advance men they like. We have seen this as a recurring theme, that men largely do not relate to women outside of a sexualized context.

Men Advance Other Men

> "What I will say is that I prefer out-front, overt -isms, whether it's sexism, racism. If somebody is shouting (in) your face like I hate you, or a racial slur or, you know, a gender slur. That is so much easier, honestly, to deal with than it is to deal with a culture of politeness that we have now that allows people to be in your face and say that they understand you and they support you, but they really are subversively pining for old times."
>
> (Catherine, *Tech*)

He's Good Enough, and They Can Go to a Strip Club Together

There have been a number of situations where I have been displaced by a male equivalent of me. And I can tell you exactly why. And they are not good, well maybe they're good but they're not excellent. By no means are they leaders in their markets for what they do. But I can understand why they have chosen them.

Because they are good *enough*, and if they are part of a bigger firm, somebody will pick up the slack. But they put themselves with someone they like. Someone else who wears Brioni suits and they can give them pats on their shoulder, and they can go to a strip club together. And they can talk about women, or cigars or watches or whatever it is that they want to talk about. And it's what they value because there's a connection.

(Natalya, *Law*)

Easier to Be an Average Man

It's actually easier to be an average man in my profession. Or an average lawyer who's a man, than being the most talented female lawyer you can be. I'm not saying that (to be) mean, but I think you have to—you don't only have to be technically good . . . you also have to be some kind of a social chameleon rather than this hammer ax guy who's pounding his fists on the table and everybody's in awe of him because he's so fucking awesome.

I've seen so many women who are technically very good, great personalities, who really to you and I would have it all. You know what I mean? They're good at what they do, they understand their client's needs, they meet those needs—quite frankly what else do you need in order to be a successful partner—who are constantly overlooked. And brassy, arrogant, mediocre lawyers who are men are advanced ahead of them. And I don't understand why.

And I think if you were to pose that question to, ultimately men who are in charge of that advancement and you say to them, "Why do you do this? Why did you make this decision?" They will make a number of justifications for it, and none of them are going to be like, "Oh because he's a guy and we really like him." It's not going to be that.

They will find a number of reasons to character assassinate the woman. "Oh she's too meek" or "I just don't feel that she's ready for it." Or "I don't feel like she has the same level of experience."

(Natalya, *Law*)

Men Can Be Average, Women Must Be Perfect

Dynamic Density

Several women discussed the hiring of average men over far more qualified women. Emile Durkheim (1895) wrote about *dynamic density*. As the world becomes more crowded, it expands and changes. More people in the world means more interactions, and in the case of executive sexism, more women reaching higher positions, territory that has been previously occupied by men. Increased competition for jobs results in more specializations, allowing for greater efficiency. Thus far, that efficiency manifests as women in low-status support roles.

With the increase in women graduating from university and getting higher degrees, that norm is no longer realistic. When women go for roles to which they are more suited, they are discovering that men with far less ability are being advanced ahead of them. According to Durkheim (1895), "traditions, economic power, or status can determine who performs what jobs regardless of talent and qualifications." Women are certainly finding this to be the case.

Women Have to Be 1,000 Times Better

Because progressing to that position . . . you're constantly compared to your male colleagues and to be a woman and progressed into partnership with progress within that particular point practice model, you have to be 1,000 times better than any man that comes up for partnership. There are a lot of average men, average lawyers who are male, who are promoted over much more talented and technically better lawyers who are females.

(Sarah, *Law*)

Systemic Changes Are Not Fair to You, Women

They can always say, "Well I have other facts and they say blah blah blah." They can always say well . . . what do you call it when you have certain quota of people, they can always say it is unfair to use quotas because women should be taken seriously for their own competence, not only for their gender. It's a very easy thing to say because it could make sense, but it doesn't because men favor men. So, we need to take actions for that to stop.

(Mara, *Politics and Culture*)

Time Will Solve It

I just find all kinds of tiresome arguments and ways of saying, "Well we can't do it because these would be the effects. . . ." Well we do have effects of the system today and the effect is that this spiral is never broken so we need to do something. And one of the most tiresome arguments is "Well time will solve everything" or "Change is coming, you just need to be patient."

(Allison, *Political Marketing*)

Hiring processes discussed in the interviews were vague and subjective. No participant I spoke with knew how to challenge the bias.

Expertise Is Disregarded

Male's Sense of Central Significance

Regardless of their achievements or expertise, men disregard women's knowledge. Instead, men hide women and shun them.

Steamrolling

Mara talks about how it is incumbent for a woman to take on behavior to adapt to men, but never the other way around. Men do as they have always done, revert to a script in calling women emotional, while nothing negative affects men.

> First of all, it's how you hand out responsibilities. Like if it's a management team or something similar, it's how you hand out tasks and how you code them with male and female. Executive sexism is also about women taking responsibilities that they don't have to. For instance, that everyone feels good and that there is a warm climate among the group. A responsibility that is not taken by male managers.
>
> And, hold on, there is a term that is a Swedish word—steamroller. Do you use that in English? Yeah, they act like steamrollers. Since they act the way they have always done, and it hasn't affected them negatively, it's the women that have to adapt and accept that way of behavior. So if a guy acts like a douchebag, a male manager acts like a douchebag in the team and there's a female manager, and she reacts negatively, the guy can always say "you're being too sensitive" or "you're overreacting" instead of reflecting on his own behavior and thinking "what can I do differently not to create this atmosphere in the team or in the room?" It is always the woman that has to adapt to the male code of behavior.
>
> (Maryam, *Marketing and Branding*)

Her Expertise Was the Men's Crisis

So I came with all this knowledge about politics and process and so forth, and the public, and they saw it as a threat. It was perceived as a threat by all these male managers coming from more traditional marketing and commercial companies. And since I had been a public figure in TV and in press, they kind of wanted to hide me. They didn't want me to continue being a public figure. So it was kind of a—let me search for the word—like when you try to control a crisis, that's how they perceived me.

Instead of, "Wow, she knows all these things, she has the number to all these politicians that we are depending on, let's use her," it was more crisis management when I entered the organization, like who is she and why does she know all of these things? She is a threat. They were threatened that I came with knowledge that they did not have. And I was not—I wasn't a coward. I could speak my mind and they were just not used to that because there had been very few managers in the organization.

(Mara, Culture and Politics)

You Don't Like Me Because I'm a Girl, and I Throw Better Than You

I think it's a real struggle between trying to be included, really wanting to be part of the gang, when the gang is all boys. And you're like, I want to show you that I can jump as high as you can, and I can throw better than you. And my God, now that you've seen that I can throw better than you, you don't like me, because I'm a girl and I throw better than you.

You know I remember this in preschool. It's kind of the same thing. But you're not in a sandbox, you're in a commercial environment.

(Natalya, Law)

Male Networks

All of the women interviewed mentioned male networks. How they imagined their accessibility to these networks varied, as did the notion of how the networks came about, but in all cases, they discussed having to make their way in male networks. Men had resources and support that women did not have, and women saw the ability to access male networks, and thus those resources, as a benefit. Following are examples of their experiences.

Women Come and Go, Male Networks Remain

We just got a new head of group manager, Executive Vice President, the top top dog of the organization. And I have seen in the past year how he has changed the organization and the ones who get to leave are the women. There are very competent women that the president of the organization had a plan for and maybe groomed into taking a higher position, but they are no longer with the company. So we have seen the group equality between our management team being lowered. And it is the men who are the pals who are still here.

(Janni, Transportation)

Nothing to Talk About, for Ten Years

Following her social conditioning, Sophia did not initiate social contact or relationship building.

> I think it goes back to my childhood. I was raised—beyond the work-place—to look at my place in that, because I think, to a lot of extent, I kind of identified myself as other and behaved accordingly. I think that goes back to I was raised pretty conservatively in a Christian home and it was kind of like this "women do not initiate" kind of mentality. Which is how I conducted my dating life. I got married pretty young, and I kind of found that that continued to exist in the workplace.
>
> I wouldn't ever initiate, "hey let's go to lunch" or "let's grab a drink" or anything like that with my male colleagues, A, because I was married and a lot of them were married and I didn't want it to look improper.
>
> (Sophia, *International Marketing*)

Although she claims responsibility for failing to so initiate social contact, she did not do so partly because of how it might be perceived, as flirty or improper. She blames herself, but likely in what she describes later as a crass, male-dominated workplace, where men did make sexual comments about women. Again, she fails either way.

> But I also came into a group that already knew each other and were really social outside of the office and now there was, you know, this woman here, and it was kind of like I didn't know how to insert myself in a way that I thought would be respectful and healthy, and I think they struggled with that as well.

She and her male coworkers struggled with how to relate to each other as people, in a "healthy and respectful way," for 7 to 10 years. Outside of sexualizing her, her male coworkers could find no relatable material to engage with a woman colleague for almost a decade.

Accessing the Network

There's still the notion that a white male's going to do the best job for people. It doesn't really matter the skin color. Across the board they just feel like "Hey, if I got a white guy . . ." In some respects I get it because for some people the reasoning is, well they all go golfing or to a country club or what-ever it is they do together so maybe when they're out there on the 18th hole they'll talk about my case and work something out and you black girl are not able to move in those circles, so thank you for the work but I know he's going to do something that you wouldn't be able to do.

The judge will see that and think, "I went to law school with that guy I'll give him a break. I didn't know the black girl." It's such a pervasive thought that they're willing to go quote unquote the cheaper route by using me, it's like the slave labor. I ran to pillar to post and did so much just because I'm willing to fight for this guy's life, and then you know, let's take it home with the white guy.

(Sarah, *Criminal Law*)

Elite Networks: Law School Outlines

You know somebody else who went to this school before you, so they got the outline and they would just pass it down.

When I was in a class I would put out a call, hey, listen, hey, do you have an outline for this? "Oh, no, no, I'm just making my own." And a year later I know, that person got the outline from whoever, another person who was in the class before who had done really well.

The years ahead of us would pass the outlines down. And I always had to create my own because I could not get them to save my life, couldn't get them. These outlines were like gold. And so when they were passed down, it was always "well, make sure you watch who you give it to."

Q: What does that mean?

I never could get an explanation as to what does that mean, other than make sure that, you know, the black girls don't get it. Basically, that's how it translated in my mind. Because what does that mean? Who will you give it to? It's not the exam, it's not the exam answers. You can't cheat from an outline. It's just a study tool.

I was living the paper chase, where they are going through, and they're like pulling the pages out of the report so others can find the information that they needed to write the brief. Yeah, that's basically what they were doing with the outline. And it's very time-consuming to create an outline from scratch, versus just to update newer case law here and there.

Most of my study time was just creating things from scratch.

And I was already at a disadvantage because I did have a scholarship to law school. But from my living expenses, I had to work so I worked full time when I was in law school, I really didn't—I would get out of class at three. And I'd have to work from four to midnight in the dining cafe, I was doing manual labor. I'm cooking on the grill and when the cafe closes I have to clean the grill and I've got to wash pots and pans and do all this stuff. And then I'd get home at like 1:30 in the morning and then try to study and fall asleep before my eight o'clock class, and then do the whole thing all over again. So almost every second of my life in law school was—it was a fight just to be able to get two seconds together to study. I guess the best way to say it is, what I learned in law school is not to expect any assistance or any help, especially not from white males in my career so I never even sought it.

(Sarah, *Law*)

"In a systematic process of escalating commitments, recruits underwent physically brutal initiation rites. At the same time they were cursed, punched, kicked, and flogged, they were also told how lucky they were to be invited into such an elite organization."

—Greek military process to train torturers
(Waller, 2002)

Men Do Not Intervene in Sexism

Sophia's is one of the few narratives that included any men acknowledging that something was wrong with another man's sexist actions. She relates how she did "bloody battle" with her boss over and over until she was eventually fired, but her voice was the only voice.

Men Watch But Do Not Intercede

In the executive committee meetings, the behaviors were well observed by all of us, but again, for the first couple of years, I guess I was the only woman on the executive committee. But two of the men would talk about them, those kinds of incidences, if I would bring them up. They would discuss them with me *outside* of the committee meetings.

One of them was former military, very proper, respectful gentleman, and he was as uncomfortable with some of the stuff that went on in there as I was. He and my current husband had similar military backgrounds, so we had that sort of alliance. So I think he was comfortable discussing it with me, sometimes when someone would say something inappropriate, he would make eye contact and look uncomfortable.

Then I had another fellow on the committee who was a friend of mine as well. We socialized, he and his wife and my husband and I, would socialize outside of the corporate scenario. And he would acknowledge the inappropriate nature. I don't recall his ever actively participating in it. But he happened to have the kind of personality where he needed the CEO's approval all the time. So he would never challenge the CEO. And some of them would come and try and, pat me on the back after meetings.

Q: Why would nobody confront this man?

He, he was pretty volatile. Charming. He was one of those—a type of CEO and blanking on the term—but he was a high-energy, charming, volatile, but passionate CEO, who tended to hire . . . a lot of his hires had been with him a long time. He must be idolized, and there are people who feel the need to idolize the person they work for. So they would forgive him his sins and love him, because he loved them back. And that was the dominant dynamic between him and his male executives.

(Sophia, *Marketing*)

Women I spoke with exhibited great courage by relentlessly challenging sexism in the face of losing their position. None of them had a similar story about men standing up against sexism. To this speaker, the men speaking to her at all was a step. In confronting sexism, speaking behind closed doors is not enough. Why do men remain silent when they claim not to support sexist behavior?

Exposing Sexist Scripts and Thought Patterns

I. No Male Equivalent to Sexism
   A. Fearing for Your Personal Safety
   B. Having a Man Masturbate to You in a Meeting

II. What Men Think Women Should Be
   A. Women Not Being How Men Perceive Gets Their Backs Up
   B. You Are an Equal and You Are the Weaker Sex
      1. Find Time or Find a Man
      2. Double Standard for Being Busy
   C. She Is an Equal at Work But Not in Personal Life
   D. He Looks at You and Thinks of His Daughter
   E. Men Do Not Understand Strong Women
   F. Less Intimidated When They Understand You

III. Men Advance Other Men
   A. He's Good Enough, and They Can Go to a Strip Club Together
   B. Easier to Be an Average Man

IV. Men Can Be Average, Women Must Be Perfect
   A. Dynamic Density
   B. Women Have to Be 1,000 Times Better

C.   Systemic Changes Are Not Fair to You, Women

D.   Time Will Solve It

V.   Expertise Is Disregarded

A.   Male's Sense of Central Significance

B.   Steamrolling

C.   Her Expertise Was the Men's Crisis

D.   You Don't Like Me Because I'm a Girl, and I Throw Better Than You

VI. Male Networks

A.   Women Come and Go, Male Networks Remain

B.   Nothing to Talk About, for Ten Years

C.   Accessing the Network

D.   Elite Networks: Law School Outlines

VII. Men Do Not Intervene in Sexism

A.   Men Watch But Do Not Intercede

Analysis

No Female Counterpart for Sexualizing a Business Relationship

For me it was always a hand on the leg, it's not like we kissed, it's not like I slept with him, we never held hands. It's not like that attention was ever invited or acceptable. I do remember me taking his hand off my leg and him putting it back on my leg, where we were having that kind of war there. It was unspoken, but we both know what we're doing.

I also remember feeling a lot dirtier and I really felt bad about it. I felt very ashamed that I had allowed that . . . you don't just pick up and move company because somebody put their hand on your leg. I could the next morning just get over it and say well, just don't go to dinner alone with him again.

"The guy's a womanizer so he's a little creepy," and you kind of laugh at it like, "Really, that was so ridiculous. I can't believe I was put in that situation. I feel kind of gross." And then you laugh at it. I never laughed at it with others, I laughed at it internally and then brushed it off.

How she begins to internalize it:

If you trust yourself and your reaction, and you trust the strength of your mental state—it's like a means to an end. We were working on projects bringing education and women's rights to the Middle East. I remember feeling very strongly of "but I'm working on a really important project" and almost a "take one for the team" kind of mentality.

Lasting effects on her personal identity and professional confidence:

I think the part that I didn't recognize, especially talking about now, is that it colored my time there and I always feel slightly ashamed. I did always doubt and wonder, even though I don't doubt my capabilities or my suitability for that job or any of the huge projects I was working on, or the amount of work I did on them or anything else. It creates a self-doubt of "Am I just here for—is that the reason he hired me? Is that the reason I didn't get this project?" It becomes so the merit system is not fully based on your work.

She feels complicit, although the behavior was an exercise of power deliberately perpetrated by him:

There's something else at play that you psychologically process in a way that is detrimental to your career, or to your relationship. Whether or not you say yes or no, whether or not you go into that hotel room, or whether you let them put that hand on your knee or whatever else; it just brings in another element that doesn't belong in the workplace.

(Mila, *Middle East Business Development*)

Your Guilt: A Silent Victory for Sexism

As a woman, reverse the role. Could you imagine sexualizing a man 30 years younger than you, trying to "wear him down" over time so he would have sex with you, whilst vaguely dangling his job as a repercussion should he outright refuse your advances? Of course not. For sexualizing a business relationship, there is no female counterpart.

This behavior is manipulative and coercive, and a clear display of high social dominance orientation, prevalent among men but not women (Sidanius and Pratto, 1999). As we have seen in other sections, the internalization of guilt and shame, the feeling that you as a woman have somehow "played along" or been complicit when dominance was being exercised against you is one of the silent victories of sexism. That feeling of being equally responsible when another person was using power and privilege to manipulate you makes you shrink away internally and doubt yourself. The internal battle begins. You are forever questioning yourself, rather than the men who manipulate you.

Why Men Like Needy Women

And it's like, they like *needy* women. I'll give you an example. Myself versus a fellow partner who's lovely, she's a great lady. She's very smart, she is very successful, but we have just completely different styles. Hers is very much you know, we have to play them at their own games. By no means is she a pushover, but she dresses and she portrays herself as a bit of a Stepford wife kind of personality.

And she twiddles her hair—if it's a case of giving a presentation . . . even though she knows very well how to set up the equipment and how to use the computer, she's like, "Oh, my God, I just pressed something, oh, gosh, this technology constantly, it defeats me." And immediately, like, five guys jump up from the partnership, trying to help her work the computer . . . and she's not perceived as a threat for some reason, you know.

Whereas I would have turned up to the meeting 20 minutes early, and I would have made sure that IT would have wired everything up and everything's working.

I wouldn't stand there going, like, Oh, my God, how do I do this—I just wouldn't . . . I would find that really embarrassing, being unprepared. as opposed to charming or ditzy kind of thing. But I think guys like that, because it's disarming, because it's charming. Whereas I think that that's perfectly fine in your personal relationship space, but not at work, because you just wasted 20 minutes of my time. I bill in six-minute segments. (Laughs) I could be earning money here.

(Natalya, *Oil and Gas Law*)

Conclusion

Why Identity Is at Odds with Gender Expectations

Sociological theorists write about role expectation. *Status* is the position you hold within your society, and *role* is what you do in that position. *Role expectation* is how individuals must learn to see themselves in the place they have been assigned (Parsons and Shils, 1951, p. 147).

As we have read in this chapter, men have in mind a certain way that women "should" be. The status given to women by sexist men is subordinate, and anything that contradicts subordination is undefinable to them. The female colleague who feigns neediness is playing the role she was assigned and the men feel comfortable with.

On the other hand, they cannot begin to relate to ambitious women. As a professional woman, the speaker in this passage cannot reconcile that role. She does not imagine herself as subordinate (nor is she), and she does not actually occupy the social space she has been assigned. In a broader sense, women cannot find a way to fit the gender role assigned to them because they do not see themselves as men see them. This becomes a problem in the professional arena because men see men as their associates and avoid women who make them feel psychologically uncomfortable. Women lose job opportunities and clients, while men lose nothing.

Creating New Scripts and Thought Patterns

- In what scenario must a man reconcile his identity to be like a woman or act against his nature to secure advancement?
- As a woman, ask yourself the same thing. If a person at your place of work was personable but you did not understand him, would that stop you from trying to get to know him?
- If men do not support sexism, why do men remain silent and not intervene?

CHAPTER NINE

How Women Try to Control Sexism

Introduction

Women being conscious of how men view them was a consistent theme in the interviews. Women thought that appearance plays a role in the way men perceive them, which in turn plays a role in how they might effectively advance in the male-dominated space. As a response to their socially conditioned cues, women reported dressing better than male counterparts and employing several other strategies to communicate through their personal appearance and presentation.

The False Pretense of Assimilation

The false pretense of assimilation was the framing concept in Chapter 7, and we discussed how psychological dominance, here sexism, makes a vague promise that women will be accepted and achieve wildly should they abandon feminine characteristics and adopt male traits. While holding up a few exceptions to the rule, the dominant group points to a few women who have succeeded in a male-dominated system, as if this opportunity for success were available equally to everyone who works hard.

This is a fallacy and it will not happen for all women, or most women, or a lot of women. Sexism sets women up to lose by creating conditions that put them at a disadvantage. As we have read so far, this comes in a variety of natural-seeming ways, from the interpersonal to the structural. Sexism is mutually enabling, self-perpetuating, and thus quite stable at this point (Tappan, 2006; Waller, 2002; Sidanius and Pratto, 1999). Women will have to continue fighting their way through sexism. In the meantime, many are still trying to fit themselves into the male frame.

When Your Characteristics Are Considered Liabilities

A sure sign of psychological dominance is when the characteristics of your identity are considered liabilities, and in response you try to alter those traits, hide them, or deny possession of them. For example, women allude to being "like one of the guys" or trying to "defeminize" themselves. Several participants talked about how certain women were "more palatable to men." Women abandon their female qualities in exchange for masculine qualities in order to succeed in male-dominated settings, such as political or economic systems. The reality is that the out-group will never be accepted. After all, according to the dominant group, they (women) have such unsavory traits. Which is why they don't belong to the better (male) group in the first place.

Altering Appearance as Act of Agency

A subordinate group does not actively seek to maintain its lesser-status role. Their self-deliberative behavior is perceived by them as an agentic response to the domination. That is, women realize the limitations they face, so they enact strategies to maneuver through a limiting power structure. In this chapter, we refer to women's strategies to change their appearance and behavior to help counter those structural limitations. What women fail to realize is how many other women have tried exactly the same strategies, with little result. In fact, rather than having the effect they sought, their attempt at behavioral and appearance change serves to reinforce the dominant group.

Women's attempt to assimilate continues the dance of one group having the power, and the other group trying to fit in so they can also have power. Women play their part in the dance by serving as a foil to men; he can only be on top if someone is below him. When a woman tries to fit in as a man, it reminds him why men are on top in the first place; it's because of his better characteristics, characteristics that are so impressive that she is trying to emulate them. She serves to remind him who he is, the natural dominant. Thus, the dance reifies the dominant group's esteem and sense of superiority because other groups are trying to be like them (Tappan, 2006; Waller, 2002; Sidanius and Pratto, 1999). This chapter discusses strategies women have enacted to achieve status in a male-centered work space.

Appearance Changes to "Be Taken Seriously"

These women discuss entering the workforce and already being aware that men will sexualize and undermine them. They also know that being subjected to that will adversely affect their careers. To counter male attention proactively, they make choices about toning down and hiding their femininity.

Avoid Beautiful Clothes

I am somebody who decided very early on in my career, because I was very conscious of not being the target of certain types of unwanted attention. I would not wear makeup to work. I would not let my hair down, literally do not let my hair down at work. I tie it back all the time.

My mother gave me a suit once when I just started out which was a beautiful suit, but it had a huge slit in the skirt. And after a few times of wearing it, I didn't wear it again. In fact, I remember why. . . . I wore it to a case once and the solicitor made some cheap remark about it as a joke.

I was in court and the client was a gangster. And I had gone to speak with him with the solicitor about something. After the solicitor said, "Well I'm sure he appreciated the slit in your skirt if nothing else." And I realized in a heartbeat that that's how he perceived me and that's how the clients perceived me. I never wore it again.

This is someone who was my age, we're not talking about some creepy old guy here, he was my age. But he was in a position—a status of power—because he was instructing me, you see. So he felt like he could say that.

I never wear heels either to court, and the clothes I wear are all pretty shapeless. Always black. So when I walk into a conference and into a court that I feel I am being perceived only as a lawyer, rather than a woman. I've felt like I had to do that to myself. I did it early in my career, right from the start.

(Isabella, *Law*)

Cover Yourself Up

I changed the way that I dress, and I still dress differently than I would have—I cover myself up quite a lot—because I want to be taken seriously. I'm also very uncomfortable with men looking at my legs and down my shirt.

Being in a male-dominated industry like I have been for the past 10 years has been competing against men in the workplace. The whole of my career, I've never wanted to be that woman who capitalizes on it by putting on the higher heels and the tight skirt even though a lot of times, I hate to say it, but they were the ones who benefited from it. They were playing the game. I didn't want to do that. That male attention made me feel really uncomfortable.

(Mila, *Middle East Business Development*)

Dress Better Than Your Male Coworkers

I've always dressed better than everyone I've worked with. That's part of me and my personality. I would probably do that anyways, but it's also to do something differently to be taken seriously. If I showed up in shorts and tee shirts and sandals like they did, I wouldn't really have my voice heard. Or be considered as professional as they are, even though it's a bunch of musicians. Very casual work environments, I didn't really ever play into that.

(Olivia, *Music*)

Be Accompanied by a Man and Dress Like a Librarian

When you say about people's perception of an expert, it's either a man who's middle-aged or a man who has some grey hair. Or it has to be a woman who looks like a librarian. If you're super nerdy and you turn up, and then again you also have to be accompanied by a man because you need a man to corroborate everything that you're saying by virtue of his presence.

It doesn't really matter what his age is, because that shows wisdom and obviously, he's battle worn. Even if he is talking utter shit, people would say, "Oh it's really great, he's really been through it, he knows what he's talking about."

(Natalya, *Law*)

NOBODY DISCUSSES A MAN'S APPEARANCE

"Have you ever heard of anyone, male or female, really commenting on a man's appearance? Not unless he turned up smelling of whiskey, shit-faced and got vomit on him—to work—you never hear anyone talking about that. But the men and women I've heard talking about the appearance of female counsel, plenty of times."

(Natalya, *Law*)

Avoiding the Male Gaze—Trying to Get Men Not to Notice You

Aware that being sexualized by a man is a bad thing for professional women, they try to shrink out of view by how they wear their hair and makeup. Important for them is that their appearance is nothing of note. More than that, by controlling their own appearance, they are under the impression that they have some level of control over men's actions. If a man is inclined to sexualize women, what she is wearing will not make him decide against that.

The first participant mentions that the situation can arise regardless of what a woman is wearing. Another woman wears a cross to ward off attention. The flawed thinking, which we also hear in rape cases, is the question of what a woman is wearing, and the notion that clothing renders a man unable to control his own behavior.

Avoid Having a Striking Appearance

I think the trick is to look good but not let your appearance be the most striking thing about you. That has always been my concern. Not because I consider myself to be a beauty, but I never, I don't want to wear very low-cut things or short things. I don't want to be judged by how I look and I don't want my relationship to be formed on those bases. I think that's dangerous. I have been in situations where, *quite frankly those situations can arise even if you're wearing jeans and a tee shirt.* But my point is that I don't want to put myself into those situations. Because if you are remotely attractive, everybody thinks it's open season. That's not a good place to be in.

(Julia, *Global Marketing*)

Don't Wear Makeup

I don't dress like a nerd, I also don't dress like I'm going to a party. I wear things I like, which I think to be professional, but I wear what I want. I barely wear any makeup. Mainly because I'm lazy, not because of anything else. I do to black tie dinners. People are really confused—one of my clients the last time I went to a black-tie dinner with him, said, "Oh my god, I didn't even recognize you."

(Olivia, *Music Industry*)

Tone Yourself Down

I try to be as professional as possible. Whatever the idea of being professional is. But it's being a bit more serious, being a bit more toned down, both in the way I act and the way I dress. . . . I guess I interpreted that this is the way you're supposed to act.

(Leah, *Political Marketing*)

Accentuate Being Religious and Married

One gal always wore a cross as a way to try to ward off sexual advances. And she was married so she wore a wedding ring. My observations are that

that does little to dissuade men who are interested in sexualized, objectifying attractive females. It's not an effective deterrent.

(Avery, Marketing)

Defeminizing Herself

These women are deliberately hiding their femaleness and trying to mas-
culinize themselves through appearance and conduct.

Things You Just Do as a Woman

There's also a lot of other things that being a woman you just *do* as part of
being a woman in a corporate workplace. The way I dress, the way I act,
it's all part of finding my role in a structure in a system.

(Allison, Political Marketing)

Hair Back, Soft Glasses

I didn't want anybody to think that it wasn't my master's degree or my experience or my knowledge or my capabilities that brought me to the role. It
wasn't because of the way I looked or the fact that you know, as a woman,
I think I kind of tried to de-feminize myself.

> I wear trousers quite often. I didn't before. I always make sure that my
> cleavage is not showing. I just read an article about how women are
> not allowed to be angry in the workplace, whereas men can because
> all of these different things around that—sorry just like coming from
> the eyeglasses. I actually bought glasses that I thought were softer
> because of this whole idea.

> I started putting my hair back in a bun, which I haven't thought
> of in a long time, but I think the whole rest of that job, I had my
> hair in a bun with my softer glasses, and my whole body covered
> up, blazers, trousers, and really being very careful about how that
> looked.

(Mila, Aviation)

Have a Strong Armor

I'm very careful with how I get into situations, how personal and private I
get with coworkers, so as to watch myself. I have been called "Ice Queen"
and "Terminator" from groups of employees who feel I'm so tough and hard.
I think probably I have a strong armor and try to be so professional and so

powerful, that they wouldn't dare step on me. I guess I adapted my behavior to protect myself. Needed or not.

(Janni, Transportation)

Become Like One of the Guys

I have quite a reputation for being a little bit tough. . . . I won't lose my temper, but I will be frank. And I'm also somebody who is not afraid of using foul language . . . I swear a lot. Sounds ridiculous, but I swear a lot. And I think that that defeminizes me.

I don't think I set out to defeminize myself but as a result of that, I'm kind of like one of the guys. I also don't have children. So I'm in a weird gray area. I'm almost perceived as not really being a girl.

(Isabella, Law)

What Your Stuff Says about You

In this section, women discuss how what they wear is supposedly reflective of their personal characteristics, as if the two are somehow related. What we hear in these passages are the judgments and evaluations of men to regulate women's appearance and implant the notion that women themselves are akin to objects. The idea that your "stuff" speaks about you is a cultural construction.

If you had to borrow someone else's clothes for a year, you would still be you. Your stuff is not you, but women are told the opposite. The silent objective sexism accomplishes here is always keeping women off balance, always guessing about themselves and their relative worth. In that way, women are not thinking about their inherent worth.

Looking Too Sharp Means You're High Maintenance

I do think that men expect—your colleagues expect you to be well polished but not too polished. Because if you turn up like sharp as a pin, they'll be like, "Oh, well she's high maintenance. Drama follows her everywhere that she goes." So it kind of goes to the point I was saying that you never strike the right balance. Likewise with your clients.

(Natalya, Law)

Skinny Glasses Means You're an Uptight Bitch

As I'm rising in the ranks as well as in office, my boyfriend said, "Whatever you do, don't get the skinny spectacle that make women in the office place look like really uptight bitches." We had a long discussion around that because we had some friends over and talked about it a couple times afterwards, "What does that even mean?" How powerful women in the workplace just have a really bad rap. You're frigid, or you're a bitch because you're wearing skinny sunglasses, but you do your work well, and you can keep up with the men.

(Mila, Aviation)

Expensive Accessories Convey Your Power, But Not Necessarily to Men

What I have is that you show your power in other ways. You stick to your plain clothing, but you do your power jewelry, you do your power handbag. That's how women have sort of evolved into showing "Don't fuck with me, I'm successful." You show your success through wealth and your power through wealth. That's how middle-ranking women show they are not to be trifled with, that they've got money. It's an outward sign of success. You wear the big jewelry, you wear the big ring, you wear the big watch . . . that's the kind of thing that shows power.

(Isabella, Law)

"No man, for any considerable period, can wear one face to himself and another to the multitude, without finally getting bewildered as to which one is true."

—Nathaniel Hawthorne, The Scarlet Letter

Men Still Interpret Women as Less

Narratives in this section remind us that despite any and all efforts by women to present themselves a certain way, men still perceive them as less. Under this invented frame of reality, men own things, not women. If a woman has something, it is because a man gave it to her. She can be talented and accomplished, but she is aggressive, so the man will still get advanced ahead of her. Her stuff is given to her and does not signify status, whereas his stuff makes him an expert genius. Masculine is positive, feminine is a liability.

Still Interpreted Wrong—His Ambition, Her Aggression

If it comes to reviews and a guy walks in, and he's like, I want this and I want that and, you know, I think I deserve it . . . they say, Oh, he's actually really driven and he's really ambitious.

When it comes from a woman, unless you are prepared to burn the place down and take some clients with you, you are perceived as *aggressive*. You're a little bit, biting off more than you can chew. A little bit like, "Well are you really sure that you are at that level?"

On the basis of the same, if you put a male associate, a male lawyer who's of the same age, the same qualification . . . why is his behavior of "Jack the lad" being perceived as that of an ambitious guy who is burning the candle at both ends, therefore, he really wants it; as opposed to somebody who actually *does* the work and does it well?

(Natalya, *Law*)

Wealth, Status, and Success—Cannot Possibly Be Yours

I married the mayor and obviously was quite established on my own. I'm the CEO of a tech company, so that presumes a level of wealth and accomplishment. And I'm married to a public servant, which presumes a level of poverty just to be candid. We do not pay our public service people enough. He was making, mayors make forty thousand dollars a year, so let's just put this in perspective. I immediately received public attacks, like actual attacks by the presumption that my then-husband was giving me things.

Gave me business or created my name. Created my brand, like he had anything to do with it! It couldn't have been Harvard. It couldn't have been MIT. It couldn't have been the two million dollars' net worth that I came to the city with on my own. It couldn't have been any of that. It couldn't have been my career. None of that. It has to be because all of a sudden, I was married to the mayor.

(Catherine, *Tech and Land Development*)

Wealth as a Communicator of Worth—a Man with Wealth

Some people really struggle with this, I don't know, they have a perception of an expert. An expert man could be anything—I mean, my god. How many men who I met wearing Brioni suits and Dunhill cufflinks, you know, and the client says, "Wow, I want him as my lawyer."

He's thick as shit, he's just given the farm away. I'm like, "I just got you the best deal in the world" and the client was too distracted by the guy's Montblanc pen to understand. "Did you see his watch?" I'm like, "*Yes*, he must be a genius."

(Natalya, *Law*)

Court Bias: Masculine Is a Strength vs. Feminine Should Be Masculinized

It's been such a long time since I've appeared in court in a way that is strikingly feminine.

That sounds odd to say but if you're a very slight-looking twenty-four-year-old then I think you seem to be more vulnerable than a six foot two, broad shouldered, twenty-four-year-old male. It's as primal as that, you look weaker.

I noticed it when I started out from the bench. I felt that younger women got a harder time from judges, both male and female judges, than their male counterparts did. I think they appeared . . . they appear to be less robust physically and I think that made a difference to how they were treated.

(Isabella, *Law*)

External Adjustments Create Internal Changes

Internalization of Oppression

If we live in a male-dominated society (which we do), then domination is part of the sociocultural landscape. Without being aware of it, we internalize the dominant lens that sees women as less and that lens becomes our lens. We exercise what power is available to us, resorting to self-concealment, isolation, and finally resignation. In addition to feeling powerless, we also feel defensive and anxious (Griffin, 1997; Lipsky, 1987).

Taking up Less Space Feels Damaging to the Self

What I decided to do to quell that response is change my appearance, change my look and not display wealth, to be honest. I learned to take up less space. What this does to your well-being sometimes is damaging. That's why I have to go home, or leave the country and go on a trip.

(Catherine, *Tech*)

Closing Yourself with Clothes Actually Makes You Closed Off

Given the fact that I shared about closing off, wearing more clothes, feeling very defensive, feeling like my status as a woman and feeling that I had certain anatomy was the reason I had certain jobs or certain positions or certain projects.

(Maryam, *Branding and Marketing*)

Playing Defense with Your Look Makes You Feel Defensive

I think I did become more closed off. More defensive for sure. I think more similar to the frigid bitch with the skinny glasses. I do think now there's a defensiveness in me, and aggressiveness in me that I notice that I bring on and I have to tone down. Kind of like that phrase, I'm the Dragon Lady.

(Mila, *Business Development*)

Being Asked to Do Menial Tasks Makes You Anticipate Being Asked to Do Menial Tasks

There were a couple times I was so aggravated over it that I started becoming a little over the top. Somebody casually saying like, "Can you grab their coat?" Almost like "Do you want to make coffee or shall I?" And me being like, "Did you just ask me to make coffee? I'm not here to make coffee. I'm not here to take their coat! Why am I the one who has to make the lunch reservation? I'm not making the reservation—you make the reservation. You can arrange the plane tickets. I'm not the travel agent here."

A lot of things when I thought I was getting them again I would jump the gun on it. Then a person might say, "I was going to ask you to make your own reservation for yourself." I was just so highly sensitive to it, being asked to do secretarial work outside my arena.

(Mila, *Business Development*)

Being Taken Advantage of Makes You Anticipate Being Taken Advantage Of

I think that dragon lady thing that I bring in where I'm immediately aggressive in the boardroom, I think I've taken that on into my personal life, too, like "What do you want from me?" and "Nobody's going to take advantage of me." I'm not going to let anybody get into that role. I'm not going to let anybody take what's mine, and I've closed off quite a bit because I felt so, maybe partially exposed, but also on some levels wronged. Yeah, I do unfortunately.

(Olivia, *Music Industry*)

Couldn't Be Feminine and Respected

Someone described me as having a core of steel . . . someone who had a rod of steel running through them. And that was his perception of me, that's how he described me to people. Steely. I felt that I couldn't be, sort of soft. I couldn't be feminine. And that was the compromise I made to be respected.

(Isabella, *Law*)

Being Sexualized Makes You Feel Sexualized

I think also a big part of it was confidence. I didn't have the confidence in myself—I was worried that they would all be looking at me rather than listening to me. And I realized that I was good enough to be listened to irrespective of how I looked, I just needed to prove that to myself. And by almost de-genderizing myself if that's even a word, so then to build up the belief that I was there because I was being listened to. I was there because I was good enough. I wasn't there because I was pretty, I wasn't there because I was sexy, I wasn't there because I was easy on the eyes.

(Julia, *Global Marketing*)

Wasted Time, Missed Opportunities

There's just so many things again I put up with. Part of it makes me a little sad, I just wasted so much time. I got put some steps back, because of the feelings around it. I know that people could say "oh it's too bad you couldn't take that job" or "it's too bad you couldn't be that person to go after this or that." I felt like if I were a man, I would have been able to accomplish that. I would be in a different position.

(Mila, *Aviation*)

Exposing Sexist Scripts and Thought Patterns

I. Appearance Changes to "Be Taken Seriously"
    A. Avoid Beautiful Clothes
    B. Cover Yourself Up
    C. Dress Better Than Your Male Coworkers
    D. Be Accompanied by a Man and Dress Like a Librarian

II. Avoiding the Male Gaze—Trying to Get Men Not to Notice You
    A. Avoid Having a Striking Appearance
    B. Don't Wear Makeup
    C. Tone Yourself Down
    D. Accentuate Being Religious and Married

III. Defeminizing Herself
    A. Things You Just Do as a Woman
    B. Hair Back, Soft Glasses
    C. Have a Strong Armor
    D. Become Like One of the Guys

IV. What Your Stuff Says About You
    A. Looking Too Sharp Means You're High Maintenance
    B. Skinny Glasses Means You're an Uptight Bitch
    C. Expensive Accessories Convey Your Power, But Not Necessarily to Men

V.   Men Still Interpret Women as Less
   A.   Still Interpreted Wrong—His Ambition, Her Aggression
   B.   Wealth, Status, and Success—Cannot Possibly Be Yours
   C.   Wealth as a Communicator of Worth—a Man with Wealth
   D.   Court Bias: Masculine Is a Strength vs. Feminine Should Be Masculinized

VI. External Adjustments Create Internal Changes
   A.   Internalization of Oppression
   B.   Taking Up Less Space Feels Damaging to the Self
   C.   Closing Yourself with Clothes Actually Makes You Closed Off
   D.   Playing Defense with Your Look Makes You Feel Defensive
   E.   Being Asked to Do Menial Tasks Makes You Anticipate Being Asked to Do Menial Tasks
   F.   Being Taken Advantage of Makes You Anticipate Being Taken Advantage Of
   G.   Couldn't Be Feminine and Respected
   H.   Being Sexualized Makes You Feel Sexualized
   I.   Wasted Time, Missed Opportunities

Analysis

Rebecca tells about when she shifted her thinking about clothes. After 20 years of not getting better results for being meticulous with her wardrobe selection, she opted instead to go back to clothing she liked. Question yourself, as you read the account, about how many men you know who think about their clothing choice to the extent of any women in this chapter.

Wasting My Life Waiting for Male Approval

I remember going shopping for a black power suit when I was defending my dissertation. It's very important to look just so, and I've always been cognizant of looking exactly right. I went into a shop looking for a black jacket. There was a sales associate who walked across the floor. She had on a seafoam green skirt that was floor length, and when she walked she looked like a goddess. I got that skirt, and that is what I wore.

I had gone through all of that, wearing the black power suits and wearing my hair back. People are still telling me I'm cute. It was obviously worth all the effort that I put into it—no makeup. Very serious. I was like, "Fuck this. I'm getting a doctorate. Will it make you feel like I'm smarter if I wear glasses? Will I be smarter if I wear a suit?"

I don't care anymore and nothing I tried works anyway. I like dresses. At that point I decided to go back to wearing beautiful things because it makes me happy, and because I never noticed a difference in how men responded to me. I'd been twenty years trying different things with my hair, different appearances, like what my body language was like, what exactly—precisely—the language I used. If they have it in their head they are not going to respect you, it doesn't matter what you've done, and it doesn't matter if you're wearing a suit. On top of that, all the things you go through, about how you act and what you wear, what man even *considers* that?

Conclusion

Women attempt to avoid the male gaze by shrinking away and trying not to be noticed physically. The assumption is flawed. They have the idea that you can control men's behavior by controlling your appearance—that you put yourself into "those situations" to be sexualized or even noticed. This leads to judgment of other women for how they present themselves.

Some women perceive their feelings as a confidence issue. They arrive at this fact, having forgotten the years of social cues that directed them to that thinking in the first place. And meanwhile, while women are fighting themselves and all the other women around you, men are advancing.

Documenting these narratives is important, as is noting your own feelings. Remember, you did not happen to feel this way, it was by design. External control builds subservience into the minds of the targeted group so they can police themselves. The results and emotions are byproducts and reinforcers of that effort (Pheterson, 1990, p. 35). Highlighting this aspect is not to plunge you deeper into a dark place. Rather, it is to shed light into that dark place so you can see it was not something you did or brought upon yourself. If men did not want to make women feel inferior, they can change their behavior. Seeing these dynamics for what they are empowers you to change your own behavior.

Creating Scripts and Thought Patterns

- What changes have you made to fit into a group?
  - Why did you feel you needed to make those changes?
  - Did they work?

- Think of the people in your life that you respect.
    - What do you respect about them?
    - What do they contribute to your life?
    - How would your life be different if this person was not in it?
    - What type of clothes do they wear?

CHAPTER TEN

It Isn't about a Particular Woman

Seeking: The prototypical left-wing bitch: annoying, condescending, smug, godless, sexless, hysterical, humorless, and deeply antagonistic toward strong, masculine men. You know the type. They're everywhere.

Seeking: Female, Caucasian, early to mid-20s, this gorgeous blonde is, "a sexual harassment suit waiting to happen."

Seeking: Topless girl. Huge Exposure.
                    —Actress descriptions submitted to casting agencies

Introduction

A current running throughout this book has been men sexualizing women in various forms. This chapter explores that further in the context of executive sexism. Under the frame of social domination, the accumulation of women communicates a man's value and status to other men. The woman herself does not matter; she is a thing, an object, an accessory. Men accumulate experiences with women like they accumulate cars and watches. Like his accessories, other men gauge his status, wealth, and power according to his perceived access to quantities of women. Three concepts best frame this subject.

Reduction of Human Value: People Are Grouped by Economic Status

Money reduces people to their function, so they are valued only in terms of their financial productivity. This reliance segments the workforce and separates humans into groups based on their economic positions (Simmel, 1907/1978, p. 356). Those with the greatest financial worth are in the most advantageous positions, and they are in positions to make decisions that affect people below their status. Thus, economic position serves to reinforce a perpetual system of quantified *value of accumulation* over the qualified experience of living.

Social dominance thrives on hierarchy. To be truly successful, an SDO man must reach the pinnacle of the hierarchy. He must be in the most prestigious position in order to make decisions. Making decisions about how things run is the most effective way to keep them running in a way that serves your interests. The accumulation of things signifies your financial worth, and financial worth is a visible indicator of your relative power; thus, the image of status helps men to achieve status. This is how the interplay between individual agency and society shape each other.

Fetishism of Commodity: Our Stuff Signifies Social Relationship

One's labor is translated into exchange for goods. Generally, these goods are items that people need to live and survive. Food, clothing, vehicles, housing, the goods people exchange for their labor serve a function. When commodities are fetishized, the products themselves become the function (Marx, 1867/1967). A bag, a ring, a watch, these items are not functional themselves. The function of these items lies in what they communicate: a Gucci bag, a Tiffany ring, a Rolex watch. The utility of the items is less important than the status they represent. We are communicating our high status through things.

Conspicuous Consumption: We Buy Things to Communicate Our Social Status

Conspicuous consumption is the original concept now known as personal branding. People are aware of social status, and aware that the *image* of status helps us to build status. Certain products enhance the image of status while others do not. By purchasing these products, the individual creates a personal identity that is represented by the brands and products that represent high social status (Veblen, 1899/1994). In a sexist culture, beautiful women are a commodity that represents high status among men.

Calculating Character: Everything Has a Price, So Everything Can Be Bought

Among certain people there is a notion that the value of a person's life is based solely on his or her's ability to accumulate wealth. Within this mentality, life itself is reduced to numeric value; thus there comes to exist among people a mathematical mode of thinking, a "calculating character" that supposes that a price is attached to everything, and thus every good and experience can be quantified. Because all things can be quantified, they can also be assigned a price, so to them *all things can be purchased*. The intellectuality of calculating character places greater importance on that which can be quantitively accumulated over that which is qualitatively experienced (Simmel, 1907/1978, p. 444).

It's a Numbers Game. Men who have social media accounts filled with pictures of themselves and attractive women are quantifying their worth. The identity of women, what they have to say, how they think or feel—these mean nothing; the woman is incidental to the point. The quality of the man's experience is not important to other men in calculating his worth. What assigns his higher status to other men is quantity, his perceived access to a high number of attractive women. And like watches, women can be bought. In addition to social media pictures, frequenting strip clubs, having sex with employees, and positioning yourself as the sexual partner of an employee are effective means to claim status.

We have read throughout this book how executive women have been subjected to this type of behavior from their employers. Also, how women watch as their male colleagues and clients buy women as entertainment, and bond over the experiences. This chapter delves further into the issue of commodification. The passages demonstrate how sexist men treat executive women as something to be bought for entertainment. We visit the personal dimensions of some interview participants to see their depth of character and accomplishment. We see then the personal toll sexism takes, and ultimately how sexism reduces the woman's identity into something expendable.

Men Who Commodify Women, Commodify Women

In this section, executive women talk about the fog in which sex and work are inextricably mixed. At several points in this work, the subject of personal attitudes and their relationship to work life has emerged. These narratives are continuations of that question.

Where Do You Dance?

I'm a Harvard graduate, A school, B school. An MIT alum from their most prestigious program. I came back to (city), married the mayor . . . and how people would approach me would be "Hey, how are you, what's your name, where do you dance?" Like that was the next question.

Professional circles, professional networking environment to the guy on the street who tries to pick you up at the gas station. It was just so pervasive . . . I started to get numb to it. But it's just so, like I said it's like eating at some point, eating nasty food on top of that, but that's just what there is, right?

(Catherine, Tech)

Social Media Images and Personal Life

Working in business with somebody who has social media that shows them disrespecting women, that's something I wouldn't do again. I wasn't really thinking about the depth of character. I was focused on building this company and making the best of the situation I was in rather than getting out of the situation. I'm a very loyal person. The first company I worked for it was almost ten years. I was in it and I was going to make it work. Seeing again social media pages objectifying women and working with somebody who objectifies women, that can't help but bleed over to the workplace. Because it's a mentality, and that treatment of women.

I couldn't take pride in my work anymore because I kept thinking "anything I do in this company will be benefitting and lining this guy's pockets. And then he's going to go to a new country, a new city and he's going to drink champagne and pour it down a woman's cleavage. And there's going to be a woman there who is willing to flirt with a guy for a glass of champagne at a table and I can't be part of this anymore."

The personal side of business, where we spend so much time with the people we work with. People don't always bring sexism in verbally or physically, but they do by their presence. Their mentality, and how it bleeds into other areas of corporate culture.

(Mila, Aviation)

Married Men Who Have Sex with Their Employees

Men don't like being thing called on sexual misbehavior—it's part of how they identify themselves, their sexual conquests. Pretty common, even if it's an inappropriate sexual conquest, there are bragging rights. Certainly not a topic of discussion with a female, much less female employee. I challenged that, and he wasn't happy.

He was angry. First, he laughed, and that sort of bravado, "Hey, I conquered." Then he was angry that I would challenge his integrity. The look I caught was like a little boy caught with his hand in the cookie jar, or more like his hand between a woman's legs. Even though he wore his cross on his chest, he also did things that he *knew* were not appropriate. But he felt driven and privileged to do, entitled to do.

(Avery, Pharmaceutical Marketing)

Women Are Commodities, Not Partners

My friend was the personal assistant to a millionaire. One example of her work, she arranged a birthday golf trip for a group of guys to the Bahamas. The plane dropped off the men, then came back and took over a plane full of girls. These guys took a picture of themselves on the golf course for the wives. The pretense was it was a guys' trip.

I always wondered if the wives knew, because these guys had no problem lying and then going home after. Pertinent to this theme of professional sexism, these guys all own huge companies. They lie to their wives, betray their children, cheat on their own families. They basically live a double life with a straight face. This is how they feel about women. Why would the women they work with be any different?

(Rebecca, *Senior Scientist*)

Personal Dimension of Participants

Women are asked and expected to alter their lives, their personal characteristics, and sometimes their professions. Here they discuss the effects of sexism and in terms of their personal histories and their identities.

Legacy of Strong, Accomplished Black Women

I was honored in *Unity* magazine this month. *Unity* magazine is a huge honor—Iyanla Vanzant was honored, Oprah, Michael Beckwith—amazing people. One of my friends said, "Oh, your mom is probably so proud of you."

I was like, "I would never hear my mom say that. My family doesn't believe in vanity."

I grew up in a house with no mirrors, because culturally there's a story that mirrors take your soul away. I was trying to explain it. I said, "My mom and my family really are not overly affectionate, but everybody's super accomplished."

Let me back up—my grandmother worked on the Manhattan Project, which was the founding of atomic energy, which is all the lights that are on top of us. Her sister kept forward with that, and then played the harp, baked the best, and ran the Children's Choir. Amazing accomplished women, black women, in the 1930s, '40s, and '50s. Their great aunt founded a school in Chicago.

For me, I've done nothing compared to what they've done. I've been through nothing, compared to what they've been through. That really is the thing that I hold on to, to make it make sense that black women in science and tech in the 1940s and '50s. What could I possibly be dealing with now that's like more insidious?

(Catherine, Tech)

Unladylike Profession

There are so many people I've met who say, "Oh, that's such an unladylike profession." And I'm like, "What's a ladylike profession? What should I be? A maternity nurse? That's a ladylike profession." This is so surreal, why are people even thinking that today?

She answers the inquiry:

"You do realize that the reason I do this is because I enjoy it and I'm good at it, and I make money. I didn't do it because I wanted to be like a man. I still go buy handbags. Does that make you feel better?"

(Natalya, Law)

Nurturing Partner and Fiery Lawyer

Personally, I saw my mother be really—subservient might be the wrong word to use—but she definitely catered to my father's needs. That's what I was socialized to believe that a woman should do for her husband. Period. Done. I'll bring your food and then I'll take the plate away and I'll wash it. Don't get up, I'll do everything for you. That is completely 100% me in a relationship.

Then I've got this person, this fighter lawyer in me also. That makes for some fireworks. I've had to claw and had fight in order to do that. But I think it makes me really independent ultimately. My guess is that I'm displaying independence and apparently the men like the damsel in distress. I'm nobody's damsel in distress.

(Sarah, Law)

Lilith from *Cheers*

She talks about her personal style of relating to men now, and the type of woman she wanted to be to respond when men tried to belittle or out-wit her.

Basically, being looked at as bit of a ball breaker I suppose, giving the appearance that I'm someone who's not going to take any shit. I probably overcompensated for that when I was younger. Did you ever watch *Cheers* when you were young? Remember Lilith? Yeah, I wanted to be Lilith, that's who I always wanted to be. I wanted to be that. Slicked back, quick quip, rapier-like responses to anything like that. You see what I mean? And that would put them back in their box.

(Isabella, Law)

Giggly

I dress quite differently in my free time than I do at work. I'm quite a giggly person privately. I wouldn't act like that at work because I think that people get the wrong idea. Maybe people think I'm leading them on, people find me flirty. I'd say it affects everything.

(Allison, *Political Marketing*)

Self-Made Daughter of Immigrants

In that moment I feel stripped of every accomplishment that I have ever made. Excuse me if I get emotional about it. I'm an immigrant. I'm the daughter of immigrants. I busted my butt through public school through college through law school. I got a scholarship to law school. I passed the bar on the first try. I am a hell of a lawyer. And in that moment when they look at me, and all they see is my skin and my gender. It feels like everything that I have worked 40 years of my life for, is worthless. I'm just sitting there, this nappy headed immigrant girl, that people thought wouldn't amount to anything.

(Sarah, *Law*)

Diminutive and Intimate Names

> "I have to fit into this little box because a strong female is not something that they find palatable. So somehow they've got to put me in their box and they use their words to do that."
>
> (Sarah, *Law*)

When men communicate their own status by using diminutive names, this is another way they reduce her identity. This has nothing to do with the woman; it is just because she is a woman that men feel justified in doing this. She has no name of her own. He uses the same names for all the women because to him, she is interchangeable with any other woman.

Because I'm a Woman

The reason that he talked to me any kind of way, is because I'm a woman. "Oh shoot, I forgot I was a woman." That's my way—I say it out loud—when I'm with my team or different settings. "Dang, I forgot I was a woman." I say it to let people know that I *know* that the reason I didn't get that contract is because I'm a woman.

(Catherine, *Tech and Land Development*)

Terms of Intimacy

These Terms of Endearment, these really familiar, almost terms of intimacy are being used, directed at me. When I'm in court I consistently get the "baby girl" and then "What's up beautiful" and "Good morning gorgeous." I'm your attorney, that is our relationship. We don't have any other relationship outside of attorney/client.

(Natalya, *Law*)

Overfamiliarity

You said the word familiarity. I *hate* overfamiliarity. I think that there are certain people who really overcompensate with that. I just find it really inappropriate and also you know, really intrusive.

Your Compliance Is Expected

Women reported that any woman anywhere is a potential target. Because men adhere to the behavior of reduction, they expect that women will be compliant in accepting or tolerating their advances, and their advances are relentless.

Fair Game

Coming across sexually is so inherent in them so they don't know any other way to be. It's just, it's weird to me. You're a mature man. This is how you've been socialized to believe that interactions with females are? No matter who the woman is, as long as she's not related, she's fair game. It doesn't matter what her making is or what her station is versus you. And they do it completely unashamedly.

(Natalya, *Law*)

Women at Work Are Considered Fair Game

A single woman in the office is looked at as fair game. I felt like there was always that element of looking down my shirt over the boardroom table.

"Oh, what are you doing this evening? Why don't we talk?" I can say I'm going home; my boyfriend is making dinner. I shouldn't have needed to say that to let people know that I was not on the market.

(Natalya, *Law*)

Men Expect Your Compliance

They absolutely expect it. When I'm looking at this guy, shackled at the feet and the waist and that's the confidence and sense of entitlement. Imagine if they are colleagues or someone with a little bit more power because then the world is their oyster. They can take whatever they want, "I have a little power." I mean if a guy in shackles can do it, please.

(Natalya, *Law*)

Women Are Conditioned to Ignore It

Someone who it happens to all the time has been told by the men in her life that it's not a big deal, ignore it, these women are exaggerating. So even we are conditioned that way to some extent. That's the response, "Where do you find these people?" They're everywhere. It's just if you choose to ignore it or pay attention.

(Natalya, *Law*)

So Prevalent

I have had this stuff happen to me since I started being around professional men. Men who I am talking to, about business or work matters, at the end of the conversation, the man will make a sexual move. Like that was the natural next step. I'm in private consulting. This happens all the time.

I stopped telling people. Men, women, they would say, "Where do you find these people?" Like it was *me* who was the problem, I was the common denominator. There's one of me and hundreds of them. I hope people now can start to get their heads around the fact that it's this type of men, they are the common denominator.

Where do I find them? I'll tell you. They make your laws. They own the companies you know and use on a daily basis. They are in charge of your children. One that comes to mind runs the youth branch of a prominent US think tank. You might be married to one. Someone is married to that guy.

I've had so many men, professional men in professional settings, hit on me, proposition me for sex, ask me out on a date, and in the next breath talk to me about their wives and children. They do it like I should be impressed about what great fathers they are, and he has a nice family. It's this weird positioning thing men do, to blame me at some point for making the conversation sexual. When I turn them down, they need to save face, so they blame me. It makes no rational sense and I've seen it time and again. It's a thing that men do.

But the men who want to hide it, will hide it. Your friends might be like this, your brother might be like, other men you think you know well. I'm not saying every man, but it's a lot. You would never know unless he was targeting you. These guys rarely have their wives around, though. I guess they don't take sand to the beach.

(Natalya, *Law*)

Women Can't Reconcile Their Identity with Male Expectations

> "I don't even know how to explain what sexism is for a woman who has any modicum of power and achievement, particularly in the South. It's like eating nasty food but that's all there is, and you eat it every day."
>
> (Catherine, *Tech*)

Women have a difficult time reconciling their identity with the prescribed gender expectations that inundate them. They describe this inner battle below. The reason they are incapable of integrating how a man thinks they should be with how they think they should be, is because the gender expectations were invented. They are simple, compliant, and without depth. That invented frame will never fit a real woman.

Always Trying to Put You Back in the Cage

My ex-husband looked around and said, "You notice something. None of the politicians' wives work. None of them have careers. They all stay at home, for this very reason. For *this* very reason." Ultimately, it's what tore our marriage apart, because who can deal with that on a consistent basis? I didn't want to have to lower my lifestyle and *hide* myself, which is essentially what I was being asked, in order to make someone else's career possible.

It's like you don't own your own identity and that sometimes is super frustrating. I've heard a woman describe it as the experience of being in a zoo. The world is looking at you, caged you, framed you, and then watching to see how you react. You have to react a certain way or else, right? There are consequences to put you right back in the box and in the cage.

(Catherine, *Tech*)

Be Strong, But Not Too Strong

Don't be a pushover, but don't try to overcompensate for it. Don't try and be a man because that's going to be to your disadvantage. "You will not be true to yourself, you will be unhappy. And you will be perceived as somebody who's just a bitch." I saw that that was actually interesting advice. I think he's right. It also made me realize that as a woman, it's impossible to get it right.

It's impossible because if you try, I'm going to be a real woman. I'm going to be a damsel in distress, or wear pink and channel *Legally Blonde*, you're not going to command respect from your clients, or from the people on the other side, because they just got to think that you're ditzy, you're a pushover, an easy target.

Then you think, I'm going to channel Hillary, I'm going to wear trouser suits, and I'm going to be really on it. You're seen as someone who is trying to overcompensate, trying to be a man, even though you are not a man. Actually, you are getting it all wrong, because you are just a bitch.

So, you know, how do you get into that middle zone? Where actually you are respected for who you are, and for what you do, you know, but whilst being yourself?

(Sarah, Law)

Feeling the Need to Reconcile Different Sides of Her Identity

I vacillate wondering if I'm too weak or too strong. Maybe too weak, maybe too strong. I never have a good measure of how I should be. It's really difficult because on the one hand I'm told I'm intimidating. I cannot see how. But I'm told I'm intimidating. On the other hand, I'm told I'm too soft and I am a pushover. I don't know how to navigate it.

(Emma, Casting)

Men's Reduction of a Woman's Identity

Sexist men invent many ways to communicate their worth and your worthlessness. Trying to reconcile the invented gender frame takes a heavy emotional toll on women. Women find themselves off-balance, feeling defeated, suffering low self-esteem, and not knowing how they could have done better. These are the symptoms of internalized oppression, when we unconsciously buy into the dominant frame and see ourselves as weak for not being able to figure out a system that was designed to make us feel lesser (Freire, 1970).

Take Me Down a Peg

Then I start to do the self-blame. Did I come across as flirty? Did I say something that may have been misinterpreted? Is it my fault that they are talking to me that way? Upon review in my head I realized, "No I didn't say anything or do anything that my male colleagues would not have done." Yet somehow because of my gender—somehow with the male clients, they feel like they need to take me down a peg.

(Lauren, Professor and Board Member)

Humiliated

I felt so worthless and so humiliated that someone felt like he could just do that to me. I came from nothing. I have worked since I was 11. I have no one to fall back on, just myself. I work hard. I got a PhD, I had a great job. Everything you're supposed to do to earn respect. And this guy—in addition to this nice bar where it happened, he also owns Hooters restaurants. I think that's important to say. This guy just thought he could grab me. And he did, and he laughed at me. It reduces you right back to nothing.

(Rebecca, *Senior Scientist*)

Invisible

You know what happens to me in court all the time? I am literally in line to call my case and generally it's older white males, they'll come in and just step in front of me. Like I'm not there.

Usually for a second like my eyes go wide and my jaw drops because, did this really just happen? Then I'll tap them on the shoulder like, "I was in line."

"Oh, I'm sorry, I didn't realize you were in line." Really? Because I was standing literally behind the person in front of me. Yeah, like he missed me! I'm not slight. I'm not a petite—I have some substance. I know you saw me. But you just didn't recognize "attorney" when you saw me, that's what it is.

(Sarah, *Law*)

Dehumanized

I always wondered to myself, "Are you impressed by me, or are you impressed that a black girl knows as much as she does and is as articulate as she is?" I can never quite figure that out and that bothers me. Because I don't know if they're telling me that I'm good, or I'm good for a black girl. It's dehumanizing for me, it's demoralizing for me. It is completely deflating and a very hard thing for me to work through.

(Isabella, *Law*)

Inconsequential

I feel the weight of that in the moment and then I've got to suck it up and fold all of that away, put it back on the shelf of my mind and just keep going in very confidently. They've really deflated my balloon. It really is hard. A part of me is a little bit of an elitist, so I'm looking at these people, "Do you even have a high school diploma and like, taking away all of what I've worked for? Come on."

(Maryam, *Branding and Marketing*)

Nothing More Than Your Gender

I'm sighing because talking about it with you, it is emotional. To think that for 13 years of this being my chosen career. It's the thing that I worked hard for and this is how I get treated, still to this day. I didn't just get a JD. I got a master's in criminal justice, just to make sure I understood everything that I was doing from an academic standpoint, but it doesn't really matter

It doesn't matter. And that's the hurtful thing. I can add degrees and degrees and degrees to my name. But it doesn't matter. At the end of the day. I'm still my skin color and my gender. And that's it. That's how I'm viewed regardless of anything else.

(Sarah, *Law*)

Exposing Sexist Scripts and Thought Patterns

I. Men Who Commodify Women, Commodify Women
    A. Where Do You Dance?
    B. Social Media Images and Personal Life
    C. Married Men Who Have Sex with Their Employees
    D. Women Are Commodities, Not Partners

II. Personal Dimension of Participants
    A. Legacy of Strong, Accomplished Black Women
    B. Unladylike Profession
    C. Nurturing Partner and Fiery Lawyer
    D. Lilith from *Cheers*
    E. Giggly
    F. Self-Made Daughter of Immigrants

III. Diminutive and Intimate Names
    A. Because I'm a Woman
    B. Terms of Intimacy
    C. Overfamiliarity

IV. Your Compliance Is Expected
    A. Fair Game
    B. Women at Work Are Considered Fair Game
    C. Men Expect Your Compliance
    D. Women Are Conditioned to Ignore It
    E. So Prevalent

V.   Women Can't Reconcile Their Identity with Male Expectations
  A.   Always Trying to Put You Back in the Cage
  B.   Be Strong, But Not Too Strong
  C.   Feeling the Need to Reconcile Different Sides of Her Identity

VI. Men's Reduction of a Woman's Identity
  A.   Take Me Down a Peg
  B.   Humiliated
  C.   Invisible
  D.   Dehumanized
  E.   Inconsequential
  F.   Nothing More Than Your Gender

Analysis

"The Best She Could Be Is What, an Escort?"

I see this in dating as well. I met this guy. He's a trader at Goldman Sachs. I have no idea how much money he makes but I assume he's alright. We have a drink and he asked me what I do. He knew that I was a lawyer, and I said, "I'm a partner in a law firm." And it blew his mind.

The first 20 minutes of an hour that we spent together, he kept saying to me, "What do you mean you're a partner?" And I had to explain what it is, and he said, "What do you mean, like a shareholder in a company?"

And I'm like my god, for a trader you're really stupid. "Yes, like a shareholder in the company."

And he said, "How?" And I said, "What do you mean how?"

I just came back from a trip and was a little bit jet lagged but I thought, I'm going to give him a bit of a chance. I said, "What do you mean how?"

And he said, "Well how does one become a partner. . . . Is it just by working?"

And I said, "Yes, there is an aspect of that but it's not like laying an egg. It's not made by how long you wait for it. You actually have to make money."

So, he was like, "So what do you do?" I said to him, "I'm really good at making money."

And I thought, I sound like a complete idiot, but I think that that's how I must explain it to this guy. I don't understand what the problem is.

He was really struggling, "But we're the same age, and you don't have a boss and I'm still an employee."

I just stared at my drink at this point because I don't really know what to say.

I spent quite a bit of time thinking about it afterwards and—you know he's French, he works at Goldman, he is a trader, he's very cosmopolitan, well read. . . . He plays tennis, holidays in Bahamas. . . . He's my neighbor, we live in one of the best areas in central London, so he's not exactly somebody who crawled from under a rock.

But he's really struggling because. . . . What, women are not supposed to do that? Even if somebody called you an overachiever, I can still have a life. That's what we're good at. We're really good at getting shit done and multitasking. I'm sure there's more men like him than not.

Q: His line of inquiry was very peculiar.

It was a bit offensive. Because I was thinking, he probably looked at me like, "Oh, she's blonde. She's Russian. The best I could be is what, an escort?" No, sorry to disappoint you.

(Natalya, *Law*)

Conclusion

This chapter is critical in explaining the interpersonal context of people's values, and how those values carry into executive settings. Sexism happens in social settings as well among men and women who are executives. In situations like the one explained above, Natalya negotiates energy deals on behalf of governments, and she is presumed a prostitute by a man of comparable financial status. He is perplexed and asks the same question for 20 minutes. He could not fathom that a woman was of such high status, higher than his own: "You don't have a boss and I'm still an employee."

Hers is not a one-off incident. In this study alone, three interviewees described men consistently assuming they worked in the sex industry. One was a PhD CEO, who said she is asked repeatedly, in professional settings, where she dances, because men assumed she was a stripper. The woman who told this narrative mentioned that men make that assumption about her, that she is an escort. As we have read, men regularly challenge women on their credentials and work histories. A third participant experiences this, a PhD company owner. She said men constantly assume and treat her like a prostitute and accused her of inventing her company as a cover story for her actual profession. She noted that these were all professional men, usually during the week and just coming from work. We also heard from participants who spoke of men sexualizing them in the same conversation that the men talked about their wives and children. It is important to note that these are networks of high-level professional men who own one or more major businesses. This is the behavior. Not all men behave this way, but this behavior, among this demographic, is frequently experienced by the women who deal with them. In our social settings and personal lives, sexism is a rampant dynamic. The fact that it is also present in work life is a natural conclusion.

Men communicate with women's bodies. For executive women this is problematic because they are surrounded by colleagues and clients who buy women's bodies on a regular basis. Live bodies, images of bodies, through the impression or reality of sex with colleagues and employees. Women are caught in the crossfire of men's competition with each other for social status when men are communicating with other men, though the language of commodifying women.

Creating New Scripts and Thought Patterns

- What effect does a person's disposition have in the professional world?
- When a man buys a woman's time and body, he also purchases her compliance and seeming acceptance of him. If he pays a woman a salary, why would he not expect the same from her?
- Does it matter that men buy access to women's bodies as a social/professional activity?
- How might a woman feel if in the midst of this?
- Can you think of a male equivalent that leaves a person feeling humiliated, dehumanized, invisible, inconsequential, nothing more than your gender?
- Do parts of your identity not reconcile with social expectation?
    - Specifically, what traits?
    - How do you know you are violating social or gender expectations?
    - What are the consequences you pay as a result?

(*Note: If there is no consequence, there is no conflict.*)

CHAPTER ELEVEN

How Women Are Pitted against Each Other

Introduction

Perspective Evolves

Understanding our everyday experiences in a larger context presents a challenge. Our perspective evolves. How you make sense of any subject today is different than how you thought of it five years ago. What you learn, how you experience situations, your cognitive and emotional processing, all contribute to an ongoing revelation of any subject that is personal to us. We search for a schema, a pattern, a structure, to arrange dynamics in a way that we can make sense of them. In this chapter, we will discuss the ways women act against each other and what drives them to do so. To begin, we return to social dominance to explore two concepts.

Exerting Power under Social Domination

Internalization of culture is long acknowledged among sociologists. We tend to become that which is our repetitive social experience. Under sexist social domination, the characteristics of success are undermining, sabotaging, and other traits that seek to keep women in a lower-status position.

Horizontal violence is a related concept, where members of a group will turn on their own group and perpetrate physical violence against them (Tappan, 2006). Members of the subordinate culture, women in this case, may attempt to replicate the power structures in which they are situated, and exert the same power over women that is exerted over them. This is what they have seen, so this is what they know. When dominated people see limited options, they practice power where they can.

The Insidious Nature of Sexism

A Woman Didn't Do This to You, a Man Did

Catherine describes meeting her subcontractor, who was going through tough personal circumstances, empathizing with a terrible situation, and helping her through it. Their relationship takes a turn that surprises the speaker when the subcontractor almost sabotages a construction project.

> The woman who's the architect comes into my office. And she's bruised up. She just starts crying. I don't know this woman. I've seen her in passing because the contract hired her, right? I know she's the architect, but I don't have a relationship with her. She just comes in, she starts bawling, so I just offer for her to sit down. She tells me how she's going through a divorce. Her husband's abusive, you know, so my heart goes out to her. I feel for her. I want to support her, "Oh, it'll be okay I'm going through a divorce also. It'll be fine, you know. You're beautiful. You're smart. You're an architect." Now her story is a little tragic. She was married to the guy for 15 years. She was a trained architect. Had kids, right away. She *stopped* working to take care of the kids. She has two (she) has to take care of. He found a new younger woman and literally cut her off and kicked her out. "It's over. Go figure it out."
> Now she's got to go back into the workforce, that's how my contractor found her. and he's tutoring her, helping her get her license and situated. She didn't have a home to stay in. I offer, "Oh well I have storage. You can store your stuff in my space. I have guys that work for me, they can come and help you pack up and move. No problem." Right. This was six months ago. . . . Now my plans are due. She comes to me to finalize the contract. She asks me to pay the amount in full. I know she has financial trouble, but that's not how we do business. She refuses to do any more work until she gets paid in full. I'm like, let me just pay her in full so we can move this forward. Her invoice says that she's going to get it done in two weeks.

The architect is nowhere to be found for three weeks. She reaches back out to her contractor. When they do make contact, the architect has personal things to say.

> She told me how horrible I am—first she tells me how lucky I am, that I have the building anyway. And don't worry, it's going to get taken care of, I'm just being anal. . . . I'm watching how diligently and blushing she works for the contractor. And I'm watching how she responds to men, and I'm

watching all this and it just hit me one moment that my ability to work through pain . . . my ability to work through the divorce and still be successful was shocking to her and upsetting to her, to the point where she (was) almost trying to sabotage my job.

Unbelievable response from a woman. That to me is the insidious nature of sexism. This woman was abused by men. A woman didn't beat her. A woman didn't kick her out on the street. A man did that to her, but she takes all that pent-up anger and rage on a woman.

Her response is, "Let me make a man love me and like me enough to never do that again." With men, she's completely approbator. She's completely submissive. If you listen to her . . . she presents well, she's an architect. She's got a reputable firm. You saw her on the street, you will be like "oh god she's a wonderful woman" right? No.

In reality, her only value exists in contrast to men. But as it relates to women, her responses (are) negative, tearing them down. Why? Because her husband cheated with the woman, who was younger than her.

She's pointing all her anger in that direction, and not to the actual perpetrator. That to me is where the real damage is happening, and I would love to see like how we address that. How do we share that? How do we deal with that with other women? Because that's when things are going to change and move forward.

Is This What We're Doing to Each Other?

A larger issue for me than men being sexist to women, is women embodying sexism, right? People who should be your allies who are internalizing those issues and then spewing them back out.

(Catherine, *Land Development*)

"I Had to Take It"

Almost like hazing, women continue the cycle of doing to other women what men did to them.

Certain female judges, life for them was pretty atrocious . . . where they got horrendous treatment from the bench, that there's almost this, "Well I had to take it and it toughened me up and so I'm going to apply the same stance to you" sort of thinking.

Another participant also describes disparate treatment by a woman judge:

Out of curiosity I would observe her in trial with other people, especially males, just to see how she would treat them and I—none of them ever got that treatment. And then spilled over from trial into just regular day-to-day courtroom interactions. Like I said I'd walk into the courtroom and she would start calling my cases. I mean thank god I have a very good memory so I'd be able to address them with her very quickly. Then she realized she couldn't rattle me that way so no longer, she's not doing that. But she would do things like if I told her I had a trial in front of another judge she called the judge to verify like I'm lying to her.

They noticed the disparate treatment that she gave me in particular. I had a supervisor come down, this was with the Regional Council office, I had a supervisor come down and literally asked me, "Do you want me to pull you out of that courtroom? Do you want me to talk to her?" I said, "Absolutely not. I don't want anybody to fight my battle for me. . . . I'm just going to stay here, I'm gonna hold my ground." But it was interesting because again, I'm looking at her as a woman and I'm thinking, 'Really? Is this what we're doing with each other?'

> "And I and I truly believe, this could just be the empathetic person in me, but men are envious of women . . . and other, women, definitely we have moments of enviousness of women . . . like what's going on and what people are really doing, and how they use the tools to try to like tear you down."
>
> (Sarah, *Law*)

Why Women Judge Each Other

It's Just That You Wear So Much Lipstick

Here Mara judges another woman based on her clothes, and then backtracks on what she clearly said. While women cognitively know judging other women is wrong, a sexist value system has become so internalized that we hold each other to men's standards.

I spoke to a friend of mine about this and we talked about our different experiences. What she said never happened to me. She said, "My problem when I step into a room all the directors, everyone, they just want to sleep with me. They are not taking me seriously, they just want to sleep with me." We talked about her experience and we talked about mine and I said it's never happened, but I wonder if it's because I just have this aura of "don't even come close or I'll bite your head off." If I just get the chance to walk into the boardroom, if I get to that level, they tend to listen to me. That's what I told her.

She of course took it as an insult, "What you are saying is the way I look and the way I dress is the reason for them to approach me or not take me seriously." I said, "Oh no, that's not what I meant," even though the men in their twisted minds do believe that is the case, because you come in a skirt and red lipstick, and I always dress in black and not much makeup on. It's not your responsibility that they think the way you dress means something. You know that they can say things that are not appropriate. That they can behave that way.

Mara's assertion was the other woman's male colleagues treated her a certain way based on her appearance. In this passage she suggests that, because the speaker alters her appearance and demeanor, men will respect her; she need only get in the room. She stated many times throughout her interview that this was not the case. Men spoke over her, undermined her, ignored her input, and made her feel stupid. She never mentioned what she was wearing when she got disregarded. In fact, in the two-hour interview she only mentioned her appearance here, when she compares herself to another woman. She assigns herself power for knowing how to dress, how to follow the rules.

When Mara told this story, she asked me what I thought. I said I did the same things she did, wore plain black clothes, hair back, no makeup. I spoke in a stoic manner. Yet I still have the problem her friend has. I walk in and the men express their desire to sleep with me. Appearance is an element that women feel they can control, and thereby control the behavior of men, but this thinking is a fallacy. Women do not have control over a man's mind, or his perception of having a superior status. Sexism is his choice. By judging other women, all we do is support his sexism.

Her Hooker Heels

Mila talks about being wary of women in her workplace, and not knowing what side they are on and what they might be about; whether they are playing into men's expectations.

Certain times when men said, "This woman can do the job. I think she's going to do really great" in front of these men, but I also like that's because she wears low-cut tops and hooker heels. Now from my own standpoint that kind of makes me sad, that I felt like somebody's choice of dress meant something, that it meant she was trying to capture that attention, and maybe it's just her fashion choice, right?

Being unsure of other women could be turned to a strength. How different could a work environment be if women were collaborative rather than competitive?

Don't You Ever Wonder Why He's Promoting You?

Women are subjected to cruel comments from other women, including this situation, where female colleagues suggested she had her position because of her appearance rather than her credentials.

I do remember getting that unwanted attention and this was around the time that I started experiencing some jealousy from women as well in terms of my role, this powerful role with the billionaire in his headquarters, repping his projects, and some of the women within the corporation and then outside of it, they would say things to me like, "Don't you ever question why he's promoting you or gave you this project. Because I would, especially if I looked like you." Just somehow my blonde hair had something to do with that, I have no idea how, and so I got it from women as well.

They Must Be Sleeping Together

Rebecca was set up with an interview call, and the person she was meeting with made an assumption about her and the man who recommended her. The interview was effectively over before it started, and she has no recourse.

I was recommended to apply for a strategic philanthropy position by the primary funder of this branch of the organization. My dissertation research directly pertained to the position, and my other professional experience correlated with this organization's initiatives with major donors. It was a perfect fit, I spent the day writing a cover letter and submitted my resume. My friend set up a call with the Executive Director he usually deals with who does the hiring.

I knew by her first question I was never going to work at that organization. "So, *how* do you know (man)?" She asked in a way that candidly suggested I knew him from some inappropriate way.

I answered her, and she said kind of slow, "Yeah." And then we proceeded with a complete bullshit conversation. She completely disregarded my experience and kept asking me what my tie to philanthropy was. I had done my dissertation topic on it, worked for a private foundation, and served as a philanthropic advisor. She just kept acting like I was lying to her or something, like I was forcing my way in when I had no right to be there. She only has an undergraduate degree in English. If somebody in our conversation was making a leap into the field . . . she just kept acting like she couldn't seem to get her head around why I would be interested in that job. She was demeaning and ridiculous to me. The interview process went nowhere.

I have no idea how to overcome that. For me, I don't get many jobs suited to my professional path. She makes an ugly assumption and goes on with her day. If the donor had recommended a male applicant, that conversation and outcome would look very different.

(Rebecca, *Senior Scientist*)

Suspicious of Other Women

I think it had to do with the fact that I have never worked in a place that has not been male dominated. I've never worked with as many women as men. I've worked with very few women, so I think there's a natural feeling when you work with very few women of being either wary of each other. women are either very difficult to work with or how is it going to play out with this woman because she must be a strong character to get to this point. Whether we do that to each other or whether it's circumstantial, I'm not sure.

(Mila, *Aviation*)

Her point is worth reflection. Have you ever been suspicious of a woman because she is a woman? If you have, you are exhibiting the bias used by sexist men. Men assign women a few different roles: mother, whore, uptight bitch, queen bee. By wondering what role a woman will fall into, you are collapsing her identity into prescribed boxes. These boxes were created by men. Consider how well your identity fits into any of those boxes.

All about Him, at Her Expense

He Liked the Drama, and Liked That It Was about Him

Describing an all-woman company, Rebecca talks about being used as the entertainment for the boss.

This pains me to talk about. I had a boss, I was a director. There were six employees, all women. Four of us were in our thirties, the other ladies were older. When I started—three of us got hired at once and the others didn't get this, just me—everyone kept telling me how the one employee, we'll call her Jen, wouldn't be happy. "Oh, she can't be happy about you." People just kept saying that when they met me professionally. Our boss was a gross-looking man, he looked like a massively overweight turtle. And I came to understand that people were referring to some kind of competition between me and "Jen" for our boss's attention, but in a personal way. I was in no such competition. But there would be work things that were problems, caused by her, and he would always be in the middle of it, like nothing could be handled without him. I'm stupid, I thought we were there to work. No. We were his entertainment. It was one problem after another and he loved the attention. It was repulsive.

(Rebecca, *Senior Scientist*)

I Have Sisters, I Know What This Is About

Mara talked about being reduced to a male counterpart knowing about women because he has sisters:

I worked in a senior position for a company owned by a man and woman. I've known them for years and worked with them both before the company. At some point, the woman co-owner cuts off from me. She used the words, "Stand down" in an email. Very hostile. I want no part of whatever her problem is, so I back away. I have no idea what it's about, nor do I ask because I don't want to do business with anyone who speaks to me that way. A couple months later the man calls me to ask about a project and his partner would be part of it. He says to me, "I have sisters, I think I know what this is about." I have five sisters and no idea what having sisters has to do with it. Just the way he framed it infuriated me, plus he cast me as being part of her problem. I never had this impression of him before that phone call, but he framed it like the pretty girls were fighting over him. I lost a lot of respect for him in that call. We no longer do business together.

(Sophia, *Tech Marketing*)

It's Always Like This When Two Pretty Girls Get Together

Emma described a similar situation in which her professional life became the subject of gossip, positioning her in sexual competition with another woman:

I was working at a philanthropic foundation and there was some weird thing happening with a fundraiser from one of the nonprofits we funded. I like working with women. I know I don't enter in with any bad attitude. I like getting to know people and how to get everyone to the best place. But she had this odd disposition toward me, always closed off, never friendly. Just that very cold, distant demeanor, this is when we are sitting next to each other at dinner. She's just being impolite.

After months of this, someone in her organization says something about it. I say, "Yeah, what is that about? I can't get her to warm up." He says something akin to how, when two pretty girls are in proximity there's always a fight for the status to be the prettiest. And I said, "What are you talking about? I'm not doing anything like that." He assured me it was fine, we could all play football together, as an organization, and get to know each other and smooth everything out.

Okay, so let me put this in context. First of all, I am in the power position here. I work for the funder and I don't *have* to be friendly with you at all. I am, because that's what I'm about, but I am under no obligation to make a relationship with you. Second, the mere fact that I was the other person involved in this non-transaction does not mean that *I* was doing what *she* was doing. I found it sexist and petty for him to say such a thing, and inaccurate. I mean seriously, we're in this line of work having these conversations?

It's so ugly. I got cast in that role as if it was reality. Then it was up to me to defend myself that I wasn't trying to be the prettiest. I'm not even in that conversation! I was the subject of it. I'm not involved. That looks and feels so bad professionally. I felt like I was fodder for their gossip. I stepped far away after that conversation. Later a board member said that my boss used to call that fundraiser all the time, but it stopped when I got hired. Maybe they got more money when I wasn't around. Maybe that was her problem.

(Emma, *Casting*)

Treated by Other Women Like a Sexual Threat

Interviewees who used networking for their business cited the difficulty in networking effectively in mixed company.

The place where I've seen it most frequently is not with coworkers, but in a business space where I don't have a plus-one. Maybe hospital galas or whatever else. I had to say several times as feedback, I can't make any connections or contacts in those environments. I find that unusual, where people can't just talk to each other. The men won't talk to me, and the women immediately go sidle next to their husbands.

(Mila, *Aviation*)

Men Are Cold and Distant When Wives Are Present

Rather than being a person talking about business with another person, women were regarded as a single woman trying to meet a man. Emma describes this:

I find it very difficult to deal with men when their wives are around because I can't get to know them, I can't strengthen the relationship. The ones who are cutthroat sharks, I don't often see them in an environment when their wives are there . . . they don't bring their wives with them. This is going to show how I've been conditioned, but in my mind there's two types of men to deal with in the workplace. One kind is easier to deal with, because they're open and friendly and accepting of women in the workplace.

The second are cutthroat sharks, who are a little chauvinistic and ready to cut you down and steal your ideas or degrade or downplay your role or whatever else. They're cold and they're distant and they're watching their guard. I find it very difficult to talk business when their wives are around.

Let us examine this section further, for here is an ideal example of how the personal/social and the business aspects collide. If you have been in a social setting where someone made an inappropriate advance toward your partner, there are two ways it can go. Either your partner corrects the behavior or the partner indulges the behavior. No partner can be stolen away. It is his or her choice to go.

Clarity is that no partner can be stolen away if he or she doesn't wish to be stolen. It is the conduct of our partner that we watch. Another person at an event, such as this situation, is simply the stimulus for a different problem. Men who have no problem interacting with businesswomen in the presence of their wives are the same when their wives are around. On the other hand, men who ignore professional women in the presence of their wives may be a different story.

In this work, we are discussing phenomena established in research and discussing it in applied context. As in other topics we are discussing, there is a different standard of conduct here. The interviews of women in this book are fraught with examples of how men, regardless of their marital status, sexualized women. The reverse of this dynamic, in comparison, does not exist.

Husband stealing among professional women may be another myth that generates animosity among women. That would be characteristic of a person with high SDO. The only way to know is to talk to the woman, rather than stereotype her.

Women Do Not Think in Terms of Sexism

Not all women feel like they have experienced sexism. In part, this has to do with the notion that sexism is sexual and about sex, rather than being about power differential and inequality. Not discounting the feelings of women and their perceptions of experience, however, very few of them considered sexism as the network of dynamics and behaviors. Had they been aware of this expanded definition beforehand, they may have answered differently. The fact they identified the behaviors but did not link them to sexism illustrates (1) women are experiencing sexism regardless of whether they personally define it as sexism, and (2) they do not think in terms of sexism.

This could be an intentional negation of the idea of being victimized or targeted. The interviews and research suggest that sexism is far from a "go-to" explanation of problems women are experiencing. They name the behaviors or dynamic but assign many other reasons for why it is occurring. In several interviews, the participant would describe the same type of situation. When it was happening to another woman, the other woman was a target of sexism. When it happened to her, the interviewee would dismiss it as no big deal. Unless they were sexualized, women did not immediately think of themselves as being immersed in sexism, nor did they largely reflect on their own circumstances. This had more to do with the way the women defined themselves and maintaining a sense of agency.

Deny Being Ignored

Ignoring my suggestions but ignoring my presence, no. I think that's part of me as well. Maybe I'm ignored but I don't notice it. I don't go into situations where I should be ignored. *I think it's a lot of how I perceive myself*, so I don't think they do ignore me.

(Natalya, *Law*)

Women Do Not Immediately Self-Identify with Sexism

I contacted Mila and asked if she or anyone she knew who fit the criteria would be interested in sharing their experiences. She thought of other women first, and then realized that she had perspective to contribute as well.

I thought potentially that I might know women who would be able to help. Then I thought, well, the best place to start, is probably me. I started thinking of other women, without immediately thinking about its relevance to me, it did make me start thinking about other women. spoke to a few women, and I was really amazed by the number of women who either, it immediately resonated with, or immediately said, "Oh, I wouldn't have any experience like that." Now I'm thinking about the connotation around that, what that might be, and how some people understand it other ways, that may be what it is.

Women who have not experienced sexualization think they have not experienced sexism, and some women who have experienced sexualization are keen to hide that fact. The immediacy and polarity of responses indicate that women do have a preconceived notion of what those experiences are about and how they should be handled. Compare that gut response with the speaker, who thought about it. She realized she had quickly overlooked herself and then reflected on her experiences and decided to contribute them to help other women who might be experiencing something similar. Also of note here is the difference in personal agency, that is, what you believe you can do with your experiences and knowledge. In bystander intervention, more knowledge means more solutions.

Sexism Happens to Other People, Not Me

This was an issue I encountered, that most women I spoke with thought of sexism only in terms of overt sexualization, not as it is expressed as structural or communication issues. There was also a defensiveness with some women. In some cases, women seemed to think that in asking them about sexism, I was suggesting they were a victim, and were quick to distance themselves. Julia describes her thinking:

"This is something that happens to other people but not me." As women, we're so empathetic and verbal, and we get on with the job. We don't read between the lines and see how we're personally being affected. I find it hard to imagine that you know, not every woman has been affected in *some* way. They say "Oh, I don't know what you're talking about," or "it's not relevant to me." In my experience, it's very relevant to every woman who is in a workplace.

Defense Mechanism

Women do not stop and contemplate their situation during it. They are too busy trying to survive:

People don't self-identify with it. Like a defense mechanism, I know women who are going through this. When you're surviving or dealing with or having to navigate through the boardroom or through your company, you don't necessarily have the time to stop and think about it. You can kind of shoulder it and get on.

(Olivia, *Recording*)

Hard to See While It's Happening

Several women discussed how they did not recognize sexism until after being out of the situation. She notes those women were working with female leaders.

Always as an empathetic woman, "I can handle it, it's not a big deal." I think that, for me, is one of the biggest things. I asked a few women; they said, "Oh I don't know, I've never really come across anything like that."

I know some women who have been working with incredible female leaders over the course of their career and they haven't really seen it. And I'm kind of surprised because I don't think I realized how my career has evolved and how affected I was until really having this conversation and thinking about it.

(Maryann, *Marketing*)

Fight for Others, But Not Herself

Another dynamic was the willingness to defend other women, but the avoidance of advocating for yourself. Janni discusses her reluctance to act on her own behalf:

I think if we had one more woman in the management team then I would do it because I'd be doing it for someone else. Only for me, it's just not worth it.

This could have to do with the identity of the individual. In many of the interviews, the women's lives and careers reflect a readiness to defend others and a practice of doing so. At the same time, with few exceptions these women also display enormous hesitancy at confronting everyday situations in their own lives, both in personal aspects and professional situations. So how we think of ourselves and how we would handle something are often different from how we do handle things. That disparity requires reflection on our identity and relational settings.

Ways Women Inadvertently Contribute to Sexism

We as women inadvertently contribute to sexism when we play into it. What seems like harmless behavior to you may not seem so to other women. Below are some ways in which traditional sexist office behavior reinforced by women undermines the women who are trying to stand against it.

Competing through Subservience

By disagreeing to menial tasks, Mila was reflecting her status as an equal to her male counterparts. Refusing to bring men food and drink as a gender-assigned lower-status role takes nerve. When other women swoop in to perform the task for the man, they are in essence complying with the notion that this is a woman's task, and the woman who refused was wrong to do so.

> Within this first job, a lot of the women were given either secretarial roles or they were given roles within his charitable foundation. I think that because I took a different vein—I said no I'm not making coffee, and then another woman would swoop in and make the coffee.
>
> (Mila, *Aviation*)

"They Mean No Harm"

Staying with an antiquated and sexist culture when you have the chance to interrupt it is another way women reinforce men's status. Natalya describes her summer placement at a firm during law school. In this case, she as an outsider was struck by the disparity in levels of professional respect.

> I just, I was actually quite horrified by the way that the male lawyers spoke to their female colleagues. It was really quite in a patronizing way. Not rude or aggressive but calling women babycakes and things like that. It was just strange. It completely lacked the level of professionalism that they afforded to their male colleagues.

From the outside she was struck by the disparity, but then was informed that is "just how it is."

> I subsequently joined that firm, different team, but I remember speaking to the lady in question . . . and I said to her that "I find it really striking and really different because it's really patronizing."
> She said to me, "That's just how it is. They mean no harm by it."

Should this situation arise in your career, suggest a different organizational norm. "The way it is" could be mutually respectful. Regardless of whether men mean harm by it, speaking in patronizing and unprofessional ways is a strong daily form of sexism that reinforces the notion that inequality is normal.

Calling Each Other Diminutive Names

Catherine makes the point that even when men do not respect women's names and titles, women can do that for each other:

That to me is when it becomes more hurtful. Like when the man calls you "sweetie." You're at a commission meeting and the commissioner's like, "Oh sweetie come up to the mike." (laughing) And you're like, "Did you just say that at a public hearing?"

You can laugh at that, but when a woman does it, it just feels different. It feels like, how do we fix this. It just kind of lives with you longer, and is more devastating.

"Resentful" Leader

Sophia is in charge of an initiative for a company that employs 30,000 people. From the outside it appears as if this company is doing *something* for women, but exactly what is unclear. Also, she does not want to be in charge.

> I don't like that I have to think about it really. I am somebody who just wants to get in there and do the work because I like the work and the fact that I have to think about this is an annoyance.
>
> I've accidentally fallen into being an advocate and a leader in this space. It's hard because I do care about it because it affects me, but I wish I didn't have to care about how it affects me. I'm not passionate about it for its own sake. Yes I love giving to women and mentoring them, things like that. It's such a big conversation I wish we didn't have to have it. I do it somewhat resentfully because it's just not where I want to be spending my time.

Not clear on why and how sexism is a problem, she uses sexist language of "militant and aggressive" to describe women who believe strongly that sexism is a problem. Categorizing women in those terms reinforces stereotypes and strengthens negative perceptions.

> But I think there are a lot of women, you know you get women on a spectrum. Some of them are like, "I don't get it, I don't even see that this is a problem," like "why do we have to talk about this all the time?" Then you get people who are more like militant and aggressive and everything. My company is global, right, so just because I've had opportunities as a woman in the United States I don't—I can't assume that my female colleagues in India or Asia or the other nations where we work (that) they will have the same opportunities as I do. So that is a reason to care about it more.

She is in charge because men gave her the project, assuming she would know what to do because she is the only woman. Another example of men thinking one woman is interchangeable with any woman. Inequality is not her expertise, nor is she particularly interested in it. Her profession is tech. She doesn't want to be doing this job, and she does not understand it. Further, she is working under a vague, unclear directive from men who themselves, according to her, were very hesitant to let a women become part of management. For how many other companies is this the case?

Stonewalling Women

Catherine describes how a city worker will not provide the service—do her job—when the speaker comes into her office. The city worker treats a male contractor differently.

> I'm working with a contractor to get permits for a facility that I have. He's an attractive Colombian man, and he's able to maneuver people in a way that's really beautiful. He just has this energy.
>
> I go down to the city and there's a woman over the account. I can't get her to come out front. I could sit there for an hour. She's not coming.
>
> I send Frank down there and the girl invites him into her office, they sit down and chat. He told me she likes him. He tells me, "I don't know what you think I'm going to do or how far I'm going to go. I know you need this permit but I've got a wife." Literally, this is the conversation we're having. About a woman who wouldn't even come out front for me.
>
> You work for the city, which means you work for me because I pay my taxes. And we're talking about a permit for a business that's going to improve the culture—No, who cares about that. She sees an attractive man and she's ready to jump through all kinds of hoops. Now if I didn't have him, how would I move forward with my business?

Our Understanding Evolves over Time

It's Like Doing a Circus Act

Natalya discusses a project when she was advising a large country, and describes the lead of that country's team of bankers. At the time, the woman seemed like a bitch.

> One of them was a lady. I don't keep in touch with her. I never knew her. She was very aggressive. She was more aggressive and had more masculine energy than all the other 15 guys in the room. To the point that it was quite counter-productive. I think everybody just thought that she was a bit of a bitch.
>
> I think because she was the leader of that team, she really felt like she had to be even meaner than all of them put together in order to command respect from her own team. Also to show the other side that she means

business. I thought that that was quite interesting. I hadn't experienced that much of this, at that point in time.

She describes her life now, much later in her career, when she has to fight for authority and legitimacy that her male counterparts get just for being men.

> I had to work harder than every single motherfucker in that room. I had to prove that I was everything. I was smart, I was charming, I was some-body who they couldn't take advantage of, that I was not a silly girl, that I thought I was a capable lawyer, I was a good negotiator, I was a good every-thing. But at the same time wasn't pushy. It's like a circus act.

She is referring to the multiple roles of competency and femininity that women are expected to display. For a man, being competent is enough. A woman must do this "circus act" described here. In Chapter 12 we explore this further.

Used to Judge Women's Appearance

Isabella describes how her point of view about women changed over time. She refers to a beautiful suit her mother gave her, which she stopped wearing because a male superior made a sexual comment about her. In the rest of her interview, she describes defeminizing herself to ward off male attention, because she thought that was the way to be taken seriously.

> In fairness, if I may say so, being completely honest, the women I used to see come in with high heels and full faces of makeup and super feminine, I would almost look down on them. "What are you doing? What are you playing at? Can't you see what we're up against here?" I'd almost feel like they were portraying a negative image of us by properly embracing our gen-der. That's the extent to which my thinking was converted.
>
> I started out, back in the era when I wore my mother's suit, I berated myself for doing that and not being clear. For putting myself in that posi-tion. Therefore, I automatically assumed that all women who bought things like my mother's suit and who were very feminine knew that they were also putting themselves in that position and therefore were trying to capitalize on it. My thinking was, "Why are you doing this? You know what people are like, you know what they're going to think about you. Therefore, you're using this as currency."
>
> I completely bought into the whole idea that being feminine was a nega-tive. I slowly but surely realized that that was complete bullshit. That women can wear whatever they want to wear in court, wear makeup, look however

they want. The fact that I didn't do it was my own issues with myself. . . . Just because I didn't have the confidence to do what they're doing, I shouldn't be looking down my nose at them. In fact, at least they're being truer to themselves, truer to their own gender.

Exposing Sexist Scripts and Thought Patterns

I. The Insidious Nature of Sexism
    A. A Woman Didn't Do This to You, a Man Did

II. Is This What We're Doing to Each Other?
    A. "I Had to Take It"

III. Why Women Judge Each Other
    A. It's Just That You Wear So Much Lipstick
    B. Her Hooker Heels
    C. Don't You Ever Wonder Why He's Promoting You?
    D. They Must Be Sleeping Together
    E. Suspicious of Other Women

IV. All about Him, at Her Expense
    A. He Liked the Drama, and Liked That It Was about Him
    B. I Have Sisters, I Know What This Is About
    C. It's Always Like This When Two Pretty Girls Get Together
    D. Treated by Other Women Like a Sexual Threat
    E. Men Are Cold and Distant When Wives Are Present

V. Women Do Not Think in Terms of Sexism
    A. Deny Being Ignored
    B. Women Do Not Immediately Self-Identify with Sexism
    C. Sexism Happens to Other People, Not Me
    D. Defense Mechanism
    E. Hard to See While It's Happening
    F. Fight for Others, But Not Herself

VI. Ways Women Inadvertently Contribute to Sexism
    A. Competing through Subservience
    B. "They Mean No Harm"
    C. Calling Each Other Diminutive Names

D. "Resentful" Leader

E. Stonewalling Women

VII. Our Understanding Evolves over Time

A. It's Like Doing a Circus Act

B. Used to Judge Women's Appearance

Analysis

> Women do not immediately see sexism as the problem—even the feminists.

Allison works for a leftist political party. While she was very comfortable speaking abstractly about culture and hierarchies and gender, how it manifested more personally in her own life was not readily evident to her. The passage demonstrates the larger repercussions of gender bias in communication and performance evaluation.

The narrative tells an incident of being verbally attacked in a meeting by a male colleague. She requests a meeting with her supervisor to discuss the matter. The female supervisor tells this woman that she is difficult to get along with, and should compensate for the man's behavior. The speaker was penalized twice. This interview portion is included to demonstrate how her mind identified the man's behavior as sexist but did not realize the female supervisor's behavior also was sexist.

> A couple of weeks ago we had a meeting with our agents. I was told off by a male colleague of mine in front of the agency, "You're overstepping your mandate here, you shouldn't be saying these things." In a way that I found very inappropriate. And that other people in the room also found very inappropriate. They reacted, "God that was really unprofessional."
>
> In a way I think maybe had I been a man that wouldn't have happened.

Q: What was the meeting about?

It was just a general status meeting with the agency and I had some ideas about how we could move the work forward.

Q: Who was present?

There were six or seven people in the room, so fifty percent from my office and fifty percent from the agency or the contractor's office.

Q: It's a time when anyone is allowed to give comments and you give comments.

Yeah yeah, definitely.

Q: And then what exactly was it that he said to you?

He said you're not in charge here. It's not your job to say what to do, even though he wants exactly that.

Q: And people in the room knew this was inappropriate?

Oh yeah.

Q: How did they respond?

No, they actually called me afterwards and said, "God, how are you? That was awful. That was like bullying. Are you okay?"

Q: Did you have anyone to tell about this?

I told my manager, I said, "This was completely out of line. We need to sit down and talk about this." We did, which was good.

Q: What happened as a result?

I think it was good because the air was cleared. I said, "I think the way you acted towards me was completely out of line," not to do that again. I felt like—can you use that expression in English—glass ceiling? Yeah, basically what happened in that meeting was that I hit the glass ceiling and I got to feel the consequence of doing that.

Later in the interview I revisited the issue. Because sexism expresses itself in bias against women's communication, I wanted to check if this was the case with her. Consistent with the methodological aspect of teaching and epiphany, my line of questions here are leading her since she is unaware of sexism in this sense.

Q: Why was it that nobody said anything to him when it happened, publicly?

In that instance, I asked myself this because what I did was lessen it, "All right all right, fair enough." I saved his skin a little bit. Instead of saying, "You're being completely out of line, why are you saying this?"

Q: So in a sense you backed him up?

Yes basically. I think that's because I often think that's a woman's role, that you don't want this tension in the room. We want everyone to be happy and the spirits to be high. You don't want to be the person who wrecks the mood for everyone else kind of thing.

Notice she believes it will be she who "wrecks the mood" by calling attention to his behavior.

Q: Right. So he embarrassed you. He tried to cut you down. So *he* didn't care about that. And yet your response was what the response of many of us is—can we explore that a bit?

You mean why I did it?

Q: Yeah.

I don't know. I don't know. I've asked myself the same thing.

Q: This isn't a way of picking at you or suggesting that you should do everything differently. It's just this—we as women, and it's well researched—we have that tendency. Almost every person I've spoken with mentions exactly that. That it's up to us to make everything calm, it's up to us to make everything nice. We don't want anybody to be embarrassed. Regardless of what gets thrown at *us*, we still have that social instinct to calm everything down and not embarrass people. Even though they just tried to take us out at the knees.

I feel, I've got to say in my family I'm a middle child and I find myself often having that role. If a discussion gets a bit heated around the dinner table I will try to change the subject or . . . interpret, "Well I think what he means is actually this." I think it's partly because I'm a middle child but it's also hard being a woman.

She ascribes blame to herself. Another prevalent dynamic of the interviews was women assigning their personal characteristics as a reason why sexist behavior happened with them. There were no correlations of the personal traits, nor of the type of sexism, but it was another way that women blame themselves when men behave in sexist ways. Next, she mentions being unprepared, something many other women cite as well. The interview continues:

Q: Reflecting on it now, if you're in that situation, do you feel like it's appropriate to correct him or to stand for yourself?

Definitely. That's exactly the kind of thing, when you leave the room and think of two thousand things I should have said. But there and then you just go to your gut reaction, which is to make everything nice again.

Q: If you had a chance to do it over?

I would have said, "You're out of line, don't raise your voice at me."
    I said all the things which felt better but you know, I just wanted to say it in the room. There's also the social aspect of it that I wanted other people in the room to see that I can stand up for myself.

Q: Right. Because what he did was a status move, communication wise. So regardless of what happens after, he still got the public status.
    Later I was asking about gendered communication differences, one of the interview protocol questions, and she chose to revisit this story. The follow-up with her manager illustrates full circle the problem of gendered communication bias. In taking issue with being treated unprofessionally, the supervisor talks out of both sides of her mouth. What is supposed to be a meeting about the man's behavior in the meeting turns into a criticism of her having problems cooperating.
    Q: Have you ever had critiques on your relational style? You're icy or you're aggressive or you sound angry?

I've told that I'm a bit too pushy. I've been asked—it was the situation with my male colleague where I said, "I want to sit down with you and I want to have another person in the room and I want to talk about what happened." Then I was asked afterwards whether I normally had problems cooperating.

Q: So it became, not that he spoke to you in that way in the room, but it was your cooperation problem?

Yeah.

Q: How did that strike you?

Wow, it pissed me off, it pissed me off.

Q: Who was it that suggested that?

It was a manager who is higher rank than both of us, "Oh you know he can be a little bit square but I can see you have problems cooperating with him. You just need to try harder. You just have to make up for what he lacks." I just found that really unfair.

Q: She completely backed him up?

Yeah more or less.

Q: How do you interpret the result of that interaction?

Well I still feel I'm glad that I did it because at least for my own integrity I got to say, "This was wrong." But I don't know, business wise, whether I actually gained anything from opening my mouth to be honest.

Conclusion

Although she feels personally empowered, the likelihood is that her career progression will be impacted negatively by her having spoken up about her male colleague. On the one hand, this interviewee is told she is difficult to get along with and that is why the problem exists (not that the man spoke so sharply to her in a meeting that several people called her afterward to comment on it). On the other hand, the supervisor also tells her the man "is a bit square" but that she should compensate for "what he lacks." In addition to it being her fault in those two ways, she further faces problems because advancement within the party is relationally based, that is, how well she is perceived to get along with others.

Creating New Scripts and Thought Patterns

- What makes you afraid to confront?
    - What labels are you avoiding?
    - How would your life be affected if you did?
- How would the lives of the people you confront be affected?
- If you are the target of sexism, what does that say about you?
- What are your thoughts about working with other women?
    - What influenced your answer?
    - What experiences led you to think this way?
- Notice if you answered by wondering which category the woman might fit.
- In your experience, have other women helped or hindered your advancement?
    - What are specific examples?
    - Have you helped, hurt, or been complacent with women you have worked with?
- What made you choose to act that way?

CHAPTER TWELVE

The Double Bind of Advancement

Introduction

When discussing sexism, one way of distancing from the topic is to suggest that man vs. woman is an age-old story relegated to the symbolic realm. In fact, sexism costs women material loss in their careers. They face various forms of bias, they are regarded as lower status and competency regardless of their actual abilities, and refuting sexism often has immediate and long-term consequences.

Negotiating Advancement

Consistent in the interviews were that women did not know how to advance in their current positions. Several women compared their salaries to a those of a male counterpart. The man's salaries were higher, and the women attributed this to them not negotiating or advocating for themselves, where they thought the men probably had. The process was unclear, and women were only offered critiques of their interpersonal skills by their male supervisor. They were not told how to advance and were not keen to ask about it for fear of sounding too ambitious.

The Cost of Women Who Seem Ambitious

Women face subtle bias when they are viewed through a sexist frame. The participants reported how their technical expertise, history of work performance, and quality of work always come secondary to a man's bravado. Women's communication, regardless of how they adjusted it, was also treated by men as being lower status to men. These are professional inhibitors women face when they are evaluated through a sexist lens. In addition to these factors, women's interpersonal traits are also inhibitors to advancement.

Among this body of work is an aptly named article, "Prescriptive Gender Stereotypes and Backlash toward Agentic Women." The authors describe interview situations in which women and men present *identically*. Women are perceived as cold and socially deficient. Their ambition was perceived as also indicating their lack of communal skills, and thus they were deemed unfit to lead others for lack of social competency. Men were not evaluated on their interpersonal skills at all. Finally, both women and men in the study were biased against women (Rudman and Glick, 2001).

The power roles for which women were interviewing require them to exhibit leadership and authority, and at the same time they are expected to be feminine and communal. The researchers noted this balance is almost impossible to strike, and the attempt alone requires great mental energy from women (Rudman and Glick, 2001). This chapter will look at what women experience in the interview process, the vague process of career advancement, and sexism that women must endure to mitigate financial loss. We will also address how psychological factors affect performance, and the relationship between SDO and negotiating of service fees.

Sexism in the Interview Process

Although not citing this type of bias directly, the interviews describe starkly different types of interview processes, evaluative criteria, and hiring procedures used for women than are used for men.

Different Interview Questions

Natalya talks about the differences in how women must qualify their experience, but men are not asked to do that.

> If I turn up and I say to them all this is my practice, this is what I do, everybody gets out their skeptic glasses and they're like, "Well, can we have some client references, somebody to back up your revenue stream?" Or, "Well how is that possible, you're so young. Can you tell us about the origin of your clients? How long have you known them, where have they come from?"

All reasonable questions, but I know for a fact because I have sat in on interviews where we are interviewing a man, those questions are not asked. It's like his word was taken as gospel. He's always able to walk in, flash a smile, talk some bullshit and everybody's like, "Well that sounds good to me. Bring him in."

Being Sexualized during the Interview

Natalya also describes an important interview in which a man sexualizes her. She wants the job and is unable to answer him as she sees fit. As a woman, she is forced to be polite and be subjected to his inappropriate glances and comment.

I went for an interview, hugely reputable international firm. This guy sits up to me, "I like your glasses. They really bring out your eyes." I said to him, "Thank you I really like your tie. It really brings out yours." You could see that he was looking at me trying to size me up. One of his colleagues started laughing.

I thought it was funny, and I was like come on, *really?*

When I told my mother the story, she said "Why did you say that? He's just being a gentleman, he's given you compliment. Part of being a woman is accepting a compliment."

I told her no, he made it very clear that he sized me up basically, from entering the room. He wasn't thinking of my CV, he was looking me up and actually if he could have done, he probably would have gone "Oh nice tits." But he chose to say "nice glasses" because that's more politically acceptable. He could say, "I like your glasses," because both of us wear glasses. . . .

Saying "They really bring out your eyes," that's a little too personal of an observation, let's put it that way. It's really difficult to react to this in any other way. . . . You can't look at him and say, "Actually, David, that's really creepy that you stared so deeply into my eyes that you are able to assess whether my glasses bring them out or not."

Because they'll be like "Oh she's really prickly, she's really confrontational. What woman doesn't know how to take a compliment? God I was just trying to be nice. I was just trying to break the ice and she's just you know, really blew up in my face."

She illustrates the typical thought pattern that places the woman at fault for pointing out the behavior. She is to blame for the discomfort if she spoke up, not the man who spoke to her inappropriately, and it would be she (who) would suffer the negative repercussions of not getting the position because *she made a partner uncomfortable.*

Must Be Collective Decision to Hire a Woman

Isabella discusses the interview process, of which she is part, and the difference between how female and male job applicants are treated. Men will hire a male candidate on the spot but need a consensus of other men to hire a female candidate.

> "Well she had exactly the same experience as this person, actually more." They say, "Well I don't know, let's go ask another five partners what they think about her."
> Let me get this right. When it comes to this guy you're prepared to make a decision by yourself. But when it comes to a woman, you need to have like, this canvassing. It has to be a decision by majority. Why?
> You're afraid to put yourself on the line and say, "I think she's good. It's a done deal, I put my name to it." You need to have at least five of your buddies to back you up. So when someone else comes along and says, "Why did you choose her instead of him?" the answer is not going to be "because I think she's bloody good." It's going to be, "Because I think she's good and five of them think so, too."
> That's what it comes down to, and I have got to say this has been the story of my life. Even right now in the interview process, they're like "We need you to meet another seven partners." And I'm like, "Oh right, because it has to be a collective decision. Because you don't want to be responsible for making the decision by yourself."

How Sexism Impedes Advancement

This section highlights the culmination of the last three, showing the material loss that results from consistently challenging a woman's professional competency, credentials, and right to be there at all, and the consequent internal deteriorating of the very idea that she has the right negotiate.

Dangling a Perpetual Carrot Wastes Years

As the sole female partner in her law firm, this woman has the desire to guide other women to partnership. They ask her specific questions about the process, which she cannot provide because the male partners do not actually intend for them to learn the process. Instead, the male partners want to enact a token initiative to address their organizational sexism, without really doing anything to address it.

I believe in progressing female associates, and in helping people have transparency into the process and understanding what is required of them and giving them the necessary assistance in order to get them there. I'm all about that . . . what I'm not really interested in at all, is being part of some kind of token initiative, which has no interest in people's progression and is just a complete waste of my time. . . . and very clearly this is what it was. It was for them to feel better, that they were doing something because of the . . . outcome of the report that they commissioned.

At the same time, when you're asked to report on it in a partners meeting, and I say, "Most of the female fee owners want at a certain level, what they really want to know is, what is their path to partnership? What is it that is tangibly required of them in order to get on to that path, what are the roadblocks, what is the process?" Because ultimately there is always a process.

One of the things that law firms really function on is this ambiguity. It's like, dangling this perpetual carrot in front of you that you never get. And people are not stupid, they can see it. That's why they leave. You don't have to be a genius to work it out.

When women discover they are chasing a perpetual carrot, they leave. They waste the time of this woman by having her work on something meaningless, and they waste the time of women who are pursuing a partnership that they will never achieve.

Different Rules Affect Preparation Time and Performance

This attorney discusses how rules are arbitrarily applied based on the judge's discretion. In this passage she explains how rules applied differently, like they are for other (white male) attorneys, result in more or less time to prepare for a case.

A continuance, if it's done in writing, should be done within 10 days. Most judges will take them overnight as long as it gets it off their calendar. I have to make sure I'm doing a motion to continue that I'm doing it that day because I don't want that to be a basis for denial. It has been.

I've seen judges do that to me, where because of the way they have accepted other people's motions, I won't necessarily observe the 10-day time frame and then I'll get my motion denied because I filed it within seven days instead of 10 days. . . .

. . . I'm thinking, but Judge, other people have done that. It's like, "Oh the rules are the rules," and I cannot dispute the fact that the rule is the rule, and so I end up with a different outcome than some of my other colleagues who are similarly situated except different gender or different skin color.

Q: So the rules are the rules, but the rules are applied and enforced differently?

> Yes, absolutely. It's generally just with continuances but it's—The reason I bring (it) up (is) because they're so important in some cases. And I've been forced into trial on a matter that other people would have got additional time to prepare so I don't have to have the time to prepare, I just have to go for it. Shoot from the hip so to speak, and a party to this is my client."

The consequence is her having less time to prepare. In this case, sexism impacts her career advancement and ability to get better cases, as well as the client who may suffer because she had to "shoot from the hip."

Disparate Treatment Causes Women to Lose Clients

Sarah describes in an earlier story that she cautiously confronted a judge who was interrupting her during jury selection and undermining her in front of potential jurors. Subsequently, the treatment from this judge became worse, and observable by clients. She loses clients because of how a judge treats her, so sexism costs her money and impedes her advancement.

> I had one judge who picked on me so bad as soon as I would enter her courtroom, she'd call me up. Literally I'm walking through the doors. I haven't put down my coffee. I haven't put down my purse. I haven't opened the file. She would just, "Oh Miss James!" She would call my cases right off the bat. My clients used to hate it and they wouldn't want me to represent them anymore in her courtroom because they saw how differently she was treating me compared to my male colleagues and didn't want me to represent them for fear that her disdain for me would lead to a harsher sentence for them.
>
> (Natalya, *Law*)

Avoiding Sexualized Activity Means She Loses Clients

Men maintain bonding over sexualized activities, and women miss out on building client relationships because they do not want to be in sexual situations with clients and coworkers. The risk in this case is that she will be replaced by a man who does enjoy participating in sexually based bonding activities with the client. Isabella describes this problem:

> Yeah, I think as a woman you have to hold your shit together all the time—there's no letting your guard down.

My clients go to strip clubs all the time. We were doing a deal somewhere and they came knocking on my door. "Oh my god, there's this great place, you'll love it." We got there and it's a strip club. It's not a strip club where people were stripping, they were already naked.

Why would you think I would love this? What part of this situation suggested that I enjoy it? They said, "All they serve is Cristal champagne here."

I said, "I could go to Harrod's and buy a bottle of champagne and enjoy it. I don't really need this." And I think because I was just so not impressed with it, they never invited me again. They go out all the time, just without me.

Losing Donation for Rejecting Advances

Lauren, who serves on a board of directors for a nonprofit that helps women and children survivors of domestic abuse and human trafficking related how a donor requested that the female founder have sex with him as a condition for him to make another donation. In addition to straight-forward sexual propositions, the organization also loses money because adjacent requests are made.

> I know she has had people who are not so forward as that, but definitely had situations where people would hint at, "I'd give you money if you did this" or "if you go out with me." She had a judge once who really wanted her to go out with him, she was like, "You know that's not what I'm doing, so. . . ." But as an organization we miss out because they keep their funds. Or they go give it somewhere else.

When considering whether or not to give money to an organization, donors check on who else is donating to them. They also watch whether donations remain steady, increase over time, or stop. Sudden stops to major funding, such as the $50,000 annual gift stopping after two years (discussed in Chapter 2), would be a major red flag that something is amiss. No way exists to convey under what circumstances the funding stopped, so blame would be placed on the organization. Donors are never wrong. Whatever problem there might be will be attributed as something negative concerning the organization.

If Sexism Is a Problem, You Can Leave

Name Sexual Harassment and Asked to Leave

This woman discussed a deteriorating executive situation and planning her exit strategy.

A VP delighted talking about his sexual exploits with his wife's orifices. He brought it up the first time and I told him to stop. Another time he brought it up, and I left the room. I knew my relationship with the CEO then was really bad and I had been hanging in there to get a final bonus that was very substantial. Because if you resign, you don't get the bonus. I knew because of the corporate culture that if I complained about this man's behavior, and named it as sexual harassment, I would be asked to leave, and I would get my bonus. That's what happened.

(Avery, *International Marketing*)

Do the Work and Shut Up

The party I work for we have values of feminism . . . but in a way, as most workplaces, they just want someone who will do the work and shut up about it. You know, they don't want anyone to cause problems. I think that probably goes for most workplaces.

(Allison, *Politics*)

Speaking up Is Your Ticket Out

Mara describes how political jobs are relationally based. The jobs you get and your advancement in the field are dependent on who likes you. Speaking about inappropriate behavior of men is an automatic ticket out of the whole industry.

When I was in politics men had free reign. They could do anything they wanted and everybody knew it. They were relentless, straight-up sex propositions. You would never dream of telling anyone because you would lose that job and then get blackballed. The whole field is relationship based.

Did they like you—that was the biggest factor if you got a job. And my god, you certainly wouldn't say anything when something happened. I always thought it was funny they were the party of family values. (Laughs) Oh god. No, I never dreamed of saying anything.

The field is at-will employment, so terminating employees at will is legal. If a woman gets terminated, she will be unable to find work elsewhere in the industry.

First, you have no one to report to. If you are working on a campaign, they would just cut you loose, without thinking twice. You just understand that's the penalty. If you have a political job, like an office job, you always work "at the pleasure" of your employer. That means they can fire you at any time, for any reason. That's why representatives and senators can be so abusive to their staff. Staff has no protection from any type of treatment. They would disappear you without thinking twice. There is no HR, no reporting process, no legal repercussions, *and* no one else will hire you. If you want to work in politics, that's how it is.

She cites the men adjacent to the job from whom she had to fend off sexual advances and avoid offending them while doing so:

I fought through it for years, but my problem was they always wanted to sleep with me. Always. I tried working around it, but there weren't that many women. You had the office holders to deal with, the candidates if it was during a race, male staff, contributors, at one point it was a senator's son. They would make a move, I would need to get out of it. If I offended them, that was the end of the job. I moved on. I had 10 years invested in that field and I just couldn't imagine a future there. (Laughing) I thought it would be better somewhere else. I was so wrong.

(Rebecca, *Senior Scientist*)

His Sex, Her Reputation

Avery talked about a four-year advertising campaign featuring the owner as the face of the company. The campaign was based on integrity, and he lied about having extramarital sexual relationships with his staff members.

Had I pursued the original ad campaign, it could have backfired not only on the company. I did point that out, it could have backfired on me as well as a professional in that field. Clearly the point was made because he agreed to change. The fact that he agreed to change the campaign was admission of guilt.

The professional repercussions of his sex life could have become a professional problem for her. "Backfiring" means that she had not done her due diligence and created a flawed campaign when that was not the case on her part.

Tolerating Sexism to Mitigate Loss

These women are aware of the constraints the are under, but choose to participate because they cannot withstand the material losses should they confront the sexism.

Patronizing Language

Natalya describes one example of diminutive language by her client. Although she preferred he did not speak that way, correcting the behavior would cause her to lose the client.

> One of my really good clients, he's not even Eastern European, he says, "I'm sure you're busy, busy girl, you have to run." I'm just going to let it slide. It's ridiculous. I haven't been a girl for 30 years. And he's like 50. I wouldn't say to him, "Oh you're a busy boy." That's absurd. You have to watch what you say, because he will think of it as an overreaction. I would lose the clients, I would lose a revenue stream . . . good girl, smart girl. "Aren't you a clever girl!" I'm not a dog.
>
> (Natalya, *Law*)

Intimate Language

Sarah was subjected to a man using intimate language with her. She, too, was faced with the choice of correcting him and suffering material losses or disregarding it and faring better in the negotiation.

> This morning I met with the city attorney of Opa-locka and within two minutes of me sitting down to discuss my client's civil forfeiture case, he was already calling me baby girl—"How did we get here?" (Laughs) "What happened? How did we get here?" We had a conversation on the phone on Friday to set up the appointment for today. I went, I sat down, we're having a professional conversation here and I'm diminutive again, I'm baby girl. Once again I felt like I couldn't challenge him in that moment because I'm really trying to negotiate and get my client's money back. I was just like, "Ah ha ha, baby girl."
>
> I kind of fell into a routine with that, well let me twirl my hair and bat my eye a little bit and maybe I can get more money back for my client— if that's what it takes then okay. And I hate that. But yeah, I fell into that. It kept resonating in my head, like, "Did he really just call me baby girl?"
>
> (Natalya, *Law*)

Limited Potential for Advancement Being a Primary Caregiver

Isabella described the professional fate many of her female peers faced. The legal system is set up in a way that the only cases that have to remain on schedule have to do with sex-related crimes like rape.

Sex cases, because of their nature, have to be fixed. In other words, to have a determinant start time and they have to be heard on a particular date, as in they have to be fixed by the court and that future is very rarely broken, because the witnesses are vulnerable, you see, particularly vulnerable. In other cases . . . fixtures can be broken, the court runs out of time, the diary is full, they have to move it to other dates. But they can't do it with sex work because of the particular vulnerabilities of the witnesses.

What ends up happening is that women who are the primary caregivers to children, who need to know when they're going to work and where they're going to work to plan their diary, it's more attractive work. They end up in this ghetto of doing this kind of work, prosecuting, defending, to the exclusion of almost every other type of work.

I have watched all my (female) peers doing just that. Literally it was rape after rape after rape. They didn't really want to be doing it but it was an easy way to market for work, and it was easier for them to organize their diaries. Because if they sign up to be a primary caregiver to children they have to make sure they're going to be in X court for this amount of time, you see?

The system obstructs women in two ways. First, this line of work does not allow women the flexibility to take other cases that will enhance their career and earnings. The interviewee cited murder and fraud as particularly lucrative, but sex cases do not pave the road to being hired for those.

The second point is that women are in the position of defending male clients who largely perpetrate violence against women. According to this interview, women are preferable to try these cases because they can be far more "brutal" while cross-examining female witnesses against whom the crime was committed. The optics of a woman attacking another woman during cross-examination eliminated any mental comparison of a man attacking the woman, which is what happened.

Emotional Toll Affects Material Outcome

These women talk about the repetitive diminishment of their status. Being visibly ignored by large groups of people and having their right to be in their professional space take a toll on their psyche. In the interviews several women addressed this. They chose to give up the struggle and disengaged. Others reported, like in the first narrative, how they felt like they were starting from far behind every time they entered the room.

Reduced to a Low Place Psychologically before Starting

In that moment, I feel like I'm starting not even (at) zero, I'm starting from way behind. I'm starting from like negative 20. I have to try so much harder and work so much harder just to prove that I have a place here in the court-room. I belong here, I work hard, and what I have to say is just as valid as anybody else's point of view.

(Natalya, Law)

Disengagement Because Nobody Wants You There

Very disappointing on the personal level. When that happens, you feel like you're starting to shrink back in your chair and back into yourself, you understand that all of a sudden this isn't a conversation. It's your monologue in a room full of 30 people who are all looking at you as if they're strug-gling to understand you and maybe you should shut up.

You stop going, which is not particularly productive or conducive, because then you don't participate at the decision-making level. You feel unwelcomed and I didn't want to be there just for statistics. I want to be part of a team and part of (a) business where my voice and my opinion matters.

(Natalya, Law)

Use a Woman, Pay a Man

These accounts deal with financial compensation for work. Men and male employers are compensated differently than the women, and for vari-ous reasons. Women were expected to do work without commute com-pensation, and in other cases said they felt uncomfortable negotiating.

Prove She Can Do the Work First

Several women described having to prove themselves in a position, where their male counterparts did not. Sophia describes such a situation and being expected to take on additional work without being paid for it while she proved herself.

There were some situations. I think some of it was a function of companies not doing well, not having great budgets, things like that, but there were times that I was asked to fill a role and prove that I was willing to take that next step before compensation or title were aligned to that. I don't know if my male peers were put in that position, or if they advocated for themselves differently. I didn't negotiate salary or anything like that until this last position that I took.

"I Could Never Charge That Amount of Money"

Q: I once heard someone say that we will know that we have truly inte-grated diversity into our mindset, not when people of color and women can have the same positions as white men, but when they can be as average as white men are in these positions.

> Exactly. And that's the long and short of it. That we could be just as average as white men in the same positions and have that be okay.
>   Appalling to me, a colleague of mine, a black female lawyer, she and I were talking the other day. A federal case had come her way . . . and she referred it to a white male colleague of hers who charged $45,000 to plead the defendant out to seven years in federal prison. I was like $45,000 for that? They paid $45,000 and the guy still went to prison for seven years? I don't even understand that. I don't get it because I could never charge that amount of money with a straight face and expect anyone to pay me.
>
> (Sara, *Law*)

"They Can't Afford That"

The account Isabella provides discusses how she worked for clients who said they could not afford her fee, so she lowered it and did the work. They did not pay her but made a drastic financial move to pay a man far more money, because he was a white man and they thought he would fare better in court.

> I've had cases where I've fought for the defendant like he was my own blood. . . . I had a fee but, "Oh I can't afford that." They can't afford that. So out of the goodness of my heart I'm doing all this work. The day comes for the client to take the resolution that I have worked out, and they hire a white male colleague of mine, who I know will not step foot in a courtroom for less than $10,000.
>   I did all the work for it, and they hired him. I asked, "How did you pay for that?"
>   "Don't take it personally. We just figured maybe it would be better if we had a white male in the courtroom, so we took the equity out of our house."

Q: (Gasp)

Yes. Wow. So, you use me as a mule to do all the work and then trot in your show pony to take you home. I just don't understand.

This narrative has a few layers to it. First, the clients felt a white man would yield them a better result. We have heard in this book about judicial bias against women attorneys and about male networks, so their assumption may well be true. Regardless of that, their decision reinforces sexism.

Second, she knew they needed the service but could not afford it, so she did the work at a reduced rate. They asked her for a favor and she helped them. The man did not help them, and they take out the equity on their house to pay him. While in a business sense the decision would be considered sensible, this demonstrates a distinct value difference. Third, the family took advantage of the woman's work and paid the man, far more, a theme that repeats in this research.

More Time to Reach the Same Place

Women shared throughout their interviews how much harder they had to work, while others, usually male networks, had resources and contacts that provided resources for them.

> It takes me more time to do the same things they can get done faster because they've got people feeding them this motion that motion . . . things that I have to pay for that they are getting for free because of their connections and I know I cannot expect that. I can ask, and sometimes I do ask but it's never fruitful, so I've learned. I've been conditioned to stop asking.
>
> (Sarah, *Law*)

In earlier chapters we heard from women who have to pay men to speak in meetings for them, because the men they have to do business with would not speak to a woman or sell to a woman. We see that women face invisible barriers, and men deny the existence of these unwritten rules. Also, paying more staff and taking time to develop and train them drains money and time from the woman; whereas men do not face drains and barriers like this.

Exposing Sexist Scripts and Thought Patterns

I.   Sexism in the Interview Process
  A.   Different Interview Questions
  B.   Being Sexualized during the Interview
  C.   Must Be Collective Decision to Hire a Woman

II. How Sexism Impedes Advancement
  A.   Dangling a Perpetual Carrot Wastes Years
  B.   Different Rules Affect Preparation Time and Performance
  C.   Disparate Treatment Causes Women to Lose Clients

    D.   Avoiding Sexualized Activity Means She Loses Clients

    E.   Losing Donation for Rejecting Advances

III. If Sexism Is a Problem, You Can Leave

    A.   Name Sexual Harassment and Asked to Leave

    B.   Do the Work and Shut Up

    C.   Speaking Up Is Your Ticket Out

    D.   His Sex, Her Reputation

IV. Tolerating Sexism to Mitigate Loss

    A.   Patronizing Language

    B.   Intimate Language

    C.   Limited Potential for Advancement Being a Primary Caregiver

V.   Emotional Toll Affects Material Outcome

    A.   Reduced to a Low Place Psychologically before Starting

    B.   Disengagement Because Nobody Wants You There

VI. Use a Woman, Pay a Man

    A.   Prove She Can Do the Work First

    B.   "I Could Never Charge That Amount of Money"

    C.   "They Can't Afford That"

    D.   More Time to Reach the Same Place

Analysis

How Sexism Gradually Erodes Advancement

Mila describes the psychological process and material consequences of being devalued over time:

Overall it was a slow deterioration of my ego and self-esteem, and my own recognition of my value. What I could bring to the table. Every time I was dismissed, I started thinking there was a valid reason for it.

I got a couple of pay cuts over time. I wasn't getting my fair due, and unfortunately by that time I was so demoralized I thought I didn't deserve it.

I also felt very trapped because I had built this new company around me. I had signed the agreement with the hospital systems. I had set the company up from scratch, the bank accounts, my name. I was managing member, I was authorized agent.

I was doing everything but living on a shoestring budget. I was making very little money, which sometimes happens in a start-up. When I found out that the men hired to come in, who had the same amount of experience or less, that they were making twice as much as me, that started to become totally unbearable for me. I had done all the work.

I was told at a certain point to shut up and calm down. I was told by other people that the founder had made almost a "she needs to get laid" comment. "She's becoming very difficult to work with."

These are things that hold you back in your career if you're focusing and you're in a negative environment, regardless of why you're in that environment. In the workplace or otherwise, that's really going to hold you back.

Everything is a choice. I chose to stay in this job I was creating over the course of two years. I was creating a new company I really believed in. That conviction and dedication kind of overrode even the personal aspects.

I walked away from it in the end. I was promised I would get a third of the company by setting it up. We had a shareholder's agreement drawn up by a lawyer that sat for two years and never got signed. The founder wouldn't sign it. It went from me being CEO and co-owner of the company and managing member, and everything in my name, where he would swoop in and take the credit for it, and along with the new male employees—all male, always. I walked away from it without anything, without even my expenses reimbursed.

Conclusion

Internalized domination brings about the feelings expressed in this narrative, those of isolation, powerlessness, inferiority, and resignation. Having dominance and privilege asserted slowly drives you into the mentality of the oppressive group. We see how the woman spirals progressively downward, and how sexist conditions were explained or justified in other ways, ways that are the woman's fault. That is because the oppression infiltrates your psyche and you begin to blame yourself, because you are consistently told you are to blame (Pheterson, 1990, p. 35).

Herein lies the difficulty of dealing with sexism. Events happen so gradually that it becomes difficult to determine when she should extricate from the situation. Recognizing sexism when you are in the midst of it is comparable to being caught in an abusive relationship. The signs and steps of abuse are distinct, you just might not have known how to recognize them. Wisdom lies in understanding what sexist dynamics look like and how they play out, which is why we are lifting the veil and showing you throughout this book.

Women are asked to be two things at once, authoritative and communal. They are asked to show the strength to lead autonomously but also required to demonstrate the maternal quality of niceness. Men are asked no such thing, and the bias works in favor of men. Behaviors linked with niceness in women are those that defer to men in discussion and decision making, behaviors that maintain female subordination (Lakoff, 1990; Ridgeway and Ericson, 2000). "Nice" women also avoid occupations linked to power and resources that would gain them status, which works out well for dominant men (Pratto, Stallworth, Sidanius, and Siers, 1997).

A participant in this study said she is frequently told that her profession is not very ladylike:

There are so many other people I've met who say "Oh, that's such an unladylike profession." And I'm like, "What's a ladylike profession? What should I be? A maternity nurse? That's a ladylike profession." This is so surreal, why are people even thinking that today?

She answers the inquiry:

"You do realize that the reason I do this is because I enjoy it and I'm good at it, and I make money. I didn't do it because I wanted to be like a man. I still go buy handbags, like, does that make you feel better?"

Research says no, that does not make people feel better. That confounds people. Agentic women know this. They pay for it every day. When you are critiqued and materially penalized for having "masculine" traits, it is because you have violated the prescribed type of what a woman should be. It is not your imagination. You have challenged an enormous system that does not wish to see you advance, a system that has fail-safes built in at every level to undermine you. The biases reviewed in this chapter are but a few examples. In Part 3, we will examine how to challenge inherently biased systems.

Exposing Sexist Scripts and Thought Patterns

- What mechanisms are available to voice sexism?
  - Formal channels?
  - Informal channels?

- When no legal repercussions are available, how would you approach the problem?
- How does applying rules differently communicate about the larger system?
- Why do certain people get preferential treatment over others?
- What are the repercussions for clients or other people who are indirectly affected by sexism?
    - Employees at a company?
    - Clients of an attorney?
    - Children of the woman?

PART 3

Intervention Strategies to Activate Bystanders

CHAPTER THIRTEEN

Speaking Up

Introduction

So far, we have read accounts of how women experience executive sexism. To provide greater depth of discussion, this chapter highlights some responses used by participants and suggests strategies to readers.

Public Status Move

"You're so young and beautiful, could you please go get the coffee?" I was a negotiator for an employee organization. I had a good profession with my education, but this boss tried to reduce me into the one with the long legs and the young face who could get coffee. We meet and negotiate collective bargaining agreements and it covers about 95 percent of the Swedish labor markets. He did that in front of board members.

(Janni, *Human Resources*)

Being asked to do menial tasks is a status move. He was positioning her as inferior, to undermine her in front of the board of directors. As his co-negotiator, that seems like a shortsighted victory. Ask your coworker what their goal is in undermining you when they do it, and do not accept they "didn't mean anything by it." We know from prevalent literature and life experience, they meant exactly what they did. Intervening with sexism means to stop accepting the notion that you misinterpreted it. If they did not *mean* it, they would not *do* it.

My emotional memory of it was that they looked embarrassed, on my behalf. I didn't want them to feel embarrassed, so I pretended like that was just normal. "Of course I can get coffee. He could have asked anyone of you, too, but I'll do it."

This is not true. He would not have asked any one of them because they are board members. His request was a status move, a move enacted by men in countries around the world.

But they didn't say anything. They didn't step in or correct him or anything like that. Although they could have.

If it was important to anyone to correct him, someone would have addressed it. They didn't step in because it did not affect them. It affects you, so practice your agency. Be prepared for next time. Should you find yourself in that position again. Find someone after and ask the appropriate way to address that in the room when it happens again, because it will happen again.

That would have been embarrassing for him. Partly I think it's just Swedish culture that you don't take conflict in the big room. You take it one to one. You don't think about it. When something like this happens, you don't know how to act.

Say something humorous to acknowledge it: "Oh, right. Because I'm a woman." Then move on without acknowledging it further. Call it what it is—a status move. But be prepared to call it out.

Did I misunderstand? I contributed because I acted as if it was normal. If I didn't react negatively then why should they? That's what I think they thought.

No, you did not misunderstand. I took the trouble to write this book to show you it's not just you. You are conditioned to think you misunderstood because men want you to feel embarrassed and remain silent. Be the opposite of silent.

Q: How do you feel about that situation now?

I think that's one of the hardest parts of an organizational culture. To practice civil courage. To be the one deviating from the norm and actually speak up. The situation has invoked in me how hard it is to invoke courage among employees and managers to actually step up when—even though it's uncomfortable.

Her coffee incident happened 20 years prior to our interview. At this point she heads HR for an organization with 7,000 employees, and company core values include civil courage. Civil courage as a concept is a good concept; however, to be useful, the concept must be applied. At the time of our interview, she was experiencing sexism on her executive team. The reasons she cited for not speaking up 20 years ago are the same reasons she cites now.

She did not want to make anyone uncomfortable because *she* was being excluded. You see how ludicrous it sounds when someone else says it? You do not want to make other people uncomfortable, but they feel okay if you are uncomfortable or embarrassed. Women are rigorously conditioned to make people comfortable and not to challenge men. Note the conditioning, and then work against it.

Intervene on behalf of yourself. Start by stating the reality, that women who speak up are seen as a problem. Tell this person how reasonable he or she is, and that of course, they can see through that absurdity. Spell it out. Don't skip steps. Draw a picture of the hypocrisy. You *know* they wouldn't want this when it violates company core values. By whether they accept or reject the information, they reveal their position and you know where you stand.

Gendered Personal Attack

I had a man tell me that I was being very unreasonable and emotional. Perhaps it was because I had my period.

At a negotiation, they were selling a refinery and my client was buying a refinery. I just kept saying "No." He said, "You don't understand."

I said to him, "I'm not saying 'no' because I don't understand, but because it's a shit deal." Not like that, but that was the gist.

She speaks clearly and addressed his misconception, that the <u>content</u> of his offer was unacceptable.

He had his clients sitting next to him, and I had my client sitting next to me. The guy got pissed off. "It's really unhelpful, you have a decision maker at your side and yet you're not making any decision."

I said to him, "We do not feel this is the right time to be making decisions. Don't reel off a list of demands and expect us to agree to it. It's not your first time, that's not how it works. Move on."

She corrects the <u>process</u> of negotiation.

"You're being very dramatic and very unreasonable. Perhaps it's because it's one of your critical days." He's Russian, so in Russia that means you're having your period.

He intended for her to be embarrassed by attacking her <u>identity</u> as a woman. Instead, she elaborates on his assertion.

I said to him, "So what you're saying to me is that I'm hysterical. Just for your reference, I am not currently menstruating." My client is a guy, and he's like cringing. "What you're saying is that if I were on my period, I am completely what—unhinged, hysterical, should be sectioned, institutionalized?"

She details the <u>content</u> of what he was insinuating with the remark. Even though other men are uncomfortable, she persists.

He's starting to roll his eyes, "That's not what I said."
"Well before you say really stupid shit, maybe you should consider the fact that your client is a woman. Look to your right, that is a woman. Do you need some time out to really consider the things that you say? Because that's not okay."

Again, she points out <u>content</u>, the gender of his client. By embarrassing her, he would also be embarrassing his client. By not feeling embarrassed, she reverses the effect of the insult.

I spoke with him outside, "I understand that you're frustrated. You're frustrated because you're not getting what you want. But do not attack me personally because that's exceptionally unprofessional and I do not attack you."

She remains professional while speaking directly. Again, she cites content. She focuses on the personal attack and asserts her position clearly and succinctly. And continues with dark humor:

"I will rip your heart out right here right now, and there are no witnesses and we are in Moscow. (*Laughing*) But don't attack me in front of my client. If you think that that makes you look smart, it doesn't. It really undermines us as a profession because your client is paying 1,000 pounds an hour and my client is paying 1,000 pounds. Also, don't be a fucking idiot. We're the ones sitting with money on the table. If you want our $1.5 billion, you have to play nice."

Her intervention was direct and fact oriented. It works because no power differential existed between her and the other attorney; if anything, she was in a stronger position since her client was the buyer in the transaction. Key in this is that she not let his insult embarrass or silence her.

As Long as They Aren't Talking about Me

> We had a lovely management-level female employee, just lovely in personality. She was the face of one of our divisions to the consumers. She was my age, I'm 61. We age, we don't look the same as we did at 20. The CEO said, "If she gains any more weight, she's not going to be able to do her job."
>
> The whole team was together. We were out to lunch as an executive committee. The CEO said it and I said, "Wow, that is really sexist." He gave me a sharp look—I don't remember the words he used, it was essentially "Don't speak to me that way." I'm thinking you should not speak that way about your employees.
>
> Some people might not think of that as sexual harassment. But that's a comment that shouldn't be made in the workplace. **As the only female in the room, I took it personally.** I certainly took it in a defensive way on behalf of the woman who is being targeted.

Her intervention highlights a theme that emerged among women. Women reported being tolerant of sexist behavior in general, as long as the men were not addressing them directly. In the context of sexism, they could not be more wrong. When men make sexist comments, they are talking about you. Remember, to sexist men we are all the same woman. That you make such a distinction in your own mind is delusional. When men are sexist against women, and you are a woman, they are sexist against you.

> I knew that the CEO would demonstrate that attitude toward her. In that context it was sexual harassment, in terms of belittling her physique to the rest of the male leadership of the corporation. She just wasn't present for it. But to me, that comment represented an attitude that was pervasive of how women were treated in that organization.
>
> There were often pats and inappropriate touching on the female staff, by male staff. Inappropriate comments. The CEO was notoriously involved with some of his female sales staff. But I did challenge him, but it obviously was not effective. That was the beginning of the death nail of our relationship.

Throughout this book are stories of women trying to be the exception. Women change their appearance, their clothes, their hair, their demeanor, to the point where it changes them internally. They try to be the exception. "He's not talking about me." Yes, he is. One man's exception is another man's target. The final paragraph articulates the different forms of sexism that were present in the organization. If you are a woman, he is talking to you. Men who do not intervene and correct him are also talking about you.

A Christmas Story: Sexist Institutions

The Christmas party took place in a private gentlemen's club in St. James. They have these private clubs and they're hundreds of years old, from the 17th century, very exclusive. We got our Christmas Party in this club which only had male members. Women could be guests but not be members. I remember walking into the venue with this very senior practitioner of the old guard, walking up the staircase and him saying to me, "You know you are very fortunate to be able to use this staircase because normally women have to enter the venue via the back staircase."

I said, "Oh really? Are they concerned that the estrogen would affect the stairway?" He was so disgusted that I—a female woman—I mean he visibly looked like he was going to be sick in his mouth. Never spoke to me again. I don't mean never spoke to me again that evening, I mean he never spoke to me again ever.

The participant who told this story was a woman of color. Historically, she could be denied entrance for at least two reasons. Regardless of what era a man is from, he feels very comfortable with exclusionary institutions. He could have said, "Do you realize how backward in thinking this place is? How outdated?" He did not. He told her she was lucky to use the front entryway. Her response, sheer brilliance. Use it whenever possible.

Child Care and Work: Sexist Institutions

Women are constantly asked to make choices that men aren't required to make about their lifestyle. I think the criminal bar invades your life to such an extent that it can alter how many children you decide to have, when you decide to have your children, in a way that other professions don't.

We don't have maternity leave, we're self-employed. Your child gets sick at eleven o'clock in the morning and you're in court, someone's going to have to deal with it other than you because you're in court.

There are things that are fundamentally incompatible with being a primary caregiver which will never be fixed. Your hearing is supposed to start at ten o'clock, you think you're going to be out of there to pick up your kids by three. The case isn't ready, and the judge puts it back until four. What are you going to do? You're going to find someone else to pick up your child.

Stuff like that happens all the time and there's a massive fallout rate, particularly for women. You don't see that happening with male counterparts. That's an institutional issue.

Expressed in a systemized way, sexism seems even more regular, because our entire society is set up this way. Androcentrism is a term that describes the male perspective. In essence, androcentrism means that men are the neutral, the standard against which all else was measured (Bem, 1993). Women are a deviation from the norm. Women bear children, so through an androcentric lens, childbearing is not the neutral norm; it is something that requires accommodation. Since men do not bear children, our systems are not set up to accommodate child care. A point of interest: very few of the participants had children. Many systems and businesses accommodate families. Most people have families, and most women have children. How is that *not* the norm?

Remind me, who benefits from the status quo?

Sexist in the Spotlight

Q: When you tell other people that you're asked what club you dance at, how do they respond?

They laugh, the same way I just laughed, I mean everybody just giggles. Everyone knows that it happens. Nobody is shocked, that's for sure.

I met this participant once, years before writing this book. The day I met her, we were on a boat and her mood was solemn. At that time, she had been in the city for a year and she kept getting that question. What she said to me was, "People here can see me as stripper, but they can't see me as a PhD." I had never heard of anyone else who had that experience. She was not giggling about being mistaken for a stripper that day. When you face it alone, that assertion grates on your soul. Of all my experiences, repeatedly being told I was a prostitute leveled me.

Q: Who do you tell?

I say it on panels now! I really want things to change. I really don't think the best way to approach people . . . I tell people openly because it really happens so frequently. It still happens, it's not like a past experience, it still happens! And I'm not the only one who has that experience.

She is intervening for herself and on behalf of other women. This is what we need on panels. Sexism is not an abstract thing, it is painful and personal. Speaking its name in public yanks the veil. By speaking openly about sexism, we make it a collective experience. I remember the relief I felt knowing someone else had the same experience I did. Not that I was glad she went through it, but knowing you are not alone is a powerful force. Collective experience helps remove the stigma of shame and eliminates the power of silence. Speak candidly when you have a platform to do so.

CHAPTER FOURTEEN

Naming the Behavior

Introduction

What sexism most robs us of is our innate right to exist as ourselves, to occupy professional space that we have worked for, and to have our thoughts and ideas heard rather than be dismissed. Women have been socially conditioned to accept that our personal worth will propel us to the top and allow us to achieve. Contrary to that social belief are volumes of empirical evidence and life experience that say otherwise. Despite what we have been fed culturally as women, our knowledge and abilities are secondary to our sex.

Throughout this book, we have seen the interconnectedness of male networks, the same tactics that play out across oceans, and the same stories from executive women from different countries describing sexism in the same ways. Agentic women, those of us who take control of our lives and strive tirelessly to progress, share something in common. We are not victims. We will not be labeled as victims. That would be contrary to our very existence. Victimhood is not an identity we ascribe to, but herein lies a weakness that can be exploited. As an institution, sexism has built in a brilliant kill switch. The mere acknowledgment of sexism automatically labels you a victim. Our strength is used against us. Our courage becomes our cowardice.

Exploiting our identity is the brilliance of sexism as an institution. Acknowledge it and you are a victim. Resist it and you are a bitch. Who hates men. And is probably ugly. And a lesbian. Pick a label. Sexism takes what is important to us and twists it into something shameful. "Working mothers," as if this is a distinction. All mothers work. The disproportionate work that falls to women worldwide is beyond astounding. But a mother who is also an executive is treated with dismay; how could she care about her children if she spends so much time away? Your achievement is used against you. Strength is a characteristic that will dismantle an inequitable power structure, so women are kept weak and small, like kittens. Speak against that which you know to be inequitable and you will be labeled, shamed, shoved back down, put in your place. Our strength is used against us.

Men are taught to disrespect and dehumanize women. Boys and men are immersed in violent and degrading pornography, and the industry is getting progressively more extreme by its own admission. Men buy women in strip clubs and through escort services, many of which are now fronts for sex traffickers. Sex is a consistent part of business; more than an indulgence, it is a regularity. Men teach and police each other on hypermasculinity that reinforces and monitors maleness that openly defiles and commodifies women through words, activities, and images (Barak, 2003). Any man can step out of it at any time. They have agency like women have agency. To ignore the reality of what has become socially normal would be a choice to remain encapsulated in a chosen lie.

Consider that interactions are indeed not individual, but a network of dynamics. Acknowledge that "rules" exist, and that we abide by them ourselves and police others in accordance with them. Now throw them away. It's time we make new rules.

Current state: Adherence to previously constructed and internalized norms and rules.

Desired state: Rather being prescribed for us, the rules that govern women's interactions with each other are based on our values.

How we get there: Rather than holding each other to the standards of men, renegotiate the rules of your conduct whenever and wherever possible. Recognize that the context of sexism relies on women going to battle with themselves and each other.

Conflict Goals

When we are immersed in conflict, the first step is to get grounded. The first two parts of this work showed in detail what sexism look like in everyday situations. The situations had multiple layers to them, and the magnitude of the problem is overwhelming. We are immersed in a series of periodic, ongoing, and situational conflicts every day. This chapter is to orient you in conflict. Instead of feeling like you are lost in a fog, the following are four ways to categorize conflict. The second part of this chapter will be its application to executive sexism.

DEFINITION OF CONFLICT

"Conflict is the real or perceived blocking of goals between two or more interdependent parties. Conflict can be divided into four categories: Content, Process, Relational, and Identity."

(Wilmot and Hocker, 2001)

Content

The thing or subject matter in question

Explanation of Content Goals

Content goals include any tangible or definable items or issues that, by having or acknowledging them, will yield us a better existence. Content goals can include things like material items, money, subject matter, time, or information.

Content can be general or specific: The car, your computer, health care, salary, dinner, clothes, activities, free time, work, religion, housing, transportation, phone calls, texting, pictures, hobbies, food, human trafficking, the tax code, sexism, homophobia, education, books.

The item or issue of content may be of great importance to you, but of little or no significance to the other party. Or it could work the other way around; the content at hand means a great deal to the other party and absolutely nothing to you. In either event, a point of focus in your conflict will be a content goal.

The ability to identify the **what** of a conflict is an important first step in addressing it. Sometimes identifying content conflict is straightforward, and sometimes it is not. Knowing what to look for and how to name it are powerful allies in conflict resolution. Below are some examples of how people might verbalize when content conflict arises.

Expressions of Content Conflict

We cannot afford this.

We don't have the staff hours available to complete this project.

I don't eat chicken.

There's not enough time to eat and make the plane.

She doesn't carry purses, so we should get her a different gift.

The dirty kitchen makes it hard to prepare a meal. Can you clean it?

I want to live someplace warm, not cold.

That's not how the political process works.

You ruined my shirt!

That is a small part of a much larger subject.

That decision was based on misinformation.

Effects of Content Conflict

Some content can be pretty straightforward. If you prefer Chinese food to Mexican, eat at the Chinese restaurant. If you need other information, ask for it. If you lack the time to do several activities, prioritize your options. If properly identified, these content issues can be resolved easily.

On the other hand, some content issues are more complicated because they evoke emotional responses. Content issues may impede your professional goals. If you do not have adequate resources to complete your tasks, their incompletion will reflect on you personally and possibly impede your suitability for raises and promotions. The inability of parents to provide for their families at the level they deem appropriate can make them feel inadequate.

When the conflict involves a thing or a sum of money, we are sometimes made to feel petty for pursuing it. "It's only a dress!" or "It's just $50." The potential embarrassment we face from others often stops us from trying to recover our losses, even when the loss causes us hardship. This dynamic compounds the conflict. In addition to the material loss, now the conflict includes irritation and resentment. The emotional component becomes a meta-frame for the situation, resulting in the worn-out adage "It's not about the money," when in fact it *is* about the money. You were just made to feel stupid for making it an issue.

Content issues that have the most potential to escalate are those that impede other goals like your professional advancement or the perceptions others have of you. When possible, name the content issue. That will provide you a more solid place to work toward agreement. Also, make sure you understand the content as the other party understands it. Understanding is not the same as agreement.

Control your feelings as much as possible, and focus on the item being discussed. Also, be cognizant of how the other party might be feeling, and allow room for his or her dignity to remain intact. Respect and rationality will enhance your efforts in conflict situations regarding content.

Process

The way we do things

Explanation of Process Goals

Process refers to how we do things, and the methods we use in decision making. Processes are put in place to construct an order of how things are done, in what sequence, and to what end. They can be subject to change in an instant, or they can be codified in law. Control of the process often has great impact on the interaction itself and the ensuing result of that interaction.

Processes can be formal or informal. Informal processes include behaviors familiar to us like manners, greetings, and etiquette. These are choices we make about how we will conduct ourselves in the company of others in specific contexts. The process goals of these behavioral norms are to guide our interaction in way that promote sociability and relationship among people. When these behavioral guidelines are violated, we take note. Similarly, we take note when people do not follow workplace rules or norms, and when people break the law. Formal processes include rules, procedures, and laws. The disregard, questioning, or outright violation of processes results in process conflict.

Expressions of Process Conflict

He didn't even say hello to me!

How did we decide Saturday was cleaning day? I want to go out, not clean.

Why can't I make the bed later? Why does it have to be now?

All information must be submitted through the program director.

We always go where you want! Why don't I ever get to choose?

She did not follow the approval process for a day off work.

The evidence was obtained without a search warrant, so it's inadmissible.

The board of directors only sees the information I show them.

What is the protocol for setting up a meeting with that organization?

You are not registered to vote at this precinct.

It's not fair that we have to do things your way all the time.

We never voted on that change, and it requires a two-thirds majority.

Effects of Process Conflict

Process conflict is the questioning or altering of how decisions get made, or how communication is conducted. It occurs when we recognize that our interests are being jeopardized, and subsequently, that our goals are being impeded due to some existing procedure or decision-making mechanism. In this event, we seek to alter the process in a way that promotes an outcome more suitable to our own interests. This can be between people, within a group, or among nations.

In many ways, process is very useful. Laws govern the way people should conduct themselves for the social good, and also dictate the methods for determining whether people have violated the law. Process helps households function by delineating roles and responsibilities. The same goes for companies and office settings; in fact, understanding process is essential to your survival in regimented workplaces where breaking the rules, even technicalities, is grounds for dismissal.

Process controls the outcome of any decision by determining who has a voice, what information gets shared, and what information gets stifled. Ultimately these factors dictate in a situation what information is relevant and what is not. Parties stand to gain or lose based on where they are situated in heavily controlled processes.

In conflict, we have the ability to choose how we engage with another party, to determine what process we use. Adopting rules like active listening, mutual respect, and not interrupting are all methods we can employ to promote a healthy conflict. Being open to new information and different ways of doing things also helps to alleviate process conflict.

Carefully study process in a conflict. It shows you how people think, how they reason, and how they come to their decisions. It gives you a window into their mentality. This window sheds light on areas of agreement that you might have previously missed.

Relational Conflict

Who we are to each other

Explanation of Relational Conflict

We have certain expectations of how others with whom we are in a relationship will conduct themselves. How others act in relation to us is generally reflective of how they feel about the relationship, its importance relative to the outer issues at hand. Relational conflict occurs when another person violates your expectation of how you think they should think, act, or behave in the relationship.

Expectations of how people behave in relationship depend on the nature of the relationship.

The relationship with your boss is not the same as the relationship you have with your coworkers. The relationship with your children is different than the relationship you have with your spouse. The dynamics of a dating relationship are drastically different depending on whether you plan to marry, or if you know the situation is temporary.

Although conventions of relational conduct exist, the expectations that we have for one another are not universal. They depend on the individual characteristics of the people involved and what you wish to accomplish together. Family dynamics vary considerably. The interaction that works for some families does not work for others. In the same way, workplaces have different rules, culture, dress codes, and levels of formality. Relationships between friends are based on a myriad of factors, all peculiar to the set or group of friends. In romantic relationships, the identity of each member contributes to set the rules of tolerable and intolerable behavior, and for all couples the formula is different. Relational expectations depend on the people you are with and why you are with each other.

Expressions of Relational Conflict

How could you do that to me?

How could you do this to us?

Considering our relationship, I expected more from you.

How can you choose him over me?

Look what she did to me! How can that not bother you?

Who's more important, her or me?

How could my own father do this to me?

What they think is more important than what I think?

I told you that in confidence!

How can you let them talk about me like that?

Why didn't you stick up for me?

Effects of Relational Conflict

The threat of relational conflict is powerful, very real, and very unsettling. When we perceive that a relationship is not what we thought it was, nothing about the other person makes sense. We feel used, misled, lied to, and at the root, we feel betrayed.

Betrayal of relational expectations is disorienting. Personal relationships bind us to others, and we choose certain people to have a relationship with based on the need to share and express particular aspects of ourselves— to be accepted, to be vulnerable, to be funny, to be smart, to be giving, to be loving. When you believe the relationship is a safe place to conduct yourself in a certain way, and then find out that relationship is not what you thought it was, what you discover is that you are not as important to the other person as you thought you were.

Even the perception of betrayal can be as powerful as the betrayal itself. Relationships are based on reciprocity and trust, and the violation of either forces us to recalibrate how we should think about and interact with the other person.

Identity Goals

Who I am in the conflict

Explanation of Identity Goals

Identity is us at our core. Who we are, what we believe, what we hold dear, what we abhor, and who we strive to be. Some aspects of our identity remain intact throughout our lives, and other components change as we grow and our perspective expands. Identity is not something that is subject to others' opinions or input. It belongs solely to us.

We belong to groups because they enhance our identity. Our affiliations and activities make us more of who we want to be by including us, nurturing us, or challenging us. When the affiliation no longer suits our needs, we sometimes move on. Other times we hold on to people, groups, and places to remind us of our past.

Identity guides our actions. We behave and make choices according to who we believe we are. Along the way, people may ask you to do things that you consider contrary to character or in direct opposition to your values. When outside forces conflict with our sense of self, it evokes a strong reaction, as if our very being is in question.

Expressions of Identity Conflict

I am a woman.
What kind of person do you think I am?

I'm not that kind of man.

I am a good father.

How can you think I would do that?

I'm a conservative Republican.

I am a part of this family.

He is a priest.

I thought you were a Christian.

I don't consider myself a divorcée.

Effects of Identity Conflict

Identity makes you feel as if you belong to something bigger, some greater vision or some larger cause. Our identity can bring us to a larger group of people who share our values. This can have incredible meaning in one's life and provide a sense of comfort and belonging. Keeping people in the space of identity is very useful in promoting group cohesion, and then directing actions of the group. People of shared identities and shared values have banded together for centuries to accomplish some otherwise insurmountable goals.

At the same time, group identity can also be manipulated to bring about certain behavior. Politicians appeal to identity when running for office. Political conversations are less about the content of an issue, and more about *what kind of person you are* for thinking or feeling the way you do about the issue. While feigning to address the issue, candidates are actually telling you how you should think or feel, and in so doing are indicating how you should vote. They are invoking identity to promote a particular voting behavior.

Political identity is the cause of many contentious exchanges and the ruination of many a family dinner. The more you fight, the more entrenched your beliefs become, and the more solid you become in your position in a way that cannot be questioned. Issues that can be discussed dissolve instead into generalities and feelings. The substantive becomes the intangible. Fights about feelings cannot be won.

On a more basic level, questioning or challenging one's identity means taking the conflict into a realm where little can be accomplished. People's identities are their own. What you can do is understand the other party's sense of identity, how their identity contributes to your conflict situation, and in what ways you can work with their identity to promote a better result.

Application

Applying conflict categories to executive sexism

How to Say He's Not That Good

I'm facing this situation in my new firm. I want to grow the team, and they're saying, "Oh we found someone who we think is interesting." I don't think he is interesting. I don't think the guy has a successful practice, and I don't think he's a good fit.

He's going to talk a good talk, and because I know him, I know that he doesn't have much to back it up. This guy, he's 55, I would expect his numbers to be much higher than what they are. But I don't know how to relay that message to them without insulting their sense of judgment.

Because you can't—that's just like saying, "One of *you*, one of *your* pack, is underperforming. I want a better playmate." (laughing) I don't know how to say it, but not saying it probably means I'm going to get lumbered with this guy who is dead weight, who feels he is massively senior in comparison to me, and he's going to try to fit his authority over me, which is a bad deal.

Problem Defined:

She wants a qualified colleague (content).

The candidate may be substandard (content).

Men's bravado is accepted without men needing to prove anything (content).

If he is substandard, it will slow growth of the practice (content).

Hiring is based on whether they like you (relational).

Her new colleagues like him, and he is like them (relational/identity).

He may also practice dominant relational style (identity/relational).

Conflict Application

Process: Relationally based hiring is not qualified or quantified, it is emotionally based. Design a hiring process with metrics and utility scale, or other instruments that necessitate validating claims in a quantifiable way. Likability can be part of the scoring process without overtaking the hiring decision. **She gets a qualified colleague (content).**

Conclusion

Conflict associated with executive sexism is typically caused by identity and relational issues. The purpose in identifying the four categories of conflict is for readers to have a system for identifying and articulating conflict. These are the basic steps to organize your thoughts and be clear on your intentions.

CHAPTER FIFTEEN

Addressing the Behavior

Introduction

Characteristics of Sexism

Women who contributed to this work told parts of their life they rarely discuss. As a result of their candor and generosity of time, we have a collection of examples from which to develop further research and solve the nuances of real problems. In summation, the women's stories shared these characteristics:

- The man teaches and the women are taught;
- The man knows everything and the women know nothing;
- The man thinks and the women are thought about;
- The man talks and the women listen—meekly;
- The man disciplines and the women are disciplined;
- The man chooses and enforces his choice, and the women comply;
- The man acts and the women have the illusion of acting through the action of the man;
- The man chooses the program content, and the women (who were not consulted) adapt to it;
- The man confuses the authority of knowledge with his or her own professional authority, which he sets in opposition to the freedom of the women;
- The man is the subject of life, while the women are mere objects.

(Freire, 1970, n.p.).

For some women, the idea of sexism as a system is not yet a mindset they feel comfortable with. Each of us experiences life differently and finds the right solutions to our problems in the right time. This work is presented as a framework for understanding seemingly unrelated dynamics and incidents. If and when the time is right, the framework will remain as a possible answer for you.

In considering whether sexism is an appropriate frame, test it through conflict resolution. As a brief overview, consider the situations you are in, and determine if the type of conflict you experience is constructive or destructive conflict. The distinction is crucial. Sexism is a structural mentality, a lens through which some people see the world. A virtual reality, if you will, that sees and values others in a fundamentally different way than do people who are not sexist.

Conflict resolution can take many forms. You can maneuver independently or with another party. For now, think of the types of conflict you experience in your executive settings and weigh them as constructive or destructive.

Constructive and Destructive Conflict

When people genuinely want to solve conflict, it takes the form of constructive conflict:

Constructive Conflicts

Constructive conflicts result from satisfied participants who have engaged in a cooperative negotiating process. Usually constructive conflict can be identified by four main characteristics.

- Narrowing the focus and definition of the conflict
- Limiting the issues to those of the conflict origin and not including secondary issues
- Seeking cooperation between parties to resolve the conflict
- Trusting that both parties want mutually satisfactory outcomes

Those who do not wish to resolve conflict tend to look more like this:

Destructive Conflicts

Destructive conflict occurs when parties have not engaged in, or have failed at, addressing their conflict issue. The dynamics turn competitive and disruptive to the parties themselves and those closest to them. The characteristics of destructive conflict include:

- Expansion of the parties and issues; original conflict often forgotten
- Escalation to threats, deception, and coercion
- Polarized views and positions
- Focus shifts to hurting the other party

Five Styles of Conflict Resolution

Women interviewed showed hesitancy in addressing situations that made them uncomfortable, even when nothing of consequence was at stake. My recommendations would be conflict communication, interest-based negation, and assertion skills. For this work, I provide an overview of conflict styles for some variation in approaching conflict related to sexism. People use different styles in different circumstances. We cannot always easily recognize what conflict style is being used, because who uses each style depends on personal profile, individual implementation (personality), and motivation. Below are descriptions of the five conflict styles. Included in the descriptions are brief scenarios to demonstrate ways that you may have experienced yourself or someone else enacting the conflict style.

Prior to engaging in conflict, ask yourself the following about your position and that of the other person:

Adapt your style to the situation and people involved.

1. How invested in the relationship are you?
2. How important is the issue to you?
3. Do you have the energy for the conflict?
4. Are you aware of the potential consequences?
5. Can you live with the consequences?
6. What are the consequences for not engaging in the conflict?

Harmonizing

The relationship matters more than your goals.

Harmonizing can also be called yielding or accommodating. The harmonizer will aban-don pursuit of almost any goal in order to keep the peace. To a harmonizer, his or her opinion is never worth voicing if any risk of offending others exists. Taken to extreme, the true feelings or intentions of harmonizers can be unclear because they are so averse to taking a stand on anything.

Characteristics

Want to please others and be pleased by others.
Human connection comes before the work or task at hand.

Best for situations when:

You realize you are or were wrong about something.
The issue means more to the other party.
You can give in on this issue and build credit for a later situation.
Preserving the peace is more essential than voicing your preferences.
Keeping somebody happy is the most important thing.
A power imbalance exists, and you having less.
Expressing your point of view may initiate retaliation from which you can-not protect yourself.
You do not really care about this issue, or its outcome is not especially important to you.

Approach them by:

Using two steps. Be sure to start conversation by connecting with them on a personal level. Inquire about their life, family, or well-being. Only after the mood has been established can you move on to business.

Not your best choice when:

You will harbor resentment.
The conduct of others is unacceptable and needs to be addressed.
Someone is trying to cooperate with you, or discuss something with you. You may inadvertently make them feel controlling if you leave all the decisions to them. They also have no way of knowing whether you are ever truly satisfied with a decision because you refuse to voice your opinion about anything.
This is what you do every time conflict occurs. Your quest to please others will get old and irritating. Others even stop inquiring about your preferences and opinions if you never offer them, or if you never take a stand on anything.
Women in the study largely cited this approach, which they are socially con-ditioned to do. Try something new.

For best results:

- Focus on your personal connection.
- Appreciate the relationship.
- Assure them that their views are valuable, and you want to hear what they think.
- Reward their honest input with warmth. Expressing candor is difficult for them, and they need to know that their input is not damaging your relationship.
- Stay light. Being too heavy or serious induces anxiety and may throw them off task.

Directing

Your goals matter more than the relationship.

For people who handle conflict through directing, controlling the outcome is of the utmost importance, even to the detriment of the relationship. When engaged in conflict with a person who typically acts as a director, bear in mind the following points.

Characteristics

Task oriented and want to get the job done.
Sometimes forget the needs and feelings of others.
Prefer to handle things now.
Having a sense of your intentions puts them at ease.

Best for situations when:

The relationship is not long term.
The decision is unpopular but needs to be implemented.
The relationship is not important.
You have no question that you are right, and being right in this instance is more important than preserving the relationship.
The issue is trivial, and the outcome does not really matter.
You need to protect yourself against untrustworthy parties.
Somebody else needs protection.
The issues at hand are vital to your welfare.
Your principles are at stake.

Approach them by:

Indicating your commitment to get the job done, which in this case means addressing the conflict.

Telling them what time frame you need to have the discussion—an hour, tomorrow, next week. The delay is fine. They just like to be clear on when.

Not your best choice when:

Treating others as equals is important for the relationship.
You would be diminishing the self-esteem of a person you care about.
You care what the other person thinks, even if they see it differently.
This is what you do every time conflict occurs (aka, control freak).

For best results:

- Make sure the timing is right—do not try to engage directors when they are in the midst of a big project or are otherwise mentally occupied.
- Do not withdraw. Take the time you need, but make your intentions clear about how and when you will address the problem.

Compromising

Medium emphasis is placed on both relationship and goals.
Feeling like you got a good deal is the most important aspect.
Compromisers like to make a deal, and moreover, they like to feel like they got a good deal. This type values reciprocity, reasonableness, and fair play. They want to find solutions in a time-efficient way, and like to have a solid time limit when framing discussions.

Characteristics

Values fairness, moderation, and efficiency of time.
Wants a time frame. Does not enjoy prolonged discussion.
Keen on finding solutions and ending problems.
Reciprocity is important.

Best for situations when:

You need to work together, but resources are limited.
You must reach some agreement.
You and the other party have goals that are mutually exclusive.
Temporary settlement will suit your needs.
Intense time pressure exists.
Reaching agreement quickly is a high priority.
The issue is of moderate importance, and not worth investing a great deal of time in exploring every possible option.
Some solution is better than outright stalemate.

Approach them by:

Suggesting a time-structured conversation, such as 10 minutes each of saying your point of view, and then 15 minutes of reaching solution. Make sure that compromiser feels he or she is being treated fairly, or else the trust between you will suffer in the long run.

Not your best choice when:

Your values or principles are at stake.
The decision has long-term consequences and requires more attention, consideration, and discussion.
You cannot live with getting less than you need from this situation.
You do not want to concede what you are trading.

For best results:

- Set a structure for your conversation and stick to it.
- Concede on whatever points you can, as this will engender good will with the compromiser.
- Make sure the solution is balanced and fair; otherwise, it will be short-lived.

Compromising is often thought of as the best approach. Everybody gives a little bit. In the topic of sexism, if you are not wrong, do not concede at all that you might be.

Avoiding

Neither the goals nor the relationship matters that much; conversely, the goals and/or the relationship may be very important.

You may know people who typically handle conflict through avoidance. When dealing with these individuals, be aware of the following information and plan accordingly. Knowing how avoiders think can help you prepare for an interaction with the best possible results.

Characteristics

Need time and space to think things through.
Will not put at risk important issues and relationships by jumping into conversations for which they feel unprepared.
Will not respond well to demands.
Surprise confrontations make them withdraw.

Best for situations when:

The relationship is inconsequential.
The issue is trivial.
People need time to cool off.
The decision can be delayed.
You do not have enough time to address the issue adequately.
You have no chance of satisfying your needs, goals, or concerns.

Approach them by:

Using two steps. First, let them know you wish to discuss a particular issue, and that you want them to think about it. Later, or in a few days, revisit the issue and ask to hear how they think about it.

Not your best choice when:

The issue is important to you.
The quality of the relationship is important to you.
A residue of negative feelings will linger.
The other person would benefit from your critique.
Familial roles or job duties necessitate you to act.
This is what you do every time conflict occurs.

For best results:

- Do not take them off guard.
- Stay calm and low-key.
- Do not expect an immediate answer.
- Provide relevant information about the issue. Include precedents from past situations, options you have for the present, and how you will deal with surprise or sudden situations in the future.

Collaborating

High importance on both goals and relationship.
Collaborators are also called cooperators, the kind of person who is looking out for you as much as for him- or herself.

Characteristics

Prefers structured conversations based on listening. Also, likes to know where and when things will be happening.
Wants to hear your needs and will try to reach the best possible decision for both of you.
Has enormous capacity for processing and assumes others do as well.
Values politeness; disdains demands and criticism.

Best for situations when:

The concerns of both parties are too significant to be compromised.

Securing the solid commitment of all parties is essential.

Long-term relationship is important.

Creative outcome is needed.

You have adequate time and energy, perhaps even weeks or years, to address the issues thoroughly.

Both parties are committed to the process and to addressing concerns of the other.

The people involved are skilled in communication or are willing to learn the skills of effective communication.

Approach them by:

Letting them know you wish to discuss a particular topic and agreeing on a time and place to talk so that both of you can be at your best when you speak.

Not your best choice when:

The other person is wrong, beyond doubt or question.

The issue is trivial.

The necessary time and energy just are not available.

People essential to the process are not really committed to it.

For best results:

- Set a time and place for your discussion.
- Blend task and relationship into your conversation.
- Hear them out. They want to hear you out as well.
- State your needs, and stand up for what you want. If you give in to maintain harmony, this type will feel controlling, which is not their intention.
- Be candid, but remain polite.
- Stay connected. If you need a break, take it. Just let them know you will be back.

Intervention: Observations and Discussion

Many Individuals Will Make an Impact

Both individuals and society have a role in addressing sexism because otherwise it will never change. One single person cannot carry that responsibility on her own shoulders, but still we need individuals who will stand and confront, even though they risk professional and social repercussions. Intervening in sexism can happen at any level, and at every level individual action does makes a collective difference. Every effort matters. Women who demonstrate the courage to expose sexism in the gruesome detail it often has do a great service for other women. Each effort paves the way for the next effort, and momentum builds on itself. Never doubt that what you do matters.

Individual Contributions Matters

Consider what occurred since #MeToo became popular. The movement has been around since 2006, and the momentum women gained from it would not have been possible had Tarana Burke not created the platform and laid the groundwork over 10 years prior. The action you take matters, regardless of whether you receive publicity for it.

Not one research participant makes any part of her livelihood from sexism-related work; that is, none of them are writers or activists who get paid to discuss the issue. Interestingly, I did ask, but no writers, attorneys, or anyone who works in this field were interested in contributing to research for which they would not be paid or gain publicity. That fact may be indicative of other things, but I leave that question to future researchers.

Experts Matter

An observation I had long made, which was confirmed by the interviews, is about the women selected for panel discussions on sexism. I have yet to hear a discussion of value. And the speaker profiles could be the reason. This research showed that executive women assigned to lead inclusion and equality projects had no working knowledge of equality. Their fields were tech and law. Which of us would step into either of those fields, or be assigned such projects, had we had no working knowledge of them?

Not only did they lack the technical expertise, they also had no interest in leading these initiatives. The men who directed them indicated no clear direction, because according to the women, the executive men did not really care. They just had to be shown as doing something woman-related. The chosen activities associated with female recruitment and retention were speakers on networking and mindfulness. Those items have nothing to do with inequality.

What is unclear is if the men or the women knew the difference. Only one participant recognized that she was tasked with leading a false initiative. In selecting leaders to run those lines of effort, the women were selected because they were the only women in the room. This supports the larger trend that all women are the same. One woman is just as good as another; surely, they all know about the same things. Women are interchangeable, after all. Any one of them will do to lead a woman-related initiative.

Support Women by Speaking Openly

As people who want to see a shift in sexism, we as women and men involved in the sexist activity explained in this book *need to be willing to get uncomfortable*. At this point, the social stigma of labeling remains a strong and effective silencer, for women. Being afraid of hurting other people's feelings when sexism occurs, or not wanting to embarrass the sexist man, sounds positively absurd when said aloud. More accurately, it sounds like a person in an abusive relationship making excuses for her partner. This is not a judgment on the women who were so kind with their time and honest with their feelings. I learned about abusive partners firsthand, which is how I became educated on the subject. But if indeed this is the case, that women remain silent because they fear embarrassment for the men who belittle them, then internalized oppression has taken hold. It has been that way for many of us, much like the ever-present debate on appearance, but we are here to help each other. Our understanding of sexism is a spectrum, a reflexive continuum. We meet each other in various places in our lives and thinking. The very least we can do is support one another and speak when it matters.

For men, the unwillingness to see "regular" behavior as sexist is a choice. The current power structures enable men to maintain the status quo. Men are rewarded for playing their part and penalized for deviating from the male script. Men, too, require the enactment of social courage if they do indeed care to shift the current levels of equality and inclusion. This work is not meant as an indictment of men. Qualitative research findings serve to create a lens through which we can see the point of view of speakers. In this research, we see the consistent and coherent overlap of stories, dynamics, and trends. Perhaps as a man you had not considered the scope of systems, behaviors, and sexualization. Perhaps you were unaware of how sexism as a structure affects the material progress and mental well-being of women. Across countries and cultures, the same stories are retold. If you had not seen this view before, you have now. What you do with the information is your choice, and your actions do matter.

Conclusion

Whose responsibility it is to address sexism is a focus of this chapter. The answer is, intervening in sexism is the responsibility of every person who wants to transmute the negative effects sexism has, as articulated through this work and countless other works. The detail offered in this research highlights how many people it takes to uphold sexism. While the expression may be one-on-one, many people have to agree to participate, and we all participate in a number of ways.

We agree to certain procedures and policies, we go along with ideas that promote exclusion or exploitation, we disregard the evidence of bias (including our own), we allow the continuation of flawed processes, we remain silent when we should speak up, we laugh even though it makes others uncomfortable, we let others stand alone rather than standing with them. We adhere to outdated beliefs because it is inconvenient to change them.

The concept of mediated action states that culture and individual action are reflections of each other. People choose to behave in a certain way and express that behavior through the use of cultural tools. In choosing to intervene (bystander activation), what benefit an individual may receive or what detriment they may face in each situation is a primary consideration.

Details vs. Meaning

Details create context, and in context we can see our place and how to redirect our efforts according to our goals and values. If one chooses to focus on the *details* rather than the *meaning* (Waller, 2002), that is another way of reinforcing sexism. Take, for example, passing around a nude picture of a woman. Focusing on the details say it is just one picture, the world is not ending as a result. Calm down, don't take yourself so seriously, and so forth. The detail is a singular incident, independent of broader connotation. Focusing on the meaning, however, shifts the narrative. The deeper meaning is that men are sharing a secret. They are sending direct social cues of dominant group superiority and their ability to exclude out-group members. Sexualization represents the dominant group's social ability to commodify a subgroup, and thus grants them the ability to degrade the subgroup with speech and dehumanize them as interchangeable parts.

Social dominance theory refers to this difference as *material versus symbolic conflict* (Sidanius and Pratto, 1999). Far from an innocent joke or isolated act, sexist behavior conveys the power of some over others. To engage in sexist behavior with this knowledge is the deliberate perpetuation of dominant power expression. Men or women who oppose the behavior will typically face some consequence. Though the consequences may be different, that there are indeed consequences demonstrates that the act has power implications. If it were not an expression of power, one's decision to speak against it would not result in consequences, but such a decision does hold consequences. Participating carries a meaning, just as *not* participating carries a meaning.

The decision you make to participate or intervene also carries a meaning.

CHAPTER SIXTEEN

Destabilizing Sexist Environments

Introduction

Destabilizing sexism depends on recognizing the structures of sexism, feeling a sense of responsibility, and acting to counter it. Impeding sexist destabilization are limiting cultural beliefs that deny its reality and severity. This chapter begins with four concepts that explain those limiting cultural beliefs and how they organize psychologically. The next section describes how sexism is manifested in law enforcement and the legal system, and the conclusion revisits critical consciousness raising.

Sexism is not a set of behaviors, it is a system of beliefs expressed and reinforced at all levels of society. Women are held responsible to fight their way through a system that is largely stacked against them, and expected to handle as an individual, problems that are codified and systemic. This chapter highlights how sexism is embedded in the law, which is ultimately why the law cannot protect women. It is not set up to.

Fundamental Attribution Error

People often attribute actions to the disposition of an individual, while failing to take into account the situational context in which the individual made his or her decision. That is, we blame the person and ignore the structure. The frequency with which this flawed thinking occurs has it termed *fundamental attribution error* (Grinnell, 2016; Waller, 2002). In the case of sexism, women are blamed and held accountable for their choices in responding to sexism, while the sexism itself (the situational context of their choice) is disregarded.

Women in this study blamed themselves when men behaved in sexist ways. They cited their own personal characteristic—birth order, social awkwardness, being homeschooled, being shy, and not being confident enough—as explanations for why men were behaving in overly sexist ways. In doing so, the women ignored the sexist structures in which they were situated. Instead of identifying behavior as sexist, women blame themselves.

Men blame women, too, as evidenced throughout this book and other literature. Ignoring the situational context, the pervasive structures of sexism, is a convenient way to feign its inexistence. Men willingly blame women for imagining things, overreacting, reading too much into things; and accuse women of inventing a discriminatory concept to fraudulently advance themselves at the expense of men. These are all efficient ways to perpetuate sexism while denying its very existence.

Recall the quote from page 1:

> "The greatest trick the devil ever pulled is convincing the world he didn't exist."
>
> —*The Usual Suspects*

Avoidance of Psychological Discomfort

Perpetrators of sexism display high tendencies of SDO. The making of a socially dominant person includes the embracing of ideologies that favor hierarchy and place some people in control of others. As with any set of beliefs, there exists a psychological comfort in having a cognitive framework through which the world can be explained.

For someone who is complicit in sexism, asking them not to be complicit in sexism is a psychological adjustment. How the world made sense before would now have to be recalibrated. Accepting new knowledge means you must reconfigure what you know. Other people might appear different to you. You may appear different to yourself. Those differences may not serve your interests.

The idea of having to see yourself and others differently, and the prospect of having to behave differently, is a lot for some people. The psychological term *cognitive dissonance* refers to the mental discomfort of holding two contradictory beliefs. If a man sees himself as a good person, but his sexist behavior is an exhibition of social dominance that contradicts his inherent feeling of goodness, then the man faces two choices. To alleviate his mental discomfort, he can either adjust his point of view and his behavior, or he can seek out contradictory information to negate the new information. *Sexism does not really exist. Feminists make this stuff up to exploit good men. Women lie. They falsely accuse men all the time.* Should he choose this route, the old script is enacted.

Diffusion of Responsibility

Another concept of note is *diffusion of responsibility* (Waller, 2002). This book is not to make the case that sexism exists. I conducted this research to convey in detail what sexism looks like in our daily lives, the meaning of sexist actions, and the opportunities we as men and women have to intervene.

Diffusion of responsibility is a term developed to explain the lack of bystander intervention in violent crime. On March 13, 1964, a woman named Kitty Genovese was beaten, stabbed, and raped by an assailant. Her eventual death took 45 minutes. In that time, streetlights twice scared him off twice, but he returned to resume the assault. Thirty-eight people knew it was happening, and not one did a thing to stop it. In fact, only one person called the police after the woman was dead. When questioned, the other observers all figured someone else would act.

Sexism takes many people to support it. Sexist behavior occurs with the knowledge of people who let it slide. Sexist jokes are made to others, and in the presence of others. Sexualization occurs so often that men feel entitled to do it. Support of sexism is also found in the mundane. The hiring process, company policies, the subtleties of company culture. Our everyday conversation. Your social media accounts. Communication patterns.

Many opportunities exist to intervene, in small ways and through larger gestures. Women throughout this study talked about how permissive sexist culture builds on itself. The opposite can also be true, but it is your responsibility to intervene. No army is showing up to handle this. Who you are matters. What kind of person you are matters. Whether or not you choose to take action when you see a possibility matters.

Just World Phenomenon

The final concept that serves as a psychological impediment for intervening in sexism is the *just world phenomenon*. This thinking mandates that good things happen to good people, and bad people get what they deserve. Overall, this mindset is convinced that the world is just. If something bad happened to you, you did something to deserve it.

The more a person believes that the world is just, the more likely they are to reason that people get what they deserve. Bad things happen, but the world is a fair place. If misfortune befalls you, you must have done something to earn it. This tendency to "blame the victim" is powerful. Results have been replicated in research, where participants blamed test subjects for the loss of a coin toss all the way to them receiving electric shocks.

These experiments concluded that blame was correlated with the perceived amount of control observers felt they had to stop the suffering of another person. *As an observer, the less control you feel able to help, the more you blame the person for his or her suffering.* When the problem seems too complicated, we blame the person experiencing it and step away.

Hearing a story of sexism that is vastly unjust, our tendency is to blame the woman telling you what happened to her. When she speaks, it evokes feelings of powerlessness. After all, what can you do about a larger system full of bias and flaws? It takes mental energy just to get your head around the enormity of the problem. You cannot even see a way to understand, let alone to help her, and this causes mental distress that you wish to be rid of as quickly as possible.

The most effective way to ease your mental anxiety brought about by hearing the problem is to blame her for it. *The world is a just place. People get what they deserve. She must be leaving something out. Things like this don't just happen. She did something to get herself here.* People go so far as to misconstrue the law of attraction to blame others: ultimately, you create the life you want, so the woman must have wanted this for herself at some level and created a situation to make it happen.

Blaming an individual and erroneously attributing individual characteristics to a systemic problem are expedient ways to end an uncomfortable conversation. This head-in-the-sand mentality is not the way forward. Sexism is a momentous issue but is in no way insurmountable. One person cannot overturn it, but many can.

On the positive side, the research of just world phenomenon also suggests that we find it intolerable to watch people suffer. This speaks well of our humanity. For example, an immediate way to help is to stop blaming targets of sexism and stop labeling them as victims. Doing either of those enacts shame and silence, both of which support and reinforce sexism.

When you read the following passages regarding women's experiences with the justice system, take note of your mental and emotional response. No evidence suggests that the world is a fair or just place. The most qualified person does not always get the job. Relationships and networks often play a more influential role than work history or professional qualifications. Injustices occur at rates that should make you enormously uncomfortable. Just world phenomenon is a convenient cliché to cite when people wish not to be physically or energetically involved with a problem they cannot solve; but each person does have a part to play, and the details of these narratives can show readers where their own contribution might be.

Sexist Treatment in the Justice System

This work has featured legal and justice perspectives from different countries. This section reflects experiences the participants had regarding the treatment of themselves and other women. Although there were several more stories, these narratives most poignantly reflect sentiment expressed in the data.

Justice Is a Construct

It's not real, the idea of justice is a construct. It's something we build, and we sell it to people so they can sleep at night, but that's definitely not how it plays out. And it's not just the networks. And it's not just in terms of the people. It's built into the way things are charged. It's built into the law. It's built into all of that. I feel like I'm fighting but it's like, it's sticky, it's all over. I can't really get away from it. So I'm fighting, but I'm handicapped at the same time.

Because I have to work within this framework that has sort of been foisted on me, like this is what's there, it's how it is, and I hate to sound fatalistic and say, one person really can't change it but that's how it feels when you're working in the present. Like my voice really doesn't really matter.

(Sarah, *Criminal Law*)

Before judges were judges, they were first attorneys. Participants discussed the treatment of women attorneys by their counterparts, whose primary use seems to be in sexualizing them, but not respecting as equals or assuming any level of professional competence on the part of women.

Creating Superficial Initiatives

I find it funny they task me as the only female partner in the corporate team to organize this initiative for female fee earners.

They paid a lot of money for someone to come in and do a report—and the result of the report was that this is an inherently chauvinistic workplace. Their response to it was, "We're going to go hire some female partners because our female fee owners are saying they don't have any female role models. And we're going to task *the* female partner with organizing this initiative to make female fee owners more involved and more engaged."

It sounds like a great initiative, but it doesn't actually make people feel engaged or included when you don't listen to them, and when you just sort of do things for planning purposes, reporting and statistics. It's culture at the top level, talking about female associates not having any role models. Well, those potential role models are sitting in the room being looked at like talking monkeys.

(Natalya, *International Energy Law*)

Participants noted, and found elsewhere in this book, the disparate treatment of judges toward male and female attorneys. Women are treated as incompetent in court and during jury selection, so much that some women lost business because the clients saw how the judge treated their attorney and did not want to bear the consequence in their sentencing.

Judicial Bias

I had one judge who picked on me so bad as soon as I would enter her courtroom, she'd call me up. Literally I'm walking through the doors. I haven't put down my coffee. I haven't put down my purse. I haven't opened the file. She would just, "Oh Miss James!" She would call my cases right off the bat. And my clients used to hate it and they wouldn't want me to represent them anymore in her courtroom because they saw how differently she was treating me compared to my male colleagues and didn't want me to represent them for fear that her disdain for me would lead to a harsher sentence for them.

(Sarah, *Criminal Law*)

If a judge is predisposed to have an observable effect on the cases tried by a woman attorney, what type of justice should one expect under those circumstances?

Inequitable Sentencing

You see it and you try to call it out. This one judge, I called him out on disparate sentencing between a white guy and a black guy, drug charges, similarly situated. The black guy he gave prison, the white guy he gave probation. He said, 'You know, you're right" and gave the black guy probation. He changed the sentence. I appreciate that, but it still tells me that there was an inherent bias even initially. Thank God he was able to open his eyes and correct for it, but let's say I wasn't able to correct for it.

(Sarah, *Criminal Law*)

Women's Treatment by Police

Sophia describes when she had a stalker at work—one of her coworkers. On top of the stress that she had been experiencing for months, as well as the fear for her personal safety, she tells what happened when she went to the police for help.

> And then also just dealing with cops. The first detective I went to, his first questions were like, "Oh well, is there anyone you've been flirting with or having an inappropriate relationship with?" Kind of "is this your fault, did you do something to instigate this?"
>
> That was super shitty. It's like, okay I've just been through this horrible thing and you're insinuating it's my fault. You know, screw you. I really need to talk to someone else. So you go through something when you're horrified and scared and no idea what to do. It was the first time I had been in a police station, filed a police report, anything like that. And to deal with that was horrible.
>
> (Sophia, *Global Marketing*)

In the longer context of her interview, we discussed why women do not speak up right away, or ever. She described this situation almost as an afterthought. Even though it was traumatizing for her and spanned months of her life, Sophia was not keen to discuss it, as if talking about it made her a victim. Women who experience sexism are not victims, they are targets.

Police, District Attorney, and Social Context

Rebecca's narrative has several elements to it. She knew the perpetrator, he was adjacent to her work. She waited several months before contacting the police. She experienced negative social consequences in her personal life and received very mixed messages from the justice system.

> This venue I held events at, one night I was the last patron there. The owner came over and we chatted for a few minutes and then he reached over and grabbed my breast. I froze. I was in shock. He made a big "O" with his mouth and put his hand over it, like he was making fun of me. I was still frozen. I got up and left, then went home and freaked out. So that itself is a humiliating experience that reduces you to nothing, but it got worse.

She explained that her boyfriend at the time was a real estate developer and had potential business ventures with this man. Also, her boyfriend frequently socialized at the bar where it happened. He spent a great deal of money there. Between that and the business, the bar owner knew him well.

> My boyfriend calls him the next day and says I'm really upset about what happened. The guy responds that he was so drunk he can't even remember how he got home. Offers nothing more.
>
> This haunts me literally every day. Nobody was sorry it happened, they were sorry not to go to the bar. Four months go by. I see my boyfriend there one night (it's an outside venue), "You're here? After what this guy did to me?"
>
> He says, "Yeah, I don't really think that happened." I was speechless. I poured his beer in his lap.
>
> The next day I called the police. I thought at least I could make it easier for the next girl who reported it. The officer came and was so kind to me. He listened and explained it was a third-degree misdemeanor and I could press charges. I hadn't expected that because so much time had passed. He actually encouraged me to. He was really nice.
>
> I go through the process and talk with DA. He's also nice and tells me a lot of time has passed. I told him when I got home that night I called my sister, who is a judge, and my best friend, who is a clinical psychologist. The DA tells me to get a statement from them and submit my own, he'll see what he can do. He puts the paperwork forward, still very nice with me.

Her experience to this point is supportive, though questionable that she had to get statements from a judge and clinical psychologist, two people of status, in order to move forward. The point, what if she had not made those calls, and what if she did not know people of status. Would her claim still be credible?

She continues. The man confesses.

> In the meantime, I get a request for mediation. As a side note, I wrote the training manual for court mediators in that state, so I know what it's all about. I told them no. He had his chance to handle it informally.
>
> That night, my boyfriend gets a voicemail from this bar owner. He admits to doing it and says his apology is long overdue, to each of us. Why he might need to apologize to my boyfriend I do not know. But now we have this voicemail, and he admits doing it.

Her experience changes when she notifies the district attorney of this conclusive evidence:

> I call the DA and tell him. His tone changes. He gets aggressive. "Why are you trying to go after this guy? Did you two used to date? Did you ever have

a relationship? Did you ever do anything with him? Why is this so important to you? What won't you just drop it?"

My sister (the judge) said it sounded like somebody got to him. Very likely he knew the guy, everybody did. The social consequences were a real thing, maybe for him too.

I tell the DA I want to move forward with the charges because it was humiliating, I hated having that experience, and I want to make sure he doesn't do it to anyone else. He basically hangs up on me.

The end of the story is that man got arrested, pleaded guilty, and was found guilty. But it was weird that the DA was fine when the case was a loser, but he got nasty with me when the man confessed and he had to go through with it.

(Rebecca, *Senior Scientist*)

Her narrative voices once again reference to a male network that seeks to protect itself. Thus far we have read independent accounts of this.

How Federal Law Enforcement Handles Sexism

This section is the narrative of Alicia, who worked in counterterrorism for the Federal Bureau of Investigation. For the sake of clarity, U.S. government agencies loan to each other personnel with different expertise. Some of Alicia's stories take place when she was on loan to the Central Intelligence Agency, so when she mentions working for the CIA, this is what she means.

Alicia's narrative focuses on when she filed an Equal Employment Complaint for sexual harassment. In response, her male supervisor initiated an internal affairs investigation on her. The ensuing harassment was so bad that eventually she resigned. After that, she was blackballed from getting employment, lost her home and all her savings, and ended up working minimum-wage jobs.

In describing her road to being fired, the details of what Alicia was accused of and how the FBI blatantly disregarded tangible evidence refuting their accusations is startling. Readers will note how each step includes the sexism reported throughout this work. The barrage of sexism is the reason to tell her story.

The Problem Is Your Boss

She describes one of her first encounters at the bureau when she is sexualized by her supervisor.

When I first got into the bureau, I had a supervisor trying to make us a couple. He called me into his office and says, "Hey can we go to lunch together today? I take all my new agents out to lunch." It was three hours of him talking about how we could be an awesome interracial couple.

He says, "I have to find an apartment ordinance." I am feeling this is so wrong, but I am a new agent. We would go to the apartment and he would tell the leasing agent, "Yeah me and my girl were looking for. . . ."

I'm like, "your girl?"—get the hell out of here! When he would go looking around the apartment, I would tell the realtor, "I am an agent that works for him and this is totally inappropriate. Can I have your card?"

He got away with all that. Kidnapping an agent for three hours and trying to make me his girlfriend. Years later I was told, "You know I tried to fire him when he tried all that crap with you, but for some reason they wouldn't do it."

She has experiences that reflect the themes we have discussed throughout the work.

Double Standards: She's a Bitch, He's a Sole Charger

Work in federal law enforcement also reflects the negative characteristics placed on women.

Gender communication, it's so different. We are being forced to communicate like these guys, but then, they'll call us a bitch. I can do one thing and I'm a bitch. The guy, he's a sole charger.

He Has Potential, She's Okay Where She Is

They see the guys and say, "The potential he has." But they see the woman and they go, "She's doing okay right now." They don't think about the potential.

Undermining Her Work, National Security and Terrorism

Referring to the man who targeted her to be fired, she says he undermined her work.

For some reason. I know why. I am a strong woman and I knew what I was doing. The people in the CIA would say, "She's right on point," and you could see them sitting there squirming in their chairs. So they were undermining the cases I was working, which were active CIA cases. Meddling with national security and terrorism.

Man Is Given Credit for Her Work

She performed work with the Joint Special Operations Command, and a man who did not work on the projects was awarded and promoted.

> I was working with special ops constantly. First it was like there was no problem with me working Joint Special Operations Command, Seal Team Six, and all that. When they start seeing there's something sexy going on, they want a dude in there. Because she is a chick, she's not a guy.

A prosecutor in the attorney general's office said the same thing. She was assigned to human trafficking when nobody wanted the cases, the laws were just enacted, and convictions were difficult. When she began winning cases and getting press, a man in her office generously offered to take the subject matter off her hands.

> Typical bureau, they tried to insert this guy . . . A couple guys that are in Delta Force, they said, "We don't know you, we don't want you here." It took them a while to trust me, but then they were like you're not going to put this dude in here.
>
> Fast forward a couple years. I was nominated for the Director's award because of my work on this operation we did. I hear I got nominated, but I never got any award. I got something from the NSA Director. Right before I left the bureau, I had access to all different file folders. I find the write-up of what I did, but with that dude's name in it.
>
> He got the Director's award. He got personal commendations from two generals. I called one of the generals and he was pissed. He said, "That's your award." That guy gets the award, plus he gets $1000, and now he's head of the San Diego office. I got along with the guy while he was at headquarters. I didn't realize he was in the club.

By "the club" she is referring to a network of white males in positions of power. She threads their interconnectedness throughout the interview. The men who undermine her all know each other.

Men Working Together to Undermine Her

Before leaving the bureau, she got access to files. Here she refers to emails when the men are thinking about how to get her fired.

> I have an email string where they're going back-and-forth. What can we throw at her? One says, "She follows all of the policies." The other said, "We

can throw time and attendance at her," which is basically what they do and they have nothing.

Some agencies have flexible time and attendance policies, but at the same time the flexibility can be used against you when they need something to use against you.

I was the only female detail, and they were also doing this to the only African-American detail. They were doing an offline OPR (Office of Professional Responsibility), which is essentially internal affairs. That is against all the rules, but they were not really sticking with the laws.

She's a Bitch without the Right Experience

She has the combination of having the bitch stigma with the assertion that she is unqualified for her new position. The outgoing lead prepped his team that she would be overwhelmed because she did not have the experience for her new position:

I get selected for Counterterrorism Squad. I hold a meeting when I first get there. "What have you heard about me?" I know what they going to say.

"You're a bitch." And I say, "Yes." One of the guys said, "But that's in our favor."

I said, "Exactly. If anyone screws with any of you without talking to me, then I'm a bitch. My job is to get you what you need to do your job and buffer you."

One of the younger agents goes, "Carl"—Carl had the squad before me— "he said you would be overwhelmed. You don't have the credentials or experience to take the squad."

I said, "What do you think?" He said, "I looked you up. I think you have enough experience to take this squad."

She notes that the former squad leader and assistant director were close friends in law school.

Ignoring Her Contributions about National Security

This participant had her contributions ignored in work meetings as a status move of her superior.

She talks about the morning of the Benghazi incident. Her work was deploying specialist investigators to embassies, and a contact from Department of Defense offers her 10 seats on a plane leaving that day that will get the FBI into Benghazi. The Assistant Director of the FBI dismisses her in the meeting, and it takes the Bureau two weeks to get into Libya.

> I was dealing with Benghazi here also. They should have deployed whoever to Benghazi the morning of. There's this multiagency plane that takes off from the United States and goes to where there's a crisis.
>
> I was probably the only supervisor of about 300 supervisors that had ever deployed teams to embassies being attacked. I had them going to Beirut and I had them going to Yemen. If you are on my squad, it was because you were hand selected, because it's intense—you're dealing with death and destruction constantly.

The contact calls her on the way to work and offers her seats on the plane to take over special evidence agents.

> The morning that I thought they would be deploying, a Department of Defense guy says to me, "How many seats do you need?" Before me, they never offered seats, not for any other supervisory. I said six. I just throw that out, it's a little more than five, less than ten.
>
> He said, "Could you use ten?" I said, "Yeah I could use ten."
>
> I said, "Are you going to provide protection?" He said, "You don't need to send your tactical groups over, just your evidence and your investigators." These are usually specialized evidence people. A lot of people on my old squad spoke different languages. They were like the cream of the crop.

She goes into the meeting of FBI counterterrorism management, headed by the assistant director. She tells him the offer and he tells her nobody needs her help.

> I go to a meeting. It's all supervisors, deputy assistant supervisors, section chiefs, and the assistant director. They start talking about who's going to be handling Benghazi. Of course, they're talking about the video, which is bullshit.
>
> I said, "Assistant Director, the multiagency plane is willing to give me 10 seats." He just looks at me and he says, "We don't need your help." (He calls her by name.)
>
> I'm like, hello, this gets you into Benghazi itself. Since he just dismissed me, because of ego, it took them over two weeks to get into the country. He knew I was used to putting people on a plane within three hours of an incident.

No one said anything, thirty-some people. All counterterrorism management. The plane never took off. That's a big controversy right now with the Benghazi survivors, why it was never deployed.

Evidently if a man is going to disregard you, the subject matter is not of consequence, even when lives are at stake. She goes on to talk about the inspector general's report on gender inequality.

Sexual Harassment and Discrimination among Federal Law Enforcement

The bureau, I hate to say it, but it's the worst. CIA is pretty bad. There was a study on the CIA, the way women are treated there. The Inspector General just put out a report of gender inequality in the law enforcement agencies under the Department of Justice. The Marshals, ATF (Alcohol, Tobacco, and Firearms), FBI (Federal Bureau of Investigation), and DEA (Drug Enforcement Administration).

They found significant inequality. 43% of FBI female investigators, aka agents, have had sexual harassment or sexual discrimination done to them. 43%. That's high.

Harassment and discrimination are law, and almost half of women in federal law enforcement have had men break the law to harass or discriminate against them. The law itself is sexist and has low regard for women, as demonstrated by its own numbers.

She goes on to talk about the physical intimidation perpetrated by the man who was trying to get her fired.

Physical Intimidation

He accuses her of going to a conference to meet men and gets verbally hostile and physically intimidating toward her.

Here's some of the things he would say to me. I went down to Virginia Beach to what was a quarterly meeting of anyone working Yemen and Somalia. At the time I belong to the CIA. They tell me to go to this meeting, so I did. When I come back, he calls me over to his office. "Why did you go the day before the conference?"

I said, "Because the conference started at 8 o'clock in the morning." He said, "I know people that went down the same day."

I said, "Yeah, they didn't make it for the first half of the day. They were higher ranks, so they didn't need to be there. What is this about?"

He said, "You only went down to Virginia Beach to meet Navy Seals." Then he stands up, and this guy is like 6'5" and a big dude. He starts glowering at me. Standing over me with his arms flailing. "You better not try to pull something on me!" Then he's going on and threatening me.

He was acting like I'm trying to get something over on him by going on a trip for the CIA. I said, "No, they asked me. They're paying for it. That's part of the job."

Then he starts getting really close to me. At that point I just got a real calm and said, "You need to back the fuck up, now."

He just looked at me. I said, "Now." And he stepped back and walked out of the office. I did think like he was thinking about hitting me.

On a subsequent occasion, the same man, who was actively working to get her fired, comes into her cubicle as she is packing to leave. Another person intervened because he feared the man was going to hit her.

I'm packing up my desk at the CIA. He comes right in my cubicle which is not big. Kind of small for two people to be in. "Oh, I know you're getting pulled back for special." I just turned to him and I said, "Who are you bullshitting? Get out of my cubicle."

He stood there. He was breathing real heavy, like he was trying to calm himself down. I wasn't the only one who noticed that. The guy who is chief of Yemen ops came right over and said, "Did you not understand, get out of here."

I looked at the guy, "I thought he was going to hit me." He said, "Yeah that's why I came over here. It looked like he was going to hit you."

He was so big he would just knock me out. The intimidation he used, he had a history of intimidating people. Discriminating against people and bullying females.

Another Woman Recognized the Signs

In this passage she talks about a psychologist observing her at a meeting and seeing the physical signs that she was being bullied.

I was in a meeting and we were talking about radicalization of people here in the United States. There was a woman sitting in a classroom, a pretty blonde woman. I'm explaining that radicalization and abuse of people here is exactly like gang recruitment. They use the same exact techniques. People are like, "Oh really?" They're asking me questions. It was FBI and CIA. I'm just talking to them, and this woman is watching me.

At the end of the meeting she said, "Can I talk to you for a second?" I said, "Yeah."

She goes, "Are you being bullied or something?" I'm like, "Why would you say that?"

"You hesitated to give certain answers. You were like, maybe I shouldn't be that smart."

She tells the psychologist what is happening with the men and her work situation, and then discovers the woman is experiencing that in the CIA.

I just look at her and I said, "I have an EEO against a couple guys and now they have an internal affairs against me." It turns out she was going through the same thing. She was a forensic psychologist.

She said, "You're a pretty blonde. You know what you're talking about. It's intimidating, especially in law enforcement. I'm getting that same shit at CIA."

I told her about all the stuff that was going on. I had (guy's) statement because I was trying to read it at that part of the investigation.

I asked her to read it, because I was getting a real jacked-up feeling. She read it and said the hair on the back of her neck stood up. "This guy's stalking you. He's bringing up your dogs, he keeps bringing up your personal life."

The Equal Employment Office Complaint Process

The investigation report they are reading is the Office of Professional Responsibility (OPR), the internal affairs of the FBI. The investigation was opened when she filed a claim with the Equal Opportunity Office (EEO). The FBI handles their EEO complaints internally. She describes the process:

This is how any complaint in the FBI goes through. You file an EEO, they file an OPR, you end up getting suspended without pay or fired. I got suspended without pay. An appeal in OPR takes forever, it would have taken another year. In order to pay your mortgage or anything, even though you're on leave without pay, you have to request to get a second job, while you're on leave without pay. The bureau likes to deny those. People like me, I just said "screw this, I'm resigning." The HR lady said I was eligible for unemployment, and then they blocked it. They blocked my unemployment.

Finances Get Drained

Well I'm like, what the hell am I going to do? I have a house that I just built for myself. After 15 years I had a good amount of money in my savings fund and 401(k). I had to drain that so I could live. I sold a lot of my jewelry. Clothes that I thought would sell, I sold those. I actually sold my plasma. I would go in a couple times a week and then I would get $100. Things like that. Very degrading. I donated so much of my furniture that I worked hard to get. My house sold at a loss. I moved into my parents' extra bedroom. I went from a three bedroom 2-1/2 bath house into a 10×10 room.

No Health Coverage

For some reason they wouldn't give me health care. Because of all the stress I was having diverticulitis attacks. I tried to get it through the county or the state, they tell me, "No you have a car." I can't make the car payments. It's a lease. "Well you have a house." I can't even make a payment.

What did she do to get herself into this situation?

They threw out a time and attendance, insubordination, destructive behavior while on duty. And I'll tell you why.

Accusation: Crazy Drunk Slut

You know Tim Gunn from *Project Runway*? His father was an FBI agent. He wrote a book and talks about how his father came home one day and he heard his father saying, "If you want to out a female agent, just make her out to be a crazy, drunk, slut."

Drunk—

OPR tried to do "crazy drunk slut." First, I can't be drunk because I was running half marathons every other weekend, sometimes back to back. Everything I put into my body was fuel. And it was a running team, so everybody would know.

Crazy—

The crazy part, they're trying to say there's mental health issues with me, to find a way to say you're not fit for duty. I knew they were going to try this. I find a psychiatrist at Georgetown, expert witness for Department of Defense. He writes it up in an evaluation. "The only thing of concern is what the FBI's doing to her. And it's wrong."

So the crazy they try, drunk they try. Both of those, not happening. Then they say slut.

Here she cites the double standard of social conduct and drinking. Nothing of note happened, simply that she was with a group of men.

Slut—

What they did is, they used some of my best work against me. I was going to the National Security Council Group, and they twisted it. A male agent going to those meetings, they're not going to ask him why he's going out for a beer afterwards with a bunch of guys. But they asked me. "You're always out with a bunch of guys." I'm like, "I don't really have a choice. I'm the only woman in these meetings."

These guys were on that National Security Working Group, I'm still in touch with them. They've all written letters in support of me.

She sent me copies of the letters. Some of the men are in national headline news. All are from top security agencies. She became personal friends with one man and his wife. When she visited the wife, they accused her of being in the house to have sex with the husband.

During the OPR interview, they accused me of trying to sleep with him. I was like, where did that come from? It was tough because I am friends with his wife Ivy. They bring up certain dates. They said, "You were stalking him, you were in his neighborhood."

I said, "He's in Djibouti. He's been there for a year and a half. His wife Ivy asked me over for lunch because I did a half marathon down there." I was hanging out with Ivy, his wife, and they make it like I was trying to sleep with him.

OPR would not accept his deployment records or a statement from the wife. They proceeded under the assumption that their accusation was true.

We worked a lot of, anyone who is held in captivity that I held that desk, you work as an inter-agency team of the federal government. I've met a lot of people who have moved up in the world. The most important ones are who I would hang out with, for sushi on a Saturday. They brought that up. They said you went to go have pizza with him. I said, "Actually the pizza place was too crowded, so we went for sushi instead."

They're surprised I'm admitting this to them—the OPR interview. I said, "Yes, before I went over there, I told deputy director. I was going to brief him on an operation we were going to do on Monday. And he was going to watch our back." What a piss-poor investigation.

Her professional associations with men are assumed to be sexual relationships. The point of order, had she been having sex with all of those men, it would have been a personal matter. In no way was it illegal or grounds for disciplinary action. This gendered label of "slut" is what the

Federal Bureau of Investigation used to sabotage its own counter-terrorism female agent.

Accusation: Destructive Behavior while on Duty

She describes the final charge, an email forwarded to her friend.

> The last one, destructive behavior on duty is because I used to date the commander of seal team six. One night I'm at the CIA and it's later at night. A woman calls me over and said, "I never see you go home early on Fridays. Don't you have any dates?" I said, "No, I'm not dating anyone."
>
> She said, "Who broke your heart?" I went over and got a picture of him with his kids. She just about had a heart attack. Her stepdaughter was marrying him. All that time he was still trying to go after me.

She dated a man while they were both in Afghanistan. He lied to her—he was married—and she found out later in their relationship.

> It was an email, this destructive behavior while on duty. It was a personal to personal email, a Hotmail to Yahoo. Me confronting him. He was an adulterer when I met him, and now he's still trying to get at me even though he's getting married in two weeks. "That's fucked up, and you're going to rot in hell for what you've done."
>
> I sent it to him. Not on FBI systems, personal to personal email. The problem was someone who was there when I had met him in Afghanistan asked about him, "What's going on with you and Captain Hook?" I forwarded him the email on his FBI email. That's where they got me for distractive behavior while on duty.
>
> What they said is that I emailed a high-level official in the intelligence community with an inappropriate email. The way they word it makes it sound like I wrote to a senator or vice president, "You're a fucked-up asshole."

The man retaliates and lies about her sending the email to his chain of command. If she had, he would face military justice charges.

> Then he started saying I sent it to his chain of command. Now had I sent that to his chain of command, he would've been brought up on charges of adultery in military justice. If I wanted to be a real bitch, I could have sent it to the Navy. But I didn't. I sent it to him. And that was destructive behavior while on duty. It shows you how they do things on their part.

The man has sexual assault charges against him and is in line to become an admiral. He becomes part of the OPR investigation against this participant.

It turns out, a little karma, when he marries this girl he was screwing around on his wife with, she's a super high-level CIA. I think this had to do with why they came after me about the email. He was moving up the ranks, he was next in line to become an admiral. Two women came forward and said he sexually assaulted them. One of them, her father was one of the secretaries of defense in the past. She was forced to resign or retire. So they're putting more weight on him than me, and he's almost being brought up on charges of sexual assault.

They interviewed him for the OPR and he said, "I don't know. That email came out of left field. I only met her in Afghanistan. I don't know why she said that."

I show up, because I'm an FBI agent, with text messages, photos, and everything he sent me. "I'm going to be a better man for you, can't wait for you to meet my kids." Here's the one that really got them. My attorney put her head on the table when she saw this. He sent one "I'm walking the dog, I can't say anything sexy." I go back with what are you wearing?" He says, "A tee shirt and a hard on."

They let him change his statement. Guess what, you lied but we're still going to give you a chance to screw her. What he was trying to do was to work into the crazy part to say that I'm unfit to hold a security clearance.

Q: As in, you imagined everything, and made it all up?

Yep. That's how OPR did me in. OPR has long been a tool used against EEO complainants . . . it is so broken, and they are so corrupt. I mean, I was showing them proof of certain things and none of it is in their final report.

Every false allegation was regarded as truth by the FBI's Office of Professional Responsibility. She noted for each charge there was tangible evidence to the contrary, but none of it was admitted into the report.

Accusation: Late Night Messages

She continues with the "questionable" behavior she exhibited.

Here's a funny thing. In this interview they say, "You send emails and text messages late at night." I say, "Yeah, because terrorists are awake late at night."

Goofy emails, they said, having to do with Pakistan. The goofy email was that the defense attaché over in Pakistan, our defense attaché, had alerted me to a major prison break of people that we actually had warrants for. I didn't handle Pakistan, so I said, "Hey this just came in," and I shot it over to my supervisor. That was the goofy email.

While this investigation is taking place, this credentialed antiterrorism agent with specialized knowledge and education is assigned clerical work.

Immobilized Her Career by No Input Opportunity and No Record of Progress

While everyone else is working a case, it's like I'm sitting there hardly doing anything. I fought it and got transferred to the America unit, that dealt with homegrown terrorism. Boston bombing happens, I'm dealing with that.

Her supervisor didn't want her to have any input on the case, to immobilize her career.

He just started marginalizing me, idling me . . . they ended up sort of making a mistake. They put me as the liaison to the lab. That's the coolest job to do. You see how they made the bomb and set up bracings for that. I was looking at a Sally Beauty Supply receipt they found when they searched the house. I went through the SKUs to figure out what they bought, and it was all these different levels of developers.

I said, "This is significant," and the people I worked with were like, "Why?" I said, "How do you think you make a bomb? You need the chemicals in these developers."

Shallow Knowledge Pool—When Talent Leaves an Organization

She also tried to educate new analysts on the historical perspective of terrorism, because all the senior members of the team have left.

None of them had a historical understanding of terrorism. So in an investigation, a name comes up. It's the grandfather of offensive jihad. He was also Osama bin Laden's Iman, his spiritual advisor. His name shows up in something and everyone's like, "Who?" I'm like, "What?" I'm sitting there thinking you people are supposed to be the experts in this shit.

So many people resigned or chose not to come to headquarters, we are full of analysts that are two years in. I'm trying to educate some of these people, knowing that my OPR is about to come to a close and I figured they were going to try and terminate me.

Blackballed for Industry Jobs

Two and half years I couldn't get a job over minimum wage. I know why. They blackballed me.

We don't say they do it, but they do. Especially when you are going for a job in the security field. I interviewed with a director of security. They were calling me back for second interview, totally gung ho. My old boss called on my behalf. He said, "They love you, this is the perfect job for you." Then I don't get it.

Is this my imagination? Why am I not getting these jobs? Time and time, I try to engage an interview, and I'm not getting them. I can't prove it, but I know, and I've heard from other people, they ostracize you. They do whatever they can to make your life a living hell and make it hard for you to get a job. I mean I see it all the time now, I see how they do it.

They have tentacles going everywhere. I know a guy, he's director of security at (major company in New York). He came in as a vice president. All of a sudden, they eliminated his position. They do that shit, they come after you.

Selling Makeup at Macy's

My uncle is a corporate attorney. He said, "Until you settle your EEO they're going to continue to blackball you. You can't stay on the East Coast. You have to go somewhere else." I ended up taking a job with Macy's in cosmetics for minimum wage. Then I was at Bank of America call center for a year.

New Job, Lower Status and Pay Than Comparably Skilled Men

I get a call from a retired assistant director . . . he said, "What are you doing for work? I always wondered what happened to you." I was like, "You could've called me two years ago."

He said, "There are a couple jobs we are going to be putting out. And by the way, they are going to try to blackball you, but they have to go through me and I'm not going to let that happen." I fly out to Chicago and have a series of interviews.

The whole Andy McCabe and FBI corruption was coming today news and I saw he had violated a certain law. I pushed a complaint against him for violating local laws of election and I didn't realize my boss here was really good friends with Andy. And he didn't talk to me again. It's been a year and a half, and he's only talked to me once. I've known him since 2001.

I've been out here for about two years and I'm probably the lowest man on the totem pole. I notice that my boss brought all the guys in as senior managers but they bring me in as an analyst, not even a senior analyst. And that's bullshit. That shows, that's how it happens.

Conclusion

The preceding account detailed the way in which federal law enforcement agencies handle sexism in their ranks. These are the top law enforcement professionals in the United States. We just read some details (she had hours more) about the way our top law enforcement conduct themselves within their own ranks. Why would they treat women outside their ranks any differently?

The notion that she encountered a few poorly behaved men is not acceptable as a frame. For three hours, this woman detailed a network of men and their relationships, and how they always seemed to advance, get credit for work they did not do, and be protected from activity that was clearly illegal. A male network was in play, and the words "white male hierarchy," in that they protect and advance their own, was among the internal investigation evidence she shared with me.

The FBI conducting its own harassment complaints conveys an attitude that nobody is higher than them, and nobody will correct them. How, then, could they do any wrong? The other interviews revealed when an HR department tells a male that a complaint has been filed against him, he retaliates in harsh ways to make life unbearable for the woman. One participant mentioned that a former coworker miscarried her child due to the stress a man caused her when she filed a harassment complaint.

We can look further into the processes the FBI uses. You are put on leave without pay and have to request to get a job while you are not being paid. The process takes about a year. The woman was blackballed out of her industry, so she could not get work for which she was qualified. Instead she was reduced to selling her plasma for money and losing her house. Blackballing is another silent means of punishing those who dare defy a powerful man. I have been subjected to it. It sets you back years and gives the appearance that you just cannot get yourself together. It creates the impression of being damaged goods. And again, it sets your career back years. Labels are powerful. Silence is powerful.

This brings us to the final goals of the work.

Critical Consciousness Raising

Sexism is a structural problem that manifests in all places in society. Because that is true, the converse is true as well. At every step where sexism exists, intervention can occur. Women and men can practice their individual agency and create new images and narratives, thereby contributing to society and culture in a different way. A useful place to start is with yourself. Society does not change. People change, and then change society. Systems influence us, but systems are not self-aware. They exist because of how and what we exchange with each other.

1. **Create visibility:** Open and articulate the world of oppression, in which women are "other."

   We read firsthand accounts of executive women to understand how they experience sexism. We learned what they go through with men, and what types of situations repeat themselves across countries and languages. They guided us through their thoughts and feelings, as well as how their thinking progressed and evolved over years. By detailing the conversations and small exchanges and seemingly insignificant everyday interactions, we witnessed the way sexism creeps into all aspects of our lives as women. They told us about how they regard other women, how their perceptions shift, and what their hopes are for women moving forward. Finally, we saw the internal struggles women endure when trying to reconcile their reality with the image projected onto them when men act through a sexist lens.

2. **Compare similarities in experience:** Expose the myths that women have been socialized to accept.

   In this work we uncovered the gender-prescribed labels that have neither truth nor evidence to support them. Men make unsubstantiated claims about their knowledge and expertise on a regular basis. They assume expert status that they do not have, and continue acting as if they are indeed experts when they are not, without the slightest hint of questioning themselves. When women assume they lack confidence in themselves, it is actually because women are undermined at what seems like every possible turn.

   Women act against their own self-interest to avoid being stereotyped. Women are challenged about their position, their knowledge, and their abilities by men; whereas men do not challenge each other on these things. Women are regarded as interchangeable. Men commodify women, and communicate with other men about their status relative to one another, through the accumulation of women's bodies. All of these factors seep into the corporate work environment. The line between personal and professional becomes inextricably blurred. Anything men do socially is an attitude they bring into the executive environment.

   When women are criticized for their communication technique, it is because they will never get it right. It is impossible for women to strike the right balance, *because women and men both demonstrate bias against women.* Leadership positions require women to be both authoritative and nice, a balance that is mentally draining and impossible to achieve. For women who have made their way to executive positions, the stereotyping and inherent communication bias are particularly costly.

3. **Create new pathways to success:** Replace old scripts and ideas with new scripts and ideas.

   As individuals, we have power to mold our reality. The people, thoughts, media, discussion, activities, images, groups, purposes, professions to which and whom we direct our energy are entirely up to us. When any of these items cause you to lose yourself or doubt your abilities, redirect your energy. If you are stuck in an employment situation, take what you can from it. Get all the training, connections, resources, vacation, and health care available to you. Live a good life. Work is not your life. Give the employer your labor but keep your soul. Keep your identity. When you feel the pressure to alter your being, now you have a name for what that is. You know where that pressure originates and what it means to do to you.

Who you are is up to you.

The remainder of this page is yours. Create your new script.

References

American Psychological Association, Task Force on the Sexualization of Girls. (2007). *Report of the APA Task Force on the Sexualization of Girls*. Retrieved from http://www.apa.org/pi/women/programs/girls/report-full.pdf.

Babbie, E. (1998). *The Practice of Social Research*. Stanford, CA: Wadsworth Publishing Company.

Barak, G. (2003). *Violence and Nonviolence: Pathways to Understanding*. Thousand Oaks, CA: Sage Publications.

Bem, S. L. (1993). *The Lenses of Gender: Transforming the Debate on Sexual Inequality*. New Haven, CT: Yale University Press.

Bolton, R. (1979). *People Skills: How to Assert Yourself, Listen to Others, and Resolve Conflicts*. Englewood Cliffs, NJ: Prentice-Hall.

Burgoon, J. K., Buller, D. B., and Woodall, W. G. (1989). *Nonverbal Communication: The Unspoken Word*. New York: Harper & Row.

Caputi, J. (1989). "The Sexual Politics of Murder." *Gender and Society, 3*, 437–456.

Cope, J. (2005). "Researching Entrepreneurship through Phenomenographical Inquiry: Philosophical and Methodological Issues." *International Small Business Review Journal, 23*(2), 163–189.

De Beauvoir, S. (1952/1989). *The Second Sex*. New York: Vintage Books.

DeMaria, A. L., Sundstrom, B., Grzejdziak, M., Booth, K., Adams, H., Gabel, C., and Cabot, J. (2018). "It's Not My Place: Formative Evaluation Research to Design a Bystander Intervention Campaign." *Journal of Interpersonal Violence, 33*(3), 468–490.

Dines, G. (2010). *Pornland: How Porn Has Hijacked Our Sexuality*. Boston: Beacon Press.

Dortins, E. (2002). "Reflections on Phenomenographical Process: Interview, Transcript, and Analysis," in *Quality Conversations*, Proceedings of the 25th HERSDA Annual Conference, Perth, Western Australia, July 7–10, 207–213.

Durkheim, E. (1893/1964). *The Division of Labor in Society*. New York: Free Press.

Durkheim, E. (1895/1982). *The Rules of Sociological Method*. New York: Free Press.

Eckes, T. (2002). "Paternalistic and Envious Gender Stereotypes: Testing Predictions from the Stereotype Content Model." *Sex Roles, 47*(3–4), 99–114.

Faludi, S. (1991). *Backlash: The Undeclared War against Women.* New York: Crown.

Feldman, R. S. (1992). *Applications of Nonverbal Behavioral Theories and Research.* Hillsdale, NJ: Lawrence Erlbaum Associates.

Foubert, J. D., and Bridges, A. J. (2017). "Predicting Bystander Efficacy and Willingness to Intervene in College Men and Women: The Role of Exposure to Varying Levels of Violence in Pornography." *Violence against Women, 23*(6), 692–706.

Foubert, J. D., Brosi, M. W., and Bannon, S. (2011). "Pornography Viewing among Fraternity Men: Effects on Bystander Intervention, Rape Myth Acceptance and Behavioral Intent to Commit Sexual Assault." *Sexual Addiction & Compulsivity: The Journal of Treatment and Prevention, 18*(4), 212–231.

Freire, P. (1970). *Pedagogy of the Oppressed.* New York: Continuum.

French, M. (1992). *The War against Women.* New York: Ballantine Publishing Group.

Goffman, E. (1974). *Frame Analysis: An Essay on the Organization of Experience.* New York: Harper Colophon.

Gray, D. E. (2004). *Doing Research in the Real World.* Thousand Oaks, CA: Sage.

Griffin, P. (1997). "Introductory Module for the Single Issue Courses." In M. Adams, L. A. Bell, and P. Griffin (eds.), *Teaching for Diversity and Social Justice: A Sourcebook* (pp. 61–81). New York: Routledge.

Grinnell, R. (2016). Fundamental Attribution Error. *Psych Central.* Retrieved on November 25, 2018, from https://psychcentral.com/encyclopedia /fundamental-attribution-error.

Hardiman, R., and Jackson, B. (1997). "Conceptual Foundations for Social Justice Courses." In M. Adams, L. A. Bell, and P. Griffin (eds.), *Teaching for Diversity and Social Justice: A Sourcebook* (pp. 16–29). New York, NY: Routledge.

Huntington, S. P. (1971). "The Change to Change: Modernization, Development, and Politics." *Comparative Politics, 3*(3), 283–322.

Jones, T. S., and Brinkert, R. (2008). *Conflict Coaching: Conflict Management Strategies and Skills for the Individual.* Thousand Oaks, CA: Sage Publications.

Joosa, E., and Berthelson, D. (2006). "Parenting a Child with Down Syndrome: A Phenomenographical Study." *Journal of Developmental Disabilities, 12*(1), 1–14.

Kumashiro, K. (2000). "Toward a Theory of Anti-Oppressive Education." *Review of Educational Research, 70,* 25–53

Kumashiro, K. (2002). *Troubling Education: Queer Activism and Anti-Oppressive Pedagogy.* New York: Routledge Falmer.

Lakoff, R. (1990). *Talking Power: The Politics of Language in Our Lives.* New York: Basic.

Larsson, J., and Holmstrom, I. (2007). "Phenomenographical or Phenomenological Analysis: Does It Matter? Examples from a Study on Anesthesiologists'

Work." *International Journal on Qualitative Studies on Health and Well-Being*, 2, 55–64.

Leathers, D. G. (1979). "The Impact of Multichannel Message Inconsistency on Verbal and Nonverbal Decoding Behaviors." *Communication Monographs*, 46, 88–100.

Lipsky, S. (1987). *Internalized Racism*. Seattle: Rational Island Publishers.

Mac, R. (2015, July 14). "Tech's Hottest Lunch Spot? A Strip Club." Retrieved from https://www.forbes.com/sites/ryanmac/2015/07/14/gold-club-tech-lunch -spot-strip-club-yelp-san-francicso/#1e939fb7314c

MacKinnon, C. (1979). *Sexual Harassment of Working Women*. New Haven, CT: Yale University Press.

Manis, J., and Meltzer, B. (Eds). (1978). *Symbolic Interaction: A Reader in Social Psychology, 3rd ed*. Boston: Allyn and Bacon.

Marton, F. (1981). "Phenomenography: Describing Conceptions of the World around Us." *Instructional Science*, 10, 177–200.

Marton, F. (1994). "Phenomenography." In T. Husen and T. N. Postlewaite (eds.), *The International Encyclopedia of Education* (pp. 4424–4429). Oxford: Peamon Press.

Marx, K. (1867/1967). *Capital: A Critique of Political Economy, Vol. 1*. New York: International Publishers.

McCosker, H., Barnard, A., and Gerber, R. (2003). "Phenomenographical Study of Women's Experience with Domestic Violence during Childbearing Years." *Online Journal of Issues in Nursing*, 9(1),12.

McLaren, P. (1998). *Life in Schools, 3rd ed*. New York: Longman.

Merriam-Webster. (2018, October 18). Definition of Sexism. Retrieved from https://www.merriam-webster.com/dictionary/sexism

Ornek, F. (2008). "An Overview of a Theoretical Framework of Phenomenography in Qualitative Education Research: An Example from Physics Education Research." *Asia-Pacific Forum on Science Learning and Teaching*, 9(2), 1.

Parsons, T., and Platt, G. (1973). *The American University*. Cambridge, MS: Harvard University Press.

Parsons, T., and Shils, E. A. (eds.). (1951). *Toward a General Theory of Action*. Cambridge MS: Harvard University Press.

Pheterson, G. (1990). Alliances between Women: Overcoming Internalized Oppression and Internalized Domination. In L. Albrecht and R. Brewer (eds.), *Bridges of Power: Women's Multi-Cultural Alliances* (pp. 34–48). Philadelphia: New Society Publishers.

Pornhub.com (2018, Jan. 9). Pornhub.com/2017 Year in Review. Retrieved from https://www.pornhub.com/insights/2017-year-in-review.

Pratto, F., Stallworth, L. M., Sidanius, J., and Siers, B. (1997). "The Gender Gap in Occupational Role Attainment: A Socially Dominant Approach." *Journal of Personality and Social Psychology*, 72, 37–53.

Pruitt, D. G., and Kim, S. H. (2004). *Social Conflict: Escalation, Stalemate, and Settlement, 3rd ed*. New York: McGraw Hill Higher Education.

Rich, A. (1976). *Of Woman Born: Motherhood as Experience and Institution*. New York: Bantam.

Rich, A. (1980). "Compulsory Heterosexual and Lesbian Experiences." In C. R. Stimson and E. S. Person (eds.), *Women, Sex, and Sexuality*. Chicago: University of Chicago Press.

Ridgeway, C. L., and Erikson, K. G. (2000). "Creating and Spreading Status Beliefs." *American Journal of Sociology*, 106, 579–615.

Riger, S., and Krieglstein, M. (2000). "The Impact of Welfare Reform on Men's Violence against Women." *American Journal of Community Psychology*, 28, 631–647.

Ritzer, G., and Goodman, D. J. (2004). *Sociological Theory, 6th ed.* New York: McGraw Hill.

Rogoff, B. (1995). "Observing Sociocultural Activity on Three Planes: Participatory Appropriation, Guided Participation, and Apprenticeship." In J. Wertsh, P. Del Rio, and A. Alvarez (eds.), *Sociocultural Studies of Mind* (pp. 139–164). New York: Cambridge University Press.

Roth, L. M. (1999). "The Right to Privacy Is Political: Power, the Boundary between Public and Private, and Sexual Harassment." *Law & Social Inquiry*, 24(1), 45–71.

Rudman, L. A., and Glick, P. (2001). "Prescriptive Gender Stereotypes and Backlash toward Agentic Women." *Journal of Social Issues*, 57(4), 743–762.

Sidanius, J., and Pratto, F. (1999). *Social Dominance: An Intergroup Theory of Hierarchy and Oppression*. Cambridge, UK: Cambridge University Press.

Simmel, G. (1907/1978). *The Philosophy of Money*. Tom Bottomore and David Frisby (eds. and trans.). London: Routledge and Kegan Paul.

Silver, C. (2018, January). "Pornhub 2017 Year In Review Insights Report Reveals Statistical Proof We Love Porn." Retrieved from https://www.forbes.com /sites/curtissilver/2018/01/09/pornhub-2017-year-in-review-insights -report-reveals-statistical-proof-we-love-porn/#69a0049e24f5

Soon, C. W., and Barnard, A. (2001). "A Phenomenographic Approach to Examine the Different Ways HIV Patients Understand the Experience of Counseling." *The Internet Journal of Mental Health*, 1(2).

Tannen, D. (1990). *You Just Don't Understand: Women and Men in Conversation*. New York: Quill.

Tappan, M. B. (2006). "Reframing Internalized Oppression and Internalized Domination: From the Psychological to the Sociocultural." *Teachers College Record*, 108(10), 2115–2144.

Tatum, B. (1997). *Why Are All the Black Kids Sitting Together in the Cafeteria?* New York: Basic Books.

TED Talks. (2015, April 28). *Growing Up in a Pornified Culture, Gail Dines*. Retrieved from https://www.youtube.com/watch?v=_YpHNImNsx8

Thompson, B. W. (1994). *A Hunger So Wide and So Deep: American Women Speak Out on Eating Problems*. Minneapolis: University of Minnesota Press.

Veblen, T. (1899/1994). *The Theory of the Leisure Class*. New York: Penguin Books.

Vygotsky, L. (1978). *Mind in Society: The Development of Higher Psychological Processes* (Cole, M., V. John-Steiner, S. Scribner, and E. Souberman, eds.). Cambridge, MA: Harvard University Press.

Vygotsky, L. (1987). *The Collective Works of L. S. Vygotsky, Vol. 1: Problems of General Psychology* (R. Rieber, ed.; R. van der Veer, trans.). New York: Plenum Press.

Vygotsky, L. (1997). *The Collective Works of L. S. Vygotsky, Vol. 4: Problems in the Theory and History of Psychology* (R. Rieber and A. Carton, eds.; N. Minick, trans.). New York: Plenum Press.

Walkerdine, V. (1990). *Schoolgirl Fictions*. London: Verso.

Waller, J. (2002). *Becoming Evil: How Ordinary People Commit Genocide and Mass Killing*. New York: Oxford University Press.

Welch, C., Marschan-Piekkari, R., Penttinen, H., and Tahvanainen, M. (2002). "Corporate Elites as Informants in Qualitative International Business Research." *International Business Review, 11*(5), 611–628.

Wilmot, W. W., and Hocker, J. L. (2001). *Interpersonal Conflict, 6th ed.* New York: McGraw Hill Higher Education.

Wolf, N. (1991). *The Beauty Myth: How Images Are Used against Women*. New York: William Morrow.

Yates, C., Partridge, H., and Bruce, C. S. (2012). "Exploring Information Experiences through Phenomenography." *Library and Information Research, 36*(112), 96–119.

Young, I. M. (1990). *Justice and the Politics of Difference*. Princeton, NJ: Princeton University Press.

Index

1st Special Forces Operational Detachment-Delta (1st SFOD-D), Delta Force, 257

Accessories, communicating through, 149–150; handbags to convey wealth and power, 149; suits to convey power, 150; works for men, but not for women, 150

Addressing sexist structures but not sexist people, 80–83, 185, 191–195, 221; "as long as they aren't talking about me," 221; core values but not executive team, 80–83; fight for other women but not yourself, 185; policies but not his behavior, 221; sexism as political abstract but not your boss, 191–195

Adultery, 99, 100, 160, 265; as a norm among married executives, 160; of male bosses/colleagues, 99, 100, 265; of male clients, 99; not wanting to be associated with, 160; not wanting to do business with, 100

Advancement, men over women, 129–133; average men advance over better women, 129–130; capable woman seen as a crisis to handle, 133; men advance other men, 129; men can go to a strip club together, 130; time will solve it, 132; women must be 1,000 times better, 131; women's expertise disregarded, 132–133

Advancement, sexism and, 196–201; ambiguous/unclear process for, 196, 199–200; autonomy vs. communal traits, 197; being sexualized in interview, 198; bias against agentic women, 197; contradictory qualifications, 197; different questions, 197; different rules, 200; disparate treatment, 201; fear of asking about, 196; fear of seeming too ambitious, 196; hiring decisions, 199; interview process bias, 197; negotiation, 196, 199

Advances, unwanted, 68, 86–87, 120–121; escaping from, 68, 121; physical, 68; sexual, 120–121; sexual invitations, 86–87; social invitations, 68

Afghanistan, 265–266

Agency, individual choice, 12, 155, 217, 271

Agentic women, 197, 212, 224, 250; ambition, stereotypes about, 197; confound some people, 212; identity

Agentic women (*cont.*)
  used against them, 224; not victims,
  224, 250; stereotypes against, 197;
  strength exploited, 224; strive to
  progress, 224; take control of their
  lives, 224. *See also* Ambition
Agreeing to sexism, mediated
  action, 245; disregard evidence
  of bias, 245; exclusion, 245;
  exploitation, 245; laugh, 245; let
  people stand alone, 245; policies,
  245; procedures, 245; remain
  silent, 245
Ambitious women, bias toward, 197;
  cold, 197; held by men and women,
  197; lacking in communal skills,
  197; socially deficient, 197; unfit
  to lead others, 197. *See also*
  Stereotypes
Androcentrism, 223
Appearance, sexualizing female, 3, 7,
  24–26, 32, 44–45, 56–57, 63, 71,
  82, 98–101, 112, 144–147, 153,
  157, 221; accessories, 3, 147, 155;
  age, 82, 221; beauty, 7; blonde, 32,
  171; body, 45; clothes, 3, 57, 112,
  144, 145, 147; cute, 154; easy
  on the eyes, 153; escort, 171;
  gorgeous blonde, 157; hair, 44,
  112, 147, 155; makeup, 3, 146,
  153; pretty, 71, 153; sexiness as
  primary worth, 56; sexual
  harassment suit waiting to
  happen, 157; sexy, 153; tall, 32;
  young, 26, 82; weight, 221
Appearance, women's intentional
  manipulation of their, 143–152;
  avoid striking appearance, 146; be
  invisible, 146; cover entire body at
  all times, 144; dark clothes, 144;
  defeminize yourself, 147–148,
  152; dress better than male
  counterparts, 145; fake religion,
  146; feign marriage, 146; less

feminine, 142; no makeup, 146,
  155
Armor, survival strategy, 80, 147
Assimilation, 107–108, 142; false
  pretense of, 107, 142; guise of,
  108 (by abandoning defining
  characteristics, 107; by
  exemplifying a few successful
  cases, 107); and social dominance
  orientation, 107
Assumptions, 111–113, 115–116,
  197. *See also* Double standards
Assumptions about men, 111–113,
  115–116; accepted at his word,
  115; always go first, 112; can be
  average, 111; competent, 112;
  deferred to as experts, 112;
  deserving of respect because
  they are a man, 112, 113; give
  validation to women, 116;
  has right to be there, 112–115;
  higher status, 197; knowledgeable,
  113
Assumptions for women, 111–113,
  115–116; credentials should be
  questioned/challenged, 115, 116;
  get compliments, not respect, 112,
  113; lower status, 197; must always
  be on point, 111; must be 1,000%
  better, 111; must be validated by a
  man, 116; must perform to the
  letter, 112; presence is because of
  race/gender, 115; right to be there
  should be challenged, 115–116;
  unimportant, 113;
  unknowledgeable, 113
ATF (Bureau of Alcohol, Tobacco,
  Firearms and Explosives), 260
Avoiding the male gaze, 147–148,
  152, 155; armor, 147; defeminize
  yourself, 147–148, 152; dress,
  147; glasses, 147, 148, 155;
  hair back, 147, 155; not really a
  girl, 152

Avoiding stereotypes, stereotype avoidance, 73–75, 96, 99, 197, 258–259; angry bitch, 96; angry black female, 74; bitch, 75; cold, 197; defensive, 99; frigid bitch, 99; hostile, 75; making a fuss, 74–75; man-hating, 75; "one of those women," 73–74; overreacting, 74; socially deficient, 197; unfit to lead, 197, 258–259

Bank of America, 268
Behavior of women described by men, 3, 48, 56, 73–75, 96, 99; aggressive, 48; angry bitch, 96; angry black female, 74; bitch, 75; defensive, 99; difficult, 48; frigid bitch, 99; hostile, 75; making a fuss, 74–75; man-hating, 75; "one of those women," 73–74; overeating, 56, 74; no sense of humor, 3; too sensitive, 3
Behavior, sexist, 7, 48, 63, 98–102; assumption that female is in support role, 98; behaving with female colleague as if you are a couple, 99, 100; degrading to women, 64, 96; invitations, inappropriate/personal, 60, 86; regulating femininity, 48; sexualizing employees, 91; suggested sexual involvement with female colleagues, 63, 98–102; suggestion that female is in support role, 98
Benghazi, Libya, 258–259
Blackballing, 12, 64, 255, 267, 269; label from, 269; national defense, 255, 267; philanthropy, 64; politics, 12; stigma attached, 269
Blame, women experiencing, 12–13, 76–77, 87; for sexualizing professional conversations, 12–13, 87; from others, 12–13; self-blame, 76, 77

Boundaries, 27, 76–77, 86–87, 98–99, 100, 159–161, 171; ambiguous social, 76–77, 100; attitudes of female commodity carried into work, 160–161; men disregarding, 27, 86–87, 98–99; women feel responsible for, 76; women hurt by, 27; work and personal life, 159, 171; touching, 99
Bureau of Alcohol, Tobacco, Firearms and Explosives (ATF), 260
Burke, Tarana, 243
Bystanders, individual choice, 10–11, 83; communicating values, 83

Calculating, 66, 76, 82
Calculating character, 158–159; all things can be purchased, 159; all things have a price, 159; Simmel, George, 159; and social media, 159; social value of qualitative accumulation, 159; women as status symbols, 159; women's value is buyable/quantifiable, 159; women's value is expendable, 159
Central Intelligence Agency (CIA), 255–256, 261–262, 266
Challenging sexism, speaking up, 75, 136, 218, 220, 223–225, 244; courage of, 218; deviating from the norm, 218; lift the veil of sexism, 223; men do not speak up in this study, 136; perpetrator has done it repeatedly, 75; preparation and practice, 218 (anticipate shock/being taken by surprise, 218; embarrassment as a silencer, 218, 220; not knowing what to say, 218; shame as a silencer, 224–225, 250); say it publicly, 223; speak openly, 223, 244; stop it happening to others, 75; support to other women, 244

Characterizations of women made by men, 4, 14, 56, 130, 132, 157, 219, 224, 232, 250, 263–265; annoying, 157; antagonistic, 157; bitch, 4, 224; condescending, 157; crazy, 263; destructive, 265; dramatic, 219; drunk, 263; emotional, 219; failure, 14; godless, 157; hates men, 224; humorless, 157; hysterical, 4; lesbian, 224; meek, 130; mental health issues, 263; mistaken, 56; not ready, 130; on period, 219; overreacting, 132; prototypical left-wing bitch, 157; sexless, 157; slut, 265; smug, 157; too sensitive, 132; ugly, 224; unable to comprehend, 219; unreasonable, 219; victim, 224, 250; wrong, 56. *See also* Stereotypes

Chicago, 268

Child care, parenting, 32, 205–206, 222–223; inhibits ability to advance, 205–206, 222–223; maternity leave, 32; relegates women to certain work, 222–223; working mother stigma, 222–223

Citations, formative experiences of women, 8–9, 12–13, 207–208, 210; context, 9; feelings, 8, 13; internalized reactions, 13, 207–208, 210 (emotionally low, 207; disengaged, 208; questioning self, 208; unwanted, 208); reactions from others, 12–13; triggers, 8, 13

Cognitive dissonance, psychological discomfort, 248–249; avoidance of, 248; holding two contradictory beliefs, 248; psychological discomfort of, 248–249; resistance to integrate new knowledge, 248

Commodification of women by male colleagues, 88, 90–91, 101, 159, 160–161, 172; accumulation of sexual female images, 160; attitudes bleed into work life, 160–161; as communication of status among men, 158–159, 171–172; disrespect female partners (wives), 161; giving impression of having sex with female colleagues, 159, 172; hiring female employees to have sex with/sexualize them, 90–91, 159, 172; mentality, 160–161; "numbers game" among men, 159; organizational culture, 160–161; sex with female employees, 159, 172; sexual images of women, 160; social media, 160; women as entertainment, 88, 90, 101; women to "change the dynamics," 90; women's company a service for men to enjoy, 89, 90, 161

Compensation. *See* Payment

Compliance of women as they perceive it, 61, 62

Compliments, physical, 27, 44, 56, 198; judgements, as, 44; sexualizing, 56, 198; women should be grateful for male attention, 27

Conflict, constructive and destructive, 235–236

Conflict, material vs. symbolic, 246

Conflict context; detail vs. meaning; contextual meaning, 245; ability to dehumanize subgroup, 245; commodify subgroup, 245; degrade subgroup, 245; purchase subgroup, 245; strip/redefine subgroup identity, 163, 168, 169, 245

Conflict goals, 225–232; application of, 232–233; content, 219–220, 226–228; identity, 231–232; process, 219, 228–229; relational, 229–231

Conflict resolution styles, 236–242; avoiding, 241; collaborating, 242; compromising, 240; directing, 239; harmonizing, 237

Consensual disagreement, 38
Consensual ideology, 37
Conspicuous consumption, 158;
  beautiful women as a brand, 158;
  as personal branding, 158; Veblen,
  Thorstein, 158
Contextual meaning; detail vs.
  meaning; conflict context, 245;
  commodify subgroup, 245; define
  identity of subgroup, 163, 168,
  169, 245; degrade subgroup, 245;
  dehumanize subgroup, 245;
  purchase subgroup, 245
Control over sexism (as perceived by
  women), 78, 83, 98–99, 183–185;
  by avoiding the issue, 83; "choose"
  vs. "accept" sexism, 78; delusion of,
  78, 183–184 (not being ignored,
  183; not happening to me, 183;
  other women experience this,
  183–184); fight for other women
  but not yourself, 185; overlooking/
  ignoring sexism, 98–99; sense of, 78
Costs of sexism to women, 7, 13, 17,
  28, 95, 102, 153, 199, 202, 205,
  209, 244; anxiety, 7; depression, 7;
  expend more resources, 28;
  financial, 13, 202, 205; health, 7;
  inability to advance as quickly, 28;
  material, 244; mental, 244;
  opportunities missed, 153; stress,
  7; time lost, 28, 102, 153, 199, 209;
  work twice as hard, 95
Cost to women for confronting sexism
  or rejecting advances, 63, 66–68,
  70, 72, 94–96, 202–205, 210,
  254–255; damage to career, 66;
  demotion, 68; lose business, 72, 95,
  202, 205; lose job, 63, 95–96,
  203–205; miscarriage, 68; pay cut,
  68, 210; personal life, effect on, 70,
  254–255; professional reputation,
  94–95, 204; ruins business
  relationship, 66; stress, 68

Counterterrorism, 258–259;
  Counterterrorism squad, 258;
  undermining woman's work in, 259
Covering up sexism, hiding sexism,
  26, 63–64; culture, woman will not
  fit with, 26; legal opinion, 63–64;
  philanthropy, 63–64
Critical consciousness raising, 13–14,
  269–271; create visibility, 13, 270;
  myths, 14; new pathways, 270–271;
  scripts, 14, 270–271; similarities in
  experience, 14, 270
Cultural scripts, 5, 14, 36, 86–87;
  definition, 14; familiarity with, 5;
  used to sexualize work relationship,
  86–87
Cultural tools, 11–12, 14, 160, 245; to
  communicate social dominance,
  245; images, 12, 160; jokes, 12;
  movies, 12; phrases, 12; myths, 14;
  words, 12
Culture, male-dominated, 22, 25–27,
  32, 34–35; child care, 32;
  Christian, 26–27; construction of,
  22, 34, 35; invisible, 27; maternity
  leave, 32; normal (perceived as), 27;
  sexist, 27; systematizing, 22, 34;
  women do not "fit in," 25, 26
Culture, organizational, 73, 91–92,
  94, 96, 159–161, 172, 218–219,
  221, 244; courage, 218–219, 244;
  role in women reporting sexism,
  73; permissiveness in sexualizing
  women, 91, 92, 94, 96, 160; sex
  with employees, 159, 161, 172, 221;
  sexist mentality, 221; touching
  female employees, 221

DEA (United States Drug Enforcement
  Administration), 260
Defensive strategies; protective
  strategies; survival, 80–81; armor,
  80; ignoring, 81; package it, 81; put
  it away, 81

Delta Force; 1st Special Forces
  Operational Detachment-
  Delta (1st SFOD-D), 257
Department of Defense (United States
  Department of Defense), 258–259
Descriptions of women by men,
  26–27, 57, 60, 164; cheap, 57; fair
  game, 60, 164; girl, a, 27; play toy,
  102; should be grateful for male
  attention, 27; will not fit in, 26;
  young, 57. *See also* Sexualization
Detail vs. meaning; contextual
  meaning; conflict context,
  163, 168, 169, 245; ability to
  dehumanize subgroup, 245;
  commodify subgroup, 245; degrade
  subgroup, 245; purchase subgroup,
  245; redefine subgroup identity,
  163, 168, 169, 245
Different rules for men and women,
  108–111; assertion, 108, 109;
  drinking, 109. 110; reputation, 108,
  109, 110; work performance, 108,
  109, 111
Diffusion of responsibility, 249;
  definition of, 249; Kitty Genovese
  murder, 249
Dissensual ideology, 38
District attorney. *See* Justice system
Diversification initiatives, 34,
  251–252; are forced to hire women,
  34; do not want to hire women, 34,
  251–252; legally obligate to hire
  women, 34; looks good to hire
  women, 34. *See also* Initiatives to
  hire and retain women
Domestic abuse, 174
Domination. *See* Male domination
Double standards, men vs. women,
  108–112, 116–118, 130, 149;
  accepted vs. challenged, 109;
  ambitious vs. aggressive, 116, 149;
  average vs. perfect, 130; bravado vs.

quality, 108; challenging vs.
  difficult, 116–118; crap vs. on point,
  111; fun vs. whore, 110; loud vs.
  good, 109; mediocrity vs.
  perfection, 110; potential to advance
  vs. not quite ready, 112; respected
  vs. must prove yourself, 112
Durkheim, Emile, and dynamic
  density, 131
Dynamic density, 131

Escaping from physical situations, 68,
  78; kissing, 68; playing dumb, 78
Exclusion, forms of, 28–30, 34, 38,
  61, 80–81, 85, 102, 134; activities,
  80; assignments/projects, 102;
  closed meetings, 61, 81; circumvent
  women in decision making, 30;
  male networks, 34; male-only
  invitations, carried over from work
  settings, 85; nudity, 80; sauna, 80;
  silence, 28–29; strip bars, 38, 85;
  women not confronting, 83; work
  conversation, 134
Expertise, women's, 132–133;
  capable woman seen as a crisis
  to handle, 133; women's expertise
  disregarded, 132–133
Experts, 243–244; absent from many
  panel discussions, 243–244; not
  always present in sexism discourse,
  243–244; on inequality needed,
  243–244
Exploiting inexperience/youth for
  sexual gain, 60

Federal Bureau of Investigation (FBI),
  255–269
Federal Bureau of Investigation,
  sexism in, 255–269; accusations,
  false, 255, 263–266 (characterized
  as "crazy drunk slut," 263–265;
  destructive behavior, 255–266;

disregard woman's evidence, 255, 264–266; having sexual relationships with male colleagues, 260, 264; mental health issues, 263–264); blackball, 255, 267, 269; bullying, 261–262; characterized as a "bitch" without the right experience, 258; counterterrorism, 258–259, 258; discrimination, 260; dismissed knowledge and expertise, 258; double standards of same personality trait, 256; ego, male, 260; financial depletion from, 262–263 (lost health care, 263; sold clothes, 262; sold furniture, 262; sold home at loss, 263; sold jewelry, 262; sold plasma, 262); give man credit for woman's work, 257 (pay man bonus for work woman did, 257; promote man for work woman did, 257); harassment, 260; immobilized woman's career through task assignment, 267; invent case to fire woman, 255; male networks and, 255–258 (friends from law school, 258; getting credit for women's work, 257; getting paid and promoted for women's work, 257; protecting other men from consequence, 255; "the club," 257); male superior tries to become a couple on her first day, 255; physical intimidation, 260–261; stalking, 262; suppressing female contribution, 259, 267; undermined woman's work, 256, 258

FBI Equal Employment Opportunity (EEO), 261–262

FBI Office of Professional Responsibility (OPR), 262–267

Federal Elections Commissioner, 58

Feelings of women, internalized oppression, 13, 26, 31–32, 70, 76, 78, 80–83, 98–102, 127, 129, 139, 151–152, 138–139, 207–208, 210–211, 218, 244; ashamed, 76, 139; black sheep, 26; closed off, 151; complicit, 78, 139; concerned for others' feelings, 69–70, 80–83, 218, 244 (clients, 70; colleagues, 69, 70, 80, 82, 218, 244; male offender, 69, 70, 80–83); defensive, 151; disengaged, 208; disrespected, 82–83, 152; emotionally low, 207; erosion of self-esteem, 211; explain life choices, 31–32, 127 (no children, 31–32, 129; unmarried, 31–32, 129); failure, 13; humiliation, 98–102; justify your time, 31–32; odd one out, 26; prove your right to be there, 207–208; questioning yourself, 102, 210; rejection, 82–83; self-blame, 211; self-doubt, 139; there to look pretty, 26, 98, 101–102; unwanted, 208; wrongdoing on your part, 13

Femininity as a liability, 152

Fetishism of commodity, 158–159, 171–172; communicating status through objects, 158; communicating status through women, 158–159, 171–172; Marx, Karl, 158

Fundamental attribution error, 247–248; blaming individual factors (personal characteristics), 248; disregarding context, 248

Gaslighting, 81, 87, 108, 120–122; denying a woman's reality, 108, 120–121, 122; woman turned a professional conversation sexual, 87

Gender expectations of women, 60, 123–129, 132–133, 140, 164–166, 168, 171–172, 198, 219; accept sexism as normal, 165; being "fair game" to male advances regardless of setting, 60, 164; and benevolent sexism, 123; children, 129; compliance in sexism, 164–165; create a "warm climate" at work, 132; family roles, 123; fathers and daughters, 123, 127; home appearance, 127; identity of women at odds with, 140, 166; make others comfortable, 198, 219; marriage, 129; mixed messages about equality, 123; needy women not a threat to men, 140; socialization of, 123; time management, 123; women not supposed to be better at work than men, 133, 171; women's feelings are less important, 219

Gender expectations violation of, 126, 128, 198, 162, 212; challenging sexist people or systems, 212; confounding to some, 212; "male" traits, 126, 128, 212; making others uncomfortable (here, when they are sexist), 198; unladylike profession, 162, 212

Gender roles, creation of, 23–25, 44; balanced, 23; childbearing and, 24–25; codification of, 24, 25; creation of, 23–24; division of labor, 23, 25; early society, 23; egalitarian, 23; marketplace value, 23; mass production and, 24; physical attributes and, 24–25; regulating femininity, 44; religion and, 24–25

Genovese, Kitty, 249; lack of bystander intervention, 249; rape and murder of, 249; thought that somebody else would act, 249

Harvard University, 159
Health, CEO responsible for employees, 63
Health consequences, 7
Hooters Restaurant, 168
Horizontal violence, 173–174; replicating domination patterns, 173–174
Human trafficking, 57, 257
Hypermasculinity, 225; monitoring, 225; policing, 225; reinforcing, 225; teaching, 225

Identity, feelings of women, 161–163, 166–168; how agentic women see themselves, 161–163, 168 (accomplished, 161; claw and fight, 162; daughter of immigrants, 163; giggly, 163; nurturing, 162; rapier-like, 162; self-made, 166–168); how women made to feel by sexist men, 166–168 (accomplishments are invisible, 168; cannot reconcile with gender expectations, 166; dehumanized, 168; humiliated, 168; inconsequential, 168; intimidating or pushover, 167; invisible, 168; like you do not own your identity, 166; men always trying to put you into a cage, 166; no middle ground, 167; not respected, 168; nothing more than your gender, 168–169; questioning yourself because of men's behavior, 167; taken down a peg, 167; worthless, 168; your voice doesn't matter, 251)

Immersed in sexism, 184; cannot see it while, 184; trying to survive while, 184

Individual choice; agency; personal agency, 12, 155, 217, 224–225, 244, 246; as a man, 155, 224–225, 244,

246; to behave differently, 12, 155, 224–225, 244, 246; to see sexism as normal, 244, 246

Initiatives to recruit and retain women, 199, 243–244, 251–252; do not address inequality, 243–244; do not focus on men or change, 243–244; for public optics, 243–244; not led by experts, 243–244; superficial, 199, 243–244, 251–252; token, 199. *See also* Diversification

Inspector General; United States Department of Health and Human Services Office of the Inspector General (OIG), 260

Internalization of culture, 173

Internalized domination, 36–37, 108–109; boasting men held in esteem, 108, 109; "brassy, arrogant, mediocre" men promoted above competent women, 109; challenging woman's credibility, but accepting a man's word for it, 109; competent women disregarded, 108, 109; definition, 36–37; explanation, 108

Internalized oppression, 151–153, 155; anticipate being taken advantage of, 152; anticipate disrespect, 152; cannot be feminine and respected, 152; close yourself off, 151; defeminize yourself, 152; defend yourself, 151; feminine characteristics considered a liability, 152; less confident, 155; take up less space, 151; tone down appearance, 151. *See also* Feelings of women

Internalized reactions, 13; compliance, 61; failure, 13; permissive, 61, 62; wrongdoing, 13. *See also* Feelings

Intervention, 88–89, 160, 245, 249–251; in rape/sexual assault, 89 (belief in false reporting, 89; belief

in "rape myths," 89; correlation with pornography consumption, 88–89; Kitty Genovese, 249; lack of, 89, 249; men hesitant to interrupt another man's "good time," 89); opportunities for, 245, 249, 250–251 (choice to act, 250–251; communication patterns, 249; company culture, 249; disregard evidence of bias, 245; exclusion, 245; exploitation, 245; hiring practices, 249; policies, 245, 249; procedures, 245; social media, 160, 249; when others laugh, 245; when people stand alone, 245)

Invitations, inappropriate, 60

Joint Special Operations Command (JSOC), 257

Jokes, 3, 12, 57; cultural tools, 12; no sense of humor, 3; sexual, 57; too sensitive, 3

Judges. *See* Justice system

Just world phenomenon; powerlessness, 249–250; blame victim, 250; definition, 249; feelings of powerlessness, 250; law of attraction misconstrued, 250; people get what they deserve, 250

Justice System, women's experiences with, 251–255; district attorney, 254–255 (accused woman of having relationship with perpetrator, 254–255); judges, 252 (inequitable sentencing for women's clients, 252; lose business due to sexist treatment by, 252; treating women as incompetent before juries, 252); police, 253–254 (accused woman of having relationship with stalker, 253; kind, encouraged woman to file charges, 254); sexualizing women in, 251; women not treated as equals in, 251

Language, sexist, 3, 7, 12, 56, 87–88, 91; jokes, 3, 12; phrases, 12; sexual inferences, 56; sexual references to make a business point, 91; violent language of pornography, 87–88; words, 12

Legal system, 7, 33–34, 57, 134–135; male networks in, 134–135; quid pro quo, 57; sentencing bias, 33–34, 134–135. *See also* Male networks

Libya, Benghazi, 258–259

Macy's, 268; former counterterrorism agent, 268

Male domination, 24–25, 34–35; codification of, 24–25; and labor production, 24; as a norm, 34, 35; origin of, 24; in religion, 24. *See also* Internalized domination

Male networks; networks, male, 30, 33–34, 123, 129, 133–145, 172, 224, 255, 257–258; court sentencing, 33, 134; decision making, 30; exclusion of women, 30; friends from law school, 258; give credit for women's work to a man, 256–257; give woman's financial bonus to a man, 257; give woman's promotion to a man, 257; judicial system, 33–34; law school outlines, 134–135; power of, 224; protect other men, 255; sexist attitudes of major business owners, 172; "the club," 257; white man middle-age club, 129; women go and men remain, 133

Marshals; United States Marshals Service, 260

Marx, Karl, 158

Massachusetts Institute of Technology (MIT), 159

McCabe, Andrew, 268

#MeToo, 243; platform that enabled discourse, 243; Tarana Burke, 243

Mediated Action; personal agency; individual choice, 11–12, 155, 224–225, 243–246; agreeing to sexism, 245; as a man, 155, 224–225, 244, 246 (exclusion, 245; exploitation, 245; disregard evidence of bias, 245; laugh along, 245; let people stand alone, 245; policies, 245; procedures, 245; remain silent, 245); choice to behave differently, 12, 155, 224–225, 244, 246; choice to see sexism as normal, 244, 246; consequences of speaking convey power, 246; impact of combined individual/collective, 11, 243, 245; individual approach, 11; structural perspective, 11

Men pitting women colleagues as entertainment, 179–181; like women "competing" for their attention, 179–181

Menial tasks, 45–46, 217; as status move, 45, 46, 217; coffee, 45, 46; food, 45, 46; scheduling, 46

Methodology, 15–20; data analysis, 16–17 (categories of description, 17; collective meaning, 17); data collection, 16 (semi-structured interviews, 16); participants, 17–20 (ages of, 17; countries of, 17; elite participants, 15–16; professions of, 18–20); phenomenography, 15; research questions, 15; sample, 15 (purposive snowball sample, 15)

Naked; nudity, 80, 85, 93, 201; bonding with female, 201; discussion/thoughts projected onto women colleagues at work, 93; executive committee, 80; sauna, 80

Names men call women colleagues, 46–47, 70, 163–164, 168–169, 205, 256; diminutive, 46, 163–164, 205 (firecracker, 47; good girl, 205; little girl, 46, 102); intimate, 47, 163–164, 205 (baby girl, 70, 205; his girl, 256); overfamiliarity, 164; to communicate status, 163, 205; to reduce identity to gender, 163, 168, 169

National Football League (NFL), 7; quid pro quo request from owner for charitable contribution, 7

National Security Working Group, 264–265

Navy Seals, 260

Networks, male, 30, 33–34, 224; court sentencing, 33; decision making, 30; exclusion of women, 30; judicial system, 33–34; power of, 224

No male equivalent, 123–139, 262; client masturbating, 123; personal safety concerns, 123; sexualizing a business relationship, 138–139; stalking by coworker, 123, 262

Nonverbal communication of men toward women, 29, 30, 32, 34; concentrating (appearing to), 29; confused by what's happening, 30; do not care what you have to say, 34; furrowing brow, 29; squinting, 29; staring back, 29; struggling to understand, 30; woman is (not an equal, 34; not there to participate, 32; not wanted there, 34)

Organizational culture, 73, 91–92, 94, 96, 161, 218–219, 221, 244; courage, 218–219, 244; permissiveness in sexualizing women, 91, 92, 94, 96; role in women reporting sexism, 73; sex with employees, 161, 221; sexist, 221; touching female employees, 221

Parenting; caregiving, 7

Participants, 15–20; ages of, 17; countries of, 17; elite status, 15–16; professions of, 18–20

Payment, women and compensation, 207–209; charge less, 207; concerned for client's ability to afford fee, 208; must "prove" their work before getting compensated, 207; used but not compensated, 207–209

Payment structures, sexist, 62

Permissiveness. *See also* Compliance of women as they perceive it, 61

Personal agency; individual choice; agency, 12, 155, 224–225, 244, 246; to behave differently, 12, 155, 224–225, 244, 246; as a man, 155, 224–225, 244, 246; to see sexism as normal, 244, 246

Personal safety, 123

Philanthropy, 57, 63

"Pimping out" female colleagues, 88; feigning social setting is a network opportunity, 88

Police. *See* Justice system

Politics, 12–13, 63; relational nature of the industry, 63; sexualization in, 12–13

Pornography, violent, 85–88, 91; consumption and increased likelihood of rape, 86; desensitization to violence against women, 86; generates acceptance of violence against women, 91; language of, 87–88; pervasiveness of use, 85

Powerlessness, feelings of, 250; perceived inability to help, 250; Psychological discomfort watching another suffer, 250; and victim blaming, 250

Promising women jobs, 59

Psychological discomfort; cognitive dissonance, 248–249; avoidance of, 248; holding two contradictory beliefs, 248; resistance to integrate new knowledge, 248

Quotas, to explain a woman hire, 131

Reduction of human value, 157–158; and hierarchy, 158; objects as power, 158; Simmel, George, 158; and social dominance, 158; and status, 158; value of accumulation, 158
Rules, 28–29, 35, 112–116, 200–201, 209, 225, 243; applied differently, 200; making new, 225; as a network of dynamics, 225; that maintain male ownership, 28–29; that maintain male power, 28–29, 35; unwritten/unspoken, 35, 209. *See also* Assumptions

Saint James Club, 222; Christmas party, 222; estrogen, 222; women to use back stairs, 222
Sally Beauty Supply, 267; bomb ingredients from, 267
SEAL Team Six, 257
Sexism as a livelihood, 243; activists, 243; attorneys, 243; no participation in this study, 243; writers, 243
Sexual assault, 65–66, 249, 254, 258, 265; charges, 258, 265; Kitty Genovese, 249; reporting parallel to sexism, 66; silence surrounding, 65–66, 254
Sexual comments, 49, 75–76; on period, 49; swallowing, 75–76
Sexualization, 55–57, 59–61, 63–64, 88–101, 159–171, 256; commodifying women, 55, 159–171; communicating power

over another, 64; dismissing, 56; entertainment, women as, 56, 88–90; exploiting inexperience/youth for sexual gain, 60; fake girlfriend, 63, 99–101, 256; gaslighting about, 56; minimizing, 56; objectification, 56; play toy, 102; pornography, 55; "pimping out" female colleagues, 56; quid pro quo, 56–57; reverse accusations, 56; sexual (accessibility to female colleague, projected by men, 57, 63, 89–101; appeal as primary worth to another, 55; conversations, 56; references, 56; requests, 57; proximity to female coworker, projected, 57, 63); sexuality as primary identifier, 55; sexuality imposed, 56, 93; sexualizing business relationships, 59–63; showpiece, women as a, 61; touching, 57, 59, 61, 168
Sexualized, how it feels to women. *See also* Feelings of women, 92; being undressed mentally, 92; subjected to it as the only woman, 92
Sexualizing business relationships, 12–13, 59–63; advertising, 59; casting, 60; international development, 59, 60–61; pharmaceuticals, 59; philanthropy, 63; politics, 12–13, 60; script used to, 86
Sexualizing work place, 84, 91–92; sexual images passed around boardroom, 84, 92; sexual language to make a business point, 91
Silence, 28–30, 78, 250; as business strategy for women, 30; as exclusion, 28–29; avoid being blamed, 250; avoid being labeled, 250; avoiding sexist confrontation, 78; so men can feel in charge, 30; so man can save face, 78

Silence, why women do not report/
confront sexism, 66–68, 71–71, 76,
78, 81–82, 93, 202, 204–205, 250,
253–254; avoid being blackballed,
254; avoid being blamed, 250;
avoid being labeled, 250, 253;
better somewhere else, idea that
sexism is just in your field, 78;
boundaries unclear/violated, 66, 68
(feel complicit, 82; feel responsible,
76; professionally associated, 66;
ruins business relationship, 66;
social settings, 66); feeling that
sexism occurs just in your industry,
78, 81; feeling you are strong, you
"can handle" it, 76, 93; immersed,
do not see it, 72, 76; material loss
(damage to career, 66; ego damage
fallout, 66–67; hurts women's
clients, 67; lose business, 72, 202,
205; lose charitable donations, 202;
lose job, 202–204); not sure how to
handle, 75; nothing will happen,
71, 73, 80 (no expectation of result,
66, 80, 81; no point, 72, 80);
perpetrator more valuable to
company, 12–13, 82; personal cost,
70 (gossip, avoiding, 66; privacy, no
assurance of, 66, 70, 81; rumors,
avoiding, 66; shame, 66, 250);
realize sexism later, but not at the
time, 82; shock, unprepared, 76;
stereotype avoidance, 73–73 (angry
black female, 74; bitch, 75; hostile,
75; making a fuss, 74–75; man-
hating, 75; "one of those women,"
73–74; overreacting, 74); would
defend another woman but not
yourself, 82
Simmel, George, 158–159
Social dominance, 9
Social Dominance Orientation (SDO),
9–10, 12, 107, 139, 248; assigning
values, 10; definition, 10;
differentiating traits, 10; favor
hierarchy, 248; higher among men,
139; internalized traits, 10;
internalized values, 10
Social messages, false cues, 250–251;
experience/qualifications matter
more than connections, 250; most
qualified person gets the job,
250–251
Socialized sexism; pervasiveness, 4–7,
9, 11, 164–165; business, 4–5;
culture, 4, 5, 7, 9, 11; female
colleagues as "fair game," 164;
media, 4, 6, 7; prevalence, 165;
politics, 4, 6, 7; society, 4, 11;
women blamed for initiating sexual
conversation, 165
Speaking up; challenging sexism, 75,
136, 218, 223–225, 244, 250;
courage of, 218; deviating from the
norm, 218; lift the veil of sexism,
223; men do not speak up in this
study, 136; perpetrator has done it
repeatedly, 75; preparation and
practice, 218 (anticipate shock/
being taken by surprise, 218;
embarrassment as a silencer, 218,
220, 250; not knowing what to say,
218; shame as a silencer, 224–225,
250); say it publicly, 223; speak
openly, 223, 244; stop it happening
to others, 75; support to other
women, 244
Stalking by male coworker, 72–73,
124, 262
Status, 37–42, 45, 50–51, 53,
196–197, 207–209, 217, 256, 268;
communication and, 196–197;
gendered assumptions of, 42–44
("doctor" is a man, 42; female agent
will be your girlfriend, 256; female
lawyer is the crime victim, 42;
female lawyer is the inmate's
girlfriend, 44); junior title for

Status (*cont.*)
   woman with same qualifications,
   268; lower pay for women,
   207–209, 268; treating men as
   high, 37, 53 (directing questions to
   men, 38, 40; men assuming expert
   status of men, 38; men citing
   inaccurate information, 39);
   treating women as low, 37, 50–51,
   53 (assuming women not credible,
   39; assuming women not
   knowledgeable, 39; challenging
   women, 53; ignoring women, 38,
   40–41; questioning women, 45;
   requesting menial tasks, 217)
Stereotype avoidance, 73–75
Stereotypes of women, sexist,
   73–75; angry black female, 74;
   bitch, 75; hostile, 75; making a
   fuss, 74–75; man-hating, 75; "one
   of those women," 73–74;
   overreacting, 74
Strip Clubs, 38, 84–85, 95, 130, 201;
   for client entertaining/relationship
   building, 85, 95; *Forbes* article, 38;
   male bonding, 130, 201; men hire
   other men who will go with them
   to, 130; prevalence of use in
   professional life, 84; for
   professional lunches, 38; tech
   industry and, 38
Stripper; prostitute; escort, 160–161,
   170–171, 223; CEO assumed to be,
   171; executive women assumed to
   be, 171, 223; Harvard University
   graduate assumed to be, 159; law
   partner assumed to be, 170–171;
   Massachusetts Institute of
   Technology graduate assumed to
   be, 159; PhDs assumed to be,
   160–161, 223
Structures, sexist, 22, 25–28, 31–35,
   102; aviation, 27; business
   development, 32; finance, 27–28;

government, 27; job assignments,
   22, 31, 102; land development, 28;
   legal, 25–26, 27, 32, 33–34;
   marketing, 26; perceived as normal,
   22, 35; pharmaceuticals, 26;
   philanthropy, 32; politics, 31;
   systematizing, 22, 35
Suppressing women's contributions,
   28–29, 48–50, 102, 132–133, 256,
   258–259, 267; accept same idea
   from man, reject from woman, 50;
   changing subject when woman
   speaks, 50, 258–259; disregard
   women talking, 50; disregarding
   women's knowledge, 132–133,
   258–259; embarrassing women,
   49; excluding women in decision
   making, 48; ignoring women, 50,
   133; immobilized woman's career
   through task assignment, 267;
   interrupting women, 49; job/project
   assignments, 102; making decision
   prior to meeting, 50; silence,
   28–29; talking over women, 49;
   undermining women's work, 256,
   258; withholding information, 48
Survival strategies women use,
   65–66, 71, 75, 81, 101, 160, 200,
   250, 267; distancing socially, 101;
   leave job, company, industry, 71,
   200, 267; make the best of the
   situation, 160; silence, 65–66, 75,
   250; stop fighting, 81

Touching, inappropriate or forced,
   59, 61, 68, 121, 253, 260–261;
   between legs, 59; escaping from,
   68, 121 (hit man with laptop, 121;
   played dumb, 68); grabbing breast,
   253; kissing, 59, 68; knee, 61; leg,
   59; personal space, 68; physical
   intimidation, 260–261; pinned
   against car, 59; pinned against
   wall, 121

United States Department of Defense (DOD), 258–259, 263
United States Department of Health and Human Services Office of the Inspector General (OIG), 260
United States Drug Enforcement Administration (DEA), 260
United States Marshals Service, 260

Veblen, Thorstein, 158
Victim blaming, 250, 253, 254; label as a silencer, 253, 254; and perceived ability to help, 250; and psychological discomfort, 250
Virginia Beach, 260

Women contribute to sexism, 174–178, 181–182, 185–190; acting like or saying sexism is acceptable, 185–186; assuming woman has a sexual relationship with superior, 178, 181–182; competing through subservience or menial tasks, 185; diminutive names for women, 186–187; disregarding other women's experience or expertise, 187–189; inequitable standards for other women, 175–176; judging appearance of women, 176–177, 189–190; sabotaging other women, 174–175; stonewalling other women, 188; using sexist terminology, 187

YaWaH, 24–25; gender neutral, 24; turned masculine, 24–25
Yemen, 261

About the Author

Elizabeth C. Wolfe, PhD, is a specialist in conflict analysis and resolution. She is senior scientist at a human security company that creates instructional material for pre-deployment Green Berets at the John F. Kennedy Special Warfare School and Center. Wolfe serves as a consultant to nonprofit organizations and philanthropic foundations and publishes on issues of donor engagement. She works with private clients across sectors including private defense, yachting, aviation, real estate, and finance. She facilitates discussions on sensitive topics including LGBTQ issues, youth and workplace bullying, homophobia, inequality, and gender violence.

Wolfe's previous work was in political campaigning, fund-raising, strategy, and press. In only one of her professional positions has she not encountered overt sexism.

Her earlier work in the philanthropic field explored human trafficking in India, Europe, and the United States. Prior to that, Wolfe worked to counter postwar communal violence in West Africa through traditional tribal engagement efforts. Wolfe's other areas of focus have been former child soldier reintegration, genocide prevention, and countering violent extremism.

She enjoys using dramatic problem solving, a theater-based conflict resolution technique, for groups and families. You can reach her at www.8HouseElan.com.